MEANINGS FOR MANHOOD

Beats / gender

MEANINGS FOR MANHOOD

Constructions of Masculinity in Victorian America

Edited by

Mark C. Carnes and Clyde Griffen

The University of Chicago Press
Chicago and London

Mark C. Carnes is associate professor of history at Barnard College. **Clyde Griffen** is the Lucy Maynard Salmon Professor of History at Vassar College.

The University of Chicago Press, Chicago 60637
The University of Chicago Press, Ltd., London
© 1990 by The University of Chicago
All rights reserved. Published 1990
Printed in the United States of America

99 98 97 96 95 94 93 92 91 90   5 4 3 2 1

Library of Congress Cataloging in Publication Data

Meanings for manhood : constructions of masculinity in Victorian
   America / edited by Mark C. Carnes and Clyde Griffen
      p.   cm.
   Includes bibliographical references.
   ISBN 0-226-09364-6 (alk. paper). — ISBN 0-226-09365-4 (pbk. :
alk. paper)
   1. Men—United States—History—19th century. 2. Masculinity
(Psychology)—History—19th century. 3. Men—United States—
Psychology—History—19th century. I. Carnes, Mark C. (Mark
Christopher), 1950–   II. Griffen, Clyde, 1929–
HQ1090.3.M43 1990
305.31'0973'09034—dc20

                                                90-32943
                                                CIP

Contents

CONTENTS

Introduction

In 1977 Gerda Lerner spoke for many when she criticized the historical profession for its neglect of women in the past. To rectify this omission of half of humankind, she called for a historical inquiry centered on women. But this was to be a "temporary strategy." "What is needed," she explained, "is a new universal history, a holistic history which will be a synthesis of traditional history and women's history." It would compare, ideally, the historical experiences of men to those of women, and encompass the interactions of the sexes.[1]

For proponents of the new social history, however, this formulation contained an important methodological ambiguity. Traditional history, social historians insisted, was a domain inhabited mostly by the famous men of statehouse and boardroom, of academy and pulpit. A union of traditional history (i.e., famous men) with women's history could not possibly yield a truly "universal" history, for it would leave out the laborers, farmers, mechanics, clerks, and shopkeepers who composed much of society.[2]

No one could have anticipated how brilliantly women's historians would succeed in achieving their half of Lerner's proposal. They have unearthed new sources, spawned entirely new fields of inquiry, and greatly expanded the theoretical underpinnings of the entire discipline of history. Most important, they have demonstrated beyond question the importance of gender as both tool and subject of historical analysis. But the "universal" history Lerner proposed awaited a parallel expansion of work on masculinity.

Lerner was herself one of the first to perceive the need to bring the experiences of men into the study of gender. Her account of the origins of patriarchy underscored the importance for women's history—and for "human" history—of examining the context of women's relations with men.[3] But such work has been all too rare. Until very recently, much of what has been written about the manhood and masculinity of the Victorian era cannot serve as even a rudimentary foundation for more elaborate analytical models such as those that have transformed women's history.

The new social history requires that, whenever possible, inferences be based on the actions and words of those being studied. Even social historians who do not sing the merits of "history from the bottom up" reject the opposite assumption that the American people, or some subset thereof, share the motivations, beliefs, or customs of their leaders. Yet work on men and masculinity has often been plagued by this "top downward" approach.

Historians have commonly held that the president of the nation exemplified the aspirations and values of all men. Andrew Jackson has been described as "a cultural symbol" who embodied "the manliness ethos" for antebellum men more generally.[4] And Teddy Roosevelt is said to have personified "the essentials of the American masculine ethos," thereby giving rise to a "bull moose mentality."[5] A more subtle approach holds that the psychological concerns of a popular president are widely shared by the people. Thus Abraham Lincoln's repressed anger toward his own father is thought to have enabled him to channel the patricidal anxieties of an entire generation into a war against a slave system tolerated by the founding fathers.[6]

"Top downward" studies of the president–as–common man variety usually make either of two assumptions: that men seek confirmation of their own manhood by endorsing the masculine style of leaders who share their traits, or that men emulate vigorous presidents as compensation for their own sense of deficiency. These assumptions are not merely contradictory; they neglect that many men voted against the individual who became president or selected their candidate without regard to characterological factors.

A variant of this line of reasoning substitutes literary or cultural heroes (usually frontiersmen or sports figures) for political ones. A commonplace of historical writing maintains that a nation of frontiersmen and independent producers naturally enshrined free-spirited individualists such as Natty Bumppo, Daniel Boone, and Davy Crockett. More recently, some scholars have argued with equal plausibility that American men clung to the example of mythical rugged individualists precisely because those traits were lacking in their own lives.[7]

The essential question remains: did these cultural symbols provide sustenance to men secure in their masculine style, or did they offer psychological compensation to men fearful of their softness? It cannot be answered by examining the rhetoric of political leaders or the products of popular culture, but only by delving deeper into the actual experiences and opinions of men in different historical circumstances and periods.

Historians have sought other types of analytical shortcuts to arrive at an understanding of masculinity. Some have examined contexts (such as competitive sports) where gender segregation has been obvious and its rhetoric freighted with combative and aggressive phrases and images. Others have focused on Victorian physicians and scientists who wrote extensively on male and female physiology.

An early example of the latter approach is G. J. Barker-Benfield's *Horrors of the Half-Known Life*. Subtitled "Male Attitudes toward Women and Sexuality in Nineteenth-Century America," the book, based on the writings of some twenty physicians, purports to explain how Victorian men viewed sexual relations and their own sexuality. For example, after describing physicians who mutilated women's sexual organs for ostensibly therapeutic purposes, Barker-Benfield proposes that the psychological impulses and personal goals of such doctors were "typical of democratic American men." Why this should be so is not explained.[8]

More troubling than the excesses of a Barker-Benfield is the tendency of even sensitive social historians to generalize from fragmentary evidence when writing about men. An example is Christine Stansell's subtle analysis of the support networks and survival strategies devised by working-class women in antebellum New York City. Throughout her *City of Women*, evil men lurk in the background, looking on "balefully" at the women who occupy the most vulnerable positions in society. It is to protect themselves from unregenerate men that these women eventually assume the task of transforming male attitudes and behaviors.[9]

Although men are a precipitating factor in Stansell's thesis, they are too often an unexamined one. For example, in seeking to show that "male license for sexual aggressiveness" increased after the Revolutionary War, she suggests that men's antagonism toward women was unconscious, being "expressed within a structure of feeling rather than a body of explicit ideas." To illuminate this hidden structure she cites the trial testimony of men charged with rape (two cases), with murdering their wives (two cases), and with kidnapping a young woman for sexual purposes. Stansell buttresses these sources with inflammatory quotations from two English documents, one of which first appeared in 1675. She concedes that such extreme testimony might not be representative of male attitudes in general, but claims without further citation that other men "spoke in a similar vein." Whatever the merits of her hypothesis, the evidence cited is not sufficient to prove it.[10]

Stansell's failure is significant partly because her work is otherwise exemplary. Unlike literary or cultural historians who infer the characteristics of the common man from the example of a few, she was acutely conscious of the need to understand women by working "from the bottom up." One of her explicit goals was to "illuminate" the lives of women who were formerly "submerged" in the histories of others (p. xiii). But her commitment to understanding the complexities of women's lives did not extend to men, whose motivations were nevertheless crucial to her argument.

It would be unfair to ask Stansell (or any other women's historian) to rewrite her work to incorporate the parallel complexities of men's lives. Were she to try, moreover, the paucity of solid research on this and other aspects of nineteenth-century masculinity would prove a formidable obstacle. Just as Lerner was obliged to call for a "woman-centered" historical inquiry fifteen years ago, remedial work is needed today to bridge the gaps in our understanding of the historical construction of masculinity.

There have been some promising beginnings. The pioneering collection of essays edited by Elizabeth and Joseph Pleck a decade ago conveyed the expansive potential of this new field, but no single period within the book received sufficient attention to generate the broader conclusions to which social history aspires.[11] Peter N. Stearns's insightful, early synthesis, *Be a Man!* (1979), was by his own admission hampered by the absence of a body of research, particularly for the Victorian era, on which to base his conclusions.[12] Similarly, John Demos recently complained that the historical study of fatherhood was "waiting to be born."[13] Other signal contributions have tended to come from historians of courtship and marriage, who have most nearly approached the "holistic" history envisioned by Lerner,[14] and from historians of leisure, sports, and exclusively male voluntary institutions—subjects with accessible and well-known primary sources.[15]

For the editors of the present volume, however, the transformational event of the history of masculinity was the publication in 1981 of Mary P. Ryan's *Cradle of the Middle Class: The Family in Oneida County, New York, 1790–1865*. In order to understand the relations of men and women during the rise of mercantile capitalism, Ryan applied the techniques of the new social history to an unusually rich collection of local primary sources. The resultant work, rooted in social detail and informed by gender perspectives, brilliantly described a shift in attitudes from "patriarchal authority" to "domestic affection." By wedding the new social history to the relational study of men and women at moments of change in the home, workplace, and community, Ryan provided a methodology and thematic focus that begged to be applied to other topics.[16]

We imagined that other scholars, unknown to us or even to each other, were pondering the implications for men's history of recent developments in women's history. To this end we issued a call for papers in the spring of 1987 for a conference on masculinity in Victorian America at Barnard College, Columbia University. By focusing on male gender roles and attitudes, we sought to promote the "holistic" history of humankind espoused by

Lerner. In limiting the subject to the Victorian era, we hoped that the papers would collectively provide the contextual richness essential to social history. We believed that a Victorian culture in the United States was ushered in by the evangelical revivals, its cohesion derived from a confident moralism, didacticism, and optimism about America that persisted into the Progressive Era.[17]

As the proposals for papers appeared, we knew that our high expectations for the conference were justified. What astonished us was our contributors' diverse fields of specialization, which included the history of women, law, medicine, reform, theology, sports, technology, and labor. Few if any identified themselves as practitioners of "men's history." Many had never before written on gender issues.[18] Most had been patiently engaged in research in their specializations when, often to their surprise, they discerned the salience of issues pertaining to masculinity and male gender roles.

Yet when these scholars looked for scholarly monographs on male gender roles and masculinity during the Victorian era, they could find precious little. That this should be true, nearly three decades after the onset of the new social history and two after the flood of work on women's history, came as a challenge to them.

All of our essays are rooted in social history—in the concrete details of everyday life rather than its intellectual or literary manifestations. Some of the essays examine exclusively male worlds; in omitting women or consigning them to the role of unexamined and distant causal forces, this approach entails some distortion of gender dynamics. But women's historians have amply demonstrated the utility of intensive scrutiny of a single sex.[19] Other essays more nearly follow Gerda Lerner's call for a history emphasizing the relation of men to women.

Some essays focus on formal institutions, such as lawyers' associations, psychiatric hospitals, fraternal orders, or labor unions. Only two explicitly consider the institution of marriage, although issues of childhood and family appear throughout the book. Other essays explore informal social networks ranging from boys' gangs to abolitionist friendships. Rather than organize the book according to an institutional perspective, however, we have underscored the developmental aspects of the acquisition of manhood. Part 1 looks at the transition from boyhood to manhood; part 2, adult friendships and marriage; part 3, work and the workplace. A final section offers an interpretive synthesis of Victorian masculinity as well as the reflections of a prominent women's historian.

This book does not attempt to encompass the wide variety of Victorian male worlds. Most of our essays focus on the white middle class. The absence of essays on blacks and on homosexuals is glaring: it is indicative of the work to be done on these subjects.[20] Nor do our essays offer detailed descriptions of their topics. Rather, their purpose is to examine the formation of gender, to analyze the evolution of cultural definitions of what it means to be male.

Our emphasis on the social construction of masculinity does not grow out of a conviction that biological factors are irrelevant to male behavior. Even cautious psychologists believe it "well established" that males tend to be more aggressive than females, probably due to higher levels of testosterone. But human physiology admits of infinite variation; the sociobiologist's statistical mean is an intellectual construct rather than a physiological reality. In fact, many women have higher testosterone levels than many men; even among men, hormonal variations are remarkably large. The assumption that biology—or a biologically conditioned psychological process—imposes on all men a single role or behavior is unwarranted.[21]

The essays in this book provide abundant evidence of widely divergent and socially sanctioned male roles and behaviors. The flinty, sexually repressed patriarch has nowadays become synonymous in the popular mind with "Victorian," but it appears that a far wider range of male behaviors and gender roles was acceptable during the mid-nineteenth century than a century later.[22] The gun-toting frontiersmen who loomed so large in the mythology of the Jacksonian era were counterbalanced by the abolitionist clergy, whose homosocial friendships were characterized by sensitivity and emotional intensity. Young men who fled farms enshrined an individualistic manliness that was fundamentally at odds with the immigrant worker's commitment to community. And lawyers and doctors, who shared the goal of professionalizing their trades, responded to the "encroachment" of women by devising different—even antithetical—"masculine" styles and strategies.

Not only did different groups conceive of masculinity in different ways, but the various gender roles and styles themselves underwent significant changes during the nineteenth century. Industrialization, by substituting machinery for skilled labor and thereby facilitating the introduction of unskilled women and children to the factory, undermined traditional paths to manhood among skilled workers. The emergence of great corporations stabilized working conditions for many employees, pulling the fangs out of the dog-eat-dog world of Darwinian America. But this relative economic security also deprived men of "manly independence" and forced them to devise new conceptions of masculinity. The gradual advance of women into public life further obliged men to reexamine their relationship to work, to politics and government, and to marriage and the family. How male dominance remained essentially intact despite these many transformations is one of the central issues confronting scholars in this field.

Most of our essays present tentative hypotheses about causation. They contend that changes in gender roles, in family structure, in capitalism, and in the nature of organizations and work led to shifts in the way men and women understood masculinity. Less frequently expressed is the possibility that causation also worked the other way—that changing conceptions of masculinity influenced broader social, economic, and political processes.

Determining where and to what extent gender is an independent variable is one of the most difficult tasks awaiting students of masculinity. Beyond that lies the challenge of understanding what different constructions of masculinity meant to their adherents. Were conceptions of masculinity strongly held and deeply satisfying—affirmations of a positive sense of self? Or, at the other extreme, were they compensatory and escapist—ways of evading the realities of class, economics, or gender?

The answers to all such questions must grow out of a close reading of social detail. Our essays and the sections that preface them are meant to stimulate further debate and research. We have not attempted to impose on the subject, in either the selection or the editing of the essays, any single theoretical and interpretive viewpoint. Theory may enrich research, and political values and personal interests give it passion and relevance, but in the end we depend on what the historical record may yield.

Constructions of Masculinity from Boyhood to Adulthood

Women's history has shown the growing importance of women in the education of the young both at home and at school during the nineteenth century, and in doing so has raised questions about how this shift affected the development of males from boyhood into adulthood. The ideology of separate gender spheres, in particular, posed a sharp contrast between the gentle virtues of the home and the moral perils of the larger world in which sons would move as adults. During the past decade some historians have questioned whether the pervasive language of separate spheres reflected the reality of gender relations, but few dispute the sharp normative contrast between men and women or doubt the preeminent influence of mothers in inculcating the gentle virtues.

Did this gendered contrast pose a serious conflict for boys? Did conflict in reconciling gender norms persist into adulthood? If so, how was it expressed, and what means did boys and men devise to resolve it? The four essays in this section address some of these questions by examining (1) the world middle-class boys created for themselves when free from adult supervision, (2) a popular ritual from one of the secret fraternal orders which proliferated during the last half of the nineteenth century, (3) the gendered diagnoses and therapeutic regimens of a state insane asylum in the South, and (4) a redefinition of masculinity which grew out of the coming-of-age struggles of social gospel clergymen.

Historian E. Anthony Rotundo has discovered in adult male reminiscences and autobiographies abundant evidence suggesting that boys from middle-class families devised, between roughly age six and adolescence, a culture of their own. This "boy culture" was of greatest significance during the mid-Victorian years, when men increasingly worked away from home but before age-graded schooling was common and before adults made concerted efforts to organize their children's play. Rotundo finds that outside of school hours, boys pursued aggressive and often cruel play and created rules and rituals antithetical to adult preaching about self-control and piety. Apart from its frequent violence and even sadism, the most striking characteristic of this boys' world was its degree of separation—spatial, cultural, and psychological—from the surrounding adult world of relatives and neighbors.

The very sharpness of this separation raises important questions about Rotundo's description and the sources on which it depends. He suggests that the existence of a "boy culture" can be construed as evidence of boys' ambivalence toward the authority and interventions of their mothers. But references to women, including sisters and "tomboys," are notably absent. This is only one reason for wondering about the selectivity of memory. When adult men reminisced nostalgically about their childhoods, did they fail to record instances of friendly interaction with adult relatives and neighbors?

This suggests an opposite reading in which the memoirs can be understood as a projection back into childhood of adult needs and attitudes. For example, did men who chafed at the discipline and imposed hierarchy of the workplace wax rhapsodic about the imagined freedom and peer-determined pecking orders of their boyhoods? And did middle-class men who sat at a desk or stood behind a counter all day fantasize about the exuberant physicality and violence of a dimly remembered boyhood? Rotundo's reconstruction of "boy culture" from this rich body of evidence should push historians to define more precisely where and how far the memoirs' biases distort the complex relationships of dependence, power, and affection that existed between middle-class boys and their peers, parents, female siblings, and neighbors during much of the nineteenth century.

Rotundo's emphasis on escape from the constraints and gentle virtues of home is echoed in Mark C. Carnes's interpretation of the psychological meaning of successful fraternal rituals in the mid-nineteenth century. The thematic content of these rituals and the importance young and old members apparently attached to them lead Carnes to view them as one means men used to resolve gender-role tensions that persisted into adulthood. He focuses on a ritual of the Improved Order of Red Men that evolved into a psychodrama in which tribal elders subjected new members to an "ordeal" before admitting them to the tribal family. Carnes faces a problem of evidence opposite to Rotundo's. Direct testimony about how men felt about these secret rituals is almost nonexistent. The rituals' cultural and psychological meanings must be inferred from a close reading of the rituals, in this case informed by theory drawn from anthropological analysis of sex roles and comparative studies of male initiation rites. As is invariably the case, however, social scientists have offered alternative hypotheses to explain male initiation ceremonies, and these might yield different explanations of the phenomenon.

The elaboration by women's historians of the feminization of the middle-class home provided a point of departure for Carnes's investigation; the recent questioning by some women's historians of the extent of separation of gender spheres in practice, and their current concern with gender interaction in all contexts of everyday life, provide points of departure for questions about Carnes's interpretation. Are the rituals primarily means of resolving a cross-gender conflict which persists from boyhood into adulthood, or are they also deeply related to members' adult roles and everyday lives? What the rituals meant to participants cannot be fully determined until we know more precisely who they were, and especially what kinds of places they occupied within the changing universe of occupations and communities after the Civil War. Carnes emphasizes the psychological guidance that rituals provided for the emotional transition from evangelical homes to the stern realities of competition in business and politics. But what if many of the members worked either in the more secure employments of the emerging private and public bureaucracies or in shops or trades with close community ties? And what can we learn about the impact of their fraternal lives on their relationships with wives and children—beyond the frequent public complaints about the amount of time members devoted to lodges?

The contrast between, on one hand, the sober, rational behavior expected of middle-class men in their workplaces, and, on the other, their ritual assaults and embraces disguised as partly naked Indians or Old Testament patriarchs, suggests a complicated psychological transaction. But the exotic behavior remained secret from the rest of the world and did not jeopardize public reputation. The stresses of trying to accommodate both the gentle virtues of the home and the competitive virtues of the marketplace became more sharply and publicly visible in the labeling and treatment of men who were institutionalized as "insane" during the last half of the century, notably in the frequent attribution of their derangement to "excessive masculinity." While examining the records of the Alabama State Insane Asylum, John Starrett Hughes, a researcher in medical history, was struck with the frequency of gendered diagnoses by families who committed their relatives to the asylum and with the gendered approach to therapy taken by the superintendent and staff. Although Hughes's essay was not inspired by recent work in the history of either women or men, it provides support for the common tendency in general interpretations of masculinity in the United States during the nineteenth century to emphasize its oppression of men as well as of women.

If Hughes is correct in inferring from his Southern data that Victorian gender norms were diffused throughout the nation after the Civil War, the fact that many Alabama families attributed their male relations' madness to "excessive masculinity" suggests what a fine line Gilded Age males had to walk. Equally important for the historiography of masculinity is Hughes's emphasis on the asylum staff's central assumption in designing therapy for deranged men: that a quieter, more "feminized" and familial environment offered the best hope of cure. That assumption suggests a degree of complexity and balance in Gilded Age understandings of gender norms that "tough guy" interpretations of American ideals of masculinity since the age of Jackson have not yet recognized.

The diagnosis of "excessive masculinity" suggests that the committing families were predominantly middle-class, affirming a respectability which emphasized self-restraint. But Hughes's essay, like Carnes's, does not try to determine social origin or residence, so the full significance of his findings is not clear. Antebellum Alabama, like other Deep South states, harbored the predominantly rural and working-class "gouge-and-bite" culture which Elliott Gorn has described so powerfully, a culture which echoed in the drunkenness and brawls of Southern small-town main streets long after the Civil War. How much the "excessive masculinity" diagnosis may have owed to this inheritance cannot be estimated until we know more about the distribution of white inmates among urban and rural areas and also among social classes. We need also to know where blacks—and whites' fear of black male violence and sexuality—fit into this diagnosis, and how therapists were concerned with them, overtly or covertly.

The first three essays in this section focus on ways in which men and boys coped with the contrast between gender spheres without directly challenging and modifying the identification of masculinity with the competitive world beyond the home. Susan Curtis, in the fourth essay, describes a group of men who entered the profession most closely associated in everyday life by the last half of the century with women—the ministry. Before the turn of the twentieth century this group, the preachers of a social gospel, were a prophetic minority, but after 1900 their thought transformed mainstream liberal Protestantism. In Curtis's provocative interpretation, they redefined Christian masculinity in a way which inadvertently facilitated middle-class acceptance of the consumer-oriented, bureaucratic world of corporate capitalism.

Curtis emphasizes her subjects' struggles with growing up male. The young men who became the social gospelers were unhappy with both the individualistic standards of achievement of their fathers and the feminized Jesus of their upbringing. Curtis's historiographical point of departure seems to be Ann Douglas's depiction of the marginalization of male clergy through their dependence on and ambivalent alliance with the women who increasingly made up their congregations. But in Curtis's view, the social gospelers' reinterpretation of theology and especially of Jesus partially reversed the marginalization of their profession. Curtis resembles Douglas and also T. Jackson Lears in her view that the social gospelers' reinterpretations ultimately contributed to the further dilution and secularization of their faith.

Curtis's piece draws mostly on the theologians' reminiscences and their books about Jesus. Yet to be elaborated on is the movement that she asserts took place in the early twentieth century toward Bruce Barton's kind of bland applied Christianity. And while her emphasis on the social gospelers' preference for a more masculine Jesus is well documented, her focus on their struggles with their fathers and their doubts about their own authority as parents raises further questions. Absent are the women who played so important a role in the families and congregations of most clergymen. A discussion of the social gospelers' cooperative ethos which does not take account of gender interaction within the clerical universe is incomplete. We need to know whether Curtis's choice of focus has excluded this interaction or whether there is an extraordinary bias at work in the social gospelers' memories, perhaps reflecting a continuing need to emphasize the masculinity of their calling.

The essays in this section highlight the ways in which men did or did not come to terms with conflict in gender norms in the nineteenth century. They do so primarily through investigation of all-male worlds or of man-to-man interactions. Women often appear in the wings as interveners or causal influences, or even as part of the theoretical framework. But these essays do not investigate gender relations directly, and in that respect they seem closer in spirit and approach to the early phase of women's history, which emphasized women's separate and distinct world. This separatist tendency may inadvertently contribute to the general absence of attention to the politics of gender and the emphasis instead on some kind of "fit" between the cultural construction of masculinity in question and broader developments in American society. Rotundo suggests that "boy culture," though self-consciously opposed to adult authority figures, encouraged the spirit of competitiveness boys would need later in life. Carnes argues that the solace of fraternal ritual enabled middle-class men to accept the constraints imposed by the new family structures and work discipline. Curtis holds that the social gospelers' more cooperative ideas of God and society contributed to the ascendancy of the "other-directed" personality type in the early twentieth century. In focusing primarily on relationships among males of similar origins and interests, these essays in passing suggest antagonism on the part of these males toward those who differ in gender, class, ethnicity, or race, but they do not take us beyond attitudes into power relations with members of different groups, nor into gendered political conflict external to their separated special worlds.

ONE

Boy Culture: Middle-Class Boyhood in Nineteenth-Century America

E. Anthony Rotundo

In 1853 a popular etiquette writer called "Mrs. Manners" launched an angry attack on the boys of America. "Why is it," she asked, "that there must be a period in the lives of boys when they should be spoken of as 'disagreeable cubs'? Why is a gentle, polite boy such a rarity?" She continued her assault in that tone of embattled hauteur so common to etiquette writers: "If your parents are willing for you to be the 'Goths and Vandals' of society, I shall protest against it. You have been outlaws long enough, and now I beg you will observe the rules."[1]

For all her wounded righteousness, Mrs. Manners expressed a widely shared view. Source after source describes boys as "wild" and "careless," as "primitive savages" full of "animal spirits." They were commonly compared to Indians and African tribesmen. One writer even called them a breed unto themselves—"the race of boys."[2] Literary critic Henry Seidel Canby, reflecting on his own boyhood in the 1880s and 1890s, emphasized further the separation of the world of boys from the world of adults: "There was plenty of room for our own life, and we took it, so that customs, codes, ideals, and prejudices were absorbed from our elders as by one free nation from another."[3]

This "free nation" of boys was a distinct cultural world with its own rituals and its own symbols and values. As a social sphere, it was separate both from the domestic world of women, girls, and small children and from the public world of men and commerce. In this social space of their own, boys were able to play outside the rules of the home and the marketplace.

Technically, of course, boy culture was really a subculture. It was an enclave within Victorian society—distinct, oppositional, but intimately related. Boys shuttled constantly in and out of this world of theirs, home and then back again. And their experiences with boy culture helped to prepare them in many ways for life in the adult spheres that surrounded them. Boy culture, then, was not the only world that a young male inhabited, nor was it the only one that left its mark on him. Still, within its carefully set boundaries, boy culture was surprisingly free of adult intervention—it gave a youngster his first exhilarating taste of independence and made a lasting imprint on his character. The following essay sketches the outlines of boy culture as it existed during the nineteenth century in the northern United States, focusing especially on the internal and external forces that gave it distinctive form.[4]

Boys lived a different sort of life in the years before boy culture opened up to them. Until the age of six or so, they were enmeshed in a domestic world of brothers, sisters, and cousins. They rarely strayed from the presence of watchful adults.[5] Mothers kept an especially keen eye on their children during these early years, for popular thinking held that this was the phase of life when the basis was laid for good character. A good mother needed to fasten early and closely the bonds of affection that would secure an active conscience in later years. More overt forms of moral instruction also began during these earliest years as language and understanding developed. Thus, for his first five to seven years a boy's adult companions were female and the environment he lived in was one of tender affection and moral suasion.[6] By the time boys reached the age of three or four, their mothers were beginning to complain about their rowdy, insolent ways.[7] But however much they rebelled, these little boys were still embedded in a domestic world dominated by women.

During these early years, boys dressed in the same loose-fitting gowns that their sisters wore.[8] Such "girlish" clothing gave small boys the message that they were expected to behave like their sisters and served also as a vivid symbol of their feminization. More than that, boys' gowns and smocks inhibited the running, climbing, and other physical activities that so often made boys a disagreeable addition to the gentle domesticity of women's world. Whether boys meekly accepted the way their parents dressed them or rebelled against its confinements, they were put in a situation where they had to accept or reject a feminine identity in their earliest years.[9]

Finally, at about age six, boys cut loose from these social and physical restraints.[10] Although they would continue to live for many years in the woman's world of the home, they were now inhabitants of an alternate world as well.[11] In the cities, boy culture flourished in backyards, streets, parks, playgrounds, and vacant lots, all of which composed "a series of city states to play in." For those who lived in small towns, the neighboring orchards, fields, and forests provided a natural habitat for boy culture.[12] By contrast, indoors was alien territory. A parlor, a dining room, almost any room with a nice carpet repelled boy culture. Boys did sometimes carve out their own turf within the house—usually in the attic, where dirt, noise, and physical activity created fewer problems than on the clean, placid lower floors. And the house was not the only indoor space that was alien. Boy culture languished in the school and in the church, and it never even approached the offices and countinghouses where middle-class fathers worked.[13]

How did a small boy enter this new realm at first? One man remembered simply that he "was aware of a great change in [his] world. It was no longer contained within a house bounded by four walls . . . [but] had swelled and expanded into a street."[14] Perhaps the change came for most boys with a similar lack of fanfare. Certainly, the autobiographies and family correspondence of the time reveal no special rite of passage that marked the entry into boy culture.

As they broke away from the constant restrictions of home, boys shed their gowns and petticoats. Suddenly, the differences between themselves and their sisters seemed to be encouraged and even underscored.[15] For their sisters were still enveloped by the moral and physical confinements of domesticity and by the gowns and petticoats that were its visible emblems. With great clarity a boy saw that "female" meant fettered and "male" meant free.[16]

Boys were now beyond the reach of adult supervision for hours at a time. And they were suddenly free to pursue a range of activities that would have been difficult if not impossible in the domestic world. The physical activities that had been hindered in early boyhood now became particular passions. Hiking, exploring, swimming, rowing, and horseback riding took on special meaning for boys newly liberated from domestic confinement. And the cold Northern winters brought still other pleasures, such as sledding, skating, and snowball throwing.[17]

While boys often pursued these activities for the pure joy of exercise, they engaged in many activities that set them head-to-head in hostile combat. Friends fought or wrestled simply for the fun of it, while other boys goaded unwilling playmates into fights. The varieties of physical punishment were as numerous as the settings in which boys gathered. Youngsters in a small Ohio town threw stones at each other just for sport. And students at a late-nineteenth-century boarding school hit newcomers on their bare buttocks with paddles. Beneath this violence lay curious veins of casual hostility and sociable sadism. One of the bonds that held boy culture together was the pain which youngsters inflicted on each other.[18]

But if boys posed a danger to one another, they were downright lethal to small animals. They preferred to use guns when they hunted, but settled for slingshots, bows and arrows, and even hand-hurled stones. Youngsters also did a good deal of trapping and indulged in the gentler pastime of fishing. Much of the violence that boys perpetrated while hunting was at least a means to an end, but some was purely gratuitous. Woodchuck trapping sometimes turned into an exercise in woodchuck torture, and insect killing offered boys a chance to test their imagination on ways to inflict suffering. The pleasure that they took in the more violent elements of hunting seems closely related to the pleasure that they took in fighting and even in stoning one another.[19]

Not all of boys' play was so openly violent nor so free-form. Popular boys' games like marbles, tag, blindman's buff, leapfrog, and tug-of-war were played according to rules passed from one generation of boys to the next. But when compared to modern games, even these structured pastimes of the nineteenth century lacked elaborate rules and complicated strategies. Spontaneous exercise and excitement were more important than elaborate expertise.[20]

Other pastimes were more personally expressive. Activities that developed on the spur of the moment or that grew slowly within the context of a friendship or a gang revealed many of the preoccupations of boy culture. A favorite subject in these improvised games was warfare.[21] The most popular imitation of war was the struggle between settlers and Indians. Boys even relished the role of the Indian—assumed by them all to be the more barbarous and aggressive.[22]

Settler-and-Indian games allowed boys to enter and imagine roles that were played by real adult males. Such imitative play was a vital part of boy culture, and there were many other popular activities that allowed even closer emulation of adult men. Boys were also enthusiastic spectators at the militia musters for adults and joined in the action if they could. There were other settings in which boys could imitate men and even participate in their tasks. During the antebellum era, political parties pressed boys into service for their rallies and parades. While this activity was initiated by adults, boys seized the opportunity to place their own stamp on the proceedings. They often picked fights with the other party's young assistants, and they sometimes insisted on lighting victory bonfires even when their own side lost. The boys who lived in antebellum cities followed yet another exciting men's activity by attaching themselves to volunteer fire companies. The tasks were hard but stirring, and the competition between companies was so fierce that it sometimes led to violence. As eager as boys were to join in the responsibilities of grown men, they took a deeper interest when excitement was involved.[23]

Most boys took a special interest in imitating or taking part in their fathers' work. Opportunities to do this differed considerably for city and country boys. Rural youngsters, after all, lived in closer proximity to their fathers' work, and there was much greater need of their help.[24] On the other hand, affluent city boys were lucky if they could imitate any of their fathers' work activities. Not only were urban boys separated from the work world of their fathers, but most of those middle-class men did work that was too abstract to interest a youngster. Buying, selling, and keeping accounts were not activities that caught a boy's fancy.[25]

Still, beneath this difference lay the essential similarity of urban and rural boy culture, both in values and in purposes. Boys from both settings were drawn to activities that offered excitement and physical exercise. Dirt and noise were often by-products of such pastimes. And certain boys' activities provided special opportunities to enter and imagine the roles of adult males.

But, above all, the pastimes boys favored set their world in sharp contrast to the domestic, female world—the world to which they returned every evening. Where women's sphere offered kindness, morality, nurture, and a gentle spirit, the boys' world countered with energy, self-assertion, noise, and frequent recourse to violence. The physical explosiveness and the willingness to inflict pain contrast so sharply with the values of the home that they suggest a dialogue in actions between the values of the two spheres— as if a boy's aggressive impulses, so relentlessly opposed at home, sought extreme forms of release outside it; then, with stricken conscience, the boy returned home for further lessons in self-restraint. The two worlds seemed almost to thrive on their opposition to each other. And boys, though they valued both worlds deeply, often complained about the confinement of home. The world that they created just beyond the reach of domesticity gave them a space for expressive play and a sense of freedom from the women's world that had nurtured them early in boyhood and that now welcomed them home every night.

The contrast between boy culture and the domestic sphere extended to the nature and strength of the bonds that cemented each of these social worlds. The nineteenth-century home was held intact by love and adult authority. Its primary purpose of nurture tended to draw its members together in emotional support and in common bonds of conscience and self-sacrifice. By contrast, the world of boy culture was held intact by less enduring ties. The expressive play which gave boy culture its focus was conducive to self-assertion and conflict more than to love or understanding. And since the adhesive materials of boy culture were not strong ones, they created a very different sort of bond than that which held together the domestic realm.

Friendship was certainly the most important relation between boys. And within their world it took on some distinctive qualities. Charles Dudley Warner described those friendships as "fervent if not enduring."[26] Evidently, these fond but shifting ties had as much to do with availability as with deeper affinities. Alphonso Rockwell, a physician, recalled that boyhood friendships were determined less "by similarity of disposition and common likes and dislikes than by propinquity and accidental association."[27] Boys' friendships, in other words, tended to be superficial and sudden, however passionate they might be for the moment.[28]

Good companionship and unshakable fidelity, rather than confiding intimacy, formed the strength of boyhood bonds. Indeed, loyalty was so important in the competitive milieu of boy culture that these youthful relationships often took on the qualities of a military alliance.[29] Loyalty was not the only basis for friendships between boys, however. Male youngsters loved to set up clubs, which met in attics and cellars. These ranged in character from small-town cabals specializing in melon theft to the natural history "museum" established by Theodore Roosevelt. Two common purposes of many such clubs were nurture and athletics. Fellow members staged raids—sometimes elaborately organized—on local orchards and gardens, then cooked and ate their booty together. Boys formed athletic groups that staged extensive competitions among members. Ironically, these events were fierce and hostile in tone and sometimes even ended in bloodshed. In point of fact, boy culture was divided as surely as it was united.[30]

Just as friendship between boys bloomed suddenly and with fervor, so too did enmity. This instant hostility was frequently "taken out on the spot," for the youngsters preferred to settle "a personal grievance at once, even if the explanation is made with fists."[31] New boys in town often had to prove themselves by fighting, and older boys sometimes amused themselves by forcing the younger boys into combat with each other.[32]

But the fiercest fights involved youngsters from rival turf. Indeed, such "enemy" groups played a powerful role in unifying local segments of boy culture, and many boys' gangs were really just neighborhood alliances designed to protect members and turf from other gangs. In the countryside, these divisions pitted village against village, or one side of town against the other. In cities, lines were drawn between different neighborhoods. And in a large, densely packed metropolis like New York, crucial rivalries could develop even between boys from opposite ends of the same block.[33] Sometimes these geographic battle lines reflected nothing more than the simple accident of residence. But often they coincided with sharp differences of class and ethnicity that added extra layers of meaning to boyish antagonisms. Henry Seidel Canby recalled the fierce hostility between Protestant boys from the comfortable neighborhoods of Wilmington, Delaware, and the Irish Catholic boys from the nearby slums. To reach their private schools every day, the youngsters from the "better" families had to cross enemy turf and pass the public and parochial schools the Irish boys attended. Canby wrote: "Each of us, by one of those tacit agreements made between enemies, had his particular mick, who either chased or was chased . . . on sight. . . . It was an awful joy to spot your own mick."[34]

While these differences of class and neighborhood carved the boys' world into large segments, there were finer gradations within boy culture that produced fewer dramatic confrontations but occupied much more of a boy's daily attention. In particular, differences of size were a major preoccupation in boy culture.[35] In some activities, the distinction between age and size blurred—"little" and "young" usually meant the same thing with boys. And among boys who were close together in age and size, another division existed—a series of informal rankings based on skill. They rated each other by weight, height, "pluck," spirit, appearance, and all sorts of athletic skills from swimming to stone throwing to ability at various organized games. The frequent fights between boys established a vitally important kind of pecking order. And those urban boys who spent much of their time in school ranked each other's scholastic abilities on a finely graded scale. Although youngsters determined some of these ratings by open contest, they established many others through unceasing observation.[36] While this constant process of comparison did not have the deeply divisive effect on boy culture that matters such as class and geography did, it provided a basis for elaborate, crosscutting hierarchies within the group and set the stage for many personal jealousies and conflicts.[37]

In fact, the boys' world was divided and subdivided endlessly. Clearly set apart from the realms of men, of very small boys, and of the entire female sex, the realm of boyhood was split into groups by differing places of residence, which in turn reflected differences of ethnicity and social status. These geographically based chunks of boys' world were ordered internally by a shifting series of rankings. And many boys disliked one another for purely personal reasons. Linking boys across these many fissures were family ties and the loyalty of friendship. But friendships among boys were volatile affairs—intense, short-lived, and constantly shifting. To a great extent, then, boys' realm—like the grown-up world of their fathers—was based on the isolated individual. Although it was a little culture based on constant play and full of exuberance and high spirits, it was also a cruel, competitive, uncertain, and even violent world. It held together because boys adhered faithfully to a common set of values.

Boy culture embraced two sorts of values: the traits and behaviors boys openly respected in one another, and the implicit values embedded in the structure of boy culture (though rarely articulated, these values were honored through daily activities and experiences). Both of these layers of value added to the distinctiveness of boy culture, and both contributed to its legacy by leaving a permanent imprint on boys' characters. Many values which boys openly esteemed are evident from the activities they pursued. In a world which centered on physical play, bodily attributes and physical prowess loomed large. Traits such as size, strength, speed, and endurance earned a boy respect among his peers. As much as boys valued loyalty and physical prowess, though, the trait which they consciously held in highest esteem was courage. Their notion of courage really consisted of two parts, stoicism and daring. Stoicism involved the suppression of "weak" feelings—fear, pain, grief. The boys' game of "soak-about," in which a group of boys tried to hit another boy in a vulnerable spot with a hard ball, was a classic expression the demand for stoicism. The victim had to face pain without flinching.[38]

This stoic courage, a feat of self-control, contrasted sharply with daring courage, an achievement of action. Like stoicism, daring found ritual expression in games. The dare was a constant presence in boy culture, goading youngsters into bold actions that they might not have undertaken on their own. As novelist Lew Wallace put it, he and his boyhood friends were "given to [this] 'dare' habit; and the deeper the water, the thinner the ice, the longer the run, the hotter the blaze, the more certain [was] the challenge."[39] These experiences with the courage of daring may have left a lasting imprint on the boys who underwent them. A number of historians and commentators have noted that the ideal of achievement which grownups taught to boys was really the cautious, abstemious ethic of the clerk rather than the bold and daring code of the entrepreneur.[40] Young males did not learn to be venturesome from the adults who preached hard work and self-denial, but from boy culture. Boldness, like stoicism, was a form of courage that youngsters cultivated.

Of the implied values, which lay just outside of boys' consciousness, the most pervasive was mastery. For one thing, youngsters were constantly learning to master new skills. Boys' many games and pastimes helped them develop a great variety of physical abilities, and boys learned the mastery of a wide range of social skills in their intensive social contact with each other and in the negotiations that threaded in and out of their daily round of activity.

Boys' experience in their separate world also taught them how to impose their will on other people and on nature itself. Their education in social mastery went on constantly while they were among their peers. Most of the popular pastimes forced boys to seek each other's defeat and thus prove individual mastery. At another level, boys strove for mastery by trying to set the agenda for their comrades ("dare" games were an extreme expression of this impulse). And some boys exhibited their mastery through bullying.

Many of boys' most forceful attempts to master their environment, though, were directed at the physical rather than the social world. The hunting and fishing activity so popular among boys taught them to master their physical surroundings. Furthermore, the many city boys who hunted in order to enlarge their animal collections were learning to subordinate nature to their own acquisitive impulses. These collections, common among Victorian boys, served the habit of mastery in still another way. For when a boy named and classified the animals he killed, he was learning to make nature serve the cause of science. Other forms of boyhood mastery fed on this same technological drive. The building of toy ships that would actually float, the construction of snow forts, the performance of crude scientific experiments—these common boyhood activities taught youngsters the skills (and the habit) of mastery over nature in the service of human needs and knowledge. The experience of boy culture encouraged a male child to become the master, the conqueror, the owner of what was outside him.

At the same time, boyhood experiences also taught youngsters to control their inner world of emotions. Games like "soak-about" forced boys to hide their "weak" feelings. Fear of being labeled a "crybaby" restrained the impulse to seek comfort in times of stress. As boys learned to overcome pain, fear, and the need for emotional comfort, they were encouraged to suppress other expressions of vulnerability, such as grief and tender affection. Boy culture, then, was teaching a selective form of impulse control—it trained boys to master the emotions that would otherwise make them vulnerable to predatory rivals.

Their activities not only put a premium on self-assertion, but also created an endless round of competitions. Boys competed constantly with one another, both in vigorous physical pastimes and in "tame" games like chess and checkers. Even seemingly noncompetitive activities like swimming, climbing, and rock throwing yielded opportunities for comparing abilities. Youngsters learned to rank their peers, and at the same time they developed the habit of incessant struggling up the ladder of achievement. Moreover, as each boy asserted his will against others, he grew accustomed to life as a never-ending series of individual combats. More than anything that a boy experienced in the settings dominated by adults, boy culture replicated the working conditions of the commercial marketplace.

Yet much of the cruelty in boys' world was spontaneous and impulsive. As boys' aggressions were given free rein, the sheer exuberance of exercise and the pure joy of play prevailed. But needless cruelty and unthinking meanness often followed from unchecked self-assertion. Boys loved to compare themselves to animals, and two animal similes seem apt here. If boys at times behaved like a hostile pack of wolves that preyed on its own kind as well as on other species, they also at times acted like a litter of playful pups that enjoyed romping, wrestling, and testing new skills. Such play is rarely free of cruelty or violence, and the same can be said of boy culture. Playful spontaneity bred friendly play and rough hostility in equal measure.

The violence that friends inflicted on each other often meant more than the playful assertion of dominance. Ironically, this deeper meaning in some of boys' violence involved their fondness for each other. Since boys worked to restrain their tender impulses in each other's presence, they lacked a direct outlet for the natural affection of friends. This warm feeling sometimes found expression in the bonds of the club and of the gang and in the demanding codes of loyalty that bound young comrades together. But another avenue of release for these fond impulses came through constant physical exchanges. Samuel Crothers described the boys' world as a place where the "heroes make friends with one another by indulging in everlasting assault and battery, and continually arise 'refreshed with the blows.' "[41] That boys expressed affection through mayhem does not mean that violence was merely a channel for fond feeling. Boys held back their deepest reserves of cruelty when they scrapped with friends, saving their fiercest fury for enemies. In their cultural world, where gestures of tenderness were forbidden, physical combat allowed them moments of touch and bouts of intense embrace. By a certain "boy logic," it made sense to pay one's affections in the coin of physical combat, which served as the social currency of boys' world.

Even above self-assertion and aggression, there was one value that governed all conduct, that provided a common focus for boys' activities together, that served as boy culture's virtual reason for being—independence. What made boy culture special in a youngster's experience was that it allowed an autonomy he had never before experienced. Teachers and parents did try at times to extend their authority to boys' world, but most of its activities took place too far away for adults to control them. Boys were on their own in constructing a world of their choosing.

Boy culture challenged a youngster to master an immense variety of skills; forced him to learn elaborate codes of behavior and complex, layered systems of value; encouraged him to form enjoyable relationships and useful alliances and to organize groups that could function effectively; and demanded that he deal with the vicissitudes of competition and the constant ranking and evaluation of peers. But most of all, the culture of his fellows required a boy to learn all these tasks independently—without the help of caring adults, with only limited assistance from other boys, and thus without any significant emotional support. Each boy—like a middle-class man at work—sought his own good in a world of shifting alliances and fierce competition. He learned to assert himself and to stand emotionally alone while away from his family. During the part of each day that he lived among his peers, he received a strenuous education in autonomy.

This autonomy existed, however, within well-defined boundaries of place and time. Many adults tried to influence what went on within boy culture even though they did not supervise it. Often, confrontations between youngsters and adults focused on acts of vandalism. Trespass and petty theft, for instance, often grew out of the blithe disregard that boys had for private property. Outdoors, their culture did not recognize the lines that separated one adult's possessions from another's—when they stole fruit or cut through other folks' yards, they often did so in a spirit of intentional innocence about the rules of the grown-up world. When Henry Seidel Canby wrote about avoiding an enemy on the way to school, he described acts of trespass as mere details in a heroic adventure: " . . . get a quick start down Madison before he [sees] you . . . shin over the Pennypacker back fence, dodge down the Howland grape arbor, double back to the Pennypacker lawn, and if no footsteps followed, . . . sink panting on the iron grayhound [*sic*] that pointed its slim muzzle down West Street."[42] Whereas Canby blithely ignored adult boundaries, other boys were drawn to rule-breaking by the possibility of a clash with authority. They constantly dared each other to perform dangerous acts. And since a confrontation with adults was one kind of danger, risking that confrontation was a way to prove one's bravery.[43] Thus, the pleasure in raiding a garden or an orchard came from the adventure as much as from the loot, and youthful mischief-makers made a sport of avoiding officers of the law and irate property owners.

These pranks further served as skirmishes in a kind of guerrilla warfare that boys waged against adults.[44] Youthful raids on adult dignity and property gave boys a chance to assert their own needs and values and lay their claim to the outdoors as a world for them to use as they saw fit. Acts of vandalism also provided boys with an opportunity to express their hostility toward male symbols of authority—police, constables, irate property owners. In Dan Beard's town in Ohio, it was a "tradition among the big boys" to steal watermelons. Dan's peers urged him to take one from a neighbor, even though the same melons were readily available in his own yard. During the theft, he and his friends eluded capture by his neighbors and thus achieved the real reward for their adventure.[45] Such guerrilla warfare gave boys a chance to reverse roles in their dealings with men. For a moment, at least, youngsters had power—power to foil the intentions of grown men, power to work for and gain the property they wanted. And grown men could rarely control vandalism—they could only oppose it enough to make it a more exciting pastime for boys.

The confrontation between boy culture and male authority often took place at school. While few boys spent as many hours in school as boys do nowadays, many spent much of their time in school under the authority of male teachers. During that time, the boys enjoyed making life difficult for the man at the head of the classroom. "Man" is actually a misnomer here, since male teachers were frequently college students or teenagers. The problem of authority thus created by the youth of the teachers was often compounded by the age of the students—in small-town schools, "children" as old as twenty might be in the same classroom with three- or four-year-olds.[46]

With the balance of power between boy culture and authority more equal than usual, even the younger boys seized this opportunity to express their resentment toward male authority. The boys talked, passed notes to the girls, threw paper wads, and refused to join in recitations. When a teacher attempted to assert his authority over a boy, the youngster might simply get up and leave school.[47] Sometimes there were even scuffles between teachers and older students.[48]

Why did nineteenth-century boys take such pleasure in flouting their teachers' authority? For one thing, boys felt little enthusiasm for school. The work was abstract, the physical confinement taxing, the ultimate rewards unclear.[49] The stepwise progression that sent young males upward through the grades, into college, and on to a good job did not become established until the end of the century.[50] Given the lack of intrinsic satisfaction or ultimate reward, boys resented the time they spent at school as an arbitrary adult intrusion into their lives. But the running warfare between boys and their teachers was also linked in spirit and motive to the guerrilla tactics of vandalism. When boys harassed teachers, they were seeking ways to take vengeance on the arbitrary authority of adults. Boys were also able to combine vengeance with enjoyment by finding clever ways to wreak havoc. The pleasure principle was ceaselessly at work in boy culture.

Parents were the most potent enemies of boy culture. They were not distant authority figures who could be irked at little emotional cost. Instead they were (usually) the two most beloved and powerful people in a boy's life. How then did boy culture fare in its conflicts with parents? What happened when the borders of home and boys' world overlapped, or when the values of those two spheres conflicted?

Middle-class men had fewer points of contact with boy culture than their wives did, but they intruded into boys' world in spite of their frequent absences from home.[51] In rural areas, a boy was expected to work on behalf of the family, whether his father was just a plain farmer or a prominent lawyer, storekeeper, or politician. Boys might work at home or elsewhere, but it was fathers who arranged the work, and most fathers also oversaw it, punishing failures of duty.[52] Fathers also frustrated boy culture by serving as head disciplinarians in their families. For example, when young Lew Wallace was sent from his Indiana home after long years of truancy and misbehavior, it was his father, not his mother, who banished him. The father also had the duty of punishing his son when someone from outside the home—a teacher, a neighbor, an officer of the law—complained about the boy's behavior. For instance, when a Maine boy named James Barnard Blake was caught stealing fruit from a neighbor's orchard, it was his father who sat him down for a stern lecture.[53]

These intrusive duties placed the father in the role of archenemy of the hedonism that typified boy culture. But the father made a difficult target for anger because his sons both feared and loved him, so they redirected their anger toward adult men in general. Daniel Beard, founder of the Boy Scouts and a prominent illustrator, explained in his autobiography that boys as a rule "did not like men," and considered them "enemies" who always interfered with "our pleasure."[54] By targeting all adult males, boys put their fathers on the same plane with constables, teachers, and irate neighbors. This may explain why boys often tormented teachers instead of simply ignoring them, and why they played cat-and-mouse with farmers by raiding closely watched gardens instead of taking better pickings from more isolated fields. Collisions with male authority figures were inevitable because boys often sought out such confrontations.

Men were only the most visible enemies of boy culture, not the most effective ones. Mothers had more contact with boys than did their husbands. And mothers responded to situations that arose in the daily ebb and flow of family life. Women were also more effective opponents of boy culture than men because of their methods of opposition. They relied less on bluster or physical punishment and more on tenderness, guilt, and moral suasion—tactics that seemed to disarm the youthful opposition more effectively than a simple show of power. These contrasts between men's and women's tactics grew partly from a vital difference in their basic social duties toward boys: men were charged especially with maintaining good order; women, with fitting boys to be sober, hardworking Christians in a treacherous world. Huck Finn perceived this when he complained that Aunt Sally wanted to "sivilize" him. Where men sought to control boys—to "interfere" with their "pleasure," as Dan Beard put it—women intended to redeem boys from their barbarism.[55]

Inevitably, then, the home and the outdoors came to stand for much more than just two physical spaces for women and boys—the domestic threshold marked a cultural dividing line of the deepest significance. On one side lay women's sphere, a world of domesticity and civilization; on the other side, adult control gave way to the rough pleasures of boy culture. Neither space was exclusive—women entered boys' world to deliver reprimands and reminders of duties at home, while boys sometimes established their distinctive culture in the upper regions of the household. But the home and the outdoors had powerful symbolic meaning. When boys tracked mud and dirt across clean floors, they were not just creating extra housework—they were bringing a fragment of their boy world into a place where it did not belong. And mothers also viewed their sons' "priceless" collections of rocks, leaves, and dead animals as invasions into a civilized world. Women and boys therefore fought constantly over muddy footprints and other relics of the outdoors that found their way inside.[56]

But mothers did not just struggle to keep the dirt and hedonism of boy culture out of the house; they also fought incessantly to extend their moral dominion out into boys' world.[57] Fortunately for women, they had more than one tactical weapon in this battle for moral influence. Often mothers attempted to control behavior by maintaining close contact with boy culture. The women who lived in small towns and in all but the largest cities were involved in social networks that sent information about their sons back to them quickly, and since they tended to run their errands in the same neighborhoods where their boys played, mothers could even conduct occasional surveillance of boy culture.[58] So most women were in a position to influence their sons' activities in the boys' world that flourished outside the home.[59] Women also struggled mightily to exert moral power within boys' world by implanting an active conscience in their sons, and they met with great success in this effort.[60] Their moral and spiritual authority seemed immense to their sons. Mothers used every available opportunity to teach their boys lessons in ethics. When gentle teaching failed, lectures and discipline were brought to bear.[61]

Often, though, the most effective restraint on boyish misbehavior was the voice of conscience, that "tyrannical monitor" that condemned in a boy's heart every violation of the moral code he learned at his mother's knee. Dan Beard's heart sank when his mother told him to stay away from the place where his friends were going to battle the boys from the next town. "This was bad news," recalled Beard, "but I never thought of disobeying her." So confident was Mary Beard of her influence that she made no attempt to keep him home. At the appointed hour, he wandered to a spot overlooking the scene of battle: "I stood disconsolately on the suspension bridge and watched my playmates, feeling like a base deserter." Dan's conscience held fast; with no one there to restrain him, he smothered his own urge to run to the aid of his comrades.[62]

But maternal influence could not really halt the operation of the wayward impulses that drove boy culture—it could only curb them. Boys, in other words, could not subdue their surging desires. They were pulled one way by the power of impulse and tugged in another by the voice of conscience. In this struggle, the pressures of boy culture supplied a powerful counterforce to maternal influence. The worst fate a youngster could suffer at the hands of his peers was to be labeled a "mama's boy." One man wrote that "the most wicked and wanton song I knew [as a boy] was:

> Does your mother know you're out?
> No, by thunder, no, by thunder!
> Does she know what you're about?
> No, by thunder, no, by thunder!"

The boys especially liked to sing this song as they performed feats of daring. The implication was that a mother's control was powerful—but it was delightful to slip beyond her grasp into forbidden pleasures.[63]

Even mothers were aware of their oppositional place in the eyes of boy culture. "Mrs. Manners" describes a mother earnestly trying to tie a ribbon on her son's collar while the son complains that "the boys'll call me 'dandy,' and 'band-box,' and 'Tom Apronstring.'" "Mrs. Manners" replies that the local paragon of good manners "plays very heartily, too . . . he is no 'girl-boy.'"[64] Such potent ridicule gave boys a powerful weapon for forcing others to reject their mothers' influence and conform to the hedonistic norms of their own cultural world. They had a fine-tuned sense of acceptable and unacceptable behaviors, and nearly all of the unacceptable behaviors were ones encouraged by mothers.[65] Boys employed social pressure—ridicule, ostracism, hazing—to defend the values and integrity of boy culture from maternal assault.[66]

Some of the most important lessons that a youngster learned from boy culture were those about living a life divided by a boundary between the two spheres.[67] He adapted to a constant process of leaving home and returning. And he quickly discovered that this process entailed a constant adjustment to the clashing values and demands of two different worlds—back and forth from a domestic world of mutual dependence to a public world of independence; from an atmosphere of cooperation and nurture to one of competition and conflict; from a sphere where intimacy was encouraged to one where human relationships were treated as means to various ends; from an environment that supported expressive impulses to one that sanctioned aggressive impulses; and from a social space that was seen as female to one that was considered male.

So the boy learned to live in a world divided. At the same time, he was also learning to live with divided loyalties and a divided heart. Ultimately, he taught himself to cope with a world of separate spheres like the one he would inhabit as an adult, for the clash between boys' world and women's was only a louder and more dramatic version of the conflict between men's and women's spheres. It was a conflict that would form a basic part of adult life.

The end of boyhood did not come in the nineteenth century as it comes in the twentieth century. There was no sequence of events that marked the progress of boys from childhood to manhood, and there were no key ages at which all youngsters reached important milestones. In earlier times, apprenticeship had marked an end of sorts to the boyhood years (though the ages of apprenticeship were themselves indefinite). But in the nineteenth century, the ages and events which brought boyhood to a close varied widely with family and personal circumstances.[68]

The most that can be said about the terminal age of boyhood is that it came in the teens, perhaps most often in the midteens.[69] But in spite of these vague age boundaries, there were a few important events which marked the end of boyhood for many youngsters. These often had to do with leaving home or taking a first clerkship or full-time job. Alphonso Rockwell's boyhood ended when he began work as a clerk. Looking back from old age, Rockwell realized that his boyhood had stopped on the day he left his home in Connecticut to take his new post in New York City:

> The ties that held me to boyhood days and pleasures along old and familiar lines were to be broken forever. Henceforth there were to be no more trips to "Indian Rock" in the company of boy intimates, where we imagined ourselves wild Indians . . . nor would I ever in the days to come sail [the familiar ponds and streams], or swim in them, or walk their banks with the zest or sense of pleasure I had known.[70]

He was assuming new statuses and the distinctive marks of manhood—self-support and a home away from his family.

But these were not the only changes that signified the end of boyhood. A teenager also brought his time in boy culture to a close when he took his first strides toward another signpost of manhood—marriage. As boys in their midteens developed an interest in girls, the customs and habits of boy culture started to lose their luster.[71] Dan Beard recalled how his teenage outlook changed when an attractive new girl arrived in town. "Suddenly marbles became a childish game which made knuckles grimy and chapped. . . . Prisoner's base was good enough sport but it mussed one's clothes." The rhymes and rituals of boyhood now "seemed absurd instead of natural," while the services at church took on a new interest. Dan suddenly began to appear in public with his face clean and his hair neatly combed.[72]

The pubescent boy did not return to the gowns and petticoats of his earliest years, but he did compromise with the demands of domesticity and restraint. He accepted willingly the confinement of clothing that had once seemed like shackles, and he even wiped away the once-treasured grime of outdoor activity from his face and hands. As he took his first steps toward marriage, a life's work, and a home of his own, he clothed himself in the garb of "civilized" manhood and washed off the marks of "savage" boyhood.[73]

The cares and commitments of manhood now loomed up before teenage boys. And at first sight, boys approached manhood eagerly; they were suddenly impatient to leave behind them the separate world that they had guarded so jealously. As Charles Dudley Warner put it, "Every boy is anxious to be a man, and is very uneasy with the restrictions that are put upon him."[74] Boys longed for the power and prerogatives of manhood—independence, authority, and a wife. They yearned to be men, and the older they grew, the more they strained in that direction.

In fact, boy culture—as viewed in a certain way—provided a course of training for manhood. It aped many activities of adult men, it taught aggressive, self-reliant qualities needed for men's work, and it helped to provide experience at making constant transitions between the gentle restraint of home and the competitive exertions of the all-male world outside. Of course, no one planned boys' activities this way. Within their own autonomous world, boys simply evolved a culture of their own that they passed on year by year from older to younger boys. But as it developed, boy culture did bear a distinct and sometimes helpful relationship to the world of manhood that lay ahead.

Yet the relationship between boy culture and manhood could be problematic as well as helpful. There were important disjunctions between boys' world and the world of men, gaps of duty and expectation that loomed like chasms before a youth who confronted them for the first time. The experience of facing those gaps and then trying to bridge them produced one of the most trying times in the lives of nineteenth-century men—the treacherous and often prolonged passage from boyhood to manhood.

After all, the contrasts between boy culture and the world of men were sharp ones: boy culture emphasized exuberant spontaneity; it allowed free rein to aggressive impulses and reveled in physical prowess and assertion.

Boy culture was a world of play, a social space where one evaded the duties and restrictions of adult society. How different this was from the world of manhood. Men were quiet and sober, for theirs was a life of serious business. They had families to support, reputations to earn, responsibilities to meet. Their world was based on work, not play, and their survival in it depended on patient planning, not spontaneous impulse. To prosper, then, a man had to delay gratification and restrain desire. Of course, he also needed to be aggressive and competitive, and he needed an instinct for self-advancement. But he had to channel these assertive impulses in ways that were suitable to the abstract battles and complex issues of middle-class men's work. Finally, a man—unlike a boy—needed a sense of responsible commitment. He could not throw over his family, disregard his business partners, or quit his job on a whim. A man had to have a sense of duty based on enduring loyalty, not on the strongest impulse of the moment. Manhood presented a young male with challenges for which boy culture had not fully prepared him. With the leap from boyhood to adulthood, a young man gave up heedless play for sober responsibility.

Just as boy culture was part of a phase in the life of a middle-class male, so, too, it had only a limited life as a historical phenomenon. The boys of the nineteenth century, of course, did not invent mischief or adventure. What separated their world from that of American boys in earlier centuries was the shape and meaning their world assumed. If we would understand that distinctive shape and meaning in historical terms, we must first understand the social milieu which enveloped middle-class boyhood in the nineteenth century.

There were several developments—each associated with the emergence of a commercial society and a middle-class culture—which influenced the form and nature of boys' world. One such development was the growing isolation of men's world from boys'. Throughout the 1800s, there was a steady exodus of professional and commercial work from the home. This trend was certainly evident in the cities, but it was visible elsewhere, too. The men who made up small-town elites (men whose sons produced much of the evidence on which this essay is based) also spent large amounts of time away from home. The work of these men, in politics and in law as well as in business, took them farther and farther afield as they followed the spreading pathways of commerce. Thus, middle-class men, whether urban or rural, became more isolated from their sons both physically and emotionally. The father-son relationship in the nineteenth century, compared to that of preceding centuries, was based on a less familiar, less active engagement between generations of males.[75] Moreover, the father-son tie was affected by the kind of work that middle-class men did. Their work was abstract, consisting of tasks far less interesting and comprehensible to a boy than the crafts and agricultural work that formed the traditional core of men's activity in rural areas. Thus, even when middle-class fathers were able to work at home, their tasks offered little to connect them with their sons.[76] In short, middle-class boys of the nineteenth century had grown alienated from their fathers and from the world of adult males. This alienation cut boyhood adrift from one of its most vital connections to the adult world.

By contrast, the conditions of middle-class life in the 1800s fostered a closer connection between the world of boys and that of women. Much historical research has shown how a distinct women's sphere evolved at the beginning of the nineteenth century.[77] Focused on domestic tasks, child rearing, and moral uplift, this redefinition of woman's activity and of her very nature as a human being had a particular impact on her relationships with her sons.

In the eighteenth century, fathers had been charged with the responsibility for molding the moral character of their sons. Common opinion at that time held that mothers were too indulgent and thus were likely to ruin their sons. Consequently, women were discouraged from playing an active role in the lives of their boys after the early years of childhood. Once basic nurture was accomplished, eighteenth-century mothers were expected to share the raising of their children (especially their sons) with older siblings, fathers, unmarried aunts, and other kin who lived in close proximity. A great many boys were bound out as apprentices or household servants or were sent away for their education by the time they had reached their teens. This all took place in a context wherein fathers were active members of the family, where the community readily penetrated the boundaries of the household, and where the world of adult males was accessible and vivid to boys.[78]

By contrast, the middle-class household of the nineteenth century became a private space. It was no longer a site of production for trade or sale, and it was increasingly a place for child rearing, for moral and spiritual cultivation, and for the interaction of the nuclear family. Women were now expected to nurture the soul and foster the conscience of the rising generation of males. Boys were not only subjected to heavier doses of maternal influence, but were subject to it for longer periods of time: most of them lived at home well into their teenage years.[79]

For a young male, this was a peculiar combination of influences. A boy grew up in one social world which contrasted sharply with the world he would inhabit as an adult. He was raised by a woman to become a man. He lived in an environment of restraint and interdependence, but he was bound for a world of independence and aggression. Some kind of social space—

intermediate between the women's world of boyhood and the men's world of manhood—was perhaps inevitable.[80]

Social custom encouraged the development of a boys' space that was neither women's nor men's. As we have seen, middle-class parents customarily freed their sons from the confinement of gowns at about age six, at the same time reducing their supervision of the boys and giving them independent playtime outdoors. In doing so, parents nurtured independence and left room for the development of a separate social space for boys. And parents did this even as they continued to nurture self-restraint and resist much of the behavior that emerged from boys' world.

In particular, the tension between women's sphere and boy culture was ongoing. Indeed, the shape and form of boys' social realm seems in many ways a reaction to the female world where they lived. The fierce independence, the physicality, the aggression, the cruelty, the masking of affection—these defining traits of boy culture reversed the qualities emphasized in women's sphere, qualities such as interdependence, spirituality, self-restraint, kindness, cooperation, and affection. Middle-class boys, as a daily matter of course, traveled back and forth between the social worlds dominated by these two contrary sets of values. And as they made this journey, the reactiveness of boy culture continued. Although this peculiar relationship between two social spheres ended in the lives of individual boys when they left home, it lived on as a social and historical phenomenon until the closing years of the nineteenth century, when the values and demands of the adult male world began to press more and more heavily on the boyhood years.

The same forces of standardization that swept through the rest of society in the late 1800s caught up with boy culture and preserved it in a special form, one which male adults packaged and then helped to pass on to new generations of boys. As early as the 1830s, books appeared which were compendiums of boys' activities. They not only suggested hundreds of games and projects but prescribed the rules as well. At first these books seemed to have little influence, but after the Civil War they issued forth in a publishing flood too great to be denied. In the final quarter of the century, a boy could learn boy culture as easily from books written by adults as from the example of older boys.[81]

Even when boys of the late nineteenth century absorbed the lessons of boy culture from older peers, they were learning a version that was already standardized by adult males. By the 1860s, college boys and the youth of towns and cities were holding organized competitions in the boyhood games of baseball and football. Free-form at the start, the rules by which these teams and clubs played were gradually standardized, smoothing out the regional variety and local eccentricity of the games. Then, during the final decades of the century, the teams fell increasingly under the influence of college and league officials who further reshaped the sports in keeping with their own adult concerns. Thus, when school-age boys in the last third of the century looked to their older peers for cues to how to play a game, they were learning rules that were being fitted ever more closely to the specifications of young men and male adults.[82]

The standardization of boyhood by grown-ups proceeded on other fronts in the late nineteenth century. During the 1880s and 1890s, adult men formed a great number of boys' organizations, such as the Boys' Brigades and the Knights of King Arthur, and also added boys' divisions to existing organizations like the YMCA. The boys' workers, as they were called, packaged many of the traditional games and skills of boy culture together with their own moral agendas (usually Christian or nostalgic for rural life) and spread them aggressively among urban boys. The most influential result of this movement was the Boy Scouts of America, which did not come into being until the second decade of the twentieth century. But for the thousands of boys who entered similar organizations before 1900, the experience did not bear a close resemblance to the experience of a boy culture unshaped by adults. The presence of a moral program generated by grown-ups sharply separated boys' organizations of the late nineteenth century from the boy world of earlier years.[83]

Most fatal to boy culture was the increase in schooling for boys from comfortable backgrounds. As late-century male youngsters began to spend nine months a year at school for a longer span of years, their experiences in the classroom and the schoolyard replaced boy culture as the focus of boys' life away from home. The content of boy culture was molded increasingly by the academic, social, and extracurricular aspects of school, which meant that it was being shaped more and more by adult hopes and concerns.[84] Boys did not accept this school culture passively. They molded it and selected from it according to their own needs. But the fact remains that boy culture was becoming more reactive to adult agendas, and these priorities were thrust into the midst of boys' separate world in a way that would have been unusual during most of the nineteenth century.

One of the most conspicuous changes that the new system of education brought to boy culture in the late 1800s was the school's age-graded ladder of ascent.[85] Although competition and informal peer ranking continued among boys, a new hierarchy of age was imposed on their world. This hierarchy not only gave new importance to a status that was purely ascribed, but also tended to break the continuity of generations, in which older and younger boys played freely together and the older taught the younger the ways of the world. The younger boys were now just as likely to learn those ways from teachers, recreational leaders, or books.

The age-graded ladder brought adulthood into boys' world in one other crucial way: it created a new sort of continuity between boyhood and manhood. As a boy climbed onto the lowest rungs in the primary grades, he could look up the ladder all the way through high school and out into the world of men's work. The age-graded ladder bridged the distance that had once existed between boyhood and manhood.

In sum, the old gap between the world of boys and the world of men was now more readily crossed in either direction. Men molded and shaped the play and the values of boys as never before, while boys sensed a continuity between their daily world and the world of men which had not existed in the nineteenth century. Boys did not cease to struggle against the demands of adulthood, nor did they stop trying to create a world more exciting and enjoyable than the ones adults sought to impose. But with the changes of the late nineteenth century, the terms of their struggle and the limits on their creativity were forever altered. A boys' world continues to exist even in the late twentieth century, but it bears a different aspect from its forerunner of the 1800s.

TWO

Middle-Class Men and the Solace of Fraternal Ritual

Mark C. Carnes

That America emerged as a middle-class nation during the mid-nineteenth century is beyond question, although scholars still debate how completely bourgeois values permeated the working classes. What remains at issue is whether middle-class hegemony was accomplished through the almost effortless diffusion of liberal values, as consensus historians claim, or through the self-conscious efforts of an emergent bourgeoisie, as revisionists contend.[1] The revisionist position has recently been strengthened by Mary Ryan, who has shown the relation of family and gender to the ascendancy of the middle class. Ryan has argued that the hardworking and sober clerks and businessmen of nineteenth-century lore were not "self-made," but had been "cradled" in the evangelical homes of the antebellum era, where sons learned important lessons in self-sacrifice, industriousness, and temperance, and remained sheltered for as long as possible from the dissipation of tavern and brothel.

Ryan's analysis of the shift in men's attitudes toward work, leisure, and the family is a signal contribution to an understanding of middle-class masculinity during the Victorian period. For Ryan, a prominent women's historian, this crucial transformation in men was caused largely by women. Although she refers to a "family strategy" and to "parental" decisions, she makes it clear that women's influence in child rearing was paramount. The "revered mother dominated the emotional space of the home," Ryan notes, so much so that the "idea of fatherhood itself seemed almost to wither away as the bond between mother and child assumed central place in the constellation of family affection. . . . In the narrowing home sphere, at least, women had undisputed title to psychological leadership," Ryan concludes.[2] The cradle of the middle class, and of capitalism itself, had been rocked by women.

Ryan's study, drawn largely from church magazines and the minutes of women's reform societies, shows how middle-class women attempted to mold sons in ways that fit the needs of capitalism. But there is little evidence to support the inference that boys pliantly changed in response to maternal

The material for this essay was partly drawn from chapter 4 of *Secret Ritual and Manhood in Victorian America* (New Haven: Yale University Press, 1989).

preachments. That children are innately resistant to parental guidance is all too evident to anyone who has raised children. Historian E. Anthony Rotundo has shown the relevance of this point to Victorian America, where boys fashioned a "culture" characterized by violent games, turf wars, cruel pranks, and other challenges to the values of home and mother (see his essay in this volume). In any case, it is hard to imagine that the adult men who fashioned the Darwinian world of nineteenth-century business and industry had fully absorbed the gentle virtues of Christ. An important question in the history of nineteenth-century masculinity—and capitalism—remains unanswered: Did middle-class sons internalize and retain as young men the values and emotional identifications they had learned at their mothers' knees?

In autobiographies and at testimonial dinners, successful men commonly attributed their accomplishments to maternal nurture. These stylized professions ("I owe it all to my sainted mother") reveal much about the symbolic importance of motherhood, especially as refracted through the haze of distant memory, but relatively little about the emotional disposition of the men who made them. Victorian men were not given to self-analysis, moreover, and they even more rarely committed their introspections to paper. To understand the psychological orientation of these young men, it is necessary to approach the subject indirectly.

The secret rituals that were created and repeatedly performed by the millions of men who belonged to fraternal orders are important—and neglected—sources for such an inquiry. In 1897 the *North American Review,* proclaiming the last third of the nineteenth century the "Golden Age of Fraternity," reported that of a population of nineteen million adult male Americans, five and a half million belonged to fraternal orders—the Red Men (165,000), Odd Fellows (810,000), Freemasons (750,000), Knights of Pythias (475,000), and hundreds of smaller orders.[3] Millions more belonged to the Grand Army of the Republic, the Knights of Labor, the Grange, and similar organizations. The distinguishing feature and central activity of all these organizations was the performance of elaborate sequences of initiation rituals.

There is little evidence to support Lionel Tiger's hypothesis that men are biologically impelled to take part in such ceremonies.[4] Apart from nineteenth-century phrenologists, who determined that a posterior portion of the brain gave rise to "inhabitiveness," no one has seriously proposed a biological basis for male bonding. Nor is the appeal of such rituals a constant in human history. Despite the claims of enthusiasts of the orders, nearly all fraternal rituals (and most of the orders themselves) were created after the 1830s. And interest among middle-class men in these same rituals declined suddenly in the early twentieth century. The initiations of the orders must be considered a distinct product of Victorian American culture and society.

Fraternal ritual, though remarkably widespread, was chiefly a phe-nomenon of the middle classes. The rise of the rituals coincided with the orders' adoption of middle-class values. Formerly drinking societies, the Freemasons and Odd Fellows during the 1830s and 1840s banned alcohol, attempted to ascertain the moral character of new members, created juridical proceedings to expel dissolute or wayward members, and replaced the rented tavern rooms by building elaborate "temples." Scholars have confirmed that membership in most orders was drawn largely from the ur-ban middle classes.[5]

But why were such men impelled to perform elaborate initiations? Con-temporaries, such as the writer for the *North American Review,* observed that

> there is a strange and powerful attraction for some men in the mys-ticism of the ritual. There is a peculiar fascination in the unreality of the initiation, an allurement about fine 'team' work, a charm of deep potency in the unrestricted, out-of-the-world atmosphere which surrounds the scenes where men are knit together by the closest ties, [and] bound by the most solemn obligations to main-tain secrecy . . .

The lodge did not promote friendship, nor even serve the needs of business, he added. So much time was spent on initiation that members never got a chance to know each other or to cultivate contacts. Often they became so intent on satisfying a "craving" for ritual that they neglected their profes-sions or businesses.[6] Why some men were predisposed to be "charmed" by and "powerfully attracted" to such rituals he did not say.

Not all rituals elicited this powerful response. Thousands of degrees were written for the hundreds of orders, but relatively few ceremonies—prob-ably no more than twenty—were successful. These were shamelessly pirated or slightly modified by rival orders, and certain themes reappeared in scores of ceremonies. Officials were themselves at a loss to explain why certain rituals struck a responsive chord in members. But powerful rituals carried tangible benefits: They prompted initiates to return to the lodge the following week, to take still higher degrees, and to pay additional initiation fees. To gain perspective on the unexpressed meanings of the rituals, I pro-pose to examine in detail the evolution of the first degree of the Improved Order of Red Men.

The order was established in 1834 by ex-Freemasons. Its original initia-tion consisted of little more than an oath of secrecy and a promise of fellowship. During meetings members drank, told ribald stories, and occupied themselves with similar amusements.[7] By the late 1830s a middle-class faction that opposed such practices attempted to prohibit "tribes" from renting rooms in taverns. When this proposal was defeated, many of these members left the order, probably to join the Odd Fellows or Freemasons, which had recently instituted middle-class reforms. By 1840 the Grand Lodge of the Red Men attempted to recapture the disaffected middle classes by enjoining lodges from meeting in buildings where liquor was sold and by expelling members who opposed such action. Despite these concessions to middle-class sensibilities, the Red Men experienced little growth: By 1850 it had only forty-five "tribes" and 3,175 members.[8]

During the following two decades the principal work of the order was the revision of its rituals.[9] The Grand Lodge convened numerous committees on ritual, offered monetary prizes for the best submissions, and formally adopted new rituals in 1850, 1852, 1857, 1859, and 1864. None "met with the general approbation hoped for," and by 1865 the order was nearly destitute.[10] In 1868 the Grand Lodge threw out the old rituals and devised a new sequence, which commenced with what they called the Adoption Degree. This time the order immediately began to experience "unparalleled growth." Before the year had ended the Grand Lodge reported that the rituals were "giving excellent satisfaction."[11] By the mid-1870s, ten thousand new members were being initiated annually. Circulars describing the order to prospective members now emphasized its "secret work," which was "beautiful beyond description and wholly unlike that of any other order."[12] By 1900 hundreds of thousands of Red Men were finding their way into wigwams of the order each week. Annual receipts exceeded a million dollars. Officials credited the ritual of 1868, particularly the Adoption Degree, with the order's success.[13]

The question of why the earlier rituals failed to elicit "general approbation" while the Adoption Degree of 1868 gave "excellent satisfaction" is ultimately unanswerable. Outside observers can never know what any aspect of a culture means to the people who create and live with it, and fraternal leaders who had to offer monetary rewards for the creation of effective rituals were obviously incapable of explaining why some were popular and others not. The question is further complicated by the Red Men's having destroyed records of the unsuccessful rituals.[14]

Forty years after the approval of the Adoption Degree, Thomas Donnalley, a student of the order, was talking to groups of elderly Red Men about the society's origins when one of them produced a copy of the unsuccessful ritual of 1864. Donnalley knew that member dissatisfaction had led to its rejection, but it seemed to him "of a high order of merit as a literary production." He could not imagine why it had been discarded. In 1908 he published sections of the document.[15]

In the Brave's Degree, the initial degree of this ritual, the candidate was given a bow and arrow and told to bring home a hunting trophy. After he had been led around the lodge, his conductor (a lodge official) pointed toward the ceiling and told him to shoot down an imaginary eagle. On completion of this pantomime he congratulated the initiate for hitting the eagle, and told him to take a plume of feathers to the chief as evidence of his hunting prowess. Then they hiked around the lodge to retrieve the feathers. These were presented to the chief, who, on seeing the trophy, welcomed the new brother to the order.

The Adoption Degree of 1868 was considerably longer than the Brave's Degree.[16] It began with an invocation by a sachem, who prayed to the "Great Spirit of the Universe" to bring harmony to the tribe, to preserve the Indians' homes, and to "shed Thy bounties upon all Red Men of the forest." Despite these hopes, however, the ritual's main theme was death. The sachem called upon the Great Spirit to give each Red Man the "holy courage" to paddle his canoe safely to "that undiscovered country from whose bourne no traveler returns." During the invocation he returned to the subject of death:

> Teach us the trail we must follow while we live in this forest, and when it is Thy will that we shall cross the river of death, take us to Thyself, where Thy council fire of love and glory burneth forever in righteousness.

Then the council fire was kindled; in the preparation room the candidate—a "pale face"—removed his shirt and shoes and put on moccasins. A scout rapped at the "inner wicket" and motioned for the candidate to follow. They padded silently around the lodge room, avoiding a group of Indians who were "sleeping" at the far end. Then the scout tripped over one of the sleeping Indians. The awakened Indian shouted, "Spies! Traitors in our Camp!" and the group captured the candidate; the scout escaped. The Indian "hunters" then conferred around a fire:

> First Brave: This pale face is of a hated nation: let us put him to the torture!
> Second Brave: He is a squaw, and cannot bear the torture!
> Third Brave: He fears a Warrior's death!
> Fourth Brave: Let us burn him at the stake!

The discussion continued in similar fashion. At last the initiate was informed that he would indeed be consumed by fire.

They proceeded to the opposite end of the lodge, where they were led to a tepee. Just after they had been admitted, another Indian rushed at the candidate with an uplifted knife, only to be intercepted by a hunter, who assured him that the paleface would soon be tortured. "Then let us proceed, pale face, and unless some Chief interposes, you perish at the stake. Why do you tempt your fate? or is it your wish to become a Red Man?" The candidate was prompted to answer yes. The hunter warned: "Know, then, that Red Men are men without fear, and none but such can be adopted by our Tribe." After more questions the hunter demanded proof of the candidate's courage: "The honest and brave man meets death with a smile—the *guilty* trembles at the very thought."

The initiate was bound to the stake, and the hunters were encouraged to prepare their scalping knives and war clubs. The Indians commenced a scalp dance, and fagots were lit. Another Indian ran to summon the prophet. The prophet, however, emerged from the tent, halted the execution, berated the hunters for their impulsiveness, and pronounced the candidate "a man without fear." The prophet then lectured the candidate on the family of Red Men, explaining that they held property in common and were dedicated to their "brothers," the "children of the forest." However, he warned the candidate that the final decision about his adoption rested with the sachem. The prophet gave the candidate an eagle's feather as proof of his courage.

After more speeches and a pledge of secrecy, the candidate was led to another tepee in the far corner of the lodge. As he approached, the sachem threw open the flap and upbraided his guards for sleeping on duty, thereby allowing a paleface to come into his presence. The warriors did not immediately respond, and the sachem started to throw a tomahawk at the initiate. One of the hungers then grasped the sachem's arm. "No, Sachem, no! Thy children when on duty never sleep!" The hunter added that the initiate had passed the ordeal and been endorsed by the prophet. He produced the eagle's feather as proof. The sachem, realizing his error, tossed his tomahawk aside and shook hands with the candidate: "Then you are welcome to our bosom." The sachem delivered a welcoming speech stressing the protection that the order afforded members of the tribe, much as "the eagle shieldeth her young and tender brood."

The 1864 and 1868 rituals were both concerned with liminality (Arnold van Gennep's term to describe the ritual transition from one status to another). But the differences between the rituals were more striking than the similarities. If the plot of the 1864 ritual was predicated on the initiate's circuitous journey to meet the sachem, the Adoption Degree was suffused with words and activities signifying motion and transition. The "pale face," who was symbolically (and prematurely?) given moccasins, "wandered" around the lodge before he was discovered by hunters, who themselves were traveling away from camp in search of game. (The ritual included an optional "Amplified Form," which showed the sachem eagerly awaiting the return of his braves, thereby reiterating the image of travel.) The initiate journeyed from camp to camp, from tepee to tepee. His crime was one of trespass, for he was twice found "astray in the sacred home of the Red Men." He compounded this error of navigation by venturing toward the sachem's tepee, thus igniting the volatile exchange. After the sachem welcomed him to the order he added that "you have left your accustomed walks in life to range the forest with Red Men," finally noting that "all within the Order have traveled the same trail, and passed through the same ordeal."

The ritual consistently drew an analogy between motion through a forest or across rivers and the journey of life. Prior to his adoption by the Red Men, the initiate was "wandering," "astray," and "trespassing," his entire life course somehow wayward. To redirect his energies and set out on a better path, he required considerable time and effort—and the assistance of secret ritual.

Although it may appear that the initiate's role was passive, the ritual's underlying premise was that the initiate had *chosen* to embark on a new life course. An ode at the closing of the Adoption Degree concluded with these lines: "Is your mind with friendship flowing, / Freedom in your pathway showing? / Brothers' love shall never cease." The preliminary couplet, infelicitous even by fraternal standards, implied a conscious effort to link the seemingly dissimilar themes of friendship and an unencumbered "pathway." The result, taken out of context, appears nonsensical. But if the ritual is understood as an extended allegory involving personal development, the closing phrase gains a highly compressed and cogent meaning: Men must remain emotionally free to pursue a path of friendship and to avoid any obstacles that would hinder such a course.

The sachem was especially concerned with the final destination of this life journey. In his initial speech he had prayed to the Great Spirit to teach each Red Man to paddle his canoe safely to "that undiscovered country from whose bourne no traveler returns." At the close of the speech he again referred to the metaphor: "When it is Thy will that we shall cross the river of death, take us to Thyself . . . " On two occasions the candidate's initiatory journey nearly ended in death, and his eventual deliverance was predicated on his ability to transcend fear of death. The prophet retuned to the metaphor of death-as-journey in his final speech: "And when through life serenely you have passed, / And landed your frail bark beyond life's sea, / May your eternal lot be cast with those / Who know no sorrow, and can feel no pain."

The initiate, though twice spared from execution, had in a sense experienced a metaphorical death: His former self had not really survived the ritualistic journey; his previous life course had been shown to be all wrong. With the help of the ritual, he had chosen an alternative—and dramatically different—route and destination. On the simplest level, the Adoption Degree implied that the life of the paleface had come to an end. He would as a Red Man chart a more "serene" course for life's journey.

The purpose of the ritual was not to reform the initiate, but to remake him entirely, for his errant life course was due to personal deficiencies. Though apprehended for the crime of trespass, he was to be put to death for a failing of character: He was a "pale face" and a "squaw" who "could not bear torture." He was excluded from the tribe, which consisted of "men without fear," because he was unfit. Through the transformative magic of the ritual, the initiate's courage was confirmed. Now he could travel with the brethren of the Red Men.

The most important innovation of the 1868 ritual was the transformation of the sachem into a complex character. In the 1864 ritual he simply expressed joy on beholding the initiate. But in the 1868 revision the sachem's character underwent considerable development. In the earliest scenes he was portrayed as a devout religious leader who fretted over his absent hunters. The initiate, though, learned only that the sachem was menacing; the climax of the ritual occurred when he threw open the flaps of his tepee, glared at the initiate, shouted "in an angry tone" at his apparently negligent guards, and made motions to kill the "pale face."

Fraternal ritualists, though by no means skilled dramatists, could certainly detect major errors in plot development. Yet the climax of the Adoption Degree was seriously flawed—at least in terms of dramatic consistency—by the awkward pause after the sachem accused his guards of sleeping on duty. There was no reason why the guards should not have explained the situation immediately. The incident apparently was contrived to provide an opportunity for the sachem to display his lethal wrath toward the initiate. This dramaturgic device thus highlighted the sachem's emotional transformation when he learned that the initiate had passed the ordeal. The sachem's anger dissolved and he welcomed the initiate to "our bosom":

> We feel it our duty, as Red Men, to watch over and supply the wants of the afflicted of our Tribe, and to shield them from danger, as the eagle shieldeth her young and tender brood.

The paternal character of the sachem and the filial character of the brethren of the tribe had become explicit. The father-son theme, moreover, was reinforced throughout the Adoption Degree. The "beloved" prophet functioned as another paternal figure whose role was similar to that of the sachem: He delivered the "pale face" from the first crisis and identified him as a "man without fear." The Great Spirit of the Universe also assumed the characteristics of a loving father. The ritual seemed to be an exhibition of paternal redundancy: The "children" of the tribe referred to their "fathers" (prophet and sachem), who in turn prayed to the father of all Red Men (the Great Spirit). And like the sachem, the prophet and the Great Spirit initially appeared distant and imposing, yet their essential benevolence was ultimately confirmed. The use of multiple father figures ensured that even the inattentive initiate would apprehend an essential aspect of the ritual: The authority figures of the Red Men, though they might *appear* threatening, were actually loving and benevolent.

The Adoption Degree presented an emotionally charged psychodrama centering on family relations. In the final lecture the sachem explained that the degree was a pallid imitation of the actual ceremonies of the Iroquois, who made their captives run the gauntlet. Those who faltered were slaughtered immediately,

> but those who passed through the ordeal successfully were adopted into the Tribe, and treated with the utmost affection and kindness. By this means all recollection of their distant kindred was gradually effaced, and they were bound by the ties of gratitude to the Tribe which had adopted them.

So it was to be with the initiate, who by joining the brothers of the Red Men necessarily detached himself from his previous family and became through adoption a child of the Red Men, there to receive the "utmost affection and kindness" of his newfound brothers and, especially, his newfound fathers.

*   *   *

Why men derived "satisfaction" from this ritual is not self-evident. One clue is suggested by the fact that these rituals, though created and practiced by the men who were transforming America into an urban industrial society, had chosen to re-create a primitive past. The Red Men were the most obvious indication of this preoccupation, but leaders and scholars of nearly all fraternal orders assumed that their rituals had some similarity to the rites of primitive men.[17] Roscoe Pound, a Masonic scholar as well as a Harvard law professor, remarked that it was obvious that Freemasonry was related to the "development of societies out of the primitive men's house."[18] The subject of fraternal ritual thus begs to be examined in light of anthropological research on primitive male initiation ceremonies.

The most important work in this field was the cross-cultural study of cultural anthropologist John Whiting and his associates. They determined that male initiation ceremonies were most commonly found in societies where women exerted an almost exclusive control over male infants and boys, and men controlled the economic and political resources (as evidenced by patrilocal residence).[19] Whiting subsequently hypothesized that in societies where the father is absent or plays a minor role in child rearing, the male infant perceives the mother as all-powerful and comes to envy her role. Yet when that boy begins to notice the world outside the home, perhaps around the age of five, he becomes aware that men control resources and clearly occupy an enviable position. A secondary identification with the masculine role thus becomes superimposed on the female identification. Male initiation ceremonies "serve psychologically to brainwash the primary feminine identity and to establish firmly the secondary male identity."[20] In societies where this "cross-sex identity conflict" becomes sufficiently widespread, initiation rituals will emerge in response to this psychological need. The rituals, by resolving these emotional conflicts, promote the well-being of young men and, presumably, of society itself.

At first glance, Whiting's discussion of mother-son sleeping arrangements and patrilocal residence seems far removed from Victorian America. But critics have contended that Whiting's coding categories were merely manifestations of larger societal characteristics: Exclusive mother-son sleeping patterns could be viewed as an analogue for father absence in early child rearing, and patrilocal residence for disproportionate male authority in the adult world.[21]

This reformulation makes it possible to move the analysis of male initiation ceremonies beyond primitive societies. In particular, the division of gender roles in Victorian America in many ways approximated the structural preconditions for Whiting's paradigm. Women's historians have shown a deep psychological division between Victorian men and women. Relegated to the "domestic sphere" of child rearing, many women sought emotional fulfillment and personal justification by devoting themselves to their children. To the task of child rearing, mothers imparted an intensity born of religious conviction, a belief that by instilling in their children the sweet virtues of Jesus, they would ultimately reshape a masculine order that had grown neglectful of his mission.[22]

On the other hand, men, having relinquished supervision of the home, increasingly defined themselves in terms of work and political affiliations.

Economic growth and structural change contributed to the separation of men from the home during much of the day. As the distance between home and workplace increased, and the workday itself was lengthened, fathers found little time to be with their children. "Paternal neglect," one observer complained in 1842, had become epidemic.[23] And when fathers returned home they were often unable to provide meaningful guidance to sons who were striking out in the emerging professions and corporations.

Not all middle-class boys had ineffective or mostly absent fathers, or received so powerful a dose of evangelical maternal guidance. Nor did all middle-class men join a lodge or become enthralled by its rituals. But many did experience some aspects of this developmental paradigm; Victorian America corresponded at least in some general way to the structural preconditions of Whiting's cross-cultural sample.

Equally important, it is apparent that the successful 1868 Adoption Degree of the Red Men might plausibly have functioned, in Whiting's words, (1) "to brainwash the primary feminine identity": The initiate, a "pale face," a "squaw," a coward, was originally considered deficient; he underwent a metaphorical death, his recollection of his former kindred was "effaced," and now he was free to pursue an entirely different life course; and (2) "to establish firmly the secondary male identity": The initiate, having first been attacked and threatened by hostile paternal figures, finally won their approval and was "adopted" as one of the "children" into the new family of Red Men.

Given its sweeping implications, Whiting's explanation and particularly his psychological assumptions warrant closer consideration. His model is drawn from identification theories which assert that if fathers are ineffective or absent in child rearing, boys will envy the power of their mothers, imitate their behavioral traits, and identify with the feminine role.[24]

The concept of identification involves distinctions and refinements that are far removed from historical evidence; it seems doubtful that historians can ever determine whether boys or men, at the core of their being, perceived themselves as "masculine." Moreover, psychologists have recently questioned the concept of gender identification. Joseph Pleck has argued forcefully that gender roles are socially constructed; there is no core masculinity to which a "normal" male innately aspires.[25] In view of these and other criticisms, I propose to replace Whiting's "cross-sex identity conflict" model with the less problematic gender-role perspective.[26]

Restated in gender-role terms, the dilemma for boys in Victorian America was not simply that their fathers were absent, thereby depriving them of psychological guides to their core masculinity, but that adult gender roles were invariant and narrowly defined, and that boys were mostly taught the sensibilities and moral values associated with the adult female role. As teenagers, or perhaps somewhat earlier, they perceived the disjunction in adult gender roles and fantasized about how they would fit into the world of men. In the absence of fathers and of adult male role models in general, they contrived a "boy culture" which in its stylized aggression and competition provided an unconscious caricature of men's roles in business and politics.[27] As young men, they were drawn to the male secret orders, where they repeatedly practiced rituals that effaced the religious values and emotional ties associated with women.

* * *

Fraternal ritual conceivably "gave satisfaction" by promoting the young man's emotional transition from an identification with feminine domesticity and religious sensibilities to the relentlessly aggressive and competitive demands of the masculine workplace. The rituals affirmed that while woman gave birth to man's body, initiation gave birth to his soul, surrounding him with "brothers" who would lavish the "utmost affection and kindness" on him. Sometimes, as in the Adoption Degree of the Red Men, the initiate's entry into a new family was explicit. But all fraternal orders appropriated the language of family relations: Members were brothers, officers were fathers, and initiates were sons. An early version of the Initiatory Degree of Odd Fellows required that candidates regard lodge officers as "our parents and guardians," who were in turn obliged to preside over the lodge "as the head of a family."[28] The Fourth, or " Remembrance," Degree asked the "children" of the lodge to heed the "instruction of a Father."[29]

Once an initiate was reborn into his fraternal family he reexperienced through the successive degrees the stages of childhood. Masonic theorists pointed out that the Blue (lowest) lodge degrees, beginning with Entered Apprentice and concluding with Master Mason, recapitulated the traditional maturational stages. The Pythian Degree of Page similarly represented the age of seven, when the child mastered household duties and learned about religion. In the degree of Esquire, which encompassed the remainder of the initiate's "nonage," he prepared for manhood, the degree of Knight. The Order of the Knights of Honor devised an explicitly developmental ritual; its three degrees were called "Infancy, Youth, and Manhood."[30]

Every major order included at least one ritual in which the initiate was threatened by elderly patriarchs. The magic of the rituals always succeeded in dissipating the surrogate fathers' contempt for or fury toward the initiate. This was particularly clear in the Adoption Degree, where the hostility of the tomahawk-wielding sachem became transmuted into affection. In this way the Adoption Degree finally "effaced" the initiate's ties to his "distant kindred"—the feminine associations of his natural family—and replaced them with ties to his adoptive masculine family, the tribe of Red Men. The double emotional function of the ritual produced a confusing combination of roles: To cease being a "squaw," the initiate became a man; yet to resolve anxieties over the adult masculine role, he regressed to the status of a child.

The Patriarchal Degree of Odd-Fellowship similarly featured a young man's quest for the approval of surrogate fathers. The initiate, wearing sandals and a shepherd's robe and carrying a crook, traveled across a desert to meet the patriarchs of the Old Testament. As he approached a tent he was seized, bound, and taken to the camp of the patriarchs, who removed his fetters and blindfolds, offered him food and drink, and related the history of prominent elders of their tribe. A high priest finally instructed the initiate to kneel. Then he intoned: "You have toiled through the ways of doubt and error to the bosom of our Patriarchal family."[31]

The relationship between surrogate fathers and sons was expanded in the revision of 1880. It began much like its predecessor, but after the initiate had been accepted into the family of patriarchs, he was identified as Isaac, son of Abraham. Before he could "enter upon his course of life" he was instructed to request his father's blessing. The initiate, again blindfolded, traveled across the wilderness of Paran to Beersheba with a conductor, encountering the usual obstacles along the way. They finally met Abraham, who exclaimed, "You give me great joy, my son." Father and son journeyed to Mount Moriah to make a sacrifice to God. After they had erected an altar, the conductor, speaking for Isaac, asked what they would do for a sacrifice. Abraham hesitated before answering: "My son, Isaac, be not surprised; it is God's order that you shall be the sacrifice." The candidate was placed upon the altar, and torches were lit to ignite the wood. The Twenty-third Psalm was read. Just as Abraham commanded that the torch be applied, a muffled gong sounded. He then announced that God had determined that Isaac not be sacrificed, but instead become an equal member of the family. Father and son were now brothers.

This recension took considerable liberties with the Old Testament. In Genesis, Isaac never lived apart from his father. The son who was cast into the wilderness of Paran was Ishmael, Abraham's son by Hagar. The ritualists of the Odd Fellows thus fused the story of Ishmael's enforced separation to that of Abraham's sacrifice of Isaac. The convergence of the two themes was important: The removal of Isaac from his father made it possible to explore the issue of disrupted father-son ties, and the episode in which Abraham offered Isaac as a sacrifice brought the issue of father-son antagonism into clear relief. The ritual then resolved these psychological tensions by reassuring the initiate that his father, though distant and imposing, had never resented him (a source of "great joy") in the first place. The central theme was filial obedience: Isaac's duty to obey his father, and Abraham's duty to obey God. Thus Abraham's willingness to do violence to his son was an indication not of antagonism, but of paternal duty.

The creation of an emotionally compelling ritual was a process of trial and error, and experience had shown that certain themes were more likely to succeed than others. Rituals such as the Patriarchal Degree acted out anxieties that young middle-class men may have felt about their fathers and about the immeasurable emotional distance they had to travel to acquire the attributes of manhood. By emphasizing a surrogate father's benevolence and love, the ritual made it easier for the initiate to identify with the masculine role; by accepting him into the family of patriarchs, the ritual enabled him to approach manhood with greater self-assurance.

Aside from its emotional significance to the initiate, a successful ritual served the needs of members who witnessed or assisted in the initiation of others. Fraternal writers often remarked on an oddity in attendance patterns: Usually the most regular members were the youngest or the oldest. Elderly lodge members surely appreciated the symbolic "veneration" accorded patriarchs, worshipful masters, and sachems. But it is also possible that older lodge members lamented the lack of emotional ties to their own children: The gender divisions of middle-class life produced fathers without effective children as well as children without effective fathers.

Much as the rituals encouraged august father figures to accept callow initiates, they also urged young men to better understand their elders. In a modification of the Odd Fellows' Initiatory Degree in 1880, the bearded "Noble Grand," who had at first expressed his resentment toward the initiate, finally explained that he would like to become better acquainted with his new friend. He even apologized for his initial hostility: "Men are not always to be taken for what they appear. . . . Some may have a rough and unseemly exterior, but a good, true heart within." Victorian fathers who had learned to control their emotions and to affect a "manly" deportment may have been incapable of articulating affection to their own sons, but the ritual literally gave voice to such sentiments, which would otherwise remain unexpressed. The dramaturgic devices of the ritual enabled elderly sachems and patriarchs to adopt and to love as their own the younger brethren of the order, who were in turn assured that father absence should not be interpreted as hostility, and that paternal approval was available to all who joined the family of the lodge.

Fraternal leaders insisted that members experience the entire sequence of initiations provided by their order. And every major order included at least one ritual in which each of the following major themes were developed: (1) The initiate at the outset was portrayed as immature of unmasculine. (2) He overcame obstacles as he embarked on a difficult journey through the stages of childhood and adolescence. This journey/ordeal reached a climax when (3) He was killed (or nearly so) by angry father figures. Finally, (4) he was reborn as a man into a new family of approving brethren and patriarchs. In this way the emotional orientations instilled by maternal nurture would give way to the sterner lessons provided by ancient patriarchs, venerable kings, or savage chieftains.[32]

Recent scholars, after studying the public rhetoric of the orders, have concluded that they performed essential structural functions for nascent capitalism. The lodge served as a "moral policing institution" whose symbols and regulations reflected capitalism's needs for free labor; indeed, the "entire ethos and spirit" of the orders was dominated by capitalism.[33]

Although the orders unquestionably adopted the institutional and promotional mechanisms of capitalism and articulated the values of the emerging middle class, it does not follow that members joined and continued to attend because of this structural congruence. Middle-class men, or workers who aspired to that status, did not have to go to the lodge to learn the merits of hard work and self-discipline. Moreover, the rituals repeatedly contravened basic tenets of capitalism. The Adoption Degree advised initiates to emulate the "children of the forest," who, it noted, held wealth and property in common. Rather than reinforcing the forms and ideologies of capitalist social organization, the rituals often subverted them.

The fascination for fraternal ritual suggests that even as the emerging middle classes were embracing capitalism and bourgeois sensibilities, they were simultaneously creating rituals whose message was largely antithetical to those relationships and values. But this does not mean that the orders and their rituals functioned in opposition to the gender, familial, and economic structures of capitalism. Quite the contrary: By providing solace from the psychic pressures of these new social and institutional relationships, they ensured its survival.

This resembles anthropologist Victor Turner's belief that social life is a dialectical process whereby society fits individuals into structures and defines their appropriate roles; yet people long for a deeper and less restrictive range of experience and meaning, and they unconsciously react against these structures by participating in liminal rituals whose symbols are in opposition to existing hierarchies and rules. In simpler societies, "anti-structure," as Turner termed these liminal ritual states, was often expressed through ceremonies such as initiation rites, in which the ordinary regularities of kinship, law, and custom were replaced by a "weird domain" of secret symbols. "No society can function without this dialectic," Turner added.[34]

Much that seems silly, foolish, or downright preposterous about fraternal ritual gains meaning when viewed from a Turnerian perspective. Odd Fellows acknowledged that once they had wrapped themselves in biblical robes and fixed masks upon their faces they were indeed odd; and lawyers, shopkeepers, and industrialists understood that it was bizarre to pretend to be Old Testament patriarchs, Roman senators, or medieval knights. But this incongruousness provided much of the meaning of the ritual by conjuring a world that offered solace from real life—from the limited range of personal expression allowed by Victorian gender conventions and by the rigid structures and discipline of work in a capitalist society. In so doing, it helped accommodate middle-class men to a new social order that was largely of their own making.

THREE

The Madness of Separate Spheres: Insanity and Masculinity in Victorian Alabama

John Starrett Hughes

D r. James T. Searcy, superintendent of the Alabama Insane Hospital, labored hard in 1895 to explain the biological differences between (normal) men and women. In a pamphlet for laymen he focused on the mechanics of conception, explaining that "the FEMALE detaches genetic cells [i.e., eggs] that remain more or less stationary, while the MALE detaches cells [spermatozoa] that go more or less at large." These spermatozoa, he continued, had "mobile faculties, by which they seek out the genetic cells of the female to coalesce with them."[1] Masculinity therefore relied on "going at large" to seek out and coalesce with its passive, unmoving, and receptive feminine counterpart. Searcy proceeded to examine the entire life cycle and concluded that at all stages the brains of men and women embodied the complementary characteristics revealed in this moment of conception. "Cerebral efforts" of males led them "to excel in competitive, aggressive life." Feminine exertions led conversely to superiority in "home duties and not in competitive and aggressive life," for the "tendency of her EXCEL-LENCIES is within the family, and is conservative, and less aggressive and inventive in outside matters."[2] So, from the creation of life until maturation of the healthy brain, men were not only different from women, but fundamentally opposite to them.

Despite his earnest scientific pretense, Searcy, a leading authority on sanity and a stalwart of the Southern scientific community, was neither challenging nor expanding his society's conception of masculinity. His remarks were more on the order of intellectual musings than scientific findings based on rigorous research. He was in fact translating widely shared, nonexpert attitudes about masculinity into an elite-sounding exegesis. Without subtlety or nuance, Searcy's prose reflected and nearly parodied the inarticulate views shared by the nonscientific masses who committed their deranged friends and neighbors to his care. In fact, Sear-

The author gratefully acknowledges the help of Martha May and Megan Seaholm.

cy's view of masculinity reflected attitudes of Victorian America not tied to any particular region.

In recent years it has become a commonplace of nineteenth-century social history to assume, as Searcy did, that men and women occupied separate spheres. Economic transformation and rapid growth during the antebellum years resulted in new and discernibly modern dynamics: market economies, rapid geographic and social mobility, Tocqueville's celebrated "individualism," the emergence of a recognizable middle class, and the decline of traditional social controls. Among those controls most notably changed was the family, which came to be defined less as an extended group and more as a nuclear unit. Men increasingly worked outside this nuclear family "in the world," while women gained autonomy in their own sphere "at home." The one sphere was public, the other private; the first presumably amoral, individualistic, and competitive, the other moral, communal, and nurturing.

Alabama's adherence to this pattern of changing gender perceptions, while perhaps delayed beyond the timing of events to the north, was largely complete when Searcy wrote. His comments, for example, suggest an unquestioned ideal of homosocial patterns of gender interaction. During the three decades before Searcy outlined his ideas, Alabama's lay population had prefigured his stark view of sex roles as it undertook to commit family members and neighbors to the Insane Hospital. In the commitment process Alabamians distinguished some varieties of men's derangement from women's and thereby acknowledged, albeit unconsciously, the separate burdens of sanity carried by each sex.

Unlike in the twentieth century, the labeling of Alabama's insane remained primarily a layperson's prerogative. State law did require that a licensed physician formally diagnose the illness and sign a certificate of insanity before commitment could occur. But records of the nearly seven thousand commitments before 1900 show that family members, rather than physicians, defined the boundary between sanity and insanity, and determined who had crossed it and when.[3] A typical commitment proceeded according to a recognizable pattern. Distressed families generally called in their physicians after coping with insane members for months or even years.[4] By this time, family members typically had already decided to commit.

Physicians helped in the process with advice and by validating the family's decision for confinement. Alabama's general practitioners, sometimes only apprentice-trained even in the years following the Civil War, lacked any special training in mental disease. Even those few who had trained in respected medical schools seldom had taken formal courses on mental diseases. Consequently, family doctors were loath ever to overrule lay diagnoses, and more often acted sympathetically to help relieve the distress of families, which often included friends of the doctors. Subtle economic incentives also militated against crossing the families' wishes. Doctors who counseled against confinement may have feared the loss of future fees.

"Diagnoses" therefore reflected a reality more profound than doctors' abstractions. They hinted at unspoken assumptions about sanity and madness, assumptions that sometimes revealed the meaning of gender. Records of men committed as insane suggest the qualities that the inarticulate majority held to be necessary for "healthy" masculinity, or at least the point at which the limit of acceptable maleness was crossed. Because families rather than physicians actually labeled and committed the insane, the causes assigned to the condition in the commitment records hint less at medical matters than at social concerns.

Several caveats are in order. Not all deranged Alabamians who were sent to the asylum by families and neighbors suffered under some gender-defined lunacy. Many insane Alabamians were senile, retarded, or inarguably mad by standards which superseded boundaries of gender or historical period. This essay therefore presents no comprehensive gender-defined analysis of all insanity. It looks only at that significant number of cases which do reveal assumptions about gender and which therefore help us to see more clearly the mental universe of an earlier era. The analysis also relies primarily on the records of men. All of the doctors who worked in the Alabama Insane Hospital or who are known to have signed a certificate of insanity were male. So too were all the state's probate-court judges who sanctioned the taking of their neighbors' freedom. Women did participate frequently and actively, as in the commitment of husbands and sons, and commonly showed creativity and assertiveness. But the process remained under the control of male gatekeepers. One suspects therefore that those women who initiated commitment proceedings either shared the same assumptions as men or found it necessary to express their special purposes and needs in a language familiar to the men who controlled the process.

Before sending a troubled member to Searcy's hospital in the university town of Tuscaloosa, a family was required by commitment statutes to forward information that could help the superintendent prepare for the patient's admission. (When space was limited, the superintendent could and did refuse patients whose insanity was chronic and therefore presumably incurable.) In particular, the hospital solicited information regarding the specific form of insanity (such as dementia, acute mania, puerperal [childbed] mania, or melancholia) and the duration of the attack.[5] Families supplied the hospital with this preliminary information on a questionnaire titled "Interrogatories." More often than not a family member filled out the form, though the attending physician or probate-court judge sometimes assisted.

Items on the questionnaire sought the suspected causes of the mental disease. Heredity, for example, appeared most commonly as the leading "predisposing" cause. This generally meant that the patient's family included a relative whom laypersons at some time thought insane. Greater attention focused on what the form identified as the "exciting" causes of insanity. These were environmental or social factors which, unlike heredity, could presumably be altered or remedied. Descriptions of these "exciting" causes often revealed how men's insanity differed from women's. Moving as they did in a somewhat separate sphere, men lived in ways that created "excitements" different from those affecting women.[6]

The asylum's admissions book, in which this information was recorded from the questionnaire on the date of the patient's arrival, reveals some of the differences separating men's and women's lunacy. Among the most common exciting causes described by those who committed male patients were "hard work," "hard study," "business trouble," and "loss of business." All of these conditions stemmed from excessive or deficient, though normal, masculine activities of study or business. Alabama's men, it would seem, lived in peril when they performed to excess precisely what their society expected of them. In a sense, then, there was a risk in being "too male." Judging from information collected from these forms, however, Alabamians never perceived wives, mothers, and sisters to have lost their minds because of excessive work or because of trouble resulting from their special varieties of (usually domestic) "business." Men more than women, it followed, inhabited a dangerous sphere that demanded discipline and moderation.[7]

"Political excitement" presented a related reason for committing men. Analysis of all the admissions for the asylum's first five years, 1861–66, show nine admissions for this cause, eight of whom were men.[8] During these Civil War years, the potential for associated excitement was considerable. Nearly two-thirds of all patients admitted during these years, regardless of diagnoses, were men (65.9 percent, 145 of 220). But for nearly all later years after the political turmoil of war and Reconstruction had passed, there were usually as many women as there were men in the inmate population. So as the era of dramatic political excitement passed, the proportion of insane men declined and the gender ratio became nearly equal. Difficulties of disunion, war, and Reconstruction selected disproportionately for men.[9]

Alabama's women worked hard (many ran businesses) and were touched directly by the often tumultuous political situation. Despite these facts, the nearly universal impression was that women's derangement grew from other, less public sources. As Searcy would explain in the 1890s, it was the very nature of men—but not of women—to go at large, embrace risk, and occasionally exceed healthy limits. In this way, men could be considered responsible for their own insanity: Their derangement resulted from their own actions. Men's madness often appeared to be rooted in public behavior in a socially sanctioned marketplace.

Questions of sexuality, or of private behavior, also concerned the families of the insane. Nearly all the commitment stories that mentioned masturbation involved men. (Masturbation, incidentally, was listed quite logically, and without apparent irony, as the disease's "exciting" cause.) Of the almost seven thousand pre-1900 admissions, only two included a recorded suspicion of female masturbation.[10] Several reasons likely accounted for this. First, men's masturbation was easier to detect; letters of concerned family members sometimes mentioned semen on bedclothes. Moreover, by the late nineteenth century, lay as well as medical opinion expressed concern about a possible loss of vitality that could accompany the "solitary habit," with its seemingly purposeless expenditure of what many considered to be a precious, perhaps finite, bodily fluid. Masturbation therefore hinted at the troubling prospect of a loss of masculine control, even masculine self-destruction. The ideal of going publicly at large in the competitive world required standards of restraint, even private restraint. Masturbation alarmed Victorians by evidencing a dangerous decay of discipline.[11]

Excessive sexual habits other than masturbation also contributed to the labeling of men as insane. Admissions records occasionally cited "venery" as an exciting cause. Usually this was a euphemism for syphilitic insanity, which by the 1890s was usually identified more clinically and less judgmentally as "general paresis." Again, as with masturbation, commitment records never listed "venery" as figuring in a woman's case. In the rare instances of nonmonogamous sexual activity in women, doctors usually listed the more imposingly clinical description "erotic mania."[12] In short, the records suggest a more value-laden description of men, who by their own uncontrolled or excessive actions brought on their own insanity.

Families and doctors of insane women, it would seem, were more comfortable in conceptualizing women's madness as being unavoidable rather than actively appropriated through deliberate choices. Those who committed women focused more on unalterable biology, not personal choices, in explaining female derangement. Commitment records reported large numbers of menstrual, menopausal, and postpartum manias, for example. Commitment histories reveal no corresponding biological origin of madness for men.[13]

As Searcy's remarks made clear, late-nineteenth-century Alabamians tended to conceptualize qualities of masculinity and femininity as complementary, almost never as overlapping. Masculinity was the polar opposite, as it were, of femininity. Neither gender possessed sufficient attributes for independence, but relied on qualities possessed by the other. Wholeness seemed possible only in union. So the "spheres," while different in nature, were not actually separate, but united by ties of dependence. Alabamians held to notions better symbolized by gender-specific hemispheres rather than wholly distinct spheres. There was in fact only a single sphere, though with gender-specific attributes clustered at opposing poles.

One exciting cause of madness closer to the woman's pole, and which families less frequently used to describe men, was grief, that paralyzing emotional state that often accompanies a tragic event such as the death of a loved one. Nineteenth-century Alabamians, much like later generations, seem to have defined grief as emerging from almost purely domestic sources, not public ones. In the sample of admissions from the 1860s, nine persons suffered from insanity triggered by what the admissions book described as "grief" (4 percent of the sample). While far too small to be statistically significant, this group nonetheless offers some impressionistic insight. Six of these cases involved women and three involved men. Two of the three men were ministers (the only ministers admitted during the entire five-year period).[14] As such they may not have shared fully in the aggressive, competitive world that Searcy later identified as the natural masculine domain. Functioning outside the ordinary public marketplace, these ministers likely dealt with private emotions in their roles as comforters to their congregations. Perhaps the larger society allowed ministers greater license to become domestically deranged.[15]

Commitment records occasionally described victims of "bad treatment" or "ill treatment" as deranged. Significantly, no Alabama family ever committed a man for this reason.[16] Usually, these descriptions amounted to little more than a shorthand for spousal abuse by husbands or the cruel treatment of widows. But assuming that men were also ill-treated and even victimized by family members and neighbors (though not so often as women), why was this not an acceptable explanation of male madness? Perhaps, by virtue of their "going at large" in a competitive, presumably aggressive arena, men were assumed to be adept at coping with bad treatment. Women, on the other hand, were often perceived as passive recipients of treatment, good or bad. Men acted on the world—and on women. Women, according to this view, received and reacted passively to these male exertions.[17]

A dominant thread in the fabric of the masculine ideal portrayed in commitment histories was men's capacity to control their circumstances. Men could avoid bad treatment by moving on or by adjusting obnoxious elements of their environment. Alabamians seem to have perceived women as possessing little of this capacity to control their surroundings and thereby escape from, prevent, or cope with bad treatment (and indeed, many no doubt lacked the economic wherewithal). Men's behavior therefore often caused the ill-treatment of others, but the women who were often victims, not the male abusers, more likely came to be labeled insane.

Troubled men's self-destructive behaviors, more often than their mistreatment of others, prompted their families to commit them. In fact, cases of drug and alcohol abuse supply some of the keenest insights into the qualities of late-nineteenth-century masculinity. Unlike the more abstract factors such as hard work, grief, or bad treatment reported by families and their doctors, drug addictions and alcoholism could be objectively verified. Virtually all observers, regardless of bias or training, could agree on the diagnosis. Analysis of these special mental disorders therefore allows an exploration of not only the perceptions but perhaps also the reality of masculine behavior.[18]

The Alabama Insane Hospital admitted many victims of alcoholism, and in all but a tiny minority of cases the patient was male.[19] Men not uncommonly had mixed dependencies that included opium, morphine, or cocaine as well as alcohol.[20] Alcoholism, which figured in virtually every case involving male inmates with dependencies, had its origins in public behavior as men got together away from home to drink. While certainly not encouraged, public drinking (even occasional drunkenness) seldom supplied grounds for social ostracism of men—especially in the more heavily populated areas, such as Mobile, Montgomery, or Birmingham, where anonymity was increasingly possible late in the century. Alabama's women, on the other hand, had access to no corresponding arena for social drinking. Consequently, far fewer women than men seem to have developed alcohol dependencies.

Alabama women did acquire serious drug addictions. Early in this period, opium eating was common among women, though men too shared this habit. By the 1880s and 1890s, as morphine became less expensive and more available, many women even in remote rural areas became dependent. This addiction generally began under a doctor's care for menstrual pain or postpartum discomfort. In short, the typical history of "feminine" drug abuse was profoundly private, sponsored by male physicians, and restricted to home settings.[21] Masculine addictions, on the other hand, were more varied, often began in socially sanctioned and nondomestic settings, and showed greater freedom of experimentation.

Dr. Peter Bryce, who ran the hospital and saw thousands of patients between 1861 and his death in 1892, summed up the entire range of masculine derangement—from hard work to alcoholism—when he identified general paresis as the archetypal masculine form of insanity. Later physicians linked this condition primarily to the final stages of syphilis, but in the early 1870s, Bryce described a far less specific etiology when, as a pioneer of sorts, he first began to diagnose it regularly. "The causes of general paresis," he explained in 1872, "are found to prevail most among men, and at the most active time of life, from thirty-five to forty, in the majority of cases. Habitual intemperance, sexual excesses, overstrain in business, in fact, all those habits which tend to keep up too rapid cerebral action, are supposed to induce this form of disease. It is especially a disease of *fast life*, and fast business in large cities." Bryce's clinical description neatly encapsulated the disease of excessive masculinity spreading throughout the social body due to an inadequately disciplined public marketplace.[22]

As Bryce's discussion of general paresis eloquently suggests, the quality of masculine derangement resulted not from crossing gender expectations, or from becoming "feminine," but from being masculine without discipline. Only a very few male inmates under Bryce's or Searcy's care had any sort of lunacy attributed to "feminine" behavior. One man admitted in 1895 insisted that he was "a woman and that his uncle [had] attempted to ravish him. . . ." Notes in his case history reveal that he repeated this assertion again and again; Searcy's staff dismissed it as entirely delusional. The patient, after all, was clearly a man. Still, the doctors' gender assumptions led them to leave unexplored the possibility that the patient had indeed been sexually assaulted, or that his gender confusion was rooted in a real event.[23]

As might be surmised from Bryce's not-so-veiled critique of masculine behavior associated with the fast life, he and his successor, Searcy, pursued a therapeutic ideal that aimed to supply in the asylum the discipline they found lacking in the masculine world beyond its walls. From 1861, when the Alabama Insane Hospital opened, its doctors employed a therapy known as "moral treatment" (as opposed to medical treatment with drugs or surgery). Employed in most American mental institutions since the 1820s and 1830s, moral treatment had been declining in popularity outside the South. In 1872 Bryce explained that he favored moral treatment because it involved the "interruption of old modes of thought and feeling by new scenes and associations, changes of food, regular habits of living, hygiene and sanitary precautions not usually required at home, and subordination to firm, exact, but gentle and consistent discipline. . . ."[24]

Moral treatment thus placed patients under the doctors' absolute authority in a carefully constructed environment which sought to foster mental health by eliminating irritating (i.e., "exciting") influences. The therapy aimed at accentuating the best of the outside world while eliminating the worst. Both Bryce and Searcy agreed with most asylum superintendents that in this way diseased brains could acquire the rest needed for recovery. In 1876 Bryce presented an idyllic vision of his own peaceful asylum, where sanity was very nearly in the air:

> Every ward in the hospital overlooks the beautiful parterres, which with their brilliant display of colors and fragrant exhalations, never fail to charm the occupants of the wards above. In fair weather the gardens and lawns are dotted in every direction with groups of patients engaged in cultivating or gathering flowers.[25]

From a twentieth-century perspective, the striking feature of this approach is its noninterventionist quality. Aside from managing the parterres and the daily agenda, doctors in the asylum did little but care for their patients' many aches, pains, and physical illnesses. They lacked useful medical treatments for mental aberrations, except for the occasional administration of sedatives to uncontrollable patients. Bryce even bragged on occasion that the institution administered practically no drugs. Nor did any of the hospital's physicians engage in any equivalent of modern "talking" therapies such as psychoanalysis.

According to hospital statistics, moral treatment was a success. Between 1876 and 1890, for example, the institution's reports to the legislature routinely reported rates of "cure" or "recovery" at about 40 percent of annual admissions, a figure considered high for the period. Precisely what constituted cure or recovery, however, is unclear. The doctors never outlined any objective criteria. To outsiders, it often seemed that release necessarily implied recovery. But some who fell short of cure also returned home. Bryce and Searcy released patients listed as merely "improved" or even "unchanged." Still, the fact remains that from the superintendent's perspective a sizable minority of patients responded positively to moral treatment, reclaimed their sanity, and returned to society.[26]

The ultimate genius, so to speak, of moral treatment was its paternalism and rather deliberate domesticity. In a report to the governor in October 1893, the hospital's trustees employed the prevailing language of domesticity when they stated that, to a considerable degree, "the whole *house*" resembled "a neat, systematic, well regulated, comfortable *home*."[27] Five years earlier Bryce had explained that "the whole tendency . . . of modern methods is to make the Hospital a home in its highest sense, and to exhibit . . . the same kindly feeling of confidence and sympathy that every sick person is entitled to at the hands of family and friends."[28] This institutional "home," designed to be familial and friendly, was by the 1890s the largest single building under one roof in the South and housed a "family" of about twelve hundred men and women. The language that Bryce and the trustees employed was carefully chosen, but to the uninitiated (and perhaps to some patients) it might understandably have seemed like hyperbole.

Superintendent Bryce, who was the asylum's only leader during its first thirty years, carefully cultivated the image of a benevolent father to rule over this giant home. He mixed with patients on informal rounds twice each week, politely and cordially chatting with his charges. Inmates who attended morning chapel listened as he read scripture. They also joined him in singing hymns while Mrs. Bryce played the organ. The superintendent and his wife also presided as hosts at various weekly amusements, such as magic-lantern shows, minstrel musicals, or rigorously supervised dances.

Bryce also exercised this fatherly authority on occasion by punishing patients, as when he revoked the chapel privileges of inmates who displayed too much emotion at services. All but the most obedient patients also spent at least an evening or two in the "cross-hall," a bare room with no windows low enough to look out of, to which the wayward were sent to contemplate their infractions of the many rules. Patients therefore came to know Bryce—and later Searcy—as patriarchs who kept a certain distance but who also could be relied on to care for their physical and moral well-being.[29]

Within this expansive "family," the entirely adult inmate population became childlike, dependent on the "parental" staff for the necessities of life. Success or failure in such an artificial society thus had little to do with masculine success "on the outside," where independence, competitiveness, and even aggressiveness were expected. Rewards inside the hospital came most readily to those of either sex who accepted their new status and mitigated some of their "masculine" behaviors. By and large, men and women received virtually the same treatment and were expected to behave similarly in the presence of the doctors and staff.

While Bryce and Searcy clearly tried to create a wholesome surrogate home for the state's disturbed, they were careful not to allow their benevolent intentions to lapse into indulgence. They required all able-bodied patients to be useful, just as children might be obliged to contribute time and effort to the family's well-being. Men generally worked outdoors on the hospital grounds, performing such chores as landscaping (moving dirt with wheelbarrows), gardening, tending livestock, working in the asylum print shop, woodworking, or making bricks and helping hired construction workers with the practically unending renovation and expansion of the buildings. A few men lived and worked at Greystone Farm, located several miles from the hospital. Women worked exclusively indoors, largely by sewing clothes for inmates or doing fancywork.[30]

By insisting on labor, the doctors consciously economized on administrative costs, but more important, they hoped to establish the value of routine exertion in purposeful, unhurried work. Shortly after becoming superintendent in 1893, Searcy extolled outdoor work at a meeting of the trustees. He explained, "The out-door work done by the patients has little or no thought or mental effort attached to it. This gives the insane brain rest, at the same time the out-door muscle exercise contributes, better than anything else, to general health."[31] Cooperative and mentally undemanding manual labor thus benefited the men. Besides encouraging the satisfaction of a day's honest labor, it promoted values of regularity, cooperation, and industry, albeit in an artificial, noncompetitive arena where conflict was not tolerated. Rewards followed from childlike obedience, calculated to please the fatherlike superintendent, rather than from successful competition.

The asylum strove to rearrange the world in another important way. The doctors rigorously sequestered men and women on separate sides of the building. Architecturally, the Alabama Insane Hospital followed the Kirkbride linear design, wherein men's and women's wards extended outward in opposite directions from a central administrative hall.[32] Sexual segregation served in part the need to ensure propriety before a public that was perpetually suspicious of asylum practices. But even more it served the ideal of moral treatment, which required elimination of excitements and irritations. Men mixed with women only occasionally, as at the closely supervised weekly entertainments, at daily religious services, or perhaps on evening walks on the expansive hospital grounds, where groups of men sometimes encountered separate groups of women. Thus, to a greater extent than their sane neighbors, Alabama's institutionalized insane literally lived out the concept of separate spheres. Moreover, the doctors clearly looked with concern at the mixing of men and women, and took pains to eliminate the dangerous excitement it might provoke.

The total regimen of moral treatment—its avoidance of medication, its work routine, and its focus on environmental manipulation—offered a subtle and unexamined critique of the concept of masculinity presented by the lay diagnoses of the families who committed patients. Inside the hospital the male patients' therapy very nearly substituted a feminine world for the presumably dangerous masculine world of the outside. This is all the more striking when moral treatment is compared with prevailing medical practices for more ordinary ailments. Prior to the Civil War, when moral treatment rose to popularity in the United States, "heroic" medicine characterized general practice. Doctors commonly administered massive doses of toxic mercury drugs such as calomel, and opened their patients' veins in order to let large quantities of blood. General practitioners, though not the more judicious superintendents, even raised huge blisters on the shaved heads of the insane in hopes of extracting suspected "brain poisons" in the form of pus and fluid. Others bled insane patients at the temples to relieve the affliction.[33]

Routine medicine by the post–Civil War years had largely abandoned the worst of this heroic era by diminishing doses and reducing if not eliminating bloodletting. But even well-educated doctors continued to overmedicate (less with calomel but more with newer panaceas such as quinine), and in more rural areas, as in much of Alabama, many still bled their patients prodigiously. Indeed, this aggressive interventionism was the hallmark of nineteenth-century American therapeutics. Considered from a fundamentally Freudian perspective, this interventionist approach was archetypally masculine, especially when contrasted with the nonaggressive feminine nurturing more often associated with nursing.[34] Both Bryce and Searcy eschewed the interventionism of their schooling and embraced instead this more "feminine" moral treatment as they addressed the mental and behavioral aberrations of their patients.

A sort of secular evangelism also stemmed from moral treatment. Bryce clearly intended for the benefits of the hospital's therapy to extend beyond the asylum to society. Bryce hoped the institution's "feminine" example might reform society as well as the individual deviants under his care. In 1875 he explained, "Upon restoration of their health, patients are returned to their homes, and necessarily diffuse in their families and neighborhoods some of the lessons of neatness, promptness, regularity and industrial economy deeply ingrained in their hearts by the systematic daily round of life in the institution." While gender lessons failed to make the superintendent's conscious list here, he unmistakably perceived the need to reform a world into which men ventured at their psychic peril. In his domesticating method of treatment he presented, perhaps unconsciously, both a critique of and a partial solution to tension in Victorian society.[35]

Bryce, Searcy, and the numerous staff physicians who passed through the hospital carried notions about gender that extended beyond the South. Bryce, a South Carolinian, studied at Bellevue in New York City and traveled to hospitals abroad before the Civil War. Both he and Searcy, a deeply proud native of Alabama who was also educated in New York, participated actively in national medical associations and served terms as president of the overwhelmingly Northern American Medico-Psychological Association (today the American Psychiatric Association). As a result, both superintendents brought to the asylum cultural horizons that extended well beyond the region they called home.[36]

Alabama's lay population, which sent patients to the superintendents' care, had less access to either Northern or national concepts of manliness. However, Alabama was by no means either homogeneous or separate from the rest of the nation. It possessed a seasoned, even gracious, cosmopolitanism in the political capital of Montgomery, as well as in the old and busy seaport of Mobile. By the Victorian period, Birmingham, a New South city of industrial character, was rapidly rising to prominence. Each of these major cities lay well within the lanes of national cultural commerce. Most Alabamians, however, lived somewhat removed from these cultural pathways in the agricultural countryside, which sometimes resembled the more static life-style of traditional and less fluid societies. But far from being easily stereotyped, the region's character possessed diverse qualities. A static rural past, an antebellum cosmopolitanism and an emerging urban industrialism existed virtually side by side and contained a class structure that held promise for a growing middle class.

In this varied milieu the hospital's doctors were no neutral reformers. Moral treatment implicitly extolled an idealized middle class with roots neither in an underdeveloped rural life-style nor in the romantic plantation tradition. Shortly after assuming the superintendency, Searcy bemoaned the growing classes of "idle rich" and the "crowded and incapable poor" which accompanied the rise of "civilization." As we have seen, the idealized masculinity reflected in the hospital's commitment records eschewed excesses and appropriated values of the middle class. The elite who oversaw the control of the insane—doctors, probate-court judges, hospital trustees, and Montgomery politicians—supported a process and an institution that catered not to some halcyon Southern past but to an emergent middle-class future.

Important studies of mental health during this period have focused primarily on urban middle-class populations in the North. They have identified "neurasthenia," a disorder of excessive nervousness, as the archetypal Victorian ailment. In particular, Barbara Sicherman, Charles Rosenberg, and Robin and John Haller have explained convincingly how this condition fitted so well into the Victorian zeitgeist, which emphasized the growth of industries, burgeoning cities, and class stratification. For example, the Hallers asserted that "neurasthenia became, in a very real sense, a rationalization of America's new social order."[37] It provided a medical catchall that seemed to apply equally well to either sex and that located the cause of derangement in the special stresses of modern urban life. Men who engaged in purely mental endeavors as part of their business, for example, sometimes suffered from an exhaustion caused by a sort of "brain sprain." Women, on the other hand, developed neurasthenia for nearly opposite reasons. Freed by servants from domestic labors and in some cases from the burdens of child rearing, women lapsed into a sort of gender-specific ennui that destroyed their mental balance.[38]

Diagnoses of insanity in Alabama do not on the surface fit this model. Commitment records include almost no mention of neurasthenia. Several factors help to explain the absence of this common diagnostic language. First, diagnosis was largely nonprofessional. Families, more than any other group, labeled the insane. Second, major studies that have stressed neurasthenia have correctly connected the diagnosis to neurologists, or largely urban, private-practice specialists in problems of the nervous system and brain, who rose to prominence during the 1880s. Before 1900 Alabama simply had no such specialists. Leading neurologists such as George Beard and S. Weir Mitchell argued that neurasthenics did not require confinement in an asylum but could be treated with rest at home. In fact, the neurologists emerged as the nation's sharpest critics of insanity specialists such as Searcy who treated unwilling patients in vast institutions.[39] Finally, only a limited part of Alabama shared the social characteristics associated with the neurasthenic populations described in existing studies. Not until late in the period, for example, did Birmingham begin to emerge as a regional industrial center.

To summarize, the absence of a familiar diagnostic language in Alabama probably reflected different stages of both social and professional development in the region, not deep differences in the basic meaning of masculinity. Procedures for labeling the insane, dominated by laypersons, and the regimen of care, administered by an elite, both revealed anxiety about men who lived their lives without discipline or who succumbed, as Bryce described it, to the "fast life." Little in the records of the hospital suggests any considerable deviation from the findings of the major studies of populations further north. A tentative conclusion is that by the Victorian period a distinctive Southern version of manliness vividly described by studies of the antebellum era or conjured up by the crudeness of small-town main streets was becoming increasingly unacceptable or even beginning to erode.[40]

By 1895, when Searcy outlined the starkly bifurcated attributes of men and women, he encapsulated attitudes that bore little regional distinction. Indeed, his views mirror well the findings of leading modern scholars of Victorian mental health. Middle-class readers of Searcy's pamphlet, whether Northern or Southern, would likely have understood the message and found it familiar. More than he realized, Searcy facilitated acceptance of modern, national attitudes about social relationships that involved gender roles. Like Bryce, who had brought moral treatment south, Searcy too served as a conduit for ideas from the wider society. Both the glimpse of manhood provided by the hospital's records and the critique of it inherent in moral treatment referred more to what the region was becoming than to what it had been.

FOUR

The Son of Man and God the Father: The Social Gospel and Victorian Masculinity

Susan Curtis

In many ways, masculinity had become problematic in late-Victorian America. Middle-class culture, grounded in individual ambition and manly achievement earlier in the century, gradually had been transformed by the 1890s and early 1900s in response to a number of key cultural developments. As Ann Douglas has observed, men grew up in a culture that was undergoing "feminization." Women novelists penned novels that chronicled the domestic lives of middle-class women. Ministers softened the stern Calvinism of their elders with a more liberal creed, which they preached to congregations made up largely of women. Together, ministers and their female parishioners articulated a culture based on nurture, sentiment, and indulgence. This feminized culture was intended to bolster Victorian domesticity, but it inadvertently opened doors for women in careers outside the home. Social expectations, women's place in society, and Victorian ideals all were called into question in the years immediately following the Civil War.[1]

What did it mean to be a man in such a society? Boys were advised to aspire to the ideal of the "Christian Gentleman," honest and genteel, yet ambitious and self-reliant. This was consistent with the small shops, farms, and factories of the pre–Civil War economy. It also was supported by evangelical Protestantism. But this ideal was buffeted by an industrializing economy and a feminizing culture in the last third of the nineteenth century. As the new century dawned, a new masculine ideal was beginning to take shape—one based on personality, social involvement, and, in David Riesman's terms, "other-direction."[2]

Some of the young men who helped redefine masculinity were also the authors of a restatement of Protestantism: the social gospel. Social gospelers reacted against the norms of individual responsibility and self-control because as young men, they had failed to live up to these ideals themselves. By the 1880s and 1890s they recognized that it was as difficult to save oneself spiritually and morally as to make a success of oneself in the economy. The feminized version of Protestantism available to them offered some comfort as they struggled to succeed, but it did not satisfy their long-ing to emulate and surpass their fathers. They incorporated certain aspects of this feminized religion into a gospel that would appeal to men as well as to women. As Josiah Strong put it in 1901, "There is not enough of effort, of struggle, in the typical church life of today to win young men to the church. A flowery bed of ease does not appeal to a fellow who has any manhood in him. The prevailing religion is too utterly comfortable to attract young men who love the heroic."[3] Caught between the frustrating demand for indi-vidualism in industrial America and the influence of feminization in religion, social gospelers at the turn of the century hoped to create a re-ligious ideal that nevertheless did justice to their manliness.

With a few exceptions, social gospelers were middle-class Protestant men from rural or small-town America. Inspired by the work of older men like Josiah Strong, Washington Gladden, and Lyman Abbott, they coalesced as a movement in the late 1880s and early 1890s. While they made important overtures to the working class, they spoke mostly to Northern middle-class audiences. The popularity of the social gospel by the early twentieth cen-tury suggests that at least parts of their message had wide appeal.[4]

In many respects, the social gospelers were much like other boys. They romped in the fields, read adventure stories with relish, and valued spirited, but fair, play. But their recollections of childhood, recorded decades after the fact in autobiographies, emphasized some aspects of childhood over others.[5] Written in large part to show how and why they had departed from the religion of their elders, the autobiographical accounts were tinged with heightened memories of early religious experiences. Despite these distor-tions of memory, social gospelers' stories of their youthful quests for faith are worth exploring because they offer a glimpse at some of the important issues that made masculinity so problematic. An examination of the lives of men who became social gospelers further shows how the social gospel helped affirm a changing conception of masculinity.

The young men who eventually became part of the social gospel move-ment remembered most vividly the importance of individualism in their lives. As children they were exposed to an individualistic religion that warned of the tortures of hell for the unrepentant. Harry Emerson Fosdick recalled "weeping at night for fear of going to hell, with my mystified and baffled mother trying to comfort me." He joined his family's church at the age of seven. Francis John McConnell remembered the "almost wholly in-dividualistic" religion of his parents, at a time, as he put it, "when repression was thought to be a mark of genuine religion." McConnell joined his father's church in 1881 at the age of ten. Shailer Mathews de-scribed his "Puritan" training in a pious community where "hell and the devil were very real" and where "the message from the pulpit was essentially for the individual." He experienced conversion at a revival in 1877 led by George C. Needham. Walter Rauschenbusch learned from his father, August Rauschenbusch, a scholar at the Rochester Theological Seminary, that there was no salvation for the unrepentant. Accordingly, in 1878 young Rauschenbusch accepted responsibility for his own salvation, and declared, "I want to be a man."[6]

As Rauschenbusch's comment suggests, this religious individualism promised to prepare converts for work in life as well as salvation in heaven. Mindful of their fathers' attainments, these young men hoped to succeed as individuals. Rauschenbusch assumed he would become the seventh in an unbroken line of ministers in his family and successor to his father, a respected scholar. Charles Macfarland remembered his father's disciplined biblical instruction and his physical labor to erect a monument to the Pilgrims at Plymouth, which eventually cost him his life. Charles Sheldon's father worked as a minister and as a farmer in the untamed territory of South Dakota.[7] Shailer Mathews and Frank Mason North admired their businessmen fathers and planned to follow them into industry.

Although they viewed their fathers as exemplars of industry, discipline, and success, many social gospelers were deprived of an effective paternal presence. For many children of the middle class, fathers played a diminishing role in the nineteenth century. The separation of work from home meant that fathers were gone much of the day. No more did they pass along the skills of their craft. Many of the men who became social gospelers experienced this separation more intensely, for their fathers died or were otherwise unavailable before the boys reached adolescence. Charles Macfarland, Charles Stelzle, Francis Greenwood Peabody, and Washington Gladden all lost their fathers as boys. Walter Rauschenbusch and his father were separated by an ocean for many of the boy's formative years. Young Rauschenbusch studied in Germany, and when he returned to the United States his father went abroad as a missionary to struggling congregations in Germany. Lyman Abbott's father, who wanted to work in New York City, sent Lyman and his two brothers to various uncles and grandparents when their mother died. Young Abbott remembered his childhood as one of "absolute freedom" from paternal authority.

Those who were separated from their fathers because of death or the demands of work were affected in several ways. They were left with powerful boyish memories of successful fathers up to whose standards they should try to measure. Rauschenbusch and Macfarland both idealized their fathers but admitted in later years that they scarcely knew them. Rauschenbusch, for example, undertook the completion of his father's memoir because he admired him. Yet in *Leben und Wirken* (1901), he noted with surprise, "I myself had little idea how rich and interesting his life was until my father's papers and correspondence revealed it to me." Gladden was six when his father died, and he strained to remember everything he could about him. Stelzle and Macfarland tried to take their fathers' place by entering the work force when their fathers died.[8]

In these circumstances the influence of their mothers was especially important. Rauschenbusch learned religion at his mother's knee as well as from August Rauschenbusch. He also wanted to emulate one of his older sisters, who married a missionary and lived in India for many years. In his short autobiography, Peabody turned "with a sense of relief" from reminiscing about childhood with his father to the events after his death in 1857. He referred to the second phase of his youth as a period of "congenial companionship" with his mother in their newly found "convenient and agreeable" home. Macfarland, who worked for a tailor and a grocer and as a printer to support his mother after his father died, eventually accepted her gift of her wedding band, which he wore until he was well over thirty.[9] In each case, the boys experienced an intense complement of ideals—the rugged individualism of their fathers and the nurture and self-sacrifice of their mothers.

Another problem they faced was a change in the post–Civil War economy that made them think it impossible to attain the individualistic success they longed for as youths. The Civil War, by accelerating the industrial development begun in the 1840s and 1850s, shattered the market out of which it had developed and upset traditional expectations. As the century drew to a close, a wide variety of mass-produced goods, a host of public institutions, increasing vacation and leisure, and a longing to escape the monotony and degradation of work all undermined Victorian verities of hard work, self-reliance, delayed gratification, and self-control. These were also the ideals of the young social gospelers.[10]

Shailer Mathews watched his father struggle mightily (and unsuccessfully) to avert business collapse. Young Mathews gave up his elder's individual ideal, and in college experienced the pleasure of teamwork, social organization, and collective enterprise. And he studied religion instead of business. Frank Mason North lasted for only a year in the hurly-burly of business before he, too, entered the ministry. In the 1870s and early 1880s, Gladden left the ministry for magazine work, then returned to the ministry when rewards eluded him at the *Independent* and when his own periodicals, *Sunday Afternoon: A Magazine for the Household* and *Good Company,* failed. Stelzle clung to an individualistic work ethic in his job at a factory until he realized that his ambitious pace drove the piece rate down and productivity quotas up for himself and his fellow workers.[11]

These young men also began to realize that they were not alone. Industrial warfare in the 1870s and 1880s, the cross-country march of Coxey's army in 1894, and urban slums swelling with masses of impoverished working people reinforced their conclusion that hard work and self-control no longer necessarily produced success. As Henry Atkinson put it, many men "tried as hard as possible" but failed to provide "enough bread for the little ones." Gladden saw "multitudes" of "worthy people" in Columbus, Ohio, who worked and saved and prayed, but who did not succeed in "raising themselves." For Gladden this broken equation constituted the "labor question" that haunted him and his colleagues for decades. Charles Sheldon moved in 1890 to Kansas, where he sought to understand the plight of laboring men in Topeka's stagnant economy. For days he searched for work until he began to feel the weight of personal failure. "The getting and holding of a job," he declared, "had come to seem . . . the very apex of success in life." Sheldon's quest revealed to him the crisis faced by manual laborers, and raised fears of softness in himself. He complained that as a minister he felt "isolated" from the "great world of labor."[12]

As Rauschenbusch, Mathews, Macfarland, Sheldon, Peabody, and others came of age in the 1880s, they became dissatisfied with both the religious individualism and the lonely enterprise of their youth. Many began by rejecting the individualism of their religious experiences. Fosdick, for example, harbored a "hidden anger" at the church because of its "wretched play upon my selfish fears and hopes." In 1888 Rauschenbusch looked back at his initial conversion experience and decided "there was a great deal in it that was not really true." At the age of twenty-seven, he underwent a second conversion to "redeem humanity" and to "live over again the life of Christ." Mathews complained that older Baptists denounced church suppers and baseball, but ignored the social ills in their community. He rejected their "orthodoxy," a "presentation of how to get salvation in heaven," and proposed instead a "social gospel"—"the teaching of Jesus"—as a way "to give salvation on earth."[13]

Although these young Protestants opposed the individualism of their youth, they did not reject religious commitment. Like Mathews, they proposed a social gospel that would force Christians to address social problems that thwarted individual regeneration. They believed that Christians had an obligation to attack the evils that led to moral ruin. Thus, they posited that the individual and society should share the burden of responsibility for salvation. They attacked the evils of alcohol, prostitution, and gambling, which tempted young men away from upright living. They addressed poverty by providing soup kitchens, bathing facilities, visiting nurses, industrial training for boys, inexpensive used clothing, and assistance for the unemployed. They bolstered the home and tried to provide an alternative to street life by organizing social clubs and by building bowling alleys and gymnasiums on church property. And they showed their sympathy for laboring men and women by evangelizing workers at lunchtime meetings at factories and shops, by providing nurseries for children of working mothers, and by endorsing the right to collective bargaining. In short, they offered a social creed rather than an individualistic one.[14] In order to carry out this ambitious program, social gospelers established reform unions, denominational brotherhood organizations, investigative teams, and social services. Some affiliated with universities, settlement houses, or political parties; others formed organizations that demanded teamwork, and few actually limited their careers to the pulpit. Most were surrounded by men who shared their zeal for social reform, and they enjoyed the newfound sense of community.[15] They also articulated three great laws of the social gospel: service, sacrifice, and love. These feminine virtues associated with Victorian domesticity were important parts of their disavowal of individualism in work and in faith.

The social gospel was not, however, a new expression of feminized religion. The men who came to the movement wrestled with the meaning of manhood and with the legacy of their fathers. They articulated a gospel that transformed the domestic concerns of their reforms into expressions of manly endeavor. Their concerns about manhood were revealed in their portrayals of God and Jesus. Jesus, the son and brother, was central to the social gospel as an example of cooperative, righteous, and manly behavior. Jesus was viewed as a reformer who cared for the downtrodden and worked with others to save humanity. He was thus worthy of emulation. God, the Father, was "indwelling" and "immanent" but not interventionist. In many ways this God resembled the social gospelers' own impressive and distant fathers. Both Jesus and God in the social gospel served as masculine ideals in industrializing America.

The Jesus to which many social gospelers were accustomed as Victorian children was largely the product of sentimental writers. Jesus was neither fully masculine nor fully feminine. Popular depictions featured him in long white gowns with long wavy locks and a soft brown beard. Both madonna and man, Jesus represented a complement of tender nurture and manly endeavor, which helped legitimize the commitment to social service as an acceptable replacement for individual enterprise. Jesus was also a son, which made him a peer instead of an unapproachable figure of authority. But social gospelers did not accept a feminized version of Jesus. Rauschenbusch insisted that "there was nothing mushy, nothing sweetly effeminate about Jesus." Rather, Jesus was a "man's man," who "turned again and again on the snarling pack of His pious enemies and made them slink away."

"He plucked the beard of death when He went into the city and the temple to utter those withering woes against the dominant class," he added. Gladden wanted others to recognize that Jesus had dominion over economic as well as religious life. "What sort of a King of men is he who is powerless to control the largest and intensest part of their activity?" he asked in *Tools and the Man* (1893). "Under such limitations, the Christian vocation becomes largely a matter of sentiment; what wonder that it is handed over to women and children? We shall never win for our Master the allegiance of the strong men of this world until we show them that he has the power and the purpose to rule the shop and the factory and the counting-room as well as the church and the home." When Macfarland extolled the strength and courage of Jesus in 1912, he confessed, "I know it would have been a great help to me in my boyhood and young manhood had I been led to appreciate the manhood of Jesus."[16]

According to Josiah Strong, interest in Jesus had been growing since midcentury.[17] With the appearance of dozens of scholarly treatments and imaginative reconstructions of the life of Jesus, American Protestants could follow in "the footsteps of the master" from "manger to throne," or they could stand in the "shadow of the cross" and answer the "call of the carpenter." They longed to know what he had said (or might have said), how he appeared to his contemporaries, the condition of his life, and his attitudes on a wide range of social and political questions. Many even speculated as to how Jesus would respond to the confusion of modernity. Nor was interest in Christ confined to schools of theology. Novels about Jesus proliferated. The principal denominational publishing houses produced a spate of new hymnals that banished the vengeful Jehovah of Isaac Watts and featured in his stead the Nazarene of Fanny Crosby. "What a friend we have in Jesus," they joyfully intoned. To Jesus they carried their burdens, and in him they believed.[18] Protestants in both humble country churches and magnificent urban temples worshiped the carpenter more directly than ever before.

Between the beginning of the social gospel movement and the 1920s, Jesus underwent a dramatic metamorphosis from the gentle Savior to the hearty carpenter-reformer of Galilee and finally to the hale organization man of Bruce Barton's imagination. In the late nineteenth century, social gospelers concentrated on making the Savior more robust, muscular, and active than the sweet, sad man in flowing gowns featured in sentimental literature. In keeping with the trend toward realism in American culture and historical criticism in theology, authors reconstructed Jesus' life and now gave him more realistic characteristics. For instance, since Jesus was a Jew who had learned carpentry from his father and later worked with fishermen, his biographers depicted him with dark hair and eyes, a well-developed physique, and rough, calloused hands. The Reverend Thomas De Witt Talmage in *From Manger to Throne* (1890) described the Nazarene as an example of industry. "Work! Work! Work!" he exclaimed. "The boy carpenter! The boy wagon maker! The boy housebuilder! Let all the weary artisans and mechanics of the earth see thee. . . ."[19] Such a Jesus was not unlike the toiling workmen of industrial America.

Jesus' humanness and altered outward appearance resulted in a changed demeanor. Instead of sentimentalizing the soft-spoken author of the Beatitudes, social gospelers noted the activism and reforming spirit of this workingman. Jesus the Carpenter particularly appealed to laborers, progressives, and social reformers. A New York settlement-house worker, Bouck White, in *The Call of the Carpenter* (1914) imagined Jesus as a radical populist who believed in "a social gospel." "His ideal is the civic ideal," White declared. "Its goal is 'the holy city descending from God out of heaven.' Therefore the Carpenter-Christ is the fit leader of the multitudinous." At the same time that Jesus sprouted muscles and a manlier beard, and showed a passion for justice, he also became more congenial and social-minded. Writers referred to Jesus as "the Captain," as the "elder brother," and simply as a friend. He was more approachable and congenial and assumed the role of team captain—a leader among equals. Mathews recounted the evolution of Jesus in his autobiography, *New Faith for Old* (1936). At first Jesus was "clothed in a bizarre combination of piety, theology, and rabbinical exposition." Gradually he became "a mid-Victorian of the liberal type" who supported idealism as long as it was "polite." Then Jesus became a "real character." Once scholars began to understand Judaic literature, the social psychology of early Christianity, its relation to the ancient world, and "Jesus' teaching," they began to appreciate Jesus as a righteous activist.[20]

The Jesus of the social gospel was a reformer whose service, sacrifice, and love did not dissuade him from manly assertion. And although Jesus depended on disciples and followers, he could nonetheless inspire "real" men. Harry Emerson Fosdick reminded readers of *The Manhood of the Master* (1913): "The Master appeals to all that is strongest and most military in you."[21] Jesus performed his manly duties, but he did so in ways different from the individualistic examples offered by the social gospelers' fathers. Jesus affirmed the social ideal and freed men from the unrealistic psychological burden of individual success and salvation, but he was not effeminate. The young men who had struggled unsuccessfully to live up to the ideals of their parents in the 1880s helped to create and endorse a new set of masculine ideals that were more appropriate in the large-scale workplaces of turn-of-the-century America.

By 1925, Richard B. Niese, editor of the *Nashville Tennessean,* noted that "the religion of Jesus Christ is sweeping the world like nothing that has ever gone before. . . . The biggest men in the country to-day are proud to proclaim their faith in the Nazarene—and they do so without a blush or a stammer." Niese remembered when "Sunday school was looked upon as a place only for women and children" whereas today "we have weekly men's luncheon clubs composed exclusively of Bible class members who gather around the table and have an hour of fellowship where campaigns for building standard Sunday schools are planned." Stelzle, who had built one of the most effective workingmen's churches in New York City in the early 1900s, urged churchmen to appeal to young men through advertising by making them see that churches fostered "the best kind of manhood." In *Principles of Successful Church Advertising* (1908) he outlined social reforms that required willing volunteers. "We need the sort of men who can do things," he asserted, "and who do them because they like to do them. Are you that kind of man?" To any self-respecting man of the early twentieth century, the question had but one answer.[22]

The discussion of businessmen's luncheons, planning, standard Sunday schools, and advertising is evidence of a subtle shift in the movement in the 1910s and 1920s. While still dedicated to the social gospel and social reform, many younger social gospelers began to plead for efficiency and businesslike promotion of their ideas.[23] The socially responsible progressive reformer became the basis for the socially responsive man—and Jesus—of the 1920s. Under these changed conditions of the social gospel, images of Jesus underwent some subtle shifts as well. In the 1920s Jesus' charm, glowing good health, and physical strength served him well in his role as an effective leader of men. In 1920 Frederick Anderson discussed "Jesus and his career" and insisted that "the personality of the Man of Nazareth . . . is the power behind Christian history." Two years later, George Fiske offered young people "a religion of youth" in which Jesus was "the Peerless Ideal of Youth." Rufus Jones insisted in a *Life of Christ* (1926) that Christians would "respond" to the "charm of his personality." In these and other books, the ideal Jesus reflected personal traits that were valued by corporate America: charm, youth, personality, and the ability to work with others. Burton Easton's and Charles Fiske's "real Jesus," for example, was "impressive in appearance and of great physical strength." Jesus, they wrote, "was not demonstrative and gushing. Nor, on the other hand, was he narrow and censorious; no true man is. He was not sad and somber, but natural and spontaneous. He was glad and free, an out-of-doors man who loved people, was genial and companionable, unaffected, fond of the society of his day, meeting people of all sorts in the hearty comradeship of life, likable and lovable, genuine, generous, large-hearted, straightforward, and strong." Others, such as Bruce Barton and Walter Denny, emphasized his leadership. His success derived not from his skill as a fisherman, carpenter, or rabbi, and not even from his relationship to God the Father. Rather, it depended on his ability to organize and manipulate men.[24]

God's image underwent no less dramatic a transformation than Jesus'. The God of the social gospelers' youth had been a stern and distant judge, not unlike their fathers. As the boys grew to manhood and came to terms with both their fathers and their faith, they modified this God in their work. As Henry Cope put it in *The Friendly Life* (1909), "God has grown in our thinking from a giant who makes worlds to a heart that suffers with ours, a soul that seeks ours, a being who is man's friend, and who cannot be satisfied until all humanity is embraced in that friendship." In the same year, William Dawson rejected the Old Testament God "of purity, not pity; of majesty, not compassion; of supreme ineffable righteousness and power and wisdom—the God of the roaring sea, and the live lightning, and the tremendous thunder, not the Parent of little children who claim His love and render in return their filial service. The Old Testament pictures God as a King, not God as a Parent."[25] Dawson preferred God as a parent.

One of the consequences of this new portrait, however, was to diminish the importance of the Almighty to his children on earth. Josiah Strong noted in 1910 that in the late nineteenth century God had "gradually and rather unceremoniously bowed out of his universe." God's disappearance was due in part to attempts to authenticate and verify the historical accuracy of biblical events, for God himself eluded verification. Advances in science had offered alternative explanations for the creation and for the genesis of man that challenged God's power. Confidence in their ability to control and exploit the natural world made some men less dependent on and less attracted to the idea of divine intervention. But the judgmental God was also ushered out of his universe because he was too daunting and inaccessible to men who had rejected their fathers' stern individualism in religion and vocation. Lyman Abbott explained his aversion to the domineering God of his youth in *What Christianity Means to Me* (1921): "Suppose that all your life you had dreaded an awful God, or in fear submitted to a fateful God, or hesitated between defying and cringing before a hated God . . . and suddenly the curtain were rent aside and you saw the luminous figure of the living Christ, and over his head were written the words, 'This is thy God, O man.'" Abbott embraced the Son "who is upon earth" and who lived a "life of love, service, and sacrifice." Similarly, Rauschenbusch explained why he rarely wrote about God. "The God of the stellar universe is a God in whom I drown," he wrote. "Christ with the face of Jesus I can comprehend, and love, and assimilate. So I stick to him."[26]

In part, social gospelers' response to God may have been a subtle, half-conscious response to their fathers. Left as boys with little more than seemingly unfulfillable demands for individual achievement, young Protestant men rebelled at the ideal even as they tried to surpass their fathers' achievements. In that regard, Fayette L. Thompson, a prominent Methodist who helped organize the Men and Religion Forward Movement in 1911, declared that it meant much more to be a Christian in his day with industrial and social strife than it had when his father was alive. "If the manhood of this generation does not awake to the fact that in order to be a true disciple of Jesus Christ in these days it must be responsive to a bigger program than any program of the past," he explained, "it will fail utterly to realize the glorious opportunity of the present. It will not do merely to measure up to the program of our fathers," he continued. "If we are to meet the expectations of God Almighty we must match a vaster program than our fathers ever dreamed, because our vision of what constitutes a religious life is a greater vision than the fathers ever had."[27]

This passage, a straightforward call to faith and religious commitment, also illuminates a number of private tensions that characterized family relations in late-Victorian America and that informed religious belief. Phrases like "to measure up," "to realize opportunity," and to "match" programs with their fathers resonate with a yearning to reach and exceed the standard set by fathers. It is revealing that Thompson chose to speak of the "manhood of this generation" rather than simply addressing the young men of his day, for manhood implies the quality and essence of being masculine. Furthermore, he refers to the "awakening" of this manhood in connection with Jesus, the son of God. Opportunity, manhood, and religion came together for this generation in the person of Jesus. This reference takes on greater significance in light of the two sentences that follow. The first calls on men to do more than measure up to their fathers, and the second reminds men "to meet the expectations of God." By following Jesus, men could realize themselves. God, however, like earthly fathers, made known his expectations, which men then strove to meet or surpass, and in this case, Thompson insists, "our vision of what constitutes a religious life is a greater vision than the fathers ever had." Once troublesome paternal expectations were out of the way, men could pursue their real interest, and for that, they looked to Jesus.

When social gospelers became fathers themselves, they tried to define their relationships with their children in keeping with their ideal of Jesus. Perhaps to prevent the frustration they had felt toward their own fathers, social gospelers befriended their children and urged parents to treat their children as "chums." One social gospeler advised parents to appoint a "captain of the day," whose job would be to discipline siblings. They were loath to demand a standard of behavior that would set them apart from their children. Macfarland, for example, romped with his growing family, joined the Boy Scouts with his sons, and played baseball with all his children. Rauschenbusch told his son Hilmar, "There is no love available to you which is so unvarying and always trustworthy as the love of your mother and father. . . . You must help us make the transition from parenthood to friendship."[28]

This "friendship" changed the nature of the relationship between parents and their children, and it served the younger people well in a society increasingly based on interdependence. Instead of the old model, in which the son's struggle to transcend paternal authority prepared him for the competitive and individualistic workplace, social gospelers conceived of friendlier parental relationships as a means to build a cooperative and egalitarian society. Individualism, and masculinity, now took on meaning only in collective endeavor. This new relationship eased some of the frustration inherent in the masculine identity of Victorian Americans, but it failed to build a society founded on Christian cooperation. Even their children became something of a disappointment. Many chose secular careers and placed their faith in large institutions rather than in religion. Walter Rauschenbusch fretted in his final hours that his children neither loved nor understood him.[29]

Images of Jesus and ideals of manhood evolved between the 1880s and the 1920s in response to one another. Anxieties over their own masculinity prompted social gospelers to look for a manly example, which they now found in Jesus. And as the social gospelers worked through both their identity and their religion, they altered both. The new ideals they created served as important components of an evolving culture from which later generations drew strength. Thus, the social gospel had important cultural ramifications in the twentieth century. The definition of masculinity for late-Victorian men was conditioned by cultural expectations, experiences in childhood, and their own redefinition of religion and culture. They helped shift manliness away from an individual standard and toward a social, "other-directed" ideal. By the 1920s their social ideals merged with a capitalistic consumer culture, and identity formation ceased to be dominated by religion.

PART TWO

Constructions of Masculinity in Friendship and Marriage

For women's historians examining middle-class women during the nineteenth century, Carroll Smith-Rosenberg's "Female World of Love and Ritual" was a landmark. Unlike most previous scholars, who had emphasized the oppression and passivity of women, she brought to attention the importance, intensity, and creativity of same-sex friendships among women of this class, regardless of marital status. In her view these women were not simply the victims of a historical process driven by men, but were themselves important and independent participants who shaped "women's sphere" to serve their own needs and aspirations. More recently, however, dissatisfaction with the limitations of the spheres metaphor has led women's historians to take an interactive view of social processes and to seek, in Linda Kerber's words, "to show how women's allegedly 'separate sphere' was affected by what men did, and how activities defined by women in their own sphere influenced and even set constraints and limitations on what men might choose to do . . . " (Linda Kerber, "Separate Spheres, Female Worlds, Woman's Place: The Rhetoric of Women's History," *Journal of American History* 75 [June 1988]: 18).

While historians concerned with masculinity have often taken a broadly relational view of gender construction, especially in seeing preoccupation with manhood as an anxious reaction to the assertiveness and influence of women, they have only begun to look closely at the process of interaction. Not surprisingly, the first explorations come largely from historians concerned with courtship, marriage, and divorce. The meaning and relative importance of same-sex friendships among middle-class males have yet to receive comparable attention, but can be expected to benefit from the work of women's historians on the shifting patterns of homosociality and heterosociality.

The three essays in this section exemplify phases in the historiography of gender. Donald Yacovone examines how cultural and intellectual traditions influenced friendships among male abolitionists. Less significant in his explanation is the relation between men and women. By contrast, the essays by Robert L. Griswold and Margaret Marsh are explicitly interactive in studying the evolution of conceptions of marriage and divorce. Griswold emphasizes the influence of women as petitioners and witnesses in divorce cases in transforming the legal norm for responsible manhood. Marsh shows how women's criticism of absent or emotionally detached husbands and fathers helped shape an ideal of domestic masculinity which men themselves came to endorse. Because scholars of gender hotly dispute the character of the male role today, the speed with which and degree to which male norms and behavior have changed in the past remain at issue. Indeed, Yacovone's essay—which most strongly cautions historians against projecting contemporary understandings of close male friendships into the past— is also most likely to arouse controversy.

***

Yacovone documents the power at midcentury of an ideal of fraternalism which, he emphasizes, derives from Christian tradition. Although he focuses on its expression among abolitionists, he believes that effusively affectionate male relationships were much more widespread, appearing at the opposite ideological extreme among Southern secessionists. Yacovone stresses both the intellectual and cultural inheritance shaping this fraternalism and the pre-Freudian climate of opinion at midcentury because he believes that gay historians have mistakenly read an erotic dimension into the effusive affection among midcentury men. His purpose is to show that there existed an ideal of male behavior, similar in style to the ritualistic and intense friendships among middle-class women, that was radically different from the rough, tough, combative style of celebrated frontiersmen so often depicted as the dominant ideal.

How widespread this "soft" male ideal was among middle-class men remains to be determined. Intimacy and physical contact in male friendships were still promoted at midcentury by social circumstances and inherited practices (such as the sharing of beds) which are alien to modern ideas of privacy. But the intensity of affection among abolitionists and among other embattled groups zealously pursuing a mission may have been uncommon even in the heyday of romanticism. The task of systematically deciphering the language, conventions, and range of variation in male friendships for different social groups has only just begun.

Whether the boundaries between homosociality and homoeroticism were as distinct as Yacovone suggests will be argued immediately, as his own criticism of gay historians' reading of the language of agape indicates. By contrasting this cultural tradition—lost by the end of the century— with the preoccupations of a Freudian age, he suggests that male fraternalism was unproblematic for most men so long as their love did not lead to actual homosexual intercourse. His portrait emphasizes the innocent joy of male friendship, except for those men who may have had "ambivalent, disturbed, or incomprehensible sexual drives behind their friendships." He does not assume that individuals worried about the boundaries between affection, sensuality, and sexuality, or that they differed much in how they defined them, much less that their affection may have been burdened by anxiety about the intensity of their infatuations or by ambivalence about their sexual orientation.

If the readings of fraternalism by gay historians seem too present-minded to Yacovone, he finds the work of women's historians on same-sex friendships helpful in showing the importance and similarity in expressiveness of fraternalism for both sexes. This similarity was strongest among the most dedicated of the Garrisonian abolitionists, a group which also provided the strongest support for women's rights and for women's full participation in the abolitionist movement. Yacovone's analysis thus calls for study of the relationships between the Garrisonians' "theory of Christian social androgyny" and their interaction with women in their families and within the movement. Moreover, their rejection of rigid gender distinctions and spheres suggests a more frequent and easier social interaction between the sexes than characterized respectable society generally. But in the absence of direct examination of that interaction we are left to speculate, alternatively, that in a culture concerned with moral purity, heterosociality may have remained fraught with anticipated perils, normally precluding the intense expression of affection that characterized male fraternalism.

If women are offstage in Yacovone's essay, they play a central role in Griswold's study of marital norms as reflected in community testimony and judicial response in divorce cases. In the wake of an evangelicalism which increasingly emphasized female responsibility for morality, wives repeatedly brought before the courts evidence of a wide range of abuses by autocratic spouses. These women's expectations of a more companionate marital norm, affirmed by scores of witnesses and local judges, spurred appellate judges to expand the definition of matrimonial cruelty to include mental as well as physical abuse. Griswold makes clear, however, that the raising of standards for male marital behavior came about only gradually and against continuing resistance by many men.

Jurists changed the shape rather than the substance of patriarchal relations; their decisions provided more protection to women within a dependent relation rather than greater rights within marriage. And the conflict over the appropriate male role did not end with judicial redefinition, as men devised new ways to resist these assaults on traditional masculine behaviors. Griswold's study does not presume a structural fit between particular male solutions of gender-related conflict and the needs or trends of the times. Thus whereas the studies of all-male interactions in part 1 of this book often suggest that male behaviors accorded with the needs of society, Griswold instead perceives an ongoing struggle within a process of change.

Griswold extends the work of legal historians who are concerned with domestic relations and benefits also from the work of women's historians who have shown the mixed motives of nineteenth-century legislators and judges in reshaping laws affecting women, especially women's autonomy. He notes how the higher standard of middle-class manhood was shaped by women's involvement in a host of reform associations. What remains less clear in Griswold's analysis is the extent to which the rising demand for more respectful and considerate behavior by husbands was accompanied by transformation in the conception of the marital relation.

Reference by Griswold and other historians to a companionate ideal before the turn of the century may be misleading insofar as it suggests a degree of partnership and dependence on the spouse-as-best-friend that was surely uncommon before the twentieth century. Margaret Marsh's essay on masculine domesticity in the late nineteenth century argues that the economic preconditions for such intimacy were not available for many middle-class men much before 1900, when increased job security within large corporations made it easier for middle-class men to direct more of their energies to the home. Like Griswold, she suggests that men were only half persuaded by women's demands for a higher standard of male behavior, a standard which by the 1890s encompassed male involvement in household tasks. But she argues that male spokesmen, some of whom also praise forms of the hyper-masculinity exemplified by Theodore Roosevelt, now extol the pleasures of domesticity for men to an extent unusual earlier.

No one doubts that over the course of more than a century a companionate ideal of marriage has come to dominate the way middle-class men speak publicly of marriage, whatever reservations and exceptions in behavior they maintain in private. But the timing of the change, even in lip service to the ideal, remains arguable. Marsh, for example, has suggestive evidence that change in the layout of suburban homes late in the nineteenth century encouraged the family to come together rather than to separate into gender-divided spheres. Determining whether this physical rearrangement reshaped the gendered meanings of interactions in everyday life requires evidence of a different character. We still know little about the frequency with which men performed particular household tasks, especially those not associated with raising their children. Nor have we adequately specified the renegotiation of male and female responsibilities within the family during the twentieth century. When, for example, did the family vacation and male responsibility for planning it become customary in middle-class families? When did Mr. Fixit and the master of the barbecue appear, and did these circumscribed modifications in role alter the older division of gender spheres significantly?

Perhaps the most stimulating part of Marsh's argument is her emphasis on the increasing number of complaints among women writers that men contributed little to the home. Others, such as Charlotte Perkins Gilman, imagined a future in which collectivized living arrangements would free women for stimulating vocations. That men feared or resented these expansive visions requires further elaboration, although women's historians have already delineated a deep and devastating male backlash in the 1920s. That backlash poses sharply the question of how far power relations between the sexes within the middle class had changed during the hundred years after Evangelicalism's elevation of women as moral and spiritual exemplars during the 1830s.

The answer to the question of how much gender relations have changed depends, for the moment at least, rather heavily on one's contemporary political stance. Those who doubt that the attitudes and behavior of men have improved much during the past century will be skeptical of claims of changes in ideals and practices during the past century. Those who see more evidence of change may be more responsive to the arguments of Griswold and Marsh. This tension in contemporary assessments of gender relations has one advantage for historians: it is likely to produce more precise delineations of the extent and timing of changes in ideals and practices, and of the relation between ideals and practices in different periods.

But the most useful recent contribution to the study of masculinity by women's studies is its increasing emphasis, especially in the history of ideas and literature, on the way women during the nineteenth century reimagined gender relations, domestic life and the household, and women's relation to public life. We are only beginning to discover how women writers altered the gender perceptions of men as well as those of women, and how they undercut patriarchy. We have known for some time about the minority of men who championed women's rights from Seneca Falls to the passage of the Nineteenth Amendment, but we now need to investigate the ways in which and extent to which conceptions of gender relations changed among middle-class men outside that minority. Because change was slow and limited, most of these transformations will be subtle and elusive. For the most part, the resulting story before World War I is not likely to emphasize a growing male sensitivity to women's concerns as much as an increasing inability to defend beleaguered patterns of male dominance.

FIVE

Abolitionists and the "Language of Fraternal Love"

Donald Yacovone

He who abides in friendship
abides in God, and God in Him.
—ST. AELRED OF RIEVAULX

P ower, will, force, action, self-sufficiency, and struggle are words repeatedly invoked to define the historical reality of men's lives. Manhood has appeared synonymous with "authority and mastery," and womanhood with "passivity and subordination." The social roles of men and women, the nature of work, urbanization, industrialization, and, more generally, intellectual life, have changed dramatically since the early nineteenth century, yet cultural perceptions of masculinity have remained remarkably static.[1] The model man still is, as James Fenimore Cooper said of Andrew Jackson, "tough as a day in February." "All fins, and gills, and bones."[2] Most historians agree that modern definitions of masculinity developed during the so-called "Age of Jackson," when young America buoyantly swept across the continent. The frontiersman, Indian fighter, and mountain man became prototypes for the manly ethos.[3]

My study of the social and intellectual history of the antislavery community has forced me to rethink current interpretations of nineteenth-century masculinity.[4] The history of the masculine experience has been distorted, and those few historians who have studied the subject have failed to harmonize cultural definitions of masculinity with other aspects of intellectual life during the Romantic era. Friendships among male abolitionists were intensely affectionate and nearly identical to the complex relations of some nineteenth-century women.[5] The freedom with which many abolitionists expressed their love and devotion, and the open ritualistic nature of their relationships, calls for a reconsideration of the commonplace view that Victorian men were emotionally inexpressive and hypermasculine.

I do not mean to deny the hegemony of men and patriarchal culture during the nineteenth century, nor do I claim that all Victorian men conformed to the fraternal model. What the personal relationships of the abolitionists show, however, is that antebellum Americans accepted no single definition of manhood. They displayed a variety of phases or styles of masculinity which sometimes blurred gender distinctions in ways that would disturb contemporary Americans. This modern reaction to intimate male friendships underscores the profound changes which have occurred in the culture's perception of masculinity. To a surprising degree, mid-nineteenth-century social attitudes permitted great liberty in personal relations, largely untainted by homophobia.[6]

Still, there is much truth in the stereotypes we harbor concerning nineteenth-century male gender roles. Widespread belief in the doctrine of separate spheres created a sexually segregated culture dominated by men. During the 1830s, for example, Thomas R. Dew, the Southern intellectual and defender of slavery, typified popular belief when he characterized men as bold and courageous and women as possessing "grace, modesty, and loveliness." Men, Dew wrote, are "the shield of woman, destined to guard and protect her."[7]

But Dew's archetypal conceptions represented only one form of nineteenth-century masculinity. Abolitionists, especially the Boston-based group allied to William Lloyd Garrison, exhibited a very different pattern of behavior, one that belied pronouncements (such as Dew's) justifying the sharp distinction between men and women. By employing the "language of fraternal love," they expressed their personal commitment to the cause and to one another.[8] The fervent sentiments of the abolitionists originated in a Christian tradition that stretched back to the Middle Ages and beyond that to the early Christian church. As members of a profoundly religious movement, abolitionists discovered that the language of ecstasy represented the only discourse that could express the intensity of their emotions and the depth of their commitment. When they professed their undying love for one another, kissed, shed tears, or clasped hands, they reenacted a ritual as old as Christianity.

Some of the most effusive fraternal relations existed among the Garrisonian abolitionists, a heterogeneous group of ministers, editors, and professional reformers best known for their uncompromising antislavery principles. Pilloried as social revolutionaries who would jeopardize the Union to end slavery, the Garrisonians considered abolitionism a paramount obligation for true Christians. The call for the immediate end of slavery and the rejection of racism became theological tenets of a dedicated clique that advanced its radical goals by seeking to re-create the social relations it believed were characteristic of the primitive Christian church. Affection cemented the Garrisonian community and provided the emotional support necessary to challenge the social order, tolerate social ostracism, and endure personal violence. For the most committed members of the group, the language of fraternal love symbolized a rejection of rigid definitions of gender and reflected a theory of Christian social androgyny that sought to restructure American society.[9]

Reconsidering the antislavery movement in 1889, the *Unitarian Review* was struck by the similarity between abolitionist societies and traditional religious bodies with their "profession of faith and forms of observance." These organizations duplicated the ideal primitive church, merging all "distinctions of race, wealth, social position, culture . . . or sectarian belief, in a common brotherhood." Despite the fracturing of the abolitionist movement in 1840, Garrisonians preferred to remember their former unity and genuine affection. They thought of themselves as "brothers" whose "hearts all beat in unison."[10] Parker Pillsbury, an abolitionist editor and former member of Garrison's clique, recalled in 1883 how the bitter opposition of church, state, and society had helped forge the abolitionist fraternity. Pillsbury recollected that "as the subsequent tempests of proscription rose in all their terrors over us," the group became "akin to heaven itself, growing brighter, too, and more beautiful."[11]

Garrisonians patterned themselves after the early Christians, coming out of a "corrupt church" to propagate the antislavery gospel. Their societies were voluntary "congregations," a nineteenth-century version of the primitive church with Garrison as its great missionary. Typologically, they placed the movement within the context of the biblical era. They saw Garrison as the nation's savior and considered themselves to be the latter-day equivalent of the apostles. Garrisonians labored among their fellow citizens in the same way that the apostles had worked among the Jews "to bring them up to the standard of faith which they themselves acknowledge."[12]

Agape, or Christian love, suffused the Garrisonian community just as it had been a dominant motif of the primitive church. According to early Christian thought, agape originated in God's love for His children and in the faith's emphasis upon universal love. As one Boston Unitarian minister wrote in 1832, "It is to his goodness that we give our affection; or . . . in the language of St. John, we love him, because he first loved us."[13] Agape was also rooted in Jesus' love for his disciples and their love for one another. This form of Christian love, as Paul Tillich wrote, repairs the destruction wrought by the Fall and reunites humanity with God. Love for God and for one's brethren bound the early Christian community, riveting Christian unity and assuring its survival. Abolitionists of all ideological persuasions accepted the notion of agape and credited God with the authorship of their mutual love. As British abolitionist Charles Stuart declared to Theodore Dwight Weld, "You are mine and I am yours. God made us one from the beginning." In agape, their affection simultaneously joined them to one another and to "our Lord, for ever."[14]

The early Christian ritual of agape defined the pattern of Garrisonian social relationships. By modeling themselves after the early Christians, the Garrisonians imparted through their rituals a sense of timelessness and a return to innocence and purity. Group members followed the traditional Christian custom of greeting one another with a kiss on the cheek or by clasping hands. They savored the company of antislavery "saints" and sincerely regretted long absences. They fortified their bonds through expressions of love and by naming their children after abolitionist and reform-minded colleagues. When abolitionists closed their letters with phrases such as "Yours in the bonds of love," they simultaneously affirmed their Christian beliefs and abolitionist principles and nurtured solidarity.[15]

The movement's many publications bridged the great distances that often separated abolitionist coworkers. They depended on newspapers like the *Liberator* for emotional support, for information concerning close friends, and for antislavery news and propaganda. The paper also became a vehicle for public expressions of fraternalism, offering comfort to persecuted colleagues. "O! how I long to stand by your side, and the rest of the lion-hearted host that are battling for the rights of man," one correspondent wrote to his "dear and deeply loved Garrison."[16]

Abolitionist friendships self-consciously imitated the biblical love of David and Jonathan. Isaac T. Hopper, the Quaker abolitionist, explained that he had loved his friend Joseph Whithall since childhood. "I think it will not be extravagant if I say that my soul was knit with his soul, as Jonathan's was to David's." Paraphrasing Saul, a friend of Lysander Spooner's described Spooner as "delightful to meet and beautiful to look upon." Wendell Phillips freely expressed his love for New Hampshire abolitionist editor Nathaniel P. Rogers. Oliver Johnson described one Garrisonian colleague as combining "the courage of Paul with the lovingness of John."[17] Within the sacred bonds of abolitionism, the reformers could "'look upon one another's countenances, and be glad.'" Antislavery colleagues remarked that Garrison and Rogers seemed as inseparable as Siamese twins. They greeted each other "as David and Jonathan" and displayed a love that "'passed the love of women.'"[18]

Perhaps of all the abolitionist friendships none was stronger or more highly praised than the fraternal bonds of Garrison and the Unitarian abolitionist minister Samuel Joseph May. May had joined Garrison at the very beginning of the radical antislavery movement in 1830 and remained with him until May's death in 1871. Within a few months of their first meeting they addressed each other as "beloved friend" and "brother." Frederick

Douglass observed that there was "something truly admirable in the devotion of Mr. May to Mr. Garrison. Never were two men more dissimilar, yet never was one man, apparently, more devotedly attached to another than is Mr. May to Mr. Garrison."[19]

In 1837, May declared to a meeting of the Massachusetts Anti-Slavery Society that he considered his life inextricably linked with Garrison's. If Garrison were shot down "that same ball shall carry me along with him." May considered Garrison the modern incarnation of Christ, a man who had sacrificed himself for truth, a supreme martyr for right, a brother. He likened the Liberator to Germany's Black Forest, source of the mighty Danube, as the source of this country's "great anti-slavery stream." Thirty years of cooperative antislavery reform work did not diminish May's love for Garrison. Writing to him in 1860, May declared that if "I were a wealthy man I would take you in my arms, or on the wings of wind of steam—and bear you off to Egypt, Palestine, Greece, Italy, etc. etc.—that you might be taken out of your cares."[20]

Garrison returned May's affection and even asked him to perform the services at his marriage to Helen Benson. Writing to his sister-in-law, Anna E. Benson, in 1834, Garrison declared that he "who holds a large share of my love stands before me—my noble, generous, gentle Samuel J. May! Pleasant is the sight of his countenance to my soul—charming the tones of his voice to my ear." Although May had left Massachusetts for Syracuse, New York, in 1845, Garrison would not permit the bonds to dissolve. He informed one of his sons that still "my soul cleaves to his as did the soul of David to that of Jonathan." In 1852, Garrison penned a love poem to May:

> Friend of mankind! for thee I fondly cherish
> Th' exuberance of a brother's glowing love
> And never in my memory shall perish
> Thy name or worth.

As late as 1867, Garrison still kept May's photograph in his study.[21]

May's life illustrates the psychological, social, and ideological functions of fraternalism within the abolitionist movement and fraternalism's broader cultural significance. At age four, May witnessed the accidental death of his brother, Edward. Over sixty years later, May could still picture the small, well-dressed body, covered with a "clean, cold, white sheet." The brothers had been virtually inseparable; they ate together and even slept together in their mother's chambers. May recalled Edward as a "fair-haired boy, with blue eyes, bright, playful, affectionate, and particularly fond of me." Edward's death sent him into prolonged inconsolable depression. Sometime afterward, May experienced a series of vivid dreams, reminiscent of Little Eva's death in *Uncle Tom's Cabin,* in which his brother descended from the heavens and glided into May's bed amid a blaze of light and cherubs. The brothers caressed, kissed, and renewed their love. The story probably tells us more about the adult May than about the child of four; still, the incident not only reveals how the nineteenth century resolved the crises of loss and grief, but also exposes the origins of a behavior pattern that remained with May for the rest of his life.[22]

American Romantics commonly formed lifelong attachments in college. During the 1820s, Ralph Waldo Emerson, the famous Transcendentalist and author, became enamored of his Harvard College classmate, Martin Gay. About 1821, Emerson composed a private poem to his soul mate (whom, for privacy's sake, he called Malcomb) that evoked typical fraternal themes:

> Malcomb, I love thee more than women love
> And pure and warm and equal is [?] the feeling
> Which binds as one our destinies forever
> But there are seasons in the change of times
> When strong excitement kindles up the light
> of ancient memories.[23]

May developed close ties with several of his Harvard classmates. He recalled spending hours singing with Benjamin Fessenden. "We were wedded to each other not only by a true friendship, but by our mutual love of song. Our voices harmonized perfectly." He described another classmate, John D. Wells, as "pure as distilled water, and affectionate as a woman. I sometimes felt really 'in love with him.'" May formed one of his closest bonds with the future education reformer George B. Emerson. When they discovered that their ages corresponded almost to the minute, they became inseparable. When George fell ill with dysentery shortly after graduation in 1817, May cared for him and took the convalescing boy to his home in Maine.[24] Two years later, Emerson accompanied May and several other Harvard students on a romp to Mount Washington. After one of the hikers discovered a bed of cranberries near the peak, he shouted out "Come boys, let us browse." According to May, they all frolicked amid the "not forbidden fruit," rolling through the bushes and eating their fill.[25]

May also developed fraternal bonds with the young men he helped guide into the Unitarian ministry. He recovered one young man, William P. Tilden, from a Massachusetts shipyard and gave him ministerial training. For three years young Tilden saw May daily. "I read with him, studied with him, talked with him, laughed with him." Years later, Tilden vividly recalled May's loving character. "He took my hand; the sky cleared. He clasped it in that broad, warm, loving palm. . . . Oh, what a clasp that right hand had!

He never gave his finger tips. He gave the whole palm, and it carried with it a whole flood of sympathy and strength."[26] May also became the mentor of a young South Carolinian named Thomas J. Mumford. May always regarded Mumford as his "Timothy," referring to the New Testament relationship between Timothy and Paul. According to one account the two men enjoyed a relationship "with warm intimacy closer than that of brothers, lasting through life." Characteristically, Mumford wrote to May on Valentine's Day in 1860, and called his note "my love letter."[27]

For Garrisonian abolitionists like May, the language of fraternal love symbolized a rejection of Calvinist theology and patriarchal society. Abolitionism reflected a positive view of human nature, a deemphasis on—if not rejection of—a belief in innate human depravity, and advanced a human-centered theology. Christ became a feminized fraternal figure, a model man, perhaps reflecting women's strong influence within the Garrisonian community. For example, Lydia Maria Child, a popular writer and Garrisonian abolitionist, believed that Christ and his disciples were universally depicted with "mild, meek expressions and feminine beauty."[28]

May also believed in the androgynous character of Christ. He argued that Christ had "as much of the feminine as [of the] masculine grace." "Humanity is dual," May asserted, "and yet when perfected it is one. . . . A perfect character in either man or woman is a compound of the virtues and graces of each." His feminized vision of Christ, which reformulated and broadened gender roles, offered a model both for his own conduct and for society. Christ, "the revelation of the perfect man," was to serve as "our pattern in all things." Advocates of nonresistance like May who challenged patriarchal culture envisioned themselves as answering Christ's call for nonresistance, embodied in the Sermon on the Mount. Such men often were described as combining the "prudence and firmness of manhood" with the "sensibilities that belonged to woman." May's desire to reform gender roles emerged directly out of his support for women's rights, and he was the nation's first minister to advocate the enfranchisement of women.[29]

Although more religiously orthodox abolitionists may not have accepted the radical implications of Garrisonian fraternal love, they adopted its "feminized" ritualistic practices. In 1825, the forty-four-year-old British abolitionist Charles Stuart established an enduring bond with Theodore Dwight Weld, then fifteen years old. The rapturous letters the two exchanged over many years represent a model of Victorian fraternalism. After a visit with Weld in 1828, Stuart bid "Adieu, my Theodore, dearer than any ties of blood could make you. . . . My soul pants once more to embrace you." When Stuart learned that Weld had adopted abolitionism, the Englishman's commitment to immediate emancipation became linked to his passion for Weld. "I long to hear of your being engaged in the sacred cause of Negro emancipation. My soul thirsts after you beloved Theodore."[30] Weld confessed equal devotion for Stuart and proudly proclaimed it to his fiancée, Angelina Grimké. "I can hardly trust myself to speak or write of him: so is my whole being seized with love and admiration of his most worthy character."[31]

Apostles of abolitionism and their converts, regardless of personal politics and religious opinions, often forged enduring bonds. Weld's conversion of James G. Birney, a former slaveholder, cemented the men in a brotherhood they believed superior to blood relations, for their union resulted from an act of will rather than from an accident of birth. This fraternal voluntarism complemented the Protestant voluntarism of the conversion experience and of church polity. Stuart also developed a loving relationship with Gerrit Smith, the great philanthropist of western New York. In Peterboro, he had "found a brother's home and a brother's heart in Gerrit Smith." As Weld helped direct Stuart into abolitionism, Stuart persuaded Smith to throw off his lingering interest in the hated schemes of the American Colonization Society.[32]

Personality clashes and ideological conflict tore at abolitionist unity after 1837. Garrisonian abolitionists who advocated women's rights and sought to grant women full membership in abolitionist societies—bitterly opposed by many clerical abolitionists as a perversion of women's presumed divinely ordained role—disaffected conservative abolitionists who opposed the introduction of "extraneous" issues into the antislavery movement. Furthermore, Garrison's commitment to nonresistance and his insistence that true abolitionists rely solely upon moral suasion tactics alienated many former colleagues who had been drawn to political activism. The ensuing acrimony destroyed the antislavery unity established at the founding meeting of the American Anti-Slavery Society in 1833.[33] The movement was further rent by the intensity of fraternal relations, which interjected the element of personal betrayal into tactical and ideological disputes. Paradoxically, the fraternalism that originally secured abolitionist unity helped contribute to the breakup of the American Anti-Slavery Society in 1840.

Although Garrison's and Wendell Phillips's friendship crumbled under wartime pressures, fraternal love helped other men overcome their differences. Augustus Wattles and James A. Thome, key participants in the antislavery rebellion at Lane Seminary in the early 1830s, both squabbled with Weld but later restored their affectionate relations. Wattles, who had been rejected by Weld for an ill-timed marriage, several years later restored affectionate relations after Weld's marriage to Angelina Grimké. "I love him as I do my own body and willingly would lay down my life for his," Wattles declared.[34] In a similar incident during their Lane days, Weld called Thome a "Jack Ass" for considering what Weld believed to be an ill-conceived marriage. Thome, like Wattles, took the occasion of Weld's marriage to repair their friendship and admitted to Angelina Grimké Weld that "there is no *man* on earth whom I love more."[35] Weld and Charles Stuart lost the intensity of their "indivisible existence" after Weld's marriage, but both tried earnestly to restore their love. In 1837, Weld expressed his sorrow over his infrequent contact with Stuart. "His absence almost seems like the subtraction of a portion of my being," Weld admitted. In 1855, long after the rupture of their friendship, Stuart still proclaimed: "I love him—I could *almost* wish myself accursed from Christ, for him."[36]

The famous mid-Victorian preacher Henry Ward Beecher developed a pattern of fraternal relations similar to that of May. As a young man, Beecher had formed a loving "covenant" with a Byronic Greek boy named Constantine F. Newell and considered it as a type of marriage vow. As an adult, Beecher established fraternal bonds with the New York editor and reformer Theodore Tilton. Until the famous post–Civil War Beecher-Tilton sex scandal, which destroyed their friendship, the two men maintained a passionate relationship. When Beecher traveled to England, Tilton wrote the older man and described Beecher's letters as "so many kisses. . . . Send some more! . . . I toss you a bushel of flowers and a mouthful of kisses." Tilton frequently expressed his love and his longing to gaze into Beecher's eyes. The two usually kissed whenever they met or parted. On one occasion, Elizabeth, Tilton's wife, discovered Beecher sitting on her husband's lap discussing the Sermon on the Mount. When Elizabeth entered the room, Beecher rose and greeted her with a kiss and resumed his seat with Tilton.[37]

The fraternal relations shared by the liberal clergy, dissenters, and other men who lived uncomfortably at the margins of their culture fortified individual resolve and fostered unity. Ironically, the abolitionists' enemies, the sacred circle of antebellum Southern intellectuals and defenders of slavery, adopted a similar language of fraternal love. They too signed correspondence to male colleagues "Yours lovingly." "Let me hear from you soon and *lovingly*," William Gilmore Simms implored Nathaniel Beverley Tucker, "for . . . [this] sort of nourishment is . . . ever necessary to the intellect as well as the affections." Another prominent member of the group, James H. Hammond, admitted to Tucker that Tucker's letters were "part of my sustenance."[38]

We must not misunderstand the purposes or befuddle the context of this language and the nature of such intimacies. The nineteenth century understood and rejected what we would call homosexual acts but had no consciousness of a homosexual persona. The word "homosexual" was not coined until the 1860s, and as late as 1920, no clear definition of homosexuality existed. Sodomy, for example, might just as easily have referred to wanton lust of any sort.[39] In their legitimate quest to recover a usable past, many historians of gay and lesbian life have distorted our view of pre-modern and pre-Freudian sexuality and culture by mistaking the language of religious ecstasy and sincerity, or agape, for homoeroticism or outright homosexuality.[40]

We must remember, as Robert B. Martin has written, that "many Victorians managed what seems to us the difficult balancing act of believing that love between men which had no overt physical consequences was therefore untouched by physical motivation." For some individuals of the nineteenth century there may indeed have been ambivalent, disturbed, or incomprehensible sexual drives behind their friendships. But the tradition of agape and its secular manifestations are too ingrained in Western culture for historians to ignore, and preoccupation with elemental sex says more about the twentieth century than about the nineteenth. The love that bonded antislavery leaders like William Lloyd Garrison and Samuel Joseph May, or Henry Ward Beecher and Theodore Tilton, was not secret or latent homoerotic desire but the expression of a Christian tradition that originated in the "rapturous union of man and God."[41]

Nor should we be perplexed by or suspicious of motives when the rhetoric of fraternal love passed into more overt physical manifestations. Nineteenth-century Romanticism, the influence of a sexually segregated culture, the isolation of normal life in a highly mobile country, and the heritage of previous centuries, in which privacy barely existed in any recognizably modern form, all encouraged intimacy and physical contact. From the earliest years of childhood, males shared beds—as had been the practice for centuries—and continued to do so throughout their lives, without homoerotic desire or the suspicion of homoerotic intent. Men from all classes and from every section of the country regularly slept together, particularly when illness or personal tragedies were involved. Samuel J. May, for example, put his nonresistance ideals to the test by sleeping with a maniac who had threatened to murder his own family. After the death of his wife in 1865, May called upon a neighbor, "Freddy," to serve as "my bedfellow," even though May's daughter and son-in-law already lived in the same house.[42]

Intimacy in both sororal and fraternal relations received official confirmation from the popular "science" of phrenology. Franz Josef Gall (1758–1828) and Johann Gaspar Spurzheim (1776–1832), the originators of phrenology, maintained that the full spectrum of human emotion could be understood by discovering the portion of the brain that controlled specific traits and personal characteristics. According to Gall, friendship was an innate brain function of a posterior lobe common to humans and animals. The organ of friendship resided beside the one that governed the love of offspring and above the one that controlled physical love. All three worked in harmony. Men with abnormally large posterior lobes were thought endowed with an innate capacity for expansive friendships. Thus, Victorian men rested comfortably in the knowledge that their effusive and affectionate behavior was rooted in physiology as well as in centuries of Christian tradition.[43]

The reorientation of American culture at the close of the nineteenth century and the corresponding rise of European imperialist thought brought a rejection of the sentimentalized, genteel values that supported the fraternal phase of Victorian masculinity. The aggressive cult of masculinity during the Gilded Age, as represented by the fulminations of Theodore Roosevelt, rejected the feminized male ideals of the earlier era. Misogynist fraternal orders, such as urban firehouse gangs that had their origins in the antebellum period, blossomed in the last part of the century.[44] Rapid industrialization, massive immigration, profound economic transformation, and dislocation transformed the texture of middle-class life and produced a culture that worshiped muscle and might. Even the children of men who had been some of the greatest exponents of the feminized male ideal censored their parents' published writings or wrote studies glorifying hero worship and the manliness of Christ.[45]

By the century's end the rise of psychoanalysis, the popularity of the new sexologists, and notorious persecutions of avowed homosexuals like John Addington Symonds and Oscar Wilde created a startling outburst of homophobia on both sides of the Atlantic. In 1885, England formally outlawed homosexuality with the Labouchère Amendment. Yet the amendment's primary author, W. T. Stead, was surprised and disheartened by the popular hysteria surrounding the Wilde prosecution. "A few more cases like Oscar Wilde's," he wrote to Edward Carpenter, the English author, socialist, and popular sexologist, "and we should find the freedom of comradeship now possible to men seriously impaired to the permanent detriment of the race." The damage that so concerned Stead was irrevocable and destroyed the early Victorian era's generous construction of masculinity.[46]

SIX

Divorce and the Legal Redefinition
of Victorian Manhood

Robert L. Griswold

In 1882, a California Superior Court judge listened with sympathy to Annie Parker's lament that her husband "never treated me as a wife should be—that is with the respectful consideration a husband should show to his wife. His conduct was uniformly truculent and morose." This evidence helped Annie gain a divorce, and in making such an award, the judge joined his brethren in other parts of the country in endorsing an interpretation of matrimonial cruelty far more expansive than traditional conceptions would have allowed.[1] At about the same time on the opposite side of the country, a New York jury ordered the divorce of a couple named Pfeiffer on grounds of the wife's adultery. Yet despite solid circumstantial evidence—including a letter written by Mrs. Pfeiffer that left no doubt she no longer loved her husband—the judge set aside the verdict on grounds that "none of the badges which usually accompany intimacy are here found present." Her actions were reprehensible and an affront to the dignity of marriage, but they did not prove she had committed adultery. Judge Edward Hatch then ordered a new trial.[2]

One case led to a divorce, the other did not, but in both instances male representatives of the state offered a measure of protection to wives and set partial limits on men's control over women; moreover, these and similar cases illustrate how new conceptions of American manhood took shape within small-town law courts and state appellate courts. The legal system—especially the local law court—was one place, perhaps one of the few places, where Victorian gender ideology and the day-to-day lives of people became publicly entangled. By examining divorce evidence at both the local and appellate levels involving matrimonial cruelty, intemperance, and adultery, this essay seeks to explore the role the legal system played in redefining American manhood and in creating legal protections for women—protections that were, however, based on patriarchal rather than feminist

The author would like to thank professors Martha Minow, Hendrik Hartog, and Martha May for their helpful comments on an earlier version of this essay.

assumptions. At least in law, what was significant about nineteenth-century patriarchy was less its decline than its changing shape.

A war of sorts was waged over male identity in the nineteenth century, a war that took a host of forms ranging from temperance, sexual purity, and religious campaigns to issues of fertility control, gambling, and male authority within the family. A cultural redefinition of manhood was under way, a process inextricably linked to a distinctive middle-class culture characterized by distinctive male and female spheres, the valorization of wifehood and motherhood, and companionate relationships between husbands and wives. This middle-class culture—shaped in large part by women's involvement in a host of reform associations—called out for a new kind of man who would forfeit traditional male prerogatives in exchange for closer emotional and psychological ties with his wife and children. Such a man, domestic moralists insisted, had to temper his authority, respect his mate's moral superiority, and make every effort to be a true companion to his wife and children. Traditional male prerogatives and behaviors—emotional coolness, authoritarian control, drinking, gambling, and absence from home, occasional sexual dalliances—all had to be abandoned if the middle class were to reshape nineteenth-century family life. The result would be to change the shape of patriarchy, to hone its rough edges, to reconstruct it along lines more appealing to middle-class domestic sensibilities. The last point is important: the motor of change was a middle-class conception of family authority, not feminist demands for sexual equality.

Inevitably, many men fell short of the new middle-class ideal. That they might resist, that they might be unwilling to give up their patriarchal control, that they might find the saloon or the club more inviting than the hearth, meant that women and men would struggle over the definition and prerogatives of proper manhood. Many of these struggles found their way into divorce petitions—generally within cruelty complaints—and by the end of the nineteenth century, thousands of American wives looked to the legal system for relief. Taking advantage of statutory laws and expansive legal interpretations of marital cruelty, beleaguered women went into local courts to complain about insensitive, domineering, sexually unrestrained, abusive husbands. In the process, courts became a moral theater in which the contours of a new definition of manhood took shape. By offering community members a chance to express opposition to the offense, to bear witness against the offender, to reaffirm the bonds of cultural solidarity, and to increase the authority of the violated norm among citizens, divorce courts helped mark out new cultural boundaries. In a sense, the court became an arena of community self-understanding, a place where general cultural principles or perspectives took on more concrete meaning.[3]

Two such courts were in rural California. A sample of some 400 divorce cases (of which 152 included allegations of cruelty) between 1850 and 1890 was drawn from San Mateo and Santa Clara Counties.[4] In these cases, more than 450 witnesses testified about their own married life or that of their friends and neighbors, and it is this testimony—coupled with the favorable reactions of local judges—that reveals the powerful currents eroding traditional attitudes about male behavior. Cruelty cases in particular throw into sharp relief the nature of the struggle between men and women. In these cases, women, backed by scores of witnesses, gave voice to a remarkably diverse range of grievances against autocratic male behavior; that local judges affirmed the validity of these complaints, and that appellate judges, as we shall see, greatly expanded the definition of matrimonial cruelty, suggests a growing consensus about the limits of male prerogatives within the family. Implicit in this consensus was a new definition of masculinity, one less domineering and forceful and more sensitive and cooperative.[5]

Even seemingly trivial displays of male domination might make their way into court: one woman, for example, complained that her husband monopolized the only chair in the home and refused to share a keg of beer; another that her husband would not let her visit friends; and a third that her husband meddled in her correspondence.[6] Daniel Wilson's transgressions in the 1860s were even less direct. Mrs. H. S. Hanson, a San Jose housewife, chastised Wilson for not paying sufficient attention to his wife: "I thought he treated her very coldly."[7] So, too, with Joseph Tuers, who, in the opinion of hired hand William Spencer, "never appeared to be very pleasant— seemed to be sulky and I have known him to go whole days without speaking to his wife or the people in the house."[8] Men drew especially sharp rebukes when they displayed insensitivity to their wives' sexual desires or to their special needs during pregnancy. In 1869, Ellen Havely testified that her husband's excessive sexual demands had ruined her health: "He was [unkind] regardless of my feeling or conditions of illness or health—often insisting and compelling me to sexual intercourse with him when my nervous condition and ill health forbade it . . . and by such treatment my health which was robust before marriage became ruined and it became dangerous to my life to longer live with him."[9] David Savage demonstrated insensitivity of a different kind when he insulted his pregnant wife—"I never knew a cow or mare in your condition to eat so much"—and then, after the birth, left his wife alone for a week, making no arrangements for a doctor, nurse, or any other assistance.[10]

Still other men spoke unduly harshly to their wives or not at all, refused to let them visit friends or go to church, and either paid little attention to their desires and opinions or ignored them altogether.[11] One man denied his wife the use of his credit; another sold his wife's chickens without her consent; a third spent "his money about saloons playing cards and other places to his shame and disgrace."[12] Several witnesses denounced husbands for insensitivity to wives who were ill; another set of cases accused husbands of causing their wives' illnesses: in 1889, for example, a young wife testified that her husband "habitually compelled me to work on the farm far beyond my strength or what my health would permit and this he well knew and rendered my existence miserable."[13] Men's cruelty, callousness, or indifference to their children came under fire as well. Eliza Noyes claimed that her husband took their three-year-old child to a "low boarding house and bar," while Margaret Maloney lambasted her husband because his behavior to the children was so harsh that "they stand in terror, trembling in his presence."[14]

These examples could be multiplied, but the point should be clear. Courts provided a forum, a ceremony of sorts, for the articulation of a critique of male behavior: the ceremony began when a disgruntled wife sought out a lawyer; the lawyer then drafted a complaint, the clerk copied and filed it, the court commissioner consulted it, the witnesses heard it, and the judge finally assessed it. Each partook of the language of the complaint; each immediately saw that the contest was not simply between a man and a woman but between a certain kind of man and a certain kind of woman, between an irresponsible, lazy, and cruel man and a chaste, pure, and dutiful woman. So, too, with the witness testimony: divorce trials were probably the only occasion when an everyday farmer, blacksmith, or housewife actually offered his or her moral judgments about manhood and womanhood to a representative of the state. Back-fence chatter was one thing, testimony under oath quite another.

Divorce litigation thus provided a public forum for a discussion of what was and was not appropriate family behavior; in the process, the community clarified gender norms. It is also significant that the vast majority of such cases involved male cruelty to females. Because women filed over 80 percent of the cruelty suits in the two counties, townspeople's testimony about matrimonial misdeeds focused on male misbehavior. The articulation of expansive definitions of matrimonial cruelty, then, developed primarily within the context of changing attitudes about husbands' marital misdeeds and women's claims to new standards of husbandly behavior. The redefinition of cruelty, in short, was embedded in a larger cultural redefinition of manhood and patriarchy.

Although California was more liberal than most states regarding divorce, other states moved in similar directions. As in California, the forces of change came from below and above: thousands of American wives, imbued with the expectation that the marital relation would be affectionate and respectful, took advantage of cruelty statutes in the last third of the century. Local judges, for their part, found such complaints legitimate and granted the aggrieved women divorces. Finally, as cases inevitably reached the appellate level, high court justices constructed a definition of cruelty that affirmed and gave formal legal expression to the judicial decisions being made in lower courts. What they settled on was a conception of cruelty that both embodied Victorian conceptions of family life and offered a critique and an implicit redefinition of manhood. In the process, they completely overturned traditional English conceptions of cruelty.

In English tradition, only violence or threats of violence constituted cruelty, but such ideas could not long endure in a culture that enshrined women's domestic life and extolled the companionate features of ideal marriages. In the face of such attitudes, nineteenth-century jurists began reinterpreting divorce statutes: whereas the Vermont Supreme Court boldly asserted in 1816 that "a bill of divorce will not be granted where the only cause proved, is a total alienation of the affections of one or both of the parties," such traditional sentiments seemed out of place by midcentury.[15] Jurists began to argue that mental cruelty—if it resulted in bodily harm— was sufficient to warrant a divorce, even where no physical violence or threat of physical violence was present. Writing in 1849, Justice Edward King of the Pennsylvania Court of Common Pleas explicitly rejected the English idea that only violence or threat of violence justified a finding of cruelty:

> Again, a husband may, by a course of humiliating insults and annoyances, practiced in the various forms which ingenious malice could readily devise, eventually destroy the life or health of his wife, although such conduct may be unaccompanied by violence, positive or threatened. . . . To hold absolutely that if a husband avoids positive or threatened personal violence, the wife has no legal protection against any means short of these, which he may resort to, and which may destroy her life or health, is to invite such a system of infliction by the indemnity given the wrongdoer.[16]

Most courts eventually affirmed King's position, and by the last third of the century, even more expansive interpretations emerged. Emphasizing the importance of marital companionship and individual happiness, some jurisdictions maintained that mental torment justified a divorce regardless of whether the torment caused physical harm. Arguing that "the tendency of modern thought is to elevate the marriage relation and place it upon a higher plane, and to consider it as a mental and spiritual relation, as well as a physical relation," the Kansas Supreme Court in 1883 defined cruelty to include behavior which "grievously wounds the mental feelings of the other" and "so utterly destroys the peace of mind of the other" as to harm bodily health *or* destroy the purpose of marriage.[17] Several years later a California justice made this point even more forcefully. Dissenting in 1890 from an opinion that was overturned two years later, Justice T. B. McFarland refused to accept the idea that mental cruelty must cause bodily harm before a divorce could be justified: if "the anguish of the mind must have eaten through the flesh, and exhibited itself in bodily disease, before there can be any legal evidence of cruelty," then alas for women with "constitutions so robust, with bone and blood, and muscle and nerve, and heart and lung so charged with vitality that the woes of a Lear would not wear out the machinery or obstruct the currents of healthy physical life. Must such a woman suffer on forever, and only the weak, who faint at a gentle reproach, be relieved?"[18]

These more expansive definitions of matrimonial cruelty were clearly linked to nineteenth-century domesticity. The valorization of women's family responsibilities gave women some leverage to critique and to redefine "appropriate" male behavior. If women were truly the moral guarantors of society, if social stability, the welfare of the next generation, and the future of the republic rested on women's shoulders, if marriage was really a relationship founded on mutual respect and affection, then men needed to change their behavior. When they did not, thousands of women found in expanded definitions of cruelty some measure of relief, if not happiness or satisfaction. As a result, both the moral dimension and the price-rationing dimension of the law—what Lawrence Friedman called "the two faces of law"—changed to meet new definitions of gender relationships and family life.[19] Behavior that was once insufficiently grievous to end a marriage was now considered so (a moral reevaluation), and as a consequence the "price" of divorce fell to accommodate the new marital expectations of nineteenth-century American women.[20]

Conceptions of intemperance in divorce litigation were shaped by some of the same assumptions as jurists tried to give meaning to the new statutes that began to appear in the 1830s. And like cruelty petitions, intemperance suits were overwhelmingly a woman's complaint: From 1887 to 1906, women received 33,000 divorces because of their spouses' alcohol abuse, men just 3,400. These statistics, moreover, downplay the role that male drunkenness played in marital breakups: an important federal study of divorce published in 1909 estimated that male intemperance was present in fully 26 percent of all successful divorce suits filed by wives, though it was the sole cause in only 5 percent.[21]

Local California evidence confirms these statistical patterns. Throughout the state from 1867 to 1906, about one thousand wives, but only three hundred husbands, received divorces because of their mates' intemperance.[22] In the two California counties, four times as many wives as husbands received divorces because of their spouses' alcohol abuse; moreover, complaints of drunkenness routinely accompanied wives' cruelty allegations. Here, too, the local court functioned as a community forum or theater for the clarification and reaffirmation of community morality. Temperance was a Victorian virtue of the first order, and in small-town courts, people had the opportunity to describe the ravages of alcohol; in so doing, they not only highlighted women's vulnerability to male vice, but gave voice to a conception of manhood at odds with the free-drinking conviviality of all-male saloons.

An acquaintance of laborer Steven Purdy, for example, described Purdy as "an idle, profligate, intemperate man." Rather than work, Purdy spent his time drinking and gambling, and even refused to work when offered a job: consequently, his wife was destitute.[23] So, too, a longtime acquaintance of James Haun described him as "foul of liquor," a man "of an idle, lazy, and worthless disposition" who brought economic hardship on himself and his family.[24] William Allen was of the same stripe: instead of saving his money, he "spent everything he earned for liquor." A neighbor, Mary Hull, testified that Allen appeared one night in her bedroom, "Drunk in my house lying in bed with his clothes on."[25] Blacksmith Samuel Brisbine spent fully a third of his time in saloons; livery-stable operator Edward Bliven lost his business due to alcohol; miner Marlin Mattson preferred to drink and carouse though "perfectly able to work"; and one Michael Ryan was "idle and dissolute and has failed to work and labor as an industrious man should."[26] Even more objectionable was the behavior of several husbands who slipped off to the cozy environs of the local saloon instead of ministering to their ill wives.[27] There are many more examples, but the essential point is that local courts provided a place where the community reaffirmed the importance of sobriety to proper manhood. Here townsfolk drew the connection between temperance, economic respectability, and proper manhood; here justices offered a measure of protection to women by breaking their bonds to such men. To be a man, the townsfolk and jurists agreed, was to be diligent, frugal, and sober: to fail, to become a drunk, was to surrender one's claim to manhood.

Lawmakers and justices throughout the nation shared such sentiments.

State after state added intemperance clauses in the nineteenth-century, and by 1900, thirty-eight of forty-six states granted divorces for drunkenness. Nationally, intemperance suits were overwhelmingly a woman's complaint, and the appellate decisions reflected this statistical fact: almost without exception, they focused on male alcohol abuse, and in the process affirmed an inextricable connection between true manhood and sobriety. Three themes run through these interpretations. First, insobriety need not be constant to meet statutory definitions of intemperance. The Arkansas Supreme Court, for example, opined in 1881 that "[he] is addicted to habitual drunkenness who has a fixed habit of frequently getting drunk, and he may be so addicted though he may not oftener be drunk than sober, and he may be sober for weeks."[28] Likewise, the Kansas high court in 1885 conceded that a man might occasionally get drunk without being a drunkard, but that a man might well be a habitual drunkard without getting drunk all the time.[29]

With temperance reformers, jurists shared the conviction that alcohol destroyed a man's breadwinning abilities; this was the second major theme running through the appellate decisions. These abilities had become especially important since the emergence of a wage-based economy characterized by a sharp division between home and work. Married women's economic dependence left them vulnerable to their husbands' failures, and if failure came because of moral turpitude—the 1909 report on divorce estimated that intemperance was present in over 20 percent of successful nonsupport suits filed between 1887 and 1906—courts offered redress. For example, in 1862 the California Supreme Court rejected a lower court's decision that drunkenness was not sufficient grounds for divorce unless it completely destroyed a man's ability to make a living. Such a definition was too stringent: if a man's insobriety kept him "from attending to his business during the principal portion of the time usually devoted to business, it is habitual intemperance—although the person may at intervals be in a condition to attend to his business affairs."[30] The moral shortcomings of Alexander Handy, for example, received a sharp rebuke by Louisiana's high court in 1887: the court noted that Handy was a traveling salesman whose "business qualifications appear to be fair." The jurists were certain he could have supported his family quite comfortably, "but from the evidence it may be fairly assumed that he spent the most of his means in gambling, dissipation, and riotous living."[31] Alcohol, in short, destroyed the work ethic central to nineteenth-century middle-class ideology: instead of being industrious, frugal, and self-denying, alcoholic men were often a "reckless, wandering" breed who lacked the ability to hold a steady job. The court's final judgment in an 1892 case from Kentucky reflected the sentiments of virtually all justices: "While we hold in highest regard the sanctity of the marriage bond and know that courts should be cautious in severing it, we feel that the good of society does not demand or require a wife, without fault in her marital relations, to be bound for life to a drinking, shiftless husband."[32]

Alcohol abuse not only destroyed a man's ability to support his family; it also poisoned affective relations within the family. Drunkenness rendered some men "quarrelsome, profane, profuse in threats of violence"; an "amiable and intelligent gentleman" might even become "absolutely crazed and maddened" under the influence, thereby making his presence within the home "repulsive and intolerable."[33] In fact, the government report of 1909 estimated that intemperance appeared in one-third of divorces granted to wives on grounds of cruelty.[34] An 1886 decision from Michigan offers perhaps the best sample of this third strand of judicial thinking. The court first acknowledged that the husband was a good man when sober and a remarkably successful farmer in spite of his drinking habits. When he went on his weekly drinking spree, however, he became "morose and ugly, sometimes brutal." His wife, for her part, was frugal and industrious, but she was not "of the most refined character"; sometimes she swore and she "had not remonstrated with him as she ought, or rebuked him for using liquor to excess." Still, the court reported, her behavior "furnishes no adequate excuse for the abuse that defendant has heaped upon her in his drunken moods, which are too frequent not to be habitual."[35]

These decisions recognized female vulnerability to male abuse, but they did so from a nonfeminist perspective that assumed that women needed legal protection from besotted, misguided males. The behavior of these husbands was unacceptable, but the ideal standard was informed by Victorian conceptions of womanhood and manhood, not by feminist ideals of gender equality. In this, the jurists and the temperance reformers shared ideals: both asked that men temper their excesses and strive for middle-class respectability; both expected wives to be ladylike and to minister to the moral needs of their families; neither demanded or even desired a radical alteration in power relations within families.

The safeguards that local and appellate justices built for women in cruelty and intemperance legislation enabled wives to free themselves from unworthy husbands. Justices erected another line of defense—albeit a thin one—for women involved on either side of adultery suits. Divorce court was one place where the Victorian insistence that men accept a single standard of sexual morality received a hearing. Where else might townspeople testify about the predatory sexual behavior of their neighbors? Where else might husbands' visits to prostitutes be publicly disclosed? Religious leaders might agitate from the pulpit, and women might pray on the brothel door-step, but local courts provided a public forum in which common Americans of both sexes reaffirmed their allegiance to the ideal of male sexual fidelity and control.

Language about men and sex was not as common in California courts as language about women and sexual impropriety, but it was present. Al-though lawyers' complaints seldom referred to men's sexual character (occasionally an elliptical reference to a husband's "faithfulness" might ap-pear), members of the community sometimes described how men adhered to or deviated from Victorian standards of male sexuality. Some complaints about husbands' inability to exhibit proper sexual self-control were rela-tively trivial. Witnesses chastised David Trayer, a soda-factory worker, for flirting with young girls who visited the factory and for occasionally visit-ing "lager beer girls." Another husband was censured for helping "young ladies" on a hike rather than extending such aid to his wife.[36] Other testi-mony was more damning. Several cases involved adultery allegations against husbands accused of having sex with prostitutes. In these trials, wit-nesses described husbands who violated all standards of manly Victorian decency, and in the process reasserted the community's commitment to a single standard of sexual morality. For example, a witness in an 1869 divorce suit against Orrin Dennis testified that Dennis told him "that he could not get enough at home and had to go outside to get it."[37] In another case, a man named P. M. Davenport told how he and Seward Jones (the defen-dant) decided to take a visitor to a bordello, whereupon Jones announced that "he was going to have some fun with the girl" and withdrew to a back bedroom. After twenty-five minutes or so, he returned and announced to his friends that "he had finished pounding her, and she was a good pounder."[38] For men like Seward Jones, divorce court represented a forum of censure, a place where the "manly" prerogative of sexual license ran headlong into the assumptions of Victorian morality.

For every Seward Jones, however, many more wives were accused of adultery. Despite a declining percentage of divorces granted to both hus-bands and wives on grounds of adultery, the fact remains that as late as the turn of the century, 28 percent of all divorces granted to men came about because of their wives' adultery (the figure for women was 10 percent), sug-gesting that men, and the wider culture, remained committed to the sexual double standard. Although men increasingly turned to cruelty allegations in the late nineteenth and early twentieth centuries, they continued to take advantage of the cultural emphasis on female sexual fidelity. In light of this reality, high court justices tried to erect evidentiary safeguards that would protect women from their husbands. They did so, it appears, because they believed that false allegations, if allowed to stand, could ruin a woman's life. In addition, justices realized that power relations within families were unequal: underlying many key decisions, in fact, was a deep fear that men would use their power to destroy their wives' sexual reputations. To prevent this calamity, justices erected a new form of patriarchal protection that resided within the judiciary itself.[39]

This check on men was evident when jurists dealt with the evidentiary difficulties of adultery cases. Because adultery was "peculiarly a crime of darkness and secrecy [*sic*]," wrote the Iowa Supreme Court in 1857, "it is not necessary to prove the direct fact of adultery, for if so, there is not one case in a thousand in which the proof would be attainable."[40] Instead, circumstantial evidence necessarily had to suffice, and courts were left with the difficult task of judging whether a series of actions, perhaps meaningless when considered apart, together added up to a proof of adultery. When making such deliberations, judges had to be ever mindful that "when the facts relied upon are capable of two interpretations, one of which is consistent with the defendant's innocence, they will not be sufficient to establish guilt."[41]

This emphasis on the presumption of innocence in adultery suits was more than a reaffirmation of Anglo-American legal principles. It was also a recognition of the gravity of the charge, particularly when made against a woman, and a check on the zealousness of local court action against women accused of adultery. A survey of the nation's leading nineteenth-century appellate cases reveals that the judiciary took steps to protect women against unfounded charges of adultery. This protection came in the form of limits on what evidence could be used to sustain such accusations.

In practical terms, this meant that the general charge that a wife "sustained the character of a lewd and unchaste woman" had little standing unless it could be connected directly to her bearing toward her alleged paramour.[42] Otherwise, a woman whose only transgression was loose talk or flirtation with a neighbor might find herself destitute and degraded. As the Missouri Supreme Court put it in 1850, a wife accused of adultery must have every opportunity to defend her character: "I know of no situation," wrote Justice John Ryland, " . . . where general good character can be of more importance to her, than in a proceeding for a divorce, upon the charge of infidelity to her husband." Should she lose, Ryland continued, the consequences were devastating: "Convict the defendant of the charge, and the law deprives her of her property, of her children, of all that is dear to her, and turns her as an outcast upon the world, a miserable and degraded being."[43]

Appellate courts reiterated the importance of the presumption of innocence. In 1888, for example, the New York Supreme Court chastised Mamie Beadleston for improperly hugging and kissing a man named Armstrong, but then added that she "was not being tried for her general conduct or inclinations but on specific charges."[44] The court overturned the lower court's decision and ordered a new trial. In 1888, New Jersey's high court reversed a lower court divorce despite evidence that the defendant, a Mrs. Osborn, and a man named Stratton went riding together and traveled with each other to Philadelphia, Niagara Falls, and the Catskills. The evidence also revealed that Stratton had left his own wife and children and boarded with Osborn, even though her home was located far from his teaching job. Although the lower court thought it "unnatural, unreasonable, and highly improbable that he should go to this trouble and expense for the gratification of a friendly sentiment only," the high court declared that "adultery is not shown, nor are the elements of lust, lewdness, depravity or secrecy, the invariable concomitants of criminal conversation, to be found in the proofs."[45]

The judiciary's patriarchal, protective role stemmed from an awareness of women's economic and social vulnerability and, perhaps more significant, from an awareness of the basic asymmetry of power relationships within families. Despite growing female influence within the nineteenth-century family, courts recognized that husbands often exercised great control over their more innocent, less worldly wives. Through a variety of deceits, unscrupulous husbands might even try to use adultery allegations to end marriages they found oppressive or simply tiresome. Thus, courts looked with suspicion on confessions and found them insufficient to prove adultery unless corroborated by other evidence.[46] Such confessions might stem from collusion or, worse yet, from a husband's evil machinations. In an 1870 New Jersey case bristling with charges and countercharges of adultery, the Court of Chancery ruled that it was the husband who had actually committed adultery. The decision came despite Mrs. Derby's having signed a confession explaining that she had met a man named Palmer on a riverboat, that Palmer had taken a stateroom in the name of "Mr. Derby," and that they had both occupied the stateroom that night. If true, such evidence would sustain a divorce petition, but the court decided that the alleged confession had been signed under false pretenses by "a fond and submissive wife [who was] always anxious to please her husband. . . ."[47] Justice Abraham Zabriskie then went on to comment about disparities of power within families in general:

> Married women, we all know, constantly sign deeds against their judgment and wishes, only to gratify the requests of their hus-

bands, and to avoid the discomfort and annoyance which a refusal would cause, and solemnly acknowledge before an officer on a private examination, that it is done of their own free will.[48]

Zabriskie concluded by sketching a portrait of the Derby family seemingly lifted from the pages of nineteenth-century domestic fiction: "From the facts in the case, the conclusion is unavoidable, that she was not a resolute, strong minded woman, but of a yielding, unresisting nature." In contrast, the husband was "a man of decided will; strong, resolute, and violent" and knew "the value of energy and violent attitude in overruling more timid minds." The power of this iron-willed Victorian husband was "well adapted to operate upon the yielding nature of his wife, and to compel her to submit, as she had always done, to anything he might dictate."[49]

Rather than protecting their wives' virtue, some husbands tried to destroy it, in the process defiling their mates' reputations and confirming Victorian suspicions about manhood in general. In response, courts tried to protect wives from husbands whose deceit and connivance brought on their wives' adultery—in one case, for example, a husband desiring a divorce offered a cash reward to a man who would have sex with his wife—and expanded the definition of matrimonial cruelty to include a husband's false accusations of adultery.[50] Given the power of such charges, courts in the years after 1840 began to argue that such false accusations against a wife constituted intolerable cruelty. Although some courts insisted that such allegations must cause actual fears of bodily harm or observable damage to health in order to warrant a divorce, others focused on the mental anguish they created. Surely, courts reasoned, the virtuous, sensitive wife could not be expected to endure such aspersions against her character; surely such calumnies would undermine the mental welfare and physical good health of a chaste wife.[51] As the North Carolina Supreme Court queried in 1856, "And what to a virtuous woman can be more contumelious than a charge made by her husband of infidelity to her marriage vow?"[52] By the 1880s, many courts endorsed the belief that words alone could destroy health. The image of a coarse husband falsely degrading the sexual virtue of his chaste wife moved the Indiana Supreme Court to declare that a "husband could hardly, by any other means cause a sensitive wife more mental pain, torment, vexation, affliction, grief and misery than to falsely charge her with the crime of adultery, and slanderously report the same among her neighbors."[53] Here, too, courts offered protection to women victimized by men.

Jurists' caution in adultery suits clearly did not originate because of any allegiance to marital stability per se: their cruelty interpretations and the soaring divorce rate in general belie such an interpretation. Appellate decisions thus seemingly worked at cross-purposes: expansive interpretations of cruelty and new intemperance statutes undermined traditional conceptions of marital stability by lowering the "price" of divorce. Cautious interpretations of adultery evidence, by contrast, made divorces due to infidelity relatively more difficult to obtain. This contradiction disappears, however, on closer inspection: in both cases, justices' opinions offered advantages to women. Although men benefited from more expansive definitions of cruelty, far more women profited by the change: from 1887 to 1906, 84 percent of all divorces granted for the cause of cruelty went to women.[54] In contrast, adultery interpretations helped women in quite a different way: women were more vulnerable to adultery charges statistically—men received almost 60 percent of all divorces based on adultery between 1887 and 1906—and, because of the double standard, morally and socially as well.[55] In light of these realities, justices urged lower courts to be cautious about taking action that could have devastating consequences for women. By its nature, adultery was a crime of secrecy, but it was also a crime with powerful public reverberations once legal accusations were lodged. As a result, justices reasserted the importance of the presumption of innocence, underscored women's vulnerability to false accusations of adultery, and directed attention to disparities of power within families.

Although jurists' treatment of cruelty, intemperance, and adultery cases offered some clear benefits to both men and women, the limits of judicial protection for women must be recognized. What judges offered was protection, but no extension of basic rights. Women, they asserted, needed the protection of men, and if men as husbands failed to protect their wives, then men as representatives of the state would do so. The rationale for such protection reflected the patriarchal assumptions of domestic ideology: women were more moral, more sensitive, and more vulnerable to innuendo and gossip than men. The jurists challenged none of these assumptions: instead, they positively asserted them and incorporated them into their legal reasoning. The jurists' interpretation of cruelty, their condemnation of drunkenness, and their caution in adultery suits helped to change the shape but not the substance of patriarchal relations.

Nor were men eager to forgo their patriarchal prerogatives. While local courts and appellate justices tried to alter conceptions of patriarchy, millions of men flocked to fraternal organizations, jingoist clubs, college fraternities, rough-and-tumble political organizations, sports clubs, and veterans' organizations; other men, depending on their social class, simply spent their free time at neighborhood saloons or downtown men's clubs. In short, the struggle over the definition of American manhood was ongoing. Although courts put forth a vision of manhood congruent with Victorian assumptions about gender, many men resisted this effort to redefine the nature of masculinity, this assault on traditional masculine behaviors.

Despite jurists' having created some measure of protection for women, the fact remains that relief from misery cannot be equated with autonomy and independence. Patriarchal protection was, and is, no substitute for feminist equality. A fundamental asymmetry persisted: when men took advantage of adultery, cruelty, or intemperance suits and secured a divorce, they ended their marital woes and enjoyed the freedom that was the birthright of their sex. When women did so, they secured immediate relief, but they also encountered a society that systematically denied them autonomy and independence. It was, in the last analysis, an asymmetry that no degree of patriarchal protection could obscure. As nineteenth-century feminists so accurately recognized, more liberal divorce laws and legal interpretations would help, but they were not sufficient.[56] Such laws might partially redefine male gender ideals and curb male excesses, but only feminism could reshape manhood in ways that would foster women's true liberation.

SEVEN

Suburban Men and Masculine Domesticity, 1870–1915

Margaret Marsh

The home is man's affair as much as woman's.
—MARTHA AND ROBERT BRUÈRE, 1909

There is no reason at all why men should not sweep and dust, make beds, clean windows, fix the fire, clean the grate, arrange the furniture. . . .
—AMERICAN HOMES AND GARDENS, 1905

When historians think about American men at the turn of the twentieth century, among the images they usually conjure up are that of a bored clerk or middle manager in some impersonal office of a faceless corporation, pushing papers or counting the company's money, longing nostalgically for a time when a man could find adventure and get rich at the same time by becoming a robber baron or conquering new frontiers; and of Theodore Roosevelt, the delicate child who grew up to relish big-game hunting and war, whose open disdain for softness and "effeminacy" made him the preeminent symbol of rugged masculinity in his own time.

We owe the association of the corporate drone with the flamboyant Rough Rider to an influential essay by John Higham, who argued that one of the most significant American cultural constructs at the turn of the century was a growing cult of masculinity. Beginning in the 1890s, Higham argued, the country witnessed a national "urge to be young, masculine, and adventurous," when Americans rebelled against "the frustrations, the routine, and the sheer dullness of an urban-industrial culture."[1] He cited the growing popularity of boxing and football, a disaffection from genteel fiction, and, not least, the rise in the level of national bellicosity, as important indicators of a new public mood.

Higham's article, published in 1970, triggered an interest in the historical meaning of masculinity. His insights, and those of others who have followed his interpretive lead, have been of undeniable value.[2] Nevertheless,

An earlier version of this chapter appeared in *American Quarterly* 40 (June 1988): 165–86. © 1988, American Studies Association. A fellowship from the National Endowment for the Humanities funded the research for this essay. The University of Pennsylvania also provided support.

their work defined an entire generation of middle-class men—young and middle-aged, married and single, urban, suburban, and rural—in terms of anxieties about manliness. Those anxieties, and the men who faced them, undoubtedly existed, but in the course of my research on suburban families, I have discovered a different manner of middle-class man. There is evidence to suggest that historians will need to supplement the image of the dissatisfied clerk with a picture of a contented suburban father, who enjoyed the security of a regular salary, a predictable rise through the company hierarchy, and greater leisure.[3]

Although the cult of masculinity does offer an explanation for some elements of middle-class male culture, other elements are better explained by the model of masculine domesticity.[4] Masculine domesticity is difficult to define; in some ways, it is easier to say what it was *not* than what it was. It was not equivalent to feminism. It was not an equal sharing of all household duties. Nor did it extend to the belief that men and women ought to have identical opportunities in the larger society.[5] It was, however, a model of behavior in which fathers agreed to take on increased responsibility for some of the day-to-day tasks of bringing up children and spent their time away from work in playing with their sons and daughters, teaching them, taking them on trips. A domestic man also made his wife, rather than his male cronies, his regular companion on evenings out. And while he might not dust the mantel or make the bed except in special circumstances, he would take a significantly greater interest in the details of running the household and caring for the children than his father had been expected to do.[6]

The evidence for the growth of masculine domesticity comes from a variety of places. Prescriptive literature is one important source. Tantalizing clues from domestic architecture, records of community groups in the suburbs, letters, and diaries are others. The first category includes the later writings of the influential literary domestic Harriet Beecher Stowe;[7] the essays of Abby Morton Diaz, a Boston feminist and popular author of juvenile fiction; widely read child-rearing manuals; and the advice of successful men to their aspiring juniors in the Progressive Era, from figures as disparate as the reformist senator Albert Beveridge and the sensationalist publisher and "physical culture" hero Bernarr Macfadden. If the image of domestic man came only from this prescriptive literature, it would still be important as a sign of changing cultural models. But suggestions of changing male roles also appeared in the reconfiguration of interior space in suburban houses, in the rise of suburban institutions which included both husbands and wives, and in the daily lives of suburban families.

Masculine domesticity required three conditions for its emergence: (1) an ideal of marriage that emphasized companionship instead of either patriarchal rule or the ideology of domesticity (see below), both of which encouraged gender separation; (2) an economic system that provided sufficient job security for middle-class men so that husbands could devote more attention to their families; and (3) a physical location in which the new attitudes toward family could find their appropriate spatial expressions. It was not until the power relations within middle-class marriage underwent subtle shifts, until the rise of the corporation provided relatively secure jobs with predictable patterns of mobility, and until suburbs began to be viewed as the appropriate space within which to create the companionate family, that the development of masculine domesticity was possible. By the early twentieth century, all three of the conditions had been met.

During the middle of the nineteenth century the patriarchal family, softened by love and mutual obligation, had served as the principal model for middle-class families. This ideal of family life depended on what twentieth-century historians have come to call the ideology of domesticity, a social theory articulated most persuasively by Catharine Beecher in the 1840s. Building in part on the ideas of Sarah Josepha Hale and Horace Bushnell, Beecher attempted to unify the contradictions of a society that was both democratic and in many ways inegalitarian by minimizing class, racial, and ethnic differences while maximizing gender differences. The success of the ideology of domesticity required, in the words of Beecher's biographer, "the isolation of women in the home and away from full participation in the society." As compensation for their voluntary abdication of the right to a position in the world of men, women held sway within the home, thereby (at least theoretically) stabilizing society as a whole.[8]

The belief in separate spheres was not universal, but during the middle years of the century it dominated ideas about gender—and not only ideas. As Mary Ryan has argued, "Any cultural construct that achieved such popularity bore some semblance to social reality." Ryan's study of Utica and Suzanne Lebsock's of Petersburg demonstrate the "social reality" of gender separation at midcentury for middle-class white women.[9] The doctrine of separate spheres began to break down after the Civil War; during the past two decades, historians have extensively chronicled the incursions of women into the masculine sphere from which the doctrine had barred them. But changing roles for women also meant changes in male roles. As women entered the masculine world, men began to enter the sphere assigned to women.[10]

We can begin to understand this phenomenon—which ended in the masculine domesticity of the Progressive Era—by looking first at changes in the kinds of advice given to young men about the organization of their lives. In the middle of the nineteenth century, male advice writers (excluding the medical advisers who wrote marriage manuals) rarely concerned themselves with the roles of husband and father.[11] Instead, they emphasized economic and social mobility, urging young men to remain sober, honest, and hardworking because these qualities were essential to economic success, not because they would help a man become a better husband or father. Most male writers did not offer suggestions on choosing a suitable wife, or on appropriate behavior toward one's children. Although the moral young man understood from these advice manuals what to avoid—prostitutes, gambling dens, and the questionable pleasures of urban life—they offered him no positive assistance in settling his personal life.[12]

William Rathbone Grey, a British writer who expressed anxieties about the future of marriage, suggested that prostitution made many men "lo[a]th to resign the easy independence, the exceptional luxuries, the habitual indulgences of a bachelor's career, for the fetters of a wife, the burden and responsibility of children, and the decent monotony of the domestic hearth."[13] Rathbone's portrait of urban decadence was not unusual for the period, but his explicit expression of a fear that it would deter young men from marrying was. American writers of advice for young men generally contented themselves with painting lurid pictures of urban corruption, without correspondingly urging their readers to embrace "the decent monotony" of domesticity. Most male advice writers did not exhibit misgivings about their readers' future domestic lives in the 1840s and 1850s; books by women did, but they addressed a different audience. Catharine Sedgwick's *Home*, for example, portrayed the moral home as the only sure preventive for the dissipation that worried the male writers, but her book's readers were largely women.[14]

One of the few men who dealt with the domestic duties of husbands at midcentury, temperance author T. S. Arthur, did so for *Godey's Lady's Book*. Arthur's series, Model Husbands, explored the impact of a husband's temperament on domestic life. His "bad model" husband possessed a foul temper, was selfish and inconsiderate of his wife, left her alone every evening while he went out with his male cronies, and paid no attention to his children.[15] A "better specimen," although he began his married life impatient with his bride's inability to manage the home to his satisfaction, learned to subdue his selfishness and thereby bring about an improvement in his wife's domestic abilities.[16] If a "better specimen" was one who could learn to subdue his anger, a "good model" had none to subdue. The ideal husband took great delight in his family, spending his evening at home reading with his wife and children. Arthur insisted that men had domestic obligations that included helping around the house in emergencies as well as showing attentiveness to their wives and children and taking their plea-sures in the home with the family rather than in the city with their male friends.[17] T. S. Arthur's determined effort to combine male superiority with conjugal generosity was atypical; significantly, he published these arti-cles in a magazine read primarily by women, not by men.

In fact, it was women writers who began to refuse to pay even lip service to the patriarchal ideal. Harriet Beecher Stowe, one of the nineteenth cen-tury's most popular writers, in her last two novels ridiculed patriarchal pretensions and praised domestic men.[18] For example, one of her respected male characters in *My Wife and I* insisted that the opinions of his wife and sister were far more valuable to him than the views "of all the doctors of divinity." In the same novel, Stowe asserted confidently that "sooner or later the true wife becomes a mother to her husband; she guides him, cares for him, teaches him, and catechizes him in the nicest way possible."[19]

Stowe's novels found an echo in the advice literature of Abby Morton Diaz, a widely read author and feminist, who tried in the mid-1870s to per-suade men that egalitarian marriages were in their best interests.[20] Long before the term "togetherness" was coined to describe an ideal marriage, Diaz insisted that "a sympathetic couple are to such a degree one that a plea-sure which comes to either singly can only be half enjoyed, and even this half-joy is lessened by the consciousness of what the other is losing." Such a matrimonial state was possible only when the wife was "at least the equal of her husband" in intelligence, taste, and education. Women would have to be granted their rights to education and citizenship before there could be truly happy marriages.[21]

By the 1890s, women advice-givers were arguing that men should help out around the house and stop expecting their wives to wait on them. As one of Margaret Sangster's friends complained, she was tired of picking up after her husband, who every day "manages to give my drawing room, sit-ting room, and library an appearance of having them swept by a cyclone. One traces him all over the house by the things he has heedlessly dropped. . . ." Sangster urged her friend to tell her husband to pick up after himself, since a good husband would surely make an effort to reform, at least "to some extent."[22] Such advice, and the relationship that it implied, was far removed from a world in which a father's convenience was of prin-cipal importance.

These changes in attitude toward marriage, combined with the significant and growing public activity of middle-class women, contributed to the greater self-consciousness on the part of women that they had significant roles to play in the shaping of society. Even if she did not aspire to vote or to work at a career, a wife could justify having greater expectations of her husband. Whereas midcentury domestic writers had begged husbands not to "sear and palsy" their wives' hearts by a "tyrannical and overbearing manner," their counterparts at the turn of the twentieth century sharply informed men that husbands too "should rise above the petty . . . irritations of the day and speak with agreeable consideration for others . . ." Furthermore, they insisted, the work of a housewife was "just as important" as the husband's breadwinning job, and therefore his wife was entitled to his income: "She earns it just as truly, and has just as much a right to it as he. . . ."[23]

By the early twentieth century, some male writers concurred with many of these sentiments, paying special attention to the importance of family togetherness. As an anonymous father argued in the *Independent* in 1906, not only the family but the larger society benefited when "father and son . . . take their social enjoyments *en famille*."[24] James Canfield expressed similar views in *Cosmopolitan*. Enumerating "the three controlling desires of every normal man," he gave first priority to male domestic needs: "His home must be more than a mere shelter. . . . He must be able to make his house a home by adding a hearth—and there is no hearth for a man but the heart of a woman."[25]

The domestic lives of middle-class families reflected the changes in attitudes toward marriage. On the surface, the majority of men's and women's lives did not appear to change much; for example, women did not hold down paid jobs outside the home to any appreciable extent. But as the twentieth century drew nearer, wives spent more time outside the home, whether in mothers' groups or women's clubs, in reform activities, or simply shopping in the downtown department stores. Husbands changed their behavior patterns as well. The great age of male fraternal orders had passed by the turn of the century, according to historian Mark Carnes. Suburban men now sought their leisure closer to home, in "field" and country clubs that welcomed the whole family and in social groups that included their wives. In one Philadelphia suburb, for example, during the first decade of the twentieth century, the Men's Civic Club had difficulty in attracting members, and the Women's Sewing Society was forced to disband completely in 1903; but the Penn Literary Society, the Debating Group, and the Natural Science Club, all of which included both men and women and numbered many married couples in their ranks, flourished. So, too, did the new family-oriented tennis club, founded in the same period.[26]

Women advice-givers at midcentury had urged women to spend time socializing with other women for their *own* well-being.[27] By the 1890s the justification for the maintenance of women's outside interests was different, emphasizing the importance of the husband-wife bond. Absorption in one's domestic duties, argued the advisers, would damage a woman's relationship with her husband. Women who confined themselves to the household and to the unremitting care of children were in danger of becoming inadequate wives.[28] In the early twentieth century even moderate reformers urged women to get out of the house, to stop "fluttering about inside four walls under the delusion that these mark their proper sphere of activity," to cease thinking of the house as a "fortified citadel."[29]

Advice to men had also changed. While male advice-givers rarely insisted that men ought to take on the administrative or physical duties of running a household, they did urge them to trade the burdens of patriarchal authority and work-induced separation from family life for emotional closeness to their wives and the pleasures of spending time with their children as companions. Not all men were in agreement with such advice, but the critics' complaints inadvertently gave credence to the new male domesticity. Richard Harding Davis, writing for *Harper's* in 1894, found his married suburban friends boring because they had no interests beyond each other, their house, and their suburban pleasures. Davis found their contentment incomprehensible.[30]

Companionate marriages required new roles for both men and women, even if we cannot describe them as egalitarian.[31] Martha Bruère, an influential Progressive Era home economist, and her economist husband Robert investigated the households of early-twentieth-century middle-class America, using actual case studies of urban, suburban, and farm families. Reformers who discouraged parsimony and encouraged consumption in the pursuit of "cultivation and comfort," the Bruères believed that "the home is man's affair as much as woman's. . . . When God made homemakers, male and female created He them!"[32]

There is a considerable cultural chasm between the middle-class society of the mid-nineteenth century, in which women took responsibility for the home and for the emotional tasks of parenthood while men took on the role of firm patriarch or detached observer, and that of the early twentieth, in which men could be referred to as "homemakers." The generational contrast between the father and husband of Harriet Beecher Stowe's heroine Eva in *My Wife and I* may serve to point up the beginnings of this change in the nature of masculine domestic involvement. The father, Mr. Van Arsdell, a well-to-do businessman who supported his family in a Fifth Avenue town house, "considered the household and all its works and ways as an insoluble mystery which he was well-pleased to leave to his wife." His role in the family was quite simply "yearly to enlarge his means of satisfying the desires and aspirations of his family," the domestic appurtenances of which "he knew little and cared less."[33]

But if Mr. Van Arsdell was a shadow in his house, fleeing to his library and leaving everything else to his wife, Harry Henderson, his son-in-law, was a very different kind of man. Harry and Eva eschewed Fifth Avenue and urban fashion for a detached single-family house; its yard had "trees, and English sparrows, and bird houses," not to mention flowers and grape-vines, those necessary adjuncts to the late-Victorian suburban house. Reveling in his domesticity, Harry spent his evenings with his wife plan-ning new decorations and home improvements (not that either Henderson actually carried out any of them; the servants did the actual labor). Hender-son said of his house that during the day "I think of it . . . when I'm at work in my office, and am always wanting to come home and see it again."[34] He was completely comfortable with domesticity, proclaiming, "There is no earthly reason which requires a man, in order to be manly, to be unhandy and clumsy in regard to the minutiae of domestic life."[35]

Although Stowe's work suggests an incipient change in the ways in which men should make their presence known in the family, it is doubtful that the typical middle-class suburban husband in the 1870s could have emulated the fictional Harry Henderson. Maintaining a condition of affluence or stable respectability for a family without a hereditary income involved consider-able risk. The salaried middle-class man with a secure corporate or bureaucratic position was still a rarity. William Robinson was a case in point. Robinson was a Massachusetts journalist of no more than local re-pute, about whose life historians would know little were it not for the papers left by his wife, Harriet Hanson Robinson, who after his death be-came a suffragist of statewide importance. Like thousands of other men, Robinson struggled to provide moderate prosperity for his growing family in the third quarter of the nineteenth century. At one point, seemingly headed for upward mobility as a member of the Massachusetts state legisla-ture, he rose at 6:30 in the morning to take the train from his house in Lowell to Boston, returning home after 8:00 in the evening. Then, since he was editing a weekly paper, he and his wife spent two to three hours each evening working on it. Later, he moved his family to Malden, a Boston sub-urb, which shortened his commuting time but not his workday. Wherever he worked he put in long hours, and there was at least one period when he remained without full-time employment for several years, supporting his family by free-lance work and part-time odd jobs.[36]

William Robinson accepted the breadwinner role and its responsibilities, although the economic realities of the age meant that his work required his whole attention. Other men opted out altogether. David Lee Child, hus-band of abolitionist and domestic writer Lydia Maria Child, was perhaps an extreme example of an ineffectual provider, since he failed at every occupation he tried. Nevertheless, the reaction of his wife, a prominent public figure, indicates the great importance of masculine economic success in the mid-nineteenth century, even to a woman capable of providing for herself. Child complained bitterly to David's sister after David died: "For the last forty-five years I have paid from my own funds, all the expenses . . . ; food, clothing, washing, fuel, taxes, etc. . . . [David] had no promptitude, no system in his affairs; hence everything went into confusion. After many years of struggling with ever recurring pecuniary difficulties, I reluctantly became convinced that there was *no help* for these difficulties."[37] Lydia Maria Child, with a husband so absolutely unfit for the demands of the marketplace economy, took over and retained, with some considerable resentment, the role of breadwinner.

Child's resentment exemplifies the contradictions of this age for middle-class men and women. She was a talented (and reasonably well paid) writer and first-rate editor, but having to support her husband because of his fecklessness angered her. Child was not alone. When Hattie Robinson, William Robinson's daughter, married Sydney Shattuck in 1878, she quit her job so that he could be the sole breadwinner. After a period of living with the bride's mother, the young couple bought a suburban house, and Shattuck, in business for himself, prospered. But his business failed, and although he spent years trying to recapture his early success, it always eluded him; at the time of his death the couple lived in a shabbily genteel boardinghouse, his wife having become a bitter, querulous, and nearly friendless woman. After his death, she was forced to throw herself on the charity of her niece.[38]

These few examples, while they do not indicate that middle-class men were abandoning the breadwinner role in any numbers, nevertheless suggest the precarious nature of middle-class status in the middle years of the century. Statistical portraits have made a similar point. As Michael Katz has said of the male citizenry of Buffalo, a reasonably prosperous city which nevertheless witnessed a downward mobility rate of 27 percent in the 1850s and 43 percent in the 1860s, "Neither staying wealthy nor failing, many men struggled from year to year, their economic state marginal and fluctuating."[39] Both men and women might be unable to live up to their assigned (or hoped-for) roles. When they failed to do so, they became dispirited and resentful. Still, Stowe's Harry Henderson did have some real-life counterparts. One was Charles Cumings, an insurance-company executive whose family moved from Boston's South End to suburban Jamaica Plain in 1877.

Charles Cumings was a precursor of the early-twentieth-century domestic man. We know of him principally because he made entries in his wife's daybook, entries that showed him to be intensely interested in the doing of his children and that revealed his delight in their new suburban house. His joyful notes about the children's first steps, anxious ones about their illness, and proud little comments on the progress of the house and lawn are complemented by Augusta Cumings's remarks, including one written during one of his infrequent absences from home, when she noted that everyone, but especially three-year-old Gertrude, missed him very much.[40] By the early twentieth century there would be more men like Charles Cumings. In the 1870s he was a rarity—an organization man during the heyday of entrepreneurship; a private man during the great age of public male socializing; and a father involved in the details of his children's lives at a time when most men still believed that children were a mother's responsibility.

The connection between Cumings's occupation and his domesticity is significant. As the century came to a close, and the American upper middle class shifted away from its mid-nineteenth-century base of entrepreneurs, independent professionals, and clergy, other men could be like Charles Cumings. By then, particularly in the suburbs, the typical early-twentieth-century middle-class father was salaried and had some security in his position, more or less regular hours, and relatively predictable patterns of occupational mobility.[41]

As middle-class men gained respite from the economic pressures that had plagued the previous generation, they had the time to give their families greater attention. This change, along with the prodding of feminists, triggered the recognition of the importance of male domestic responsibility. Abby Diaz had remarked in the 1870s that people were always asking her why, if women needed education for motherhood, men did not need similar training for fatherhood. Men, she responded, did indeed need such training, but she was too busy to provide it. She added derisively: "If men feel this need, there is nothing to prevent them from assembling . . . to inquire how they shall best qualify themselves to fulfill the duties of fatherhood. [I am] . . . under the impression that men's clubs do not meet especially with a view to such discussion."[42] And Harriet Beecher Stowe, although less a feminist than Diaz, remarked during the same period, "We have heard much said of the importance of training women to be wives." She would have liked "something to be said on the importance of training men to be husband's."[43]

By the 1890s, acerbic tones had diminished, to be replaced with sympathetic anecdotes about families in which the men shared domestic duties. Margaret Sangster approved of a family of her acquaintance in which "everyone shared the housework, even the boys . . . ," while in another household the son, "a manly young fellow," did the ironing.[44] Martha and Robert Bruère took the idea of masculine domesticity at least as seriously as did Sangster, insisting that "a knowledge of housekeeping is not a matter of sex, but science," so "all ought to know [it], men and women alike." High schools, they argued, ought to require boys to take home economics courses, because men should also become "homemakers."[45] But even the (male) editor of the suburban-oriented magazine *American Homes and Gardens* announced in 1905, "There is no reason at all why men should not sweep and dust, make beds, clean windows, fix the fire, clean the grate, arrange the furniture," and cook. The editor refers to domestic servants, not husbands. Still, he intended to make a point about male involvement in the home, and not merely about servants; he continued the same theme in his editorial for the following month: "The responsibility for the home is not [the wife's] alone," he insisted, "but is equally the husband's."[46]

It is not clear that the average middle-class man, young or old, was induced to do the ironing because of examples like those cited by Margaret Sangster, or to take home economics courses on the advice of the Bruères. Men were, however, becoming more involved in the internal workings of the household, as Joan Seidl discovered. She has examined the personal papers of Minnesotans of the turn of the century, many living in suburban Saint Paul, and found that husbands of the early twentieth century took a far greater interest in the home than did those of the 1880s. Her focus is on house decoration; in the earlier period men cared little about it, but by the first decade of the century they were active participants. The recently married Helen Sommers, for example, wrote to her sister in 1909 about decorating the house into which she and her husband had moved: "Harry & I are working every thing out together. . . ."[47] Household decoration, however, according to Seidl, was a symbol of the growing involvement of men in the home. "Most remarkable," she argues, "given the standard interpretations of the period, is the degree to which husbands took an active role in domestic arrangements. . . . Fixed hours of work allowed leisure for Walter Post to dry the dishes and for James Andrews to paste up the wallpaper."[48]

Women, however, wanted men to do more than share in the process of making decisions about household furnishings. They also wanted them to be nurturing fathers. Some of them pinned their hopes on the next generation. Kate Wiggin, who before she wrote *Rebecca of Sunnybrook Farm* had been a kindergarten teacher, attempted to develop "the father spirit" in little boys. At school, her charges played a bird game, in which "we had always had a mother bird in the nest with the birdlings. . . ." Wiggin then introduced a "father bird" and similarly reorganized other games. Finally, she incorporated the boys into "dolls' day," previously a girls' game only. Wiggin asked one of the boys to play "father" and rock a doll to sleep. To her delight, all the other little boys then wanted to play.[49]

Wiggin published her kindergarten techniques and they enjoyed wide circulation. Perhaps it was the imagined sight of thousands of little boys rocking dolls to sleep that encouraged men to start getting involved in rearing their children, in order to save their sons from such influences. In fact, some of the motivation for greater fatherly involvement with children was surely a desire to balance the preponderant female presence in the lives of young children. But the word is *balance,* not *overshadow.* Masculine domesticity, as it had evolved by the early twentieth century, was incorporated into the concept of manliness, as men became convinced that in order to have their sons grow up to be "manly" they should involve themselves more substantially in their children's upbringing.[50]

Senator Albert Beveridge was one of a growing number of men who applauded masculine domesticity in the early twentieth century.[51] These men encouraged fathers to form direct and immediate bonds with their children by playing games with them, taking them on camping trips, and simply spending time with them. Of course, before the entrenchment of the ideology of domesticity in the middle of the nineteenth century, fathers had maintained a large role in family government, but in the earlier period the emphasis was on obedience, discipline, and the importance of the father's role as head of the household. In the early twentieth century the stress was on friendship: Fathers were encouraged to be "chums" with their children—especially, but by no means exclusively, with their sons. Male writers on parenthood differed from their female counterparts in that they placed greater importance on independence, approving of boys' having, from about the age of seven on, a sort of freewheeling companionship with other boys—a "gang" or "bunch," to use the terms of the period. They argued that a father could encourage such freedom because the new closeness of father and son would prevent the boy from falling into evil ways. His father would play baseball with him, take him and his friends camping and swimming, and in general play the role of a caring older companion rather than that of a stern patriarch.[52]

Within this new definition of fatherhood, aggressiveness was channeled into safe outlets. The concepts of masculine domesticity and "manliness" were in many ways more complementary than antithetical: One might hypothesize that men, as their behavior within the family became less aloof (or patriarchal) and more nurturing and companionable, would develop a fantasy life that was more aggressive. The rage for football and boxing, and the reading of adventure novels, might have provided that vigorous fantasy life, masking but not contradicting masculine domesticity; that subject remains to be investigated. What is clear, however, is that some of the advocates of masculine domesticity did think about its implications for manliness, but stood their ground nonetheless. Senator Beveridge, in his advice book for young men, told the story of a "resourceful Oriental" who had suggested that "the influence of women on the Occidental man is effeminizing our civilization." Beveridge countered with his own view: "Even if what this Oriental assailant of our customs terms the overcharge of femininity in Occidental society does mellow us," he said, "it does not follow that it weakens us."[53]

Bernarr Macfadden epitomized the connections between the cult of masculinity and masculine domesticity. Macfadden was a major figure in the mass culture of the early to middle twentieth century, amassing a publishing empire based on his ownership of the *New York Daily News* and the magazines *True Story* and *True Romance*. In the second decade of the twentieth century he published *Physical Culture* and other books on health and what we now call "fitness." A self-proclaimed savior, Macfadden addressed his gospel of "physical culture" to women as much as to men. And just as women ought to develop physical strength, he believed, so too men ought to develop their nurturant capacities, since both men and women had emotional and nurturant functions within the family.

Macfadden insisted that husbands should even be present at childbirth, and he further warned, "Whenever you find a man who is without an innate love for children, you may rest assured that there is something wrong with his character."[54] An early (and authorized) biographer of Macfadden claimed that his subject regularly devoted his evenings to his family, always leaving work "between five and seven. . . . He is a home-loving soul. . . . Sane, happy American family life is one of his ideals . . . , and his own [seven] children are a constant source of pleasure to him."[55] Whether Macfadden's biographer accurately described his subject's habits is less significant than it mattered deeply to Macfadden that readers believe in the overarching importance of his family life. In the mid-nineteenth century, a self-made man like Macfadden would have stressed the tenacity and arduousness of his economic struggle, rather than his willingness to set it all aside at a specific time each day in order to be with his family.

The final condition for the development of masculine domesticity was spatial. The suburbs began to be viewed as the natural habitat of domestic man. Macfadden claimed that the purchase of a "modest little home" would give the young married man a sense of stability as well as the necessary physical distance from urban temptations. Having come to New York City from the

Midwest to make his fortune, Macfadden himself moved to the suburbs at the first opportunity, and held resolutely antiurban sentiments.[56] Albert Beveridge had expressed similar views. Devoting an entire chapter of his advice book for young men to "The New Home," he informed his readers that "'Apartments' cannot by any magic be converted into a home. . . . Better a separate dwelling with [a] dry goods box for table and camp-stools for chairs than tapestried walls, mosaic floors, and all luxuriousness. . . ." Furthermore, once the young man had got himself a wife, a nice suburban house, and some children (because "a purposely childless marriage is no marriage at all"), he "will spend all of [his] extra time at home," listening to his wife play the piano, reading, and, not least, playing with the children.[57]

Two things are important about the domestic advice of Macfadden and Beveridge: first, here were successful men advising their juniors to cultivate domestic habits; second, they were advising them to do so in the suburbs. Macfadden and Beveridge were among a growing number of Americans in the early twentieth century who viewed urban life as a direct threat to family happiness. As late as the 1880s, the city had still seemed redeemable to urban residents and social critics alike. When people moved to the urban fringe they were often waiting for the city to catch up to them, not trying to escape it. But by the turn of the century the suburban flow had an escapist quality; one symbol of that escapism, as Kenneth Jackson points out, was the decline of annexation as a means of holding city and suburbs together.[58] And a number of sociologists who specialized in the study of the city during the first decade of the twentieth century contended that urban life and stable family life seemed incompatible. In 1909 the American Sociological Society devoted its annual meeting to questions about the family. While the scholars in attendance were not entirely agreed about the nature of the changes that were affecting the family, a number of the participants warned explicitly that city life and family togetherness had become mutually exclusive.[59]

The advice-givers and academics hoped that middle-class fathers, with more secure careers and houses in the suburbs, would spend their time with their wives and children rather than with male friends. The great popularity of family-oriented recreational activities around the turn of the century and afterward suggests that suburban families wanted to play together. According to the most comprehensive study of American leisure, in this period croquet and roller-skating were more popular than baseball (and many families, including the girls, apparently tried to play baseball on the lawn). Bicycling did not become a craze until it became a sport for girls and women as well as for boys and men. Suburbs institutionalized the relationships that marked the companionate family by creating various kinds of clubs, such as "wheel clubs," athletic fields used by both sexes, and golf and tennis clubs. (If early-twentieth-century photographs and real estate advertisements are reliable, men played golf with their wives, not with business associates.)[60]

Cordelia Biddle, who was a child in the years before World War I, had an atypical upbringing because she was part of Philadelphia's self-proclaimed gentry. Probably most fathers did not teach their daughters how to box, as hers did. "The center of activity at our house," Biddle later recalled, "was the boxing ring, . . . where I was initiated into the mysteries of the solar-plexus punch, the left jab, and the right cross. Instead of dolls, I played with barbells; instead of hopscotch and ring-o-levio, I was learning to patch up cuts under the eye." But if she remembered that boxing was an unusual sport for girls, she also remembered "that women of that period were so athletic." Biddle's parents belonged to a bicycling club called the "Century Club" because it "specialized in hundred-mile trips," during which her mother "easily kept up" with her father.[61]

Togetherness meant more than sports and outdoor recreation. In suburban Haddonfield, New Jersey, where commuters to Camden and Philadelphia swelled the population from about 2,700 in 1900 to more than 4,000 by 1910, husbands and wives joined cultural and social clubs together to study nature, to talk about their family trips, even to debate each other on public issues. Such clubs were popular in the community—the debating group had more than a hundred active members, and the literary society (which was mostly a social club) sometimes drew as many as forty people to its monthly gatherings. Men and women did not do everything jointly; they did not enjoy absolute togetherness. What is at issue is the degree of change that occurred over the course of the last quarter or so of the nineteenth century. And if we compare these husbands and wives of the early twentieth century to the generation that preceded them, the change is apparent. In Haddonfield, even the Mothers and Teachers Club, which normally met in the afternoon, scheduled two of its eight meetings in the evening for the convenience of the fathers.[62]

In light of all this, we must be skeptical of assertions like those of Peter Stearns, who has remarked that while it was true that suburbanization weakened patriarchy, it also, in "increas[ing] the physical separation of the man from his home . . . left the woman in greater effective control."[63] The decline of patriarchy did not lead to a decline of masculine interest in the home in the early twentieth century. Elaine Tyler May offers a contrasting view. In her comparative study of marriage and divorce in Victorian and Progressive Era America, she illustrates the ways in which Los Angeles, a suburbanized city composed principally of residential subdivisions, dealt with the early-twentieth-century fears about the collapse of the family. In Los Angeles, middle-class Americans created an intense family life in a suburban environment that they hoped would both protect the family from the dangers of urban life and allow its members to enjoy its material blessings.[64]

Architectural evidence supports May's arguments. The most striking thing about the middle-class domestic architecture produced in the second and third quarters of the nineteenth century, as Gwendolyn Wright has pointed out, was its design for separation.[65] The most striking thing about suburban houses in the early twentieth century was their design for family togetherness. In middle- to upper-middle-class homes, the living room replaced the separate parlor, study (commonly considered a male refuge), and sitting room that had characterized Victorian upper-middle-class houses. Both modest and fairly expensive new houses had more open floor plans.[66] Architects in the early twentieth century, ranging from the iconoclastic Frank Lloyd Wright to the very conservative Joy Wheeler Dow, explicitly designed houses for family togetherness. And architectural writers made the same statement in home magazines.[67] Families no longer maintained segregated social space, but the rage for marking off children's spaces with special wall coverings and accessories announced, perhaps obliquely, that women and children would no longer automatically share space. Such a change, one could speculate, might have made it more possible for men and women to share private space.[68]

The evidence described above may not persuade historians to abandon entirely the notion of an early-twentieth-century cult of masculinity, and there is no reason that they should; nevertheless, during the last years of the nineteenth century and the early years of the twentieth, masculine domesticity cropped up in advice literature by both men and women, in architectural design, in recreational patterns, in Progressive Era analyses of middle-class households, and in the personal papers of Eastern and Midwestern suburbanites. Taken as a whole, these data do suggest that we need to seek more information about the historic domestic role of American men.

The redefinition of manliness to include some traditional female functions was in one respect an attempt to counter the growing feminist movement. Masculine domesticity was a collective male response to the arguments of Charlotte Perkins Gilman and her followers, who insisted that the traditional family was anachronistic in an urban society and who demanded that women seek for themselves the sense of individual achievement and separate identity that had been reserved for men.[69] Gilman's writings and lectures received considerable attention in the periodical press of the day, although it is unlikely that all middle-class men knew her by name.

Whether they could identify her, however, is not the point; no one who read the papers could have been ignorant of the views she espoused. On the whole, men responded to those views by moving their families to the suburbs. There, fathers would draw themselves into the domestic circle, where individual needs could take second place to the needs of the family.

Masculine domesticity, in that sense, served as men's rejoinder to those feminists who insisted that women had as much right to seek individual achievement as did men. It offered an alternative to feminism: Men would acknowledge the importance of the domestic sphere, not only rhetorically, but also by assuming specific responsibilities within it. Women, however, shared only partially in the world of men. Reform activities, mothers' clubs, even voting became acceptable, but taking on roles in the larger society identical to those of men did not. I would speculate that, intentionally or not, men who espoused masculine domesticity deflected feminist objectives.[70]

Suburbanism was neither incidental nor accidental to this process. Suburban advocates in the early twentieth century preached that removal from the city would both encourage family unity and discourage excessive attention to one's individual wants. The suburb served as the spatial context for what its advocates hoped would be a new form of marriage. Husbands and wives would be companions, not rivals, and the specter of individualist demands would retreat in the face of family togetherness.

Constructions of Masculinity in Work and the Workplace

$\mathbf{M}$en's work has always been regarded as a crucial influence on their conceptions of masculinity. But historians have only begun to describe the construction of gender in occupations and workplaces. Where gender is not an obvious issue, as in the bureaucratization of white-collar work at the turn of the century, the absence of monographic literature is glaring.

Women's historians and labor historians have led the way in investigating gendered aspects of work, partly because definitions of manhood figure prominently in male workers' struggles with their employers over control of the workplace, including the limitation of women or younger male workers. These historians' investigations suggest an ongoing process of re-defining meanings of manliness in adapting to changing circumstances and conflicts. What remains to be determined, however, is how deeply rooted in workers' consciousness the new meanings became, since they often origi-nated as tactics in particular labor struggles. Even where a redefinition of masculinity resulted from gradual accommodation to changes in the orga-nization and nature of work, it frequently remains unclear whether this redefinition functioned subsequently as an independent variable.

The three essays in this section indirectly raise questions about causation in gender change and about gender as a causal factor. The essays investigate the construction of masculinity in three very different kinds of work: a pro-fession (law), a traditional craft (printing), and skilled factory work (textile work in a mill town). Comparing the three makes the reader ask further questions: How significant are the differences among occupations and classes? Is rhetoric and ideology reinforced by behavior and institutions?

Michael Grossberg's essay suggests the general usefulness of holistic ex-aminations of the institutions, rituals, and heroes by and through which members of an occupation shape and express their conception of man-liness. As the new nation extended into previously unsettled areas, judges took to circuit riding; away from home, especially in frontier areas, the in-tensified competition of courtroom performance and the camaraderie of the tavern produced a new definition of masculinity that was at odds with the profession's traditional scholarly and literary aspirations. Lawyers now chose to present themselves to the public as self-made men, deeply democratic in habits and thoroughly at home in the rough-and-tumble world of politics.

Grossberg's holistic portrayal ends with the Civil War. Grossberg suggests—but does not show—how older unifying practices, like conviviality, were undermined by increasing emphasis on expertise in the late nineteenth century. A new hierarchy emerged as the profession splintered into several strata: an elite of corporate counsel, specialists such as patent lawyers, and, now at the bottom in status, individual practitioners. Grossberg does not try to elaborate the consequences of this differentiation within the profession. Instead he focuses in the last part of his essay on how the elite reinforced its gendered definition and control of the profession through law school admissions, the case method in legal education, and opposition to women lawyers except in auxiliary positions.

The challenge for future gender research in the post–Civil War legal profession will be to determine how different kinds of lawyers interacted, on what occasions, and with what consequences for the construction of gender within the profession as a whole. Was conviviality among lawyers now segregated according to status, ethnic origin, and type of practice or expertise? If so, what were the implications for their style of masculinity and their attitudes toward women's petitions and demands? Did lawyers from immigrant or working-class origins approve of the deliberate toughness of the case method or accept the social Darwinian justification of it which Grossberg finds among the profession's elite? And how deeply rooted among different kinds of male lawyers were the exaggerated gender stereotypes employed in the opposition to admitting women to the bar?

Gender-related conflict makes shifts in gender norms, arguments, and rhetoric easier to identify, but, as Ava Baron's essay suggests, determining their significance can be much more difficult. In the printers' response to technological change at the turn of the century, a major redefinition of masculinity appeared whose practical consequences have yet to be elaborated. By simplifying typesetting, the Linotype eliminated the need for a protracted apprenticeship and spurred employers to substitute less skilled labor, including boys and women. Deprived of security, unionized printers abandoned their traditional defense of apprenticeship as the process of becoming manly through achieving competence in their craft.

But while printers acquiesced in employers' insistence that job security depended on performance rather than on certification, they sought new means of maintaining control over the work force. They now argued that certain biological and psychological (i.e., manly) traits were prerequisites even for training in the trade, and that only the union could determine which males possessed those traits. No sissies or weaklings need apply! There is a similar shift toward emphasis on physical health and ruggedness in middle-class discussions of masculinity during the late nineteenth century.

How far this new line of argument shaped journeymen printers' practices or influenced employers' policies remains unclear. Did any shop implement the demand by one unionist that physical examinations be required for new entrants to the trade? More important, what evidence is there that the new emphasis on hardiness reshaped the way printers regarded or dealt with their fellow printers? Did they abandon their former admiration for education and cultivation? (Exposure to journeymen's "appreciable degree of culture in literary matters" supplemented the technical instruction of apprenticeship in hand-set days.)

Did printers devise any rituals or tests for ensuring hardiness among themselves? By the turn of the century, did their recreation and sociability outside the workplace encourage a more "macho" ideal of manliness? Did they come to disdain, even to harass, males who seemed too "soft"? In short, did the unionized printers' new line of argument have any deep effects on the way printers conceived of themselves and so behaved, or did it remain largely a weapon in the debate with employers? The question gains importance from the employers' success in demanding that apprenticeship now consist partly of classroom instruction in publicly funded technical schools where middle-class views of the good workman were more likely.

While Baron's essay highlights the tactical value of a redefinition of masculinity, Mary H. Blewett's study of Lancashire textile workers in Fall River, Massachusetts, points up the complexity of change in gender norms. Conflict makes those norms visible, as it did in the printers' story, but here the focus on one locality and the narrative method permit a more nuanced account of change, continuity, and flexibility within the mule spinners' and weavers' ideas of manliness. The deferential behavior of Lancashire men— itself a consequence of that industrial district's historic struggles—was contemptuously dismissed by employers in New England who ridiculed the newcomers' doffed caps and servile gestures as unmanly. Mule spinners were further alienated by the unwelcome activism of women weavers who threatened their manly respectability, most extremely when they resorted to a Lancashire tradition—the food riot—alien to New England and French Canadian workers alike. These union men defined manhood by excluding females from their work and their labor organizations while eventually accepting American politics and marketplace ideology.

But Blewett can show that these same mule spinners were flexible in their practice of manliness within the household. Often married to weavers, they saw no shame in doing routine housework. And when their leadership and sense of propriety was not threatened, they also could be flexible about women's initiatives in conflicts with employers; they deferred to the weavers' strategy against the mill agents so long as it proved successful. When the mule spinners moved closer to the outlook of American labor, they did so selectively. Adopting a craft-union definition of manly behavior, they clung to the Lancashire view that a man should stay put and fight for his rights in his own community. They continued to reject the view of many native New England workers that manly independence was affirmed by moving on when conditions in one locality proved intolerable.

Blewett's essay is a useful reminder that constructions of masculinity may be transplanted to new locales, but lose part or all of their original meanings over time. Historians concerned with masculinity need to look more closely at the complex process by which gender meanings gain or lose influence. In considering particular cohorts of workers they need to ask how far they embrace old and new values simultaneously and how the balance in their commitments shifts over time. And they need to ask of each new meaning for manhood how far it reflects meanings already present rather than a fresh imagining of male gender and gender relations.

The three essays in this section illustrate how constructions of masculinity vary in different contexts within the same culture. This focus on specific occupations and workplaces may lead to an overemphasis on that which seems distinctive within those constructions compared to what may be shared with other males in the culture. For example, the masculine style of the butchers, notorious for their rough camaraderie and taste for brutal sports, contrasts sharply with the ideal of manly behavior among workers who adopted middle-class norms of piety and respectability, like the factory operatives whom Bruce Laurie labels "revivalists." But they may not have differed substantially in their commitment to male dominance and prerogatives within the family or in their views of sexual division of labor.

The historian of gender must weigh the relative importance of such common commitments and differences in style so that we do not lose sight of the "forest" of patriarchy in looking at the "trees" of differing meanings for manhood in particular occupations. This tension should spur a useful continuing debate about whether change in definitions of masculinity entails change in gender relations. The debate also will bring into sharper focus differing emphases among women's historians and labor historians in defining causal relations between gender and class.

EIGHT

Institutionalizing Masculinity: The Law as a Masculine Profession

Michael Grossberg

In 1886, attorney Charles Moore published in the *Hartford Daily Times* "The Woman Lawyer," a tale of a young woman, Mary Padelford, who wishes to practice law. She arrives in Moore's hometown, Old Litchfield, Connecticut, on a stagecoach. Upon seeing her "slender figure" and the determined look on her face, attorney Walter Perry, "a *man* vigorous in mind and body," declares that if Padelford "possesses enough physical strength" she might succeed. But it is soon evident that while she can draft superb legal documents, she is no match for the rigors of the courtroom. During a stormy trial that pits her against two tough, unscrupulous adversaries, Padelford falls from her chair in a swoon. "Oh take me away, take me away," she whispers. A physician later diagnoses her condition as "brain fever." Constant study of the law has taxed her constitution "to the utmost" and long trials have brought her "mental and physical exhaustion." She announces that, although loath to give up her profession, she must on the advice of her physician cease trying cases. Padelford forsakes the courtroom, marries Perry, and spends the rest of her life helping him in a law partnership.[1]

Moore's cautionary tale reveals assumptions about gender and the law in Victorian America that legal history needs to explore. The central issue concerns the evolution of legal consciousness in the United States: the fundamental values and assumptions Americans developed about the legal process as it took on its own distinct forms after the Revolution. Legal consciousness, as law professor Duncan Kennedy has argued, suggests that people "share premises about the salient aspects of the legal order that are so basic that actors rarely if ever bring them consciously to mind."[2] These

I would like to acknowledge the helpful comments on the initial version of this essay made by participants in the January 1988 conference, "Masculinity in Victorian America," at Barnard College, Columbia University. I have also been the beneficiary of very useful critiques by Nancy Hewitt and the members of the 1987-1988 Fellows Seminar at the National Humanities Center.

basic assumptions about the law mediate between concrete interests—social, economic, or political—and outcomes. Legal consciousness is decipherable only by recognizing that the law existed as a relatively autonomous domain within American society. That is, over time the American legal system developed its own characteristic language, institutions, assumptions, professional ideology, and rituals. To a degree, these set the legal order apart from other elements of society, and conferred on the profession a relatively autonomous source of authority.[3]

Consequently, the law was not just one more occupation; it was a distinctive endeavor with a special place and power in the republic. And there came to be embedded in American legal consciousness an underlying premise that decreed the bar a masculine domain. Indeed, masculinity was so fundamental to the profession's consciousness that for most of the century it acted as an unarticulated first principle.[4]

Only by probing the role of masculinity in the nineteenth-century legal profession and the consciousness of its members can we fully understand the origins and meaning of the tale of Mary Padelford. Though examples of the way in which masculinity defined professional identity are elusive, the evidence explored in this essay suggests some ways in which lawyers translated the changing masculine ideals of the larger society into professional beliefs and practices. This institutionalization of masculinity in the bar also illuminates some of the critical yet largely unexamined links between the public and private sides of men's lives in nineteenth-century America.

After the Revolution, lawyers carved out a powerful new place for themselves. Their swelling numbers suggest the result. The bar increased almost four times as fast as the population; the new republic was the most lawyer-ridden nation in Western society. Central to the consciousness of the expanding profession was a clearer, and in many ways increasingly masculine, conception of the lawyer's role.[5]

Unlike in the colonial era, legal practice became a full-time occupation as postrevolutionary lawyers jettisoned lingering colonial traditions of lay participation in practice and judging. Lawyers plied their trade within a newly structured legal system created by the federal and state constitutions. And, beginning in the 1790s, they produced an indigenous legal literature of case reports, treatises, and periodicals that promoted a common professional culture of shared rules, approaches, and jargon. Lawyering itself became dependent on admission to the bar, a special professional community defined by expertise, not geography, with its own changing forms of hierarchy, training, craft consciousness, and organization. These were reproduced in localities across the nation. And most important here, as in all nineteenth-century American communities, gender served as a primary means of self-identification and exclusion. As a masculine community, the bar influenced the way lawyers filled institutional roles and devised public policies.[6]

The bar's distinctive institutional form of masculinity emerged in the opening decades of the nineteenth century. A gradual disjunction between law and literature is an evocative example of the way masculinity helped shape the bar's professional consciousness. In colonial America, where law usually had been a sideline for merchants, farmers, and planters, lawyers were assumed to be men of letters conversant in all forms of discourse. As members of an ancient learned profession, they were thought to be word-smiths able to write legal briefs, philosophical essays, political satire, and even fiction. During the revolutionary era, though, this affinity for law and letters began to break down as lawyers constructed new professional forms. As the full-time professional replaced the part-timer, literary pursuits—especially novels and poetry—ceased to be recognized as fit lawyerly avocations. Clashing phrases such as "visionary versus practical" and "passion versus utility" exposed a rift between images of lawyers as men of letters and as men of action.

Vocational anxiety spread among lawyers torn between the law and literature. Trapped by a growing tendency to associate writing fiction with idleness and an unwillingness to participate in the affairs of life, they found themselves attacked by other attorneys, who questioned their morals, patriotism, and masculinity.[7] A fellow legal apprentice, confident in his own vocational choice, wrote to lawyer-novelist Charles Brockden Brown in the early 1790s, warning against literary indulgence: "Renounce, then, I entreat you, your allegiance to fancy! . . . Despise the distressing power of her wand, but bow in manly submission to the sceptre of reason."[8] Other critics paraded the model of Sir William Blackstone, whom they lauded for abandoning poetry for legal writing.

These pressures intensified as lawyers more precisely defined their vocation as a masculine, public profession. Henry Wadsworth Longfellow discovered the new definition in 1825. Despondent over being forced to study law in his father's office, he asked Theophilus Parsons, Jr., editor of the *United States Literary Gazette,* for a job with the journal. Longfellow made clear his desire to leave the law and write poetry. Parsons wrote back a stinging rebuke couched in terms of the profession's masculine ideals: "There is a stage in the progress of a bright mind, when the boy has thrown away his toys and marbles, but the young man is still so far a child as to value things more by their elegance and power of amusing than by their usefulness. He plays with his books and thinks he is working when he is only playing hard. . . . Get through your present delusion as soon as you can; and then you will see how wise it will be for you to devote yourself to the law."[9] Though such advice did not deter Longfellow or lawyers like Washington Irving, Richard Dana, or Herman Melville, the antiliterary animus did help push men like John Quincy Adams, Daniel Webster, and countless others away from a seemingly frivolous life of letters and toward the more "manly" vocations of law and politics.[10]

The aversion to the lawyer-as-novelist did not mean that the bar rejected all forms of writing. Rather, practicality served as the standard. Lawyers who penned tracts useful for practice, or elegant treatises that educated their brethren, won accolades. It was the impractical that elicited the dismissive professional epithets of the scholarly and bookish. Attorneys able to move a jury with a clever phrase or apt literary allusion won professional renown. Utility separated the manly advocate from the effete intellectual.

This professional aversion to a life of letters divorced from the realities of legal practice expressed a new vision of the successful lawyer as "a man of action and cunning, not a scholar."[11] It supplanted a colonial and early postrevolutionary image of the best of the bar as educated gentlemen who speculated in ideas as well as commerce. Cincinnati lawyer and legal author Timothy Walker made the point directly in an 1839 address to the graduating class of the local law school: "The most learned lawyer in the world would not get business, it he did not attend to it. The question with the client is, not who knows the most law, but who will manage a cause the best, who devotes most attention to it."[12]

The new ideal of the lawyer as a man uniquely able to solve the practical problems of the growing society was buried deep in the bar's professional consciousness during this formative era. It would be celebrated by the profession's chroniclers, from Tocqueville to Daniel Boorstin.[13] And it found numerous expressions, perhaps the most apparent and significant of which was the bar's growing affinity for politics. Political speeches and treatises, unlike novels and poems, were legitimate lawyerly publications. The triumph of the ideal of the lawyer as a "doer"—not a "thinker"—was a telling professional contrast to the fate of the ministry, which, as cultural critic Ann Douglas has shown, was being feminized and thus marginalized during this era.[14] In the words of Justice Joseph Story: "The eloquence of the bar is far more various and difficult than that which is required in the pulpit—it addresses the very souls of men in the most touching and pathetic admonitions."[15]

Courtroom litigation, which dominated practice in this era, is another source of information on the bar's masculine ideals. In practice and in professional lore, circuit riding epitomized the bar's early professionalism.

Ranging over wide jurisdictions, teams of lawyers and judges arrived at county seats, divided up clients and roles, and held court before rustic crowds eager for a little drama. The traveling band stayed at inns and swapped stories and professional tricks. These group forays into the wilderness helped make the law a fraternity of men who lived in close contact for long stretches of time and whose lives became tightly intertwined.[16]

In his 1849 biography of Attorney General William Wirt, John P. Kennedy captured this form of professional bonding: "The riding of the Circuit . . . gave to the Bar a sportive and lighthearted love of association which greatly fostered the opportunity and the inclination for convivial pleasure. A day spent upon the road on horseback, the customary visits made to friends upon the way, the jest and song, the unchecked vivacity inspired by the grouping together of kindred spirits—all had their share in imparting brotherhood."[17] In the same way, Pennsylvania attorney Peter S. DuPonceau, reminiscing about his circuit-riding days, recalled that "as soon as we were out of the city, and felt the flush of air, we were like school boys in the playground on a holiday."[18]

But even the playground has its social rules, and circuit-riding institutionalized professional norms that biographer Kennedy called "convivial." In an era when few formal barriers limited admission, and training occurred primarily through apprenticeship, the social life of the judicial circuit maintained discipline and enforced professional standards.[19] Even as circuit riding gave way to settled practice, the emphasis on male conviviality was replicated in courthouse cliques and bar meetings.

The bar's fraternal forms represented a two-sided struggle to find a place in the republic. Lawyers accepted the market as a means of proving individual worth, yet relied on guild professionalism to insulate members from excessive competition by instituting distinctive professional norms. Among these were such traits as camaraderie, competitiveness, physical courage, practicality, personal trust, oratorical prowess, entrepreneurial skill, and an aversion to bookishness—a litany that in many ways paralleled the larger masculine ideals of the era but that contained particular meanings for the bar. These norms assumed a rough equality among practitioners and their jobs. Lawyers looked to conviviality rather than to hierarchical specialization (the solution of the postbellum bar) to restrain competition. In 1852 Moses B. Butterfield articulated the manly attributes of lawyers in Racine, Wisconsin, in a letter to his wife: "The bar of Wisconsin are fine looking men, as fine as I ever saw anywhere—but one or two ordinary looking men. But as a general thing, I should say not too much given to hard study. Some appear to have spent much time in study but most appear to enjoy sport and pleasure and are apt to try and live by their wits."[20] Similarly, the obituaries of antebellum lawyers tended to characterize departed practitioners as "fearless," "manly," and "independent."[21]

These traits expressed a lawyerly version of what might be termed "responsible manhood." In an era haunted by the fear of male failure—characterized most repeatedly in the popular imagery of drunken husbands guzzling family wages in dingy barrooms—the ideal lawyer carefully reasoned through problems, soberly addressed difficulties, courageously defended the dependent, and acted as an independent crusader.[22]

A man's admission to the bar and professional success depended on his conforming to these masculine values. Early in the nineteenth century, Massachusetts attorney James Sullivan offered a comradely description of the bar's internal controls. He noted that when "the business of the term was nearly completed, it was customary for both Bench and Bar to assemble at the tavern for a social meeting. On these occasions, they constituted a court among themselves, appointing one of their number Chief Justice, for the trial of all breaches of good fellowship during the term."[23] In an 1831 public letter to Massachusetts bar leader Rufus Choate, Frederick Robinson offered a view of professional discipline very different from Sullivan's. A radical Democrat, Robinson spoke as an outsider. He charged the bar with exclusivity and class bias, and demanded the right to practice law without having to be accepted by local lawyers. But his challenge to professional norms made him the object of the informal sanctions Sullivan had so warmly endorsed. Robinson considered exclusion an insult to his manhood. He realized that fraternal rights could be exercised only upon acceptance by brother practitioners; outsiders remained supplicants. He railed against the "brotherhood of the bar" that had secretly met to deny him the right to appear in court since he had not been "regularly admitted to the bar." He protested to Choate: "You previously told me, you 'could not respect me as a brother.' I asked you 'to treat me as a man.'" Claiming the right as a citizen to appear in court, Robinson objected to the way in which Choate and his "fraternity have been enabled little by little, to entrench [themselves] behind an impassable barrier." He vowed to keep up his fight despite his knowledge that "the fraternity of the bar, which has waged war against me is powerful, beyond what is commonly perceived."[24] His campaign revealed how the bar's masculine code could exclude as well as include.

Though many, if not most, practitioners failed to meet the standard, the image of responsible manhood served as an internal mechanism of guild control and an external depiction of lawyers as trusted public servants.[25] The failure of formal gatekeeping mechanisms such as a graded bar, bar associations, and fee schedules, as well as ever-present fears of antilawyer outbursts, encouraged the informal controls associated with conviviality and responsible manhood.[26]

The tension between law and literature and the convivial professionalism of the antebellum bar suggest the role of masculinity as a defining characteristic of the bar. Looked at in this fashion, the recent assessment of Abraham Lincoln by historian Robert Wiebe indicates that in the martyred president may be found the most evocative example of the antebellum community of lawyers. Lincoln entered professional folklore as the symbol of the bar's version of the self-made man.[27] His professional career highlights the defining role of masculinity in the bar. Wiebe described Lincoln's democracy as "a fraternity, rooted in a man's world of law and politics and then extended nationwide. To a considerable degree Lincoln inherited these gender-laden conditions. Law and politics have long been male monopolies to which the new democracy now added a greater self-consciousness about spheres for men and women and a greater emphasis on personal connections within each sphere."[28]

Lincoln was at home in the male world of circuit-riding lawyers, where his story-telling skills, oratory, off-color humor, and fierce competition found natural expression. His law practice thrived in this fraternal yet competitive environment. Equally important, though the real Lincoln worried about his craft skills and studiously honed them, the mythic "Honest Abe" became a valued symbol of the lawyerly ideals of democracy and justice that constituted part of the professional imagery of responsible manhood. William Herndon, his law partner, helped create the myth by insisting that Lincoln, a leading railroad lawyer of his region, "knew nothing of the laws of evidence, of pleading, or of practice, and did not care about them; he had a keen sense of justice and struck for that, throwing aside forms, methods, and rules of all law."[29] The real and mythic Lincoln the lawyer converged as a symbol of the best of the bar as self-made men struggling to find justice for their clients and communities. Despite recurrent accusations of being shysters and fomenters of trouble, benevolent, democratic professionals like Lincoln helped improve the professional image of lawyers and legitimize the bar's seizure and retention of power over central parts of the republic's economic and political life. From legislatures to businesses, lawyers defined their domain broadly, and in the process became the most versatile and powerful profession in the nation.

A glance at the antebellum bench suggests how the bar's professional image of "responsible manhood" was also translated into particular institutional roles. As attorney and legal reformer David Dudley Field observed in 1844, "The character of the judges is . . . the character of the lawyers. They are made at the bar; their moral characters take on their complexion there."[30] Masculinity was part of that complexion. Looking at the bench in terms of the profession's masculine beliefs offers a descriptive language that avoids tired, often ahistorical political labels like "liberal" or "conservative," and equally problematic ones like "activist" or "strict constructionist." A gendered view of judges is one way to put the judiciary back into the social context from which the profession emerged.

Masculinity provides an insight into the nature of judicial authority. In a society that equated dispassionate decision making with responsible manhood and legitimated power through such an equation, judges performed a critical male role. Embedded in the judicial office was a set of assumptions premised on the belief that dispensing justice was a manly duty. That belief was significant because, as historian Stephen Botein argues, judges epitomized "the public ethos expected of all who pursued legal careers."[31]

The public image of the judge was bound to the emergence of a "mystique of the robe." Since the early nineteenth century, historian Maxwell Bloomfield argues, "writers have endowed the judicial role with almost magical properties of character building and intellectual enlightenment."[32] And as the scene shifted from trial courts to appellate tribunals, the imagery of veneration intensified. In plays, travelogues, death notices, and other mediums of popular culture, descriptions of judges consistently used the language of responsible manhood: wise, skillful, impartial, upright, and venerable. Each word was a gendered element in the composite definition of a judge, and each a linguistic expression of the assumption that neither women nor lesser men could fulfill the role of sage magistrate.[33]

Attorney George Sharswood made the connections clear in his 1854 book on professional ethics. In cautioning lawyers to treat those on the bench with respect, he observed: "In matters collateral to official duty, the judge is on a level with the members of the bar, as he is with his fellow-citizens; his title to distinction and respect resting on no other foundation than his virtues and qualities as a man." Yet, as Sharswood lectured members of the bar, there may well be "occasions, no doubt, when duty to the interests confided to the charge of the advocate demands firm and decided opposition to the views expressed or the course pursued by the court, nay, even manly and open remonstrance; but this duty may be faithfully performed, and yet outward respect be preserved, which is here inculcated."[34] Using more colorful prose, Joseph Baldwin captured the judicial ideal in one of his 1853 satirical sketches of flush times in Mississippi and Alabama. Speaking of an unlettered candidate for the profession, Baldwin quipped: "He was such a man as passes for a wonderful judge among the rustics—who usually mistake the silent blank of stupidity for the gravity of wisdom."[35]

While lawyers like Abraham Lincoln and Joseph Story were calling law the nation's civil religion, judges were becoming the republic's priestly class. Judges became a secular replacement for ministers of the gospel, who declined in stature and responsibilities. In a heterogeneous polity riven by economic and social change, the image of judges as venerable magistrates assuaged deep-seated antistatist fears of public authority by personalizing power in a trusted secular version of the priestly class. As Bloomfield discovered, nineteenth-century popular writers often described judges' victimization of the poor but "refused to impute class bias to the law itself. The basic problem [was] one of individual integrity; if good men filled even the lowest judicial posts, no question of unequal justice could arise."[36] The 1843 *North American Review* defended judicial independence in just such a fashion: "The natural reverence of men for justice and the instinctive moral promptings of the heart are enlisted in favor of the courts, and hold up before the judges a shield against violence or contempt."[37] Exaltation of judges may also have reflected a popular desire to conceive of the law as a glue binding an increasingly divided society, a faith in legal magistrates that legal realist and Freudian convert Jerome Frank would ridicule in the 1930s as evidence of the populace's immaturity and need for father figures.[38]

The courtroom, with its raised dais, robed judges, code of deferential silence, jury box, and solemn trappings, became a symbol of the majesty and mystery of the law in a society that deified litigation as the most appropriate form of public conflict resolution. And the courtroom was a male domain, into which women—and other men—came primarily as supplicants. The rituals of law were thus dominated by a manly brethren of robed jurists and lawyer-acolytes. An antebellum commentator described the courtroom of New York chancellor Reuben Walworth in just such masculine hierarchical terms: "The Chancellor does a great deal of talking himself, but is treated with great respect. It looked very much like a schoolmaster and his pupils, only the boys were a little too big to answer the description of the latter."[39]

In *The Pioneers* (1823), James Fenimore Cooper captured the distinctive place accorded to and assumed by American judges. The novel is significant because Cooper mined popular culture to construct an image of the proper magistrate. In writing of a constant tension between reason and emotion— "head and heart," in the language of the day—and between law and justice, he put judges on the side of law and reason. Judge Temple, when forced to pass judgment on Natty Bumppo, the man who saved his daughter's life, dismisses a plea for leniency. His words were those of a lawyer, not a father: Bumppo, he ruled dispassionately, would receive "whatever the law demands, notwithstanding any momentary weakness I may have exhibited, because the luckless man has been of such eminent service to my daughter."[40] Public and private patriarchy were not indistinguishable; in turbulent nineteenth-century America the judiciary became public patriarchs because of professional and popular acceptance of this distinction.

Judges gained further legitimacy by particularizing their role. As they faced the innumerable problems created by market and social conflict, they divided their responsibilities into various domains and assumed different poses in each. Though obviously part of the larger tendency of the profession to divide the law into ever more discrete "hornbook" categories of tort, contract, property, and negotiable instruments, the ability to assume various poses in dealing with the specifics of legal disputes also constituted a primary way in which judges personalized their power and individualized justice. If the courtroom can be termed a theater—as it surely was in nineteenth-century America—then judges performed in a series of one-act plays, donning a different persona for each performance, with each pose a version of responsible manhood.[41] The institutionalization of these judicial images during the nineteenth century led legal historian Aviam Soifer to conclude that in "proclaiming both their uniformity and their ability to distinguish between people as individuals and as members of groups, the judicial brethren became paternalistic patriarchs."[42]

Massachusetts chief justice Lemuel Shaw, one of the most influential and widely known appellate jurists of antebellum America, illustrates the point. He personified the vision of manly responsibility being embedded in the judicial office. Fittingly, Shaw, who served on the Bay State bench from 1830 to 1860, has been immortalized as Captain Vere in Herman Melville's *Billy Budd* (1891). Melville, Shaw's son-in-law, depicted Vere (much like Judge Temple) as a sage yet troubled jurist trying to reconcile the conflicting claims of law and justice, and thus made his character conform to the popular vision of the proper judge.[43] Equally significant, Shaw's career reflected the transfer of priestly social authority from ministers to judges. Although his father had been a minister, Shaw rejected the pulpit in favor of the courtroom, yet brought an evangelicalism and sense of priestly duty to his profession.[44]

Shaw's performance as a judge is recorded in volume after volume of the *Massachusetts Reports*. His published opinions indicate how he assumed the poses of responsible manhood: as public-spirited entrepreneur determined to spur commercial growth in commercial law cases like *Farwell v. Worcester Railroad* (1842); as wise policeman defending order and justice by devising tests of criminal intent in criminal law cases like *Commonwealth v. York* (1845); as just patriarch deciding whether it was best for a child to live with his mother or his father in family disputes like the child-custody case of *Commonwealth v. Briggs* (1834).[45] Shaw, like other judges, brought to each conflict a particular set of concerns, techniques, and commitments; each represented the public exercise of a form of masculine responsibility. With good reason feminist Antoinette Brown Blackwell charged in 1852 that the law was "wholly masculine," and that the very language of legal documents was restricted to the "thoughts, feelings, [and] biases of men."[46]

The professional ideals of the bar faced a crisis in post–Civil War America. The conflicts of the era compelled lawyers to articulate more clearly than ever before the gender assumptions of their profession. Values and commitments that had been buried deep within the professional consciousness of the legal community surged to the surface.

The implicit became explicit, in large part because in the last decades of the century the community of lawyers became much more fractious and stratified. A more rigorous form of professionalism significantly revised earlier notions of proper legal practice and training.[47] The new professionalism directly challenged key tenets of the bar's masculine ideals. More and more leaders of the bar conceived of themselves as experts in a way that undermined older practices like conviviality. Controversies took a variety of forms, but often centered on the meaning of being a manly advocate in industrial America.

The most unsettling change during the era was the rise of the corporate lawyer and corporate law firm. The corporate lawyer epitomized the ongoing shift in the attorney's role from advocate to counselor. For many lawyers, the new role raised fears of lost freedom—the independent professional turned hired hand. Bitter debates within the bar over the meaning of professionalism were often couched in terms of manliness: Could a lawyer on retainer to a corporation (a later generation would call him an organization man) still be a manly advocate? Could classroom learning and bar examinations produce Lincolns of the law? Would ethnic and lower-class men uphold the bar's customary honor code? Would the bar cease to be a profession and become a business?[48]

Greater stratification in the bar intensified these conflicts. Specialization encouraged a new professional hierarchy. Some specialties, such as patent law, emerged out of particular technical demands; others, such as criminal law, came to be viewed as undesirable because of the clientele. Corporate attorneys topped the hierarchy; solo practitioners, often from immigrant backgrounds and engaged in criminal and personal-injury law, were the profession's lower class. Tensions over these changes fed the debate over professional standards that compelled lawyers to articulate some of their assumptions about lawyering as a masculine profession.

A gradual shift to formal education in law school as the prescribed method of professional training acted as a lightning rod for the conflict between the new professionalism and the bar's now orthodox masculine ideals. At the heart of the new law school was the case method, which replaced lectures with teacher-directed "Socratic" dialogues on appellate cases. What historian Robert Stevens has called the "machismo view of the case method" reflected both the tough-mindedness of the era and the continuing need to defend book learning in a profession that deemed practice more manly than theory.[49] Legal science, too, reinforced the idea of law as a hard, manly occupation grounded in seemingly objective, deducible rules.

Harvard Law School dean Christopher Columbus Langdell, the father of the case method, and other champions of the new approach frankly described it as a competitive struggle. They felt compelled to argue that it took manly courage and determination to survive the Socratic dialogue just as it had apprenticeship; in either, only the fittest survived. Celebrating the triumph of the case method, the 1917 *Centennial History of Harvard Law School* emphasized how the technique fostered individualism and competitiveness. The volume presented the student as "the invitee upon the case-system premise, who, like the invitee in the reported cases, soon finds himself fallen into a pit. He is given no map carefully charting and laying out all the byways and corners of the legal field, but is left, to a certain extent, to find his way by himself. His scramble out of difficulties, if successful, leaves him feeling that he has built up a knowledge of law for himself. The legal content of his mind has a personal nature; he has made it himself."[50] The "virility" of this classroom struggle, as Harvard law professor James Barr Ames put it, contrasted favorably with the old law-school reliance on lecturing, which had not been "a virile system," for it treated the student "not as a man, but as a school boy reciting his lines."[51] In the postwar bar, even the classroom had to be made into a battlefield—a development fraught with implications as the law school came to dominate legal education.

Formal admission standards, academic rather than practical measurements of skill, and the other features of late-nineteenth-century professionalism challenged the bar's competitive ideal. These new barriers replaced the convivial professional screening processes of the antebellum bar with academic testing and certification restrictions. Elite biases were obvious. Admission requirements, particularly that of a college degree, effectively eliminated the great majority of the otherwise eligible population from consideration. This generated intense controversy among lawyers. In pointed gender terms, an Iowa lawyer defended standards of success and professional progress based on individual manly qualities rather than formal training. "What our profession needs," he contended, "is moral stamina, sterling integrity, and recognized noble manhood." Similar voices were raised in support of night law schools, part-time institutions that became the new breeders of Lincolns of the law. The dean of one night school proclaimed his students "men of heroic mold," "a goodly race, full of enthusiasm, industry, perseverance, and that fine courage which scoffs at difficulty and welcomes the fray."[52]

Advocates of the new professional standards responded to these defenses of traditionalism by mixing ethnic prejudice with industrial-era visions of competence. The influx of ethnics challenged elite standards. Writing in his diary in 1874, patrician attorney George Templeton Strong praised Columbia Law School's institution of admission tests: The requirement of a college diploma, or an examination including Latin, would "keep out the little scrubs (German jew boys mostly) whom the School now promotes from the grocery-counters . . . to be 'gentlemen of the Bar.'" In a different vein, Charles W. Needham, assistant solicitor for the Interstate Commerce Commission, insisted that "new conditions in social and political life demand new types of men, or at least, men of special training and equipment."[53] These conflicting views epitomized late-nineteenth-century struggles over the professional definition of the lawyer that often found expression in terms of masculine values.

A feminist challenge to the bar also threw the profession into crisis. In the last decades of the century a few women demanded a place in the masculine community of lawyers. Barred from the profession by custom and statute, these women mounted individual campaigns to bring down the gender barrier. They lobbied legislators and filed suits, often with success. Their challenge stirred a particularly telling mixture of resistance and support that adds another perspective on the role of masculinity in defining the nineteenth-century legal community.

The general reaction of male lawyers appears to have been one of disbelief, coupled at times with "horror and disgust."[54] This dismay underscores some of the gender realities of the profession. In an 1881 essay, "Why Should Not Women Be Lawyers?" Massachusetts law student Ann C. Southward listed the arguments most frequently used against a woman practicing law: "She lacks strength of body; She lacks strength of nerve; The practice of law renders her unrefined by contact with baser natures; It exposes her to insult; It unfits her for a domestic life; It is a source of domestic disagreement; She is intellectually unfitted."[55] In many ways the list presented the flip side of the masculine traits thought necessary for successful legal practice. These traits were a professional expression of the belief in separate gender spheres that pervaded nineteenth-century American social ideology. Countless male legislators, judges, and lawyers echoed the views of a California lawmaker who spoke against a bill that would erase the gender restriction: "The sphere of women is infinitely more important than that of men, and that sphere is the home."[56] In a profession in which gender distinctions had been so deeply embedded, much of the male bar dismissed demands by women to be lawyers as simply unnatural.

Elaborate responses to the feminist challenge came from judges forced to explain the gender barrier. The most famous pronouncement was Justice Joseph Bradley's concurrence in a decision by the United States Supreme Court, which had rejected Myra Bradwell's claim that the Illinois bar, in denying her admission, had violated her occupational rights under the Fourteenth Amendment. Bradley felt compelled to go beyond the legal reasoning of his colleagues. He sermonized that the "paramount destiny and mission of women" was to fulfill "the noble and benign offices of wife and mother. That is the law of the creator." The justice also declared that the "natural and proper timidity and delicacy which belongs to the female sex evidently unfits it for many occupations of life"; the law, of course, was a prime professional example. More suggestive of the profession's masculine self-image, Bradley insisted that a man must be "women's protector and defender," not their colleague.[57]

Wisconsin chief justice Edward Ryan also felt driven to define proper gender roles when he denied R. Lavinia Goodell the right to practice law. He explained that "nature has tempered women as little for the juridical conflicts of the courtroom, as for the physical conflicts of the battlefield." Ryan insisted that the use of masculine pronouns in statutes regulating the bar manifested a legislative intent to keep the bar a male profession. Turning to the old lawyerly argumentative device of reductio ad absurdum, the Chief Justice rejected the very possibility of reading "persons" in a gender-free fashion: "If we should follow that authority in ignoring the distinction of sex, we do not perceive why it should not emasculate the constitution itself and include females in the constitutional right of male suffrage and male qualification. Such a rule would be one of judicial revolution, not of judicial construction."[58]

Judges like Bradley and Ryan dictated gender standards by drawing on the social and jurisprudential values of their profession. The rules and statutes they interpreted were to a significant degree indeterminate and flexible. Their interpretations were not declarations of fixed rules but expressions of the bar's version of responsible manhood. As the titular leaders of the legal community, judges like Bradley and Ryan gave voice to the bar's determination to keep women out. In yet another example of the divide between law and politics, which lawyers pointed to time and again as a means of staking out their professional autonomy and expertise, the bench and bar steadfastly tried to maintain the gender line while legislators answerable to different constituencies breached it. The ban on women, like the treatment of lawyer-politicians as renegades from the profession, provided a primary means of professional self-definition. And yet the pronouncements by Bradley and Ryan also point out clashing views of the judicial role. Bradley assumed the pose of protector of the defenseless; Ryan posed as the defender of masculine prerogatives. Masculinity spoke loudly but not with a single voice from the bench and at the bar.[59]

The implications of the judicial defense of the bar as a masculine profession surfaced most clearly in the 1894 Supreme Court decision *In re Lockwood*. The case centered on whether or not women were even "persons" under the law. Belva A. Lockwood appealed to the Supreme Court because the state of Virginia refused to license her as an attorney.

The appeal capped a stormy career at the bar. Lockwood had been admitted to the bar of the District of Columbia in 1873 after graduating from National University Law School in Washington, D.C. Soon she built a practice in probate and police work, but found herself continually excluded from the courtroom. Chief judge Charles Drake had refused to let her act as counsel in the United States Court of Claims, declaring her disabled by virtue of being a married woman. When her husband came to court and formally consented to her activities, Drake was unequivocal: "Madam, women do not speak in this court. You will sit down." After several adjournments and appeals, he finally ruled that "under the laws and Constitution of the United States a court is without power to grant such an application," and that "a woman is without legal capacity to take the office of attorney." In 1875 Lockwood was denied permission to practice before the Supreme Court. She overcame this obstacle by successfully lobbying for federal legislation enabling all women lawyers to appear before the court. In 1879 she became the first woman to exercise that right.[60]

In 1894, Virginia denied her the right to practice, despite a state law stipulating that any person who had been licensed to practice in any other state or the District of Columbia could practice in Virginia. The state court of appeals decided that "person" meant "man." The United States Supreme Court affirmed the ruling and refused to order Virginia to admit Lockwood.[61] "The importance of the *In re Lockwood*," historian Joan Hoff Wilson argues, "lies in the fact that the Supreme Court chose to allow states to confine their definition of 'person' to males only. From 1894 until *Reed* v. *Reed* [1971] states could maintain that women were not legally 'persons' by virtue of this single Supreme Court decision."[62]

And yet ritualistic defenses of established gender roles and spheres failed to sustain formal barriers against women. Both Bradwell and Goodell eventually became lawyers, though by legislation that overrode judicial resistance. By the end of the century most statutory barriers fell, yet only a trickle of women actually entered the bar. Informal constraints continued to decree the law a man's profession.

Guided by doctrinaire beliefs in separate spheres, most lawyers and laypeople assumed the informal gender line to be natural. In 1889, officials at the University of Iowa expressed little surprise that few women attended the school despite their acknowledged right to do so: "But there seem to be obstacles to the practice of the profession by women, inherent in the nature of the occupation, which have discouraged the study of law by [women] so that few have availed themselves of the advantages of the [School of Law]."[63] And in 1900, the president of the University of Michigan acknowledged that some women attended the law school, but noted that few went on to practice. Instead, he asserted, they either helped in their fathers' law offices or used their legal training to be "more efficient teachers of political economy, civil government, and history in academies, high schools or colleges. It seems improbable that any considerable number of women will find it congenial or remunerative to follow the profession of law."[64] The gender realities of the legal community were evident as well in the felt necessity of the editors of the *Bench and Bar of Cleveland* (1889) to assure readers that the city's first woman attorney, identified as Mrs. Mary P. Fraser, was "a standing refutation to the tradition that a woman who enters a profession need suffer any loss of dignity, refinement, or womanly taste."[65]

Women attorneys became—in the useful language of Antonio Gramsci—a "contradictory consciousness" in the legal community, but they did not develop a "counter-hegemony."[66] The feminist challenge to male dominance resulted in the creation of a female sphere in the law as part of the profession's new industrial hierarchy; it did not transform its gender premises. Within that sphere women created alternative professional institutions: the Woman's International Bar Association, founded in 1888; the Equity Club, a correspondence club of women lawyers in the 1880s; the *Women Lawyers Journal,* begun in 1911; and female law schools like Boston's Portia School of Law.[67] All of these organizations testified to the gender segregation among lawyers. For women, as for ethnic and black men, the potent mix of prejudice and specialization resulted in professional segregation. While male Jewish lawyers found themselves relegated to criminal work and personal-injury cases, women found themselves consigned to paperwork, secretarial pools, and libraries. Yet the presence of women in the legal community, like that of ethnics, blacks, and lower-class whites, stirred internal conflicts that would increasingly engulf American lawyers. When a woman challenged her exclusion from Hastings College of Law by pointing out that an Asian student had been accepted, the lawyer for the California school promptly replied that "the Chinaman" had been thrown out too.[68] And, perhaps more to the point, women entered the legal community in large numbers as wage laborers; in the words of historian Lawrence Friedman, "the first women to appear in law offices did not come to practice law; they came to type and take shorthand."[69]

Medicine is a revealing contrast to the bar. The barriers to a medical career, though imposing, were less impassable than those blocking a life at law. Would-be female lawyers discovered, as historian Barbara Harris contends, that "practicing law was even more incompatible with nineteenth-century ideas about women than was practicing medicine. Female doctors could claim that their careers were natural extensions of women's nurturant, healing role in the home and that they protected feminine modesty by ministering to members of their own sex. By contrast, women lawyers were clearly intruding on the public domain explicitly reserved for men."[70] Thus, despite the relatively greater ease of entry and far greater number of practitioners, women constituted but 1.1 percent of the bar and yet 6 percent of the medical profession in 1910.[71]

And gender distinctions continued in professional consciousness as well as in numbers. Even some of those who championed the right of women to practice law used stereotyped differences between the sexes to support the cause. Phoebe Couzins, one of the first female lawyers in Saint Louis, told a group of women law school graduates in 1895 that women were needed to clean out the "cobwebs" in the law because "man had been trying to do the housekeeping in the Temple of Justice for years all by himself." Male dominion, she insisted, had left the law in desperate need of women's special skills: "Legal fiction is piled on legal fiction and precedent on precedent until the whole storehouse of law is in a helpless confused condition. It needs women's wit, women's fairness and women's sense of right and righteousness to put the legal fabric in order and repair."[72]

Crusading attorney Clarence Darrow voiced some of the implications of exiling women to the fringe of the profession in an early-twentieth-century address to a group of Chicago women lawyers. He counseled, "You can't be shining lights at the bar because you are too kind. You can never be corporation lawyers because you are not cold-blooded. You have not a high grade of intellect." Questioning whether women could ever command the fees male attorneys received, he wondered if they could "ever make a living." Darrow did think women could become divorce lawyers, and then conceded that there was "another field you can have solely for your own. You can't make a living at it, but it's worthwhile and you'll have no competition. This is the free defense of criminals."[73]

Darrow's distinction between masculine and feminine forms of law and practice found numerous expressions. Doctrinal categories became "hard" if they were hornbook rules on economic relations such as contract or property, and "soft" if they dealt with more problematic social relations such as family law. This distinction was part of the legacy of nineteenth-century liberal thought that associated abstract reasoning with masculinity, emotionality with femininity. Suspicion of approaches to legal analysis that deviated from strict casebook methods, particularly the use of social science, also elicited such labels. And commercial practice, as Darrow contended, was a man's responsibility; women, if they forced themselves into the bar, ought to be given marginal jobs like domestic relations or legal aid.[74] Progressive lawyer and reformer Reginald Heber Smith, director of the Boston Legal Aid Society, suggested that women should serve as legal secretaries or legal aid counsels. In a 1924 letter to the dean of Yale's law school, Smith insisted that female attorneys were out of place in a regular law firm, but the "legal aid office is different. It is much easier for women to practice in such an office and they seem to get along alright."[75] Similarly, in 1920 the other judges on the Cleveland Court of Common Pleas assumed that Florence Allen, the first woman elected to the local bench, would take over all divorce cases. They were astounded when the unmarried Allen, who prided herself on economic analysis, refused.[76] Small-claims courts, mediation, family courts, legal aid—all attempts to deal with class and economic strife by healing instead of adversarial methods—were also seen as "softer" and thus more feminine aspects of the profession and the law. Real work, commercial practice, remained adversarial and thus a male responsibility.

In these ways masculinity found new forms of professional definition. In noting the persistence well into the twentieth century of such gender distinctions in law, sociologist and lawyer D. Kelly Weisberg observed: "The qualities most admired in men—confidence, ambition, self-assurance, assertiveness, aggressiveness, competitiveness—are looked upon with disfavor in women because they conflict with the traditional image of the sex. Yet, paradoxically, these qualities historically have been and still are the qualities which are viewed as prerequisites for the successful lawyer."[77]

The nineteenth-century bar was a man's profession, masculinity a baseline of professional consciousness and community membership. Masculine values helped define the place of the lawyer in American society and legitimated his power by making it seem natural and preordained. Because judges and lawyers operated in a relatively autonomous professional realm, their version of responsible manhood had sources within and outside of the legal order. A legal system is relatively autonomous, anthropologist Sally Falk Moore points out, because it generates "rules and questions and symbols internally" and at the same time is "vulnerable to rules and decisions and other forces emanating from the larger world by which it is surrounded."[78] A particular institutionalization of masculinity, in sum, helped bind the legal community even as it appealed for public recognition of judging and lawyering as male endeavors. Institutionalized masculinity had become part of American legal consciousness.

The nineteenth-century legal community offers one story in the history of men's public roles. Just such tales, historian John Demos laments, have dominated historical discourse—"a history of public life and official behavior."[79] Demos calls for a new history of men that would accentuate the personal and private. But to rigidly separate the public and private sides of men's lives would repeat the error of social historians who so championed the study of private life that they ignored politics and power. As many social historians now recognize, an overemphasis on the private, combined with an aversion to the public, resulted in the neglect of some of the basic dimensions of historical change. It produced a history that failed to address fundamental questions of power and how the use of power affected daily lives and long-term life prospects. It further denied individuals and groups their political—and legal—identities.[80] Only by linking the public and private—indeed, by seeing these as the social constructs that they are—and by focusing on the reciprocal interactions between the two can social history fulfill its promise.

The institutional power some men exercised in the law suggests why the public role of male power cannot be ignored. To do so risks seriously misunderstanding the place of men in both the public and private domains of the past. By examining the interaction of state and society, in this case the use of masculinity to bridge the two, part of the role of men as both private and public actors can be recovered. Writing a new kind of institutional history that concentrates on the interaction of the public and the private is necessary to such an understanding of the history of American men. And doing so will clarify why attorney Charles Moore felt compelled to create Mary Padelford and show her unavoidable demise in a world made by and for men.

NINE

Acquiring Manly Competence:
The Demise of Apprenticeship and
the Remasculinization of Printers' Work

Ava Baron

T he gradual demise of the apprenticeship system during the nineteenth century had profound implications for journeymen printers. To them, apprenticeship was more than a system of acquiring technical skills; it was an important link between their work and family roles, and an essential ingredient in acquiring manhood. American printers, like other craftsmen in the colonial period, continued the traditional European custom of training boys in the "mysteries" of their craft through an extensive apprenticeship, typically lasting between five and seven years. Following the introduction of the Linotype at the turn of the century, various off-the-job training programs and schools were developed to supplement or supplant the apprenticeship system. Journeymen responded to changed economic and social circumstances by redefining masculinity and the criteria for determining worker competence. But, as we shall see, if their efforts to defend their craft and manly respectability they became mired in contradictory definitions of manhood.

Feminist research has provided much-needed information on relations between men and women workers. We also now know much about workingmen's policies to exclude women from unions and occupations.[1] But during the proletarianization that occurred in Victorian America, printers viewed boys as well as women as threats to their prestigious craft positions, to their relatively high wages—and to their manhood. Indeed, male printers expressed even greater concern and antagonism toward boys than

This essay is based on material from "An 'Other' Side of Gender Antagonism at Work: Men, Boys, and the Remasculinization of Printer's Work," in Ava Baron, ed., *Work Engendered: Toward a New History of Men, Women, and Work* (Ithaca, N.Y.: Cornell University Press, forthcoming), and is part of my book manuscript, "Men's Work and the Woman Question: The Transformation of Gender and Work in the Printing Industry, 1850–1920." I would like to thank Mary Blewett, Richard Butsch, Ileen DeVault, Nancy Hewitt, Priscilla Long, Martha May, Keith McClelland, and Sonya Rose for helpful comments and criticisms.

toward women who worked in the industry. The "apprenticeship question," as journeymen called it, involved controversies over the selection and number of boys, the length and methods of training, and most important, the criteria for determining both masculinity and worker competence. These issues filled countless columns of printers' trade journals and hours of typographical-union meetings. However, little scholarly attention has been given to these facets of gender at work.[2]

Workingmen contrasted themselves to boy apprentices as a means to gauge their manliness. Apprentices represented a threat to adult male printers' work and family positions. Yet the existence of apprenticeship also bolstered these craftsmen's class and gender positions by highlighting the value of craft skills, the significance of training, and the achievement of manly respectability through work.[3]

To members of the typographical union, completion of apprenticeship symbolized passage into manhood and simultaneously into skilled "competent" worker status. The notion of competence in these early decades of the nineteenth century referred to a man's ability to earn a livelihood for himself and his family.[4] One acquired an ability to "earn a competence" by learning an entire craft.[5] Masculinity was gradually acquired during the apprenticeship term as a boy learned the skills necessary to do manly work. Becoming proficient in a trade transformed a boy into a man by enabling him to earn a "family wage" and by providing him with a position of "honorable independence."[6]

Journeymen believed that once a boy completed an apprenticeship and was certified as a competent worker, he should have the right to earn a "man's wages." Market fluctuations and lack of business therefore were illegitimate grounds for reducing wages. During a strike in 1844, journeymen of the Franklin Typographical Society resisted their employers' efforts to reduce wages because business was dull, "as if the laborer was responsible for the decrease in business."[7]

At a mass meeting of printers in 1850, the journeymen again rejected the principle of supply and demand as the basis for determining wages. They unanimously resolved not to surrender their business "to the unregulated, unlimited operation of the vaunted 'law of supply and demand.'"[8] Instead, they insisted that wages should provide the means necessary to support their families.[9]

The power and prestige of the typographical union were premised on the competence of its members. Therefore, throughout the nineteenth century the union insisted on serving as certifier of workers' competence. The advantage of the apprenticeship system and the union's control over it, printers explained, was that it prevented the labor market from being

flooded with incompetent printers. A completed apprenticeship was sufficient to demonstrate competence, and this became the primary requisite to
gain admission into printers' associations and typographical unions.[10]

Apprenticeship socialized boys into the work culture. Without a proper
apprenticeship, one union executive feared, a boy "would not know anything about unions, nor would he have any sympathy with their rules and
regulations."[11] M. Nicholson, a printer from Cincinnati, explained how the
work process of hand typesetting had been conducive to boys' socialization
and technical instruction. Even "conversation in the composing room" was
a "great aid to the beginner, for he could hear arguments, disputes, sometimes a brief lecture, on almost every question from spelling, punctuation,
history, on and through to law, medicine, theology and other more or less
occult topics."[12] In the "hand-set" days, another printer explained, journeymen developed a sense of proper grammar and acquired "an appreciable
degree of culture in literary matters," which the boys in the office sought to
emulate. The apprentice learned that a printer who made spelling or gram-
matical errors was ridiculed. The future printers "received their cue from
this stimulating atmosphere."[13]

With the onset of capitalist printing production during the 1830s, many
employers reduced their labor costs by hiring "halfway" journeymen, or
"two-thirders." These boys, usually apprentices who ran away before completing their term, worked at one-half or two-thirds of a regular
journeyman's wage.[14] Journeymen complained that the practice encouraged boys "to elope from their masters," creating a "great grievance to
journeymen, and also certain ruin to the boys themselves." An inadequate
apprenticeship robbed the boy of skills needed for remunerative employment.[15] Boys who ran away before completing their apprenticeship
were "incapable of governing their passions and propensities," and therefore "plunge headlong into every species of dissipation, and are often
debilitated by debauchery and disease before they arrive at the state of manhood."[16] Journeymen charged that employers encouraged boys to run away
before completing their apprenticeship by taking on too many boys, by
using them only as cheap labor, and by not providing them with training in
all aspects of the craft. As a result, journeymen claimed, the trade became
flooded with those who knew only the simpler typesetting work known as
straight composition; these incompetents were unworthy and incapable of
earning the union wage.[17]

Union printers and some employers continued to seek means to strength-
en the apprenticeship system and to increase control over runaway apprentices through the 1800s. Employers in country shops and small urban job
offices desired lengthy apprenticeships. This allowed them to benefit from

the skilled work of the apprentice during the last few years of the term without paying full journeymen's wages.[18] However, employers complained about investing time in training an apprentice only to find that he would leave once his labor became profitable, while the employer had no recourse or way to hold him back.[19] One employer explained that he did not take on boys through indenture because "the boys think they are men after a few months . . . , and demand or look for men's positions. There is no way to hold boys till they become men . . ."[20]

Employers in large urban areas increasingly opposed having legal and personal responsibilities for apprentices. Apprentices, no longer sons or relatives of employers, were given wages rather than room and board. Gradually, during the nineteenth century, market relations displaced the old system of personalized mutual obligations.[21] Employers liked to be able to discharge boys without restrictions, and boys preferred to be able to leave for better job offers at will. Public sentiment, too, opposed the old style of apprenticeship with its long term of indentured service and diffuse obligations required of both boys and employers. To many, apprenticeship connoted an "un-American" form of servitude and personal dependence.[22]

When employers in large urban printing firms did take on apprentices, they turned over the task of training to the foremen or to employees in the shop. But journeyman printers typically working by piece wages were resentful of this responsibility, since employers did not compensate them for lost wages.[23] As a result, boys received minimal tutelage. Such apprenticeship deprived the boys of the satisfactory skills and adequate socialization into printers' work culture that they needed to qualify as competent printers.[24]

Martin Witter, president of the International Typographical Union, in 1886 expressed his fear that a large class of incompetents was being produced because of the lack of systematic apprenticeship training. These incompetents not only embarrassed the union but also were fatal to its prosperity and to the happiness of the new members themselves. "Dissatisfaction, jealousy, and in many cases recklessness were the result."[25] This conflict of interests between adult male printers and boys at the point of production became increasingly pronounced and more generalized in other types of printing establishments. By the end of the nineteenth century, journeymen found it increasingly difficult to maintain traditional definitions of worker competence and masculinity.

The economic recession in the early 1890s, combined with the introduction of the Linotype, resulted in increased unemployment and destroyed printers' security in their skill. By 1894, 266 Linotype machines had been installed, resulting in the displacement of 480 printers in New York City alone. Conservative estimates claim that each machine displaced two printers during the initial stages of the introduction of the machine. But even in 1908, unemployment among printers in New York State reached 21.6 percent.[26]

The typographical union sought to minimize the displacement of union printers by accepting the machine and claiming Linotype operation under union jurisdiction.[27] But the work and gender terms of the new position were drastically transformed in the process. The introduction of the Linotype set into motion conflicts between union men and employers over the skill and gender definitions of the work.[28] These conflicts resulted in new criteria for judging competence and significant shifts in journeymen's conception of masculinity.

Union men attempted to sustain older notions of competence by arguing that fully apprenticed printers were the most qualified to work on the machine. One union member told the Industrial Commission in 1899 that a card of the International Typographical Union was "prima facie evidence of a man's competency."[29]

Publishers claimed that the Linotype made possible typesetting with little training and skill. Since Linotype operation could be learned in a relatively short time period, a long apprenticeship was no longer required. Some publishers even claimed that an operator could become expert within a matter of days.[30] Further, employers sought to redefine competence in quantitative terms, measuring and evaluating workers' performance in relation to the production norm—the minimum output for machine composition. In this way, employers sought to have men prove their competence on a daily basis at work in order to obtain and to maintain their jobs.

The Linotype intensified conflicts between employers and workers over the piece wage scale. As a result, both sides supported the adoption of time wage payments. By 1909 piece rate provisions were virtually obsolete.[31]

With the time system, employers became increasingly concerned with controlling and measuring the output of each individual employee. Some employers adopted bonus systems, rewarding the speedy and accurate operator with a higher wage than the slower worker. Others measured the output and speed of each individual employee with mechanical indicators attached to the machines.[32]

Work on the Linotype threatened craft respectability. Printers had been proud of their reputations as thinkers and scholars. They were quick to point to the power and respect printers had once enjoyed. But work on the composing machine, as one printer explained, made typesetting "as mechanical as it possibly can be under human agency." The machine operator had little time to think.[33]

Under the new work conditions, journeymen were treated much like boys in indentured servitude. Denied the freedom to come and go without restraint, they sadly suffered various indignities and lack of independence at the hands of employers. "Iniquitous shop rules" lowered the social esteem of craftsmen, one printer complained. At work the printer became "practically a prisoner," deprived of the "liberty to talk freely or see his friends, no matter how great the emergency."[34]

Union men gradually acceded to new definitions of competence. A competent printer became defined as one who was "efficient and capable of performing the work assigned."[35] Production norms used to measure a man's competence were negotiated by the union and employers and were specified in union contracts.[36]

This redefinition of competence heightened the demands on the operators both as men and as workers. In earlier decades the operators stressed the difference between men and boys in terms of training and socialization. By the 1890s, they viewed competence as derived from particular biological traits associated with manhood. This definition of manly competence in terms of speed and endurance, however, meant that workers had to prove themselves as men on an ongoing basis. Competence at work became the primary criterion for hiring and firing, and for affirming masculinity.[37]

Competence was so central to journeymen's ability to fulfill their manly responsibilities and to their masculine identity that those labeled incompetent, union men believed, became despondent, broken-spirited, and even suicidal.[38] Men should be spared "the temptations and dangers which come from incompetency," concluded the ITU president.[39]

Since workers had to reaffirm their masculinity continually by working up to the production norm, workers discharged for incompetence lost their jobs and discovered that their manliness was also suspect. A foreman's right to judge competence also gave him the power to determine who was a man. If a man's competence was successfully challenged he lost all his "job property rights." The union protected the job rights of every man, "provided he does good work and can set 3,700 ems per our, leaded slugs, or 3,200 ems per hour, solid slugs."[40] For these reasons, a foreman's arbitrariness had to be controlled. James O'Leary, charged with incompetence, appealed to the Chicago Typographical Union to halt these "insidious soul-destroying practices." "For myself I do not plead, but beg for the cause of manhood," he added.[41]

The union maintained that incompetence was the only grounds for discharge.[42] Since the criterion for competence was whether a man could work up to the production norm, the union insisted that a man did not need to be "swift," or a "bonus hunter," but should simply be "capable of giving service in proportion to the emoluments accruing."[43]

Printers attempted to circumvent employers' standards by distinguishing competence from other criteria of worker performance such as carelessness, inefficiency, and inattention to the details of the work.[44] They defined a competent printer as one who could do the work, even if his actual performance fell short of average. Consequently, a foreman who discharged a man whose fitness had already been established had to "show deterioration as a workman" or prove that "general unfitness—physical, mental or moral" had appeared since initial hiring.[45]

Workingmen had redefined and narrowed the meaning of competence in light of new work standards. But in doing so, their masculinity was situated on a more shaky foundation than in previous decades. By the 1890s, even a man who had once been declared competent could lose his ability to perform his job. Masculinity and competence were no longer enduring characteristics.

Many older journeymen who could not learn to operate the new machines or who could not work up to the production standard were forced to retire or to find other means of employment. Journeymen could no longer claim they were masters of their craft. Many were simply displaced by the new technology. Others were forced to revert to the status of "learner," taking special courses, or attending typesetting schools established by employers, machine manufacturers, or typographical locals.

The new standards for judging competence on the Linotype emphasized workers' endurance and further intensified the conflict between journeymen and apprentices by favoring younger over older workers. The line between the apprentice as boy and the journeyman as man became less distinct. Journeymen justifiably perceived apprentices as their rivals in new and more profound ways. Changes in work conditions, the speeding up of production on machine work, the adoption of time wages, and new standards of worker competence intensified conflicts between journeymen and apprentices. It became even more difficult than in previous decades for journeymen to assume responsibility for apprentices' training, since it lowered their own productivity. Since printers' manhood as well as their job property rights now depended on continually working up to specified production norms, printers abandoned systematic attempts to teach boys all aspects of the job.[46]

The increased specialization of apprentices jeopardized their future claims to competence and hence to manhood. Accompanying specialization was what printers saw as "a loss of independence, and, to some extent, a sense of helplessness."[47] A union printer pointed to the serious consequences for boys in later years of having been deprived of a proper apprenticeship. Only those instructed in every branch, he said, were "practically equipped for the battle" when they reached manhood.[48]

Employers, too, were responsible for apprentices' incompetence. As union men saw it, employers were more interested in making money from the apprentices' work than in teaching them a trade. Often the apprentice was given no instruction at all but simply picked up whatever he could.[49] Once an apprentice became proficient at a particular task, the employer kept him at that position, the ITU president complained, "solely because his highly specialized service reduces the cost of production a fraction of a cent a column."[50] Journeymen blamed employers' greed for "the neglect of our boys," who were allowed "to run wild" to a greater extent than in any other business.[51] A union printer lamented, "Now the boy is not engaged for the purpose of making a man of him, but rather to make money out of his labor."[52]

Inadequate training in the entire craft and a specialized division of labor, said the ITU president, spelled "not only economic loss but the possible ruination of men."[53] A man's competence gave him a sense of manly independence that an incompetent worker lacked.[54] Furthermore, an apprentice who specialized in one aspect of the craft was deprived of his manly honor, for he was forced to "steal the trade" by working for less than union wages in order to support his family. An incompetent obtained employment through "some form of misrepresentation as to his abilities," only to be turned out as soon as the quality of his work became apparent. The man became known as an incompetent, and as a result, "The poor unfortunate has no place to go and is welcomed nowhere, except it be in a saloon of the lowest class. . . . If the incompetent is a father, then these conditions are almost sure to breed criminal tendencies among his children."[55]

For such reasons, said the president in 1911, the union should examine the effects of inadequate apprenticeship training "on the boy and the man," not just on the cost of production. A "mock apprenticeship" was the parent of misfortune. When a young man secured his first job upon becoming a journeyman and found he was not much of an artisan and probably had "no real right to call himself a printer," the knowledge came as a shock. The boy then suffered from periods of depression which enveloped him "in the dark gloom of utter hopelessness." While employers dismissed these problems as mawkish, "those who are students of the development of character and manhood," the president argued, "will not dismiss these features as negligible."[56]

Employers suggested and developed a number of solutions to the apprenticeship problem. They called for replacing the old apprenticeship requirements of proficiency in all aspects of printing with a system of certification of competence in specialized branches or types of work.[57] But the major strategy employers pursued by the end of the nineteenth century was to replace apprenticeship with school training.[58]

Employers had less incentive to maintain an apprenticeship system. Since the Linotype was designed to do straight composition, it reduced employers' desire to take on apprentices as less skilled, cheaper labor to do this work. From the employers' vantage point, mechanized typesetting had transformed the work into a science that could and should be taught in schools as a set of general principles.[59]

Union printers suspected employers of using trade schools to create a glut in the labor market, thereby depressing wages.[60] The battle fought in previous decades to have wages based on skill rather than market principles had failed. Wages now were determined by the principles of supply and demand. As a printer lamenting the advent of trade schools explained: "Skill does not fix wages, for the moment skilled labor becomes common, universal, and such must be the ultimate objective of trade schooling, it receives common wages."[61]

The typographical union found it increasingly difficult to legitimate training solely on the basis of intuition and rule-of-thumb methods of work. Union men were caught in a double bind. On the one hand, the apprenticeship system as it existed by the late nineteenth century was impractical and could not be enforced. To maintain it in its current form would have undermined the union men's craft and gender positions. On the other hand, the replacement of apprenticeship with training schools created other class and gender crises for them. As a result, union members argued the merits and demerits of trade-school education for decades. Typographical locals advocated various different solutions to the apprenticeship problem, and the national union developed no consistent position on training schools until the early twentieth century.[62]

Once the union recognized that it could no longer dismiss trade schools as "jokes," its policy was to accept them in the hope of influencing their direction. "The trade school is here," the ITU president explained in 1907.[63] In 1915 the ITU established a commission on vocational training to determine the aims, purposes, and net results of such schools. The union explained to its members: "We are face to face with a condition that will prove a menace to the trade, or an advantage to it dependent largely on how we handle the question now."[64]

The ITU had acceded to the new terms of craft legitimation. It made numerous efforts to establish training programs and schools under its own control. Printers established technical clubs which offered programs and lectures designed to increase the printers' understanding of the craft.[65] The ITU "Course in Printing," developed in 1908, translated the "mysteries of the art" of printing into predetermined guidelines. Acquiring competence required mastering these guidelines and the general principles on which they were based. Instruction at the workplace would be reduced, a union spokesman explained, since graduates of the course "will be able to reason out what should or should not be done."[66] Between 1908 and 1913, more than 4,300 students had taken the course. However, these various union efforts to maintain control over training failed for lack of money.[67]

Ultimately, both the union and employers sought state intervention to resolve the apprenticeship question. The compromise was a system of publicly funded vocational education. Employers succeeded in their efforts to create a new form of industrial training in schools.[68] The union accepted the idea of technical schools, but rejected those financed and controlled by employers. At the same time, employers came to accept the union's position that schools should be used to supplement rather than to supplant apprenticeship. Apprenticeship thus came to mean a combination of classroom instruction and on-the-job experience.[69] Despite these compromises, employers and printers continued to battle over central issues regarding the nature and organization of training schools.[70]

The central question remained how to determine competence, but the focus now was on apprentice limitations and on selection procedures for admission to the schools and apprenticeship programs. To union men in the late nineteenth century, competence was contingent on biological traits, not just acquired skills. They argued that they brought special masculine aptitudes and abilities to the work, which made some better workers than others. Simply being a male was not sufficient to qualify as a printer, since not all males were considered equally suitable for the work. Only those with the right "aptitudes" could ever become truly competent printers.[71]

These views about the relationship between masculinity and work shaped the ways in which union men dealt with the apprenticeship question. Since not all boys had the ability to become competent printers, the men sought to gauge a boy's "aptitude" for printing before an apprenticeship began.

Union men saw the decline in printers' general level of competence as the result of the wrong kind of boys being admitted as apprentices. The lack of an apprenticeship system in printing offices allowed boys to be employed indiscriminately, without regard to their "fitness" for the trade, as one printer lamented.[72] While the bosses were willing to take on any kind of boy, the union should require testing and qualifications. The best way to rid the trade of incompetents was to head them off in the beginning by requiring apprentice applicants to take an examination to ascertain their aptitude for the trade.

In addition to having his general knowledge tested, the boy should also be examined by a physician to assure that he had the "bodily capacity" for the work. Not all boys had the capacity to become "true men." Journeymen no longer argued that all boys could acquire masculinity through apprenticeship. Now they claimed that some boys were too "delicate" to be able to withstand the "long hours and constant mental and bodily strain" required by the work. The presence of effeminate boys had caused the work to be infected with "female diseases." If such unfit boys were kept out of the printing business, one printer claimed, "consumption and other tubercular complaints would not be so remarkable for their ravages in the trade."[73] The union insisted that such boys were unfit to be printers.

As a result of changes in printers' work, the union found it increasingly difficult to attract "desirable" candidates for apprenticeship. The ITU Committee on Supplemental Education identified the devaluation of skills and the loss of the craft's manly respectability as the reasons why more qualified young men did not seek to become printers. Boys "with spirit and red blood in their veins will not submit to such tyrannies." Boys seek more "manly pursuits," printers claimed. To attract the best American youths, union printers instructed employers to treat the boys "less like prisoners of necessity and more like men."[74]

The Linotype threatened job security and undermined the traditional definition of competence as the basis for employment. This further jeopardized the printers' manly respectability by undermining their positions as family providers. Samuel Gompers, AFL president, explained to the Industrial Commission in 1899: "Man, by his physical condition is the natural breadwinner of the family, and it is his duty to work; and not only is it his duty, but he has the right to work; the right to the opportunity to work." Therefore, he argued, when a "two-thirder" was hired in preference to a journeyman, society did the worker and his family a great injustice. The consequence, he continued, was boys who supported their fathers; "idle men and busy children."[75]

Printers proposed to lessen unemployment by further limiting the number of apprentices.[76] Earlier nineteenth-century notions of skill as a form of property were transformed into the belief that printers had the right to pass their craft positions to their sons, thus fulfilling their duties as family providers. A printer's job, what he called his "situation," became his property, accruing the same rights and protections given to owners of other types of property. The union's control over apprenticeship protected this property right.[77] On that basis, as a member of the New York typographical local saw it, union printers' sons should be given preference over sons of nonprinters in learning the trade. As he explained: "It is their undoubted right to be given an opportunity to follow in the footsteps of their fathers . . . "[78]

Union limitations on the number of apprentices as a solution to the unemployment problem created another dilemma for union printers, since there was thus decreased opportunity for their own sons' entry into the craft. In cities where the number of apprenticeships fell short of the demand, union men debated apprenticeship limitations and the consequences of giving printers' sons preference over sons of nonprinters.[79] One printer lamented: "Year after year the unions draw the apprenticeship limit a little tighter, until today, in some branches of the trade, at least, an enterprising and hopeful father who desires his son to become a disciple of the art preservative is met with a complete rebuff."[80] Thus employers were not entirely to blame for this crisis in men's ability to fulfill their fatherly responsibilities to their sons. In the transition to new conceptions of masculinity, the union had adopted class and gender strategies that were internally contradictory.

TEN

Masculinity and Mobility: The Dilemma of Lancashire Weavers and Spinners in Late-Nineteenth-Century Fall River, Massachusetts

Mary H. Blewett

I have stood where I could see the rustling throng issue from a mill as the bell rang, and the gates were thrown open; and what I saw were no longer manly men, but men of stooping forms and hopeless faces; women, dispirited, slovenly and aimless; and children . . . —the embryos of an emasculated adulthood—the whole crowd, where once were seen fine specimens of manhood, now a sorry spectacle of overtasked, exhausted and despondent humanity. . . .
——ANONYMOUS CLERGYMAN, 1871

Historians of masculinity have characterized the late nineteenth century as an era that enshrined manly virtues and physical prowess. But by concentrating on the experience of the middle class, scholars have neglected the different and specific meanings of masculinity among industrial workers like the mule spinners and weavers of Fall River, Massachusetts. To these workers, who toiled long hours in stifling factories, Teddy Roosevelt's call for a return to the "strenuous life" would have sounded ridiculous.[1]

The scarcity of literary evidence on the private lives of working-class people, in comparison with sources on middle-class experience, suggests that historians will have to examine the public record of labor struggles and union policies in order to understand the meanings of masculinity for industrial workers. In doing so, they will discover that class and gender are interconnected and interdependent, and that the meanings of masculinity have deeply political connotations.

Although a few labor historians have examined manhood as an ideological concept and as a system of shop-floor behavior and ethics, much of their work is concerned with a description of ideas and activities rather than with an analysis of changing conceptions of masculinity as a broad social phenomenon. And some social historians have argued that working-class men

I would like to thank Ava Baron for her interest in and critiques of this essay.

conceived of masculinity in similar terms throughout the Western world, or even that middle- and working-class men shared the same conceptions of manhood. This suggests a dissociation of the experience of gender from historical change in ways that are reminiscent of the treatment of womanhood before women's studies.[2]

Changes in the meanings of masculinity during the turbulent decade of the 1870s among working-class people in Fall River call these assumptions into question. The labor struggles of this period revealed variant conceptions of masculinity among English immigrants and among immigrant and native-born workers. The social meanings of working-class gender, unlike those of the middle class, were formulated within a nexus of complex economic forces. The social construction of masculinity was central to the conflicts over ideology and strategy of working people and was shaped by the outcome of these labor struggles.

The key struggle pitted immigrant mule spinners and weavers from Lancashire against each other. They were part of a massive emigration sponsored by British trade unions in the early 1870s and came to dominate the Fall River work force culturally and politically by 1875. Lancashire workers tried to reconstruct in New England the heritage of popular radicalism they had brought with them from old England. Simultaneously, Fall River capitalists attempted to purge their English workers of "chronic insubordination."[3] During the conflict that ensued, the meanings of masculinity within the ideology of Fall River labor protest were challenged and transformed.

Skill and physical strength, along with respectability and law-abiding sobriety, were fundamental to the manly character of many immigrant textile workers, but from the moment that Lancashire men landed in Fall River, the measure of that skill and strength was always at issue in the textile factories. The mill agents were determined to dominate the domestic market for cotton print cloth by acquiring the cheapest raw cotton and the best machinery. Then they paid the lowest wages in the region and depended on the intense physical exertions of the operatives to produce massive quantities of inferior cloth, the defects of which the printed patterns would conceal. They controlled the market by maintaining the capacity to glut it with the cheapest possible goods. Fall River became known among operatives as "the hardest place for work and the meanest place for wages" in New England.[4]

The spinners and weavers of Lancashire, England's most militant industrial region in the early nineteenth century, had opposed mechanization and centralization: the hand spinners resisted the self-acting mule while the hand-loom weavers fought the introduction of the power loom. Both also resisted the employment of women, viewing them as cheap, coercible workers. Men regarded control of the trade as crucial in struggles with their employers.

By midcentury this resistance to machines and to women workers had faded as hand spinners worked alongside the "minders" of self-acting mules, while both sexes commonly tended the steam-driven looms in Lancashire factories. Despite the general decline of popular radicalism after the passage of legislation in the late 1840s that granted limited manhood suffrage and the ten-hour workday, spinners and weavers developed different organizations and strategies to defend their interests. Issues of gender strategy remained central to their approaches. However, by the middle of the nineteenth century both groups of male workers had, as a result of the general reform of the terms of industrial work, replaced their public image as "Lancashire brutes" with that of sober, conscientious, self-educated, and serious men who operated consumer cooperatives like small businesses and enjoyed the employers' acceptance of their unions.[5]

The Lancashire spinners believed that a union dominated by small numbers of skilled male workers could control the supply of labor and thereby prevent market forces manipulated by mill agents from determining wages. While they drew the self-acting (male) minders into their organized hierarchy (renaming them spinners), they were successful in limiting entry into the trade to young men and boys. In contrast, the weavers' organizations permitted free entry to their occupation by both men and women, often cooperated with nonmembers (even nonweavers) during strikes, and recruited members from the many workers who moved freely about Lancashire in search of better work and wages. Unlike the spinners, they were fundamentally concerned with the establishment of a standard list of wages in Lancashire, not with control over who performed the work in what locale. Regional organization was more important to them than the gender composition of the union.[6]

The immigrants who arrived in Fall River in increasing numbers in the late 1860s and early 1870s transplanted the labor organizations and political values of Lancashire. They also brought with them an experience of industrial relations that had developed along with the employers' acceptance of their unions in the midcentury compromise between capital and labor. Both worker and "master" acknowledged mutual responsibilities. Workers treated their employers with deference, and employers agreed to negotiate with union men. In England, this deferential relationship involved complex behaviors that protected and secured the respectability and sober-minded bearing of working-class masculinity.[7] However, the immigrants quickly learned that the capitalists in New England regarded their doffed caps and careful politeness as marks of servility and unmanliness, rejecting their expectations of mutuality with open contempt. In the absence of deferential politics in Fall River, spinners and weavers searched for new ways to confront the power of their employers yet maintain their respectable manhood.

The complex meanings of masculinity and its relationship to geographical mobility for the immigrant mule spinners began to emerge during a strike in 1870. The spinners' union reacted to a 30 June announcement of a wage cut for all workers with an attempt to draw their employers into Lancashire-style negotiations. The five hundred spinners (speaking on behalf of thousands of other textile operatives, such as the weavers who were thrown out of work with the stoppage of spinning operations) offered to compromise.[8]

The Fall River agents, unwilling to deal with the union, refused to reply to or even acknowledge the mule spinners' formal statements. Strike leader William Isherwood, who had been blacklisted in Lowell in 1867 for ten-hour-reform activity, summed up their actions as "silent contempt."[9] The mill agents then recruited mule spinners from other textile cities and towns in New England as strikebreakers. Deferential politics and negotiation had failed.

The Fall River spinners now sought other means to preserve the respectability and sober demeanor of workingmen. Determined to avoid the use of overt violence against the strikebreakers who began to arrive at the central railroad depot, they instead appealed to the dignity and manhood of brother mule spinners, while offering to pay train fares back home.

The strategy of the mill agents was to provoke a violent reaction by the spinners in order to discredit them and convince the community that the union leaders were reckless and irresponsible men. Mill agents heightened tensions during the strike by calling in false alarms and using fire companies to drench the crowds, by persuading the mayor to hire special police and summon the state militia, and by encouraging undercover agents to spy on striking spinners and circulate reports of drunkenness and potential bloodshed.[10]

The sole incident of violence in 1870 toward a strikebreaker illustrates the care with which striking spinners and their allies among the weavers divided the responsibilities of intimidation along gender lines to protect the manly respectability of the union spinners. A strikebreaking spinner, new to the trade, had refused to join the union. To make an example of him, noisy members of a crowd of strike supporters waiting outside the mill kicked him, stoned him, and gave him "a tremendous pounding" as he left for the night after two days at work. The street crowds were composed mostly of women and children, and the attackers were probably weavers.

They supplied the howls and jeers, the fists and blows, to humble a disloyal male.

These crowds were backed up by the tenants of corporation housing nearby; armed with stones and dirt clods, they were ready to shower the strikebreakers at a signal. State police called in by the city authorities discovered that the majority were women sitting at their windows with stones concealed in their aprons.[11] The spinners, entirely absent from the tumult, remained law-abiding citizens and respectable men. The dissociation of masculinity from overt violence during the 1870 strike served class politics and emphasized a flexibility in gender meanings as long as the spinners exercised leadership and authority on behalf of other textile workers during the strike.

The striking mule spinners also resisted attempts by mill agents to link the geographic mobility of strikebreaking spinners to their employers' ideology of supply and demand. When workers complained about wages, mill agents claimed that market forces determined the supply of labor, which in turn set the wage level in Fall River. Spinners were told to go to other mill towns where their skills were in demand. The agents regarded any attempt to oppose market forces, such as intimidating strikebreakers by collective action, as "coercion" and interference with individual rights and natural economic laws.[12] But strikers feared that the dispersal of union men would cripple attempts to resist wage cuts. Strike leaders sought instead to fix the responsibility for the wage cut on decisions made by the Fall River mill agents, not by an impersonal market—decisions which the spinners believed could be changed by negotiations between the union and the mills.

Mill agents also tried to attack spinning as a manly trade by insisting during the strike that "girls" ran mules "easily and successfully" in some Massachusetts mills. The spinners responded that they worked harder and faster than workers anywhere else in New England, walking twenty-five miles and more per eleven-hour day with only one young boy to help piece up broken yarns: "a pretty good day's work for any man." The work was "so hard" that many spinners could not work the entire month at the mill, but had to "stay away from it and rest." The striking spinners continued to oppose any use of women in spinning, insisting that the exhausting work was "not a fitting employment for females."[13] Defending mule spinning as a skill that only men could perform was central to their conception of manly work.

As long as the spinners led organized protest in the city, their customary opposition to women in the trade shaped their sense of proper gender arrangements. Yet in the streets, their wives and daughters might yell and throw stones on behalf of class interests. But strike leaders, unruly or not, were blacklisted by a common agreement among the mill owners to bar pro-union workers from spinning in the city. Blacklisted spinners either left the trade or left Fall River. Those who stayed on in the community to work at less skilled jobs automatically lost their status as craftsmen and their positions in the union, diminishing their sense of manly worth.

The case of one "elderly" English mule spinner, cited by social reformer Lillian Chace Wyman in her study of the effects of secret blacklisting in Fall River, illustrates the experience of blacklisting as an assault on manhood. This blacklisted spinner was told only that he was being fired for poor work. He spent weeks seeking another place, only to be discharged again and again, until by chance he discovered his name on the blacklist in a mill office. The spinner was relieved that his dismissal and his inclusion on the blacklist were in retaliation for union activity, not a judgment on his ability to spin. "You may think it a weakness in me but that pleased me, and it pleased the old woman [his wife], and made her proud to think they couldn't find fault with me."[14] Husband and wife agreed that, despite his age, his skill and strength were the measure of his worth as a man. This association of respectable masculinity with the craft and the union proved vulnerable to the combined determination of Fall River capitalists to tame Lancashire workers by isolating their leaders.

After two months without wages or a strike fund, other textile workers slowly returned to the mills. Isherwood and all the other leaders of the spinners' union were blacklisted and evicted from corporation tenements, while the strikers reluctantly signed contracts pledging not to join a union and went back to work.[15] However, all parties to the 1870 strike took the long view: the spinners organized in secret, the weavers waited for reinforcements, and the mill agents tried to identify and blacklist all leaders.

Many immigrant spinners in Fall River apparently had wives who were weavers. One English-born mule spinner described a pattern common to such families. He rose at 5:00 A.M. to start the breakfast while his wife and children slept, helped to make dinner and put it into pails, and after work started supper before his wife got home. Defending his involvement in housework to his astonished interviewer, the spinner explained that he and his wife cooked and cleaned the house together on Sundays. Then after dinner they took a "nap," the only chance for intimacy in a workweek of nearly seventy hours. This pattern of shared housework enabled his wife, with the help of their twelve-year-old daughter, to tend ten looms, more than the usual six to eight looms of women weavers, and thereby earn more on piecework.[16] As the mills in Fall River continued to expand production and to supply plenty of factory work, changes in the traditional sexual division of labor in household work were negotiated among family members. Participation in routine housework alongside a working wife did not undermine a spinner's sense of manliness.

Failing to locate sufficient native-born labor for the twenty-two new cotton mills that were built in a frenzy of activity between 1870 and 1872, Fall River managers sent recruiters to Lancashire to hire more English operatives. But they refused to accept their unions or labor politics. Fall River agents convinced themselves that they would be able to dominate these historically unruly people as easily as they had come to dominate the national market for print cloth. A great immigration in the early 1870s swelled the numbers of Lancashire workers already resident in the city. When the depression of 1873 produced wage cuts and deteriorating working conditions, Lancashire workers were in control of local labor activity.

Hard times after the onset of the 1873 depression put enormous pressure on working-class standards of living and working, especially in terms of bodily strength and stamina. Working-class men perceived these pressures as an assault on their manly right to spin according to the requirements of the craft and as a threat to their abilities as husbands and fathers to support their families. The Lancashire immigrants who arrived after 1870 confronted unfamiliar working conditions that drove the pace of work beyond endurance. Their first reaction was to channel their political energies into the final push in 1874 for the ten-hour workday in Massachusetts textile factories. Fall River managers responded to new statutory limitations on daily labor by significantly speeding up work processes and pushing operations each day beyond the legal limit.[17]

Wage cuts during the depression of 1873 meant that overtaxed workers had less income to spend on food, especially the beef and beer that were staples of the English workingman's diet. Sweating spinners, who every day walked twenty-five miles and more back and forth at the mules in the brutally hot spinning rooms, craved beer, which supplied carbohydrates for thirsty bodies and anesthesia for overstrained nerves. Mill agents castigated the beer-drinking English for intemperance and argued that "more sickness is caused by beer than by overwork."[18] During hard times, workers were forced to eat bread and cheese instead of the red meat they believed essential for a man's physical well-being.

New England mill agents refused to supply their spinners with the helpers customary in Lancashire. Instead, a spinner had the assistance of only one young "back boy" to help repair the multiple strands of yarn spun from cheap cotton during the back-and-forth motions of the huge frames. These pressures produced a "Fall River walk," brisk and quick. Few spinners, even the young and vital ones, had the stamina to work a full month of six-day weeks (eleven hours a day) without laying off as "sick" for several days to regain their strength. Male workers designated as "sick spinners" routinely filled the jobs of exhausted men for several days each month. By pacing the work just beyond the extent of a man's physical powers, an abuse the operatives called "lashing the help," the mill agents undermined the workers' pride in manly strength and skill. Unlike the English, Fall River overseers posted the daily work records of each spinner to create competition among operatives and to encourage shame and ridicule among men about their work capabilities.[19]

After a year of hard times, the mill agents of Fall River demonstrated their market power by limiting production in order to stimulate prices. However, when other New England textile mills shifted into print cloth, Fall River factories returned to full-time work in January 1875, but cut wages by 10 percent. Their intention was to flood the market with the cheapest cloth and thereby defeat their upstart competitors. Fall River workers had already accepted an initial 10 percent wage cut in early 1874. At a meeting in January 1875 that excluded women workers, male weavers nearly accepted the additional cut.[20] In the major struggle that followed, women operatives, inspired by recollections of popular radicalism in Lancashire and their convictions about the historic effectiveness of resistance, challenged their reluctant male co-workers to strike.

In their public call for the meeting, female weavers, speaking for themselves and their children, complained about the "dilatory, shilly-shally and cowardly action" of the male leadership. Their first meeting on 16 January reverberated with direct challenges to working-class manhood. Addressing their complaints to the only man present, Lancashire-born Henry Sevey, editor of the Fall River *Labor Journal,* they shouted, "Come on, you cowards! You were [be]got in fear, though you were born in England"—a reminder to the male weavers that they were the sons and grandsons of the hand-loom weavers of Lancashire, who had fought tenaciously for their rights.[21]

The next day a group of male weavers approached Robert Borden, treasurer of the Crescent Mill, and presented their demands to him before a *Boston Globe* reporter.

> A delegation of 6 tall, blonde, blue-eyed Englishmen, they held their hats in their hands and their tongues in their mouths until the Treasurer spoke to their leader when he stepped respectfully to the counter and said in a marked North Country accent: "Wael, I suppose ye're awaere we are come to see ye, sir, about our little grievances, and thaet's about the figger thaet we think will bring us back t'our looms."

When Borden protested that the manufacturers suffered more than the weavers from hard times, the weavers' barely concealed anger flared briefly.

"More of a hardship, sir?" interrupted a giant bearded Yorkshire man, with flushed pale face and tears standing in his eyes, "more of a hardship, sir? Ah if ye knew—"

"We haeve to live upon our daily wages," another said in a low suppressed voice, "and back of thaet we've no money, sir; while you've plenty to back-set you, I hope. . . ."

As the men went away disappointed, the reported remarked to Borden: "That's a gentlemanly set of strikers." "Yes," Borden replied, "I make them gentlemanly."[22] The next day, the male weavers and the spinners joined the women's strike.

Activist women formulated the strike's successful strategy: suspend work at the three mills whose agents had instigated the wage cut, but continue work at the other mills, so that workers could then contribute a share of their wages to the strike fund. They also urged the mule spinners to organize the young women who were just beginning to spin warp thread on primitive ring-spinning frames.[23] The men had reluctantly agreed to strike, but some spinners and weavers still opposed the decision, including Lancashire-born labor reformer Thomas Stephenson, whose *Lawrence Journal* competed with Henry Sevey's paper for the support and direction of the textile operatives of New England. Stephenson pilloried Sevey's conversion to the women's position at their 16 January meeting. He described Sevey as another "Adam in the garden of old" who had been manipulated "as the weaker vessel" by "babbling Amazons." His criticism that Sevey lacked "ordinary manly courage and determination" may have echoed the views of many male workers until victory was won.[24] After the 10 percent wage cut was rescinded, the Fall River weavers controlled labor politics. Their successful use of Lancashire radicalism to best their American employers made the women weavers and their male supporters appear forceful, while their opponents seemed both wrong and weak.

Fresh from their success, the weavers, men and women, began to organize a regional association of textile operatives to standardize wages and agitate for factory legislation that would reform New England labor laws. Mill agents throughout the region shuddered at the prospect of an American Lancashire. For mule spinners, the appeal of the standard wage list and a regional organization lay in undermining the power of the mill agents to recruit other New England textile workers to break strikes. They sought especially to make both the blacklist and strikebreaking obsolete in Fall River by developing connections with mule spinners in textile centers like Lawrence and Lowell. However, for many New England–born textile workers, geographical mobility, initially from farm to factory, meant an individual's right to leave one employer or community and seek to better himself as a man. As one Fall River operative critical of English ways put it: "Individual ideas, rather than the collective, rule in this country."[25]

Many American workers, men and women, and manufacturers alike rejected as spiritless and unmanly the claims of immigrant spinners and weavers to a right to work in their trade in their chosen community. As Charles Nordhoff, labor reporter for the *New York Herald,* wrote: "No man is a slave who has the right to migrate and the spirit to do it, the courage and endurance necessary for the struggle with life." Nordhoff contrasted the attitudes of English and American workers. The Lancashire weavers knew "only weaving, and nothing else, and regard it as their only work, . . . and they will starve rather than do anything else." English trade unions taught a man that he had "a vested right in [his] trade and a right to live by it. . . . He remains in Fall River; he does not attempt any other work; he is simply a Fall River weaver, and stands and suffers on that ground." But an American worker would show "the greater pride and independence in his course. . . . He would accept the conditions, quietly do his work well, but with a determination to get out of the business as soon as he could . . . move himself away."[26]

English spinners and weavers who immigrated before 1870 had adopted from labor reformers and native-born workers the rhetoric of individual rights and of the Union cause in the Civil War. At moments of the greatest crisis in 1875, strike agitators asked: "Do you call this a free country? . . . Is this liberty? Is this republicanism? Is this what you fought for when you suffered to preserve the Union of our glorious country? Don't go to work as slaves."[27] These men had served as mediators between Yankee labor reformers and the newly arrived English immigrants. But many other native New England workers defined manhood as equality with their employers and freedom of movement, not as digging in their heels and battling it out with the employers in one community. The domination of labor protest in Fall River by the weavers from Lancashire undermined this coalition.

In the summer of 1875, as the weavers organized throughout eastern Massachusetts and Rhode Island, the mill agents decided to try again to destroy their small competitors by cutting wages back to what they were before the weavers' strike and by glutting the market with cheap goods. In response, the weavers—with the enthusiastic support of both men and women— challenged the power of the manufacturers to control the industry by collectively withholding their labor from production in their own deliberate effort to influence the market price of print cloth. On 31 July, they voted overwhelmingly for a one-month "vacation" and wildly applauded a resolution to the effect that if the Fall River mills could not pay decent wages for weaving, they had no moral right to the print-goods market. The weavers resolved that if other manufacturers could pay more for the work, then "they have the best right to it," and the Fall River mills "must stand their chance of being burst up."[28] This defiant act, drawing on their heritage of popular radicalism, denied the validity of a morally neutral market run by natural laws. As a result the mill agents determined to crush this unprecedented threat to their power.

After a month of vacation, with production booming in other mill towns and no price increase in the market, the operatives abandoned the "vacation strike." However, the mill agents, eager to demolish both the spinners' and the new weavers' organizations, declared a month's vacation of their own and locked out their employees. Within several weeks the workers were "clemming"—an old Lancashire term for literally wasting away with hunger. That hunger, and the insistence of the mill agents that no union member could work in Fall River, tapped a politically primitive response from the angry Lancashire workers.

On 27 September, the day when the mills finally reopened, the strikers responded as their forebears had done in Lancashire since the 1790s. Inspired by elderly male weavers from Manchester, England, with memories of late-eighteenth-century food riots, both men and women marched by the hundreds to city hall, yelling "Bread!" and "Tyranny!" They carried signs that read "15,000 white slaves for auction" and bore poles on which loaves of bread were impaled. They demanded their right to be fed, and if refused they threatened to take food wherever they could find it. To underscore her anger at being told to return to work or go to the state poor farm, one woman striker hit the mayor on the head with a loaf of bread. The historic significance of the food riot was clear to Lancashire people, but baffling to all others (including the mayor, who literally did not know what hit him)—all except the conservative press in Boston and Providence, whose editors well understood the revolutionary import of Manchester-style bread riots in New England textile cities.[29]

This spectacle split the textile operatives into confused and hostile camps. American and French Canadian workers were appalled and alienated by demands for bread, threats of looting, and talk of arson and violence. The defeat of the vacation strategy convinced the mule spinners that the weavers' union, with its contingent of female agitators and its unmanly, emotional displays of desperation and rage, had led the workers into disaster. Begging city authorities for bread, with violence as the only alternative to the horrors of the state poor farm, was no way for a man to behave in public or to deal with his employer. Mill owners denounced the bread rioters and could now recast all union men as "English and Irish scum." The disastrous vacation strike associated all union leaders, in the minds of many

New England operatives, with "the fomentation of incipient riot and disorderly conduct," while labor reformers hastily condemned all strikes as contrary to American values. Operatives returning to work were forced to sign away their union memberships.[30] The weavers' union disappeared, and the spinners' union went underground.

After 1875, the spinners recaptured the leadership of Fall River labor politics, which turned toward moderation and caution. Their secretary, Robert Howard, won acceptance as a leader who first made his own men "as obedient and docile and harmonious as the parts of a mule frame."[31] The weavers' dream—of a Lancashire in New England that would include equal participation of men and women workers in work and union activity—vanished along with their organization.

A spinners' strike in 1879 demonstrated the vulnerabilities of abandoning the weavers' popular radicalism and regional organization. Conducting themselves with courtesy and patience while accepting the economic laws of the marketplace, the mule spinners waited until print cloth prices had finally risen, then reminded the mill owners of their past promises to rescind wage cuts when good times returned. But their employers refused to negotiate, recruited strikebreakers from other New England textile centers, and, most important, began to change the work force and technology in their spinning rooms. They hired women and young boys to run the new ring-spinning frames. Yarn spun on ring frames meant fewer jobs for skilled mule spinners. During their strike meetings, mule spinners listened to arguments in favor of "thinning" the labor market by withdrawing all women (or at least all married women) from factory work. As one speaker insisted, "The comfort and dignity of man begins when he has a home and domestic circle engaged in promoting his happiness."[32] The working woman at her ring-spinning frame had now become the enemy.

Unable to prevent the increasingly desperate spinners from using violence to intimidate strikebreakers, the leaders of the lost strike in 1879 were all blacklisted. The act of surrendering his union membership in order to get off the blacklist signaled for one of these men a shameful abandonment of the Lancashire traditions of union activity. He lamented, "I'm humiliated,—I'm less of a man than I was!"[33] His view of respectable masculinity, based on the value of his work and his physical ability to perform it satisfactorily on his own terms, was threatened, as in 1870, by the geographic mobility of those who served as strikebreakers. His humiliation also reflected a sense of personal loss at the defeat of Lancastrian popular radicalism that was the aftermath of that bitter decade of class struggle in Fall River.

The meanings of masculinity and the uses of mobility for spinners and weavers were central to the conflicts between the cultural and political traditions of Lancashire and the conditions of work and life in Fall River during the turbulent decade of the 1870s. Initially, immigrant mule spinners attempted to transplant the deferential politics of the midcentury system of industrial relations from England to New England. In doing so, they protected their respectable masculinity in ways that they believed served class politics. They also demonstrated some flexibility in gender relationships during labor protest and in their households—as long as their leadership of the community of workers remained uncontested.

The use of popular radicalism by rebellious females during the 1875 weavers' strike revealed serious conflicts among men and women workers over the leadership of class politics.[34] The activism of the weavers offered ways to resolve the dangers of geographic mobility among New England textile workers and even challenged the ideology of supply and demand, as well as the power of their employers to manipulate the market. But female activism also threatened exclusive male control of the spinners' union, the authority of mule spinners in labor politics, and the respectable masculinity of mule spinners by association with public riot.

After the failed attempt by the weavers to influence the print cloth market, the spinners returned to a strategy of moderation that restored their sense of proper masculine leadership but offered no means to confront either the power of their employers or their ability to transform the nature of spinning by employing women on new machines. Despite a keen sense of loss among some male activists, by 1880 the mule spinners advocated a family wage paid to skilled and respectable union men who bowed to the forces of supply and demand and voted for political candidates who supported unions and labor reform. After the events of the 1870s, Robert Howard, who became the secretary of the National Mule Spinners' Association, built a career in state politics that eventually led to the state senate and a prominent role in the Massachusetts Knights of Labor.

Conflicts over the meanings of masculinity in Fall River factories and in labor protest were not simply stumbling blocks to the establishment of a Lancashire in New England; more important, they provide evidence of intraclass conflict and cultural discontinuity in gender meanings. They also represent one powerful but largely unrecognized element in the interconnections among people caught up in immigration, industrialization, and cross-cultural adjustment in late-nineteenth-century America.

The redefinition of manhood in Fall River involved complex interplays of culture and work. Employers used class power unremittingly to undermine their workers' demeanor as respectable and trustworthy men. Women weavers sought inclusion in labor protest and reminded their male coworkers, weavers and spinners alike, that to be a Lancashire man had once meant bold action and imaginative strategy. Textile workers from New England and Quebec associated masculinity with freedoms and responsibilities other than to stand and fight whatever the odds. But for Lancashire men who remembered the radical past, like Henry Sevey of the *Labor Journal,* their duty was clear: "If a man cannot knock down his oppressor, you at least like to see him try; and if you cannot knock the tyrant down who would oppress you, you can at least give him a welter!"[35]

Looking toward Future Research

A s specialized research elaborates aspects of the history of masculinity, the need to stand back and take stock increases. The newness of the subject enables it to benefit from the development of women's history during the past two decades. In this section, women's historian Nancy Cott comments on some things we can learn from that development, from its false steps as well as from its breakthroughs. Her afterword and the essay by Clyde Griffen also pose questions for future research. They do so by drawing on the essays in this volume to propose larger interpretations. Griffen focuses directly on the history of American masculinity, offering a speculative synthesis for the century after 1830. Cott suggests how new research on masculinity may clarify larger themes in American society and culture, such as the relationship between individualism and the construction of social order.

Whereas women's history was obliged to learn about women as well as about gender, Cott thinks that men's history has a simpler task, insofar as the history of men as individuals has been constantly investigated. That seems true for many aspects of male experience and behavior, but hardly for all, especially not for those at the margins of public life and within the home. For example, we know little yet about the changing forms and extent of male participation in domestic responsibilities and their variation by occupation, class, race or ethnicity, and region. This information will be essential for developing perspective on the history of male gender.

Women's history has shown the limitations of conventional distinctions between public and private and the inaccuracy of identifying men with the former and women with the latter. But Cott's hypothesis of a propensity among nineteenth-century American males to construct highly competitive pecking orders does suggest that men and women had very different approaches to the construction of social order. If Cott's hypothesis is correct, it seems likely that men would tend to segregate their home lives from their other activities in ways women would not.

Griffen, on the other hand, focuses on aspects of gender relations and those social and cultural tendencies which favored more cooperative, less competitive relationships—many of them associated with women. Rather than emphasizing a repeated pattern in male creation of groups and institutions, his interpretation emphasizes change in gender norms and its relation to change in economy and society. What is unclear at this point—given Cott's and Griffen's differing foci—is how far these interpretations conflict with or complement each other.

Perhaps the most interesting part of our uncertainty is whether the two interpretations apply to the same individuals. One of the difficulties in research on masculinity is the diversity of social worlds—workplace, home, church, voluntary associations, sports, and other kinds of recreation and entertainment—that individual men inhabit. How widely applicable are generalizations about the views of members of any male group or institution when we know so little about how those views were shaped by outside experiences? Did the men who flocked to fraternal orders, for example, also go to church regularly? Were they less often participants, even as spectators, in the growing middle-class enthusiasm for sports, and rarely visitors of saloons or taverns?

Whether we can ever get much beyond the occasionally revealing autobiography in reconstructing the everyday round of life for nineteenth-century men—even of the middle and upper classes—is unclear. The discovery by Lewis Saum of so many letters, diaries, and journals of middling folk gives some reason for hope. But even if that kind of direct testimony proves unavailable or uninformative for this purpose, historians can go further than they have so far in trying to link participation in different groups and institutions.

Other needs for future research become apparent in Griffen's essay in the spottiness of the various kinds of analyses available at this point for constructing even a speculative synthesis. For example, his interpretation emphasizes major shifts, at several points, in influences shaping gender: from the evangelical revival to the Civil War to bureaucratization in white-collar work and the general shift form moral to scientific rhetoric during the early twentieth century. The first and last have been well documented, with major contributions by women's historians, but the impact of the Civil War on veterans and of bureaucratization on male white-collar workers has not been studied in any systematic way. Indeed, as Margaret Marsh's essay on masculine domesticity has suggested, the connections between influences like bureaucratization, suburbanization, and mass-circulation magazines—and, we might add, standardization in education and the emergence of national experts on child rearing and the family— have been mostly inferred. The difficult task of discovering how they are related in the experience of individuals in different birth cohorts around the turn of the century lies ahead.

Ideally, change in gendered behavior and attitudes for particular birth cohorts should be studied across the life course, but that counsel of perfection is unlikely to be realized, except possibly in certain well-documented subjects like industrialists or intellectuals. What can and should be done, however, is to look for evidence of variation in construction of gender by age and previous experience among members of any group investigated. A businessman whose maturation was shaped by the evangelical revivals and who survived into the Gilded Age was likely to differ in conception of manliness, as he did in experience, from young men coming of age during the Civil War who went into business. Among the latter, those who fought were likely to vary in gender norm from those who deliberately avoided fighting in order to begin their careers. Historians of masculinity in Victorian America need to find ways of evoking the constantly shifting mix of old and new meanings for manhood among the individuals who composed groups and generations during the century after 1830.

ELEVEN

Reconstructing Masculinity from the Evangelical Revival to the Waning of Progressivism: A Speculative Synthesis

Clyde Griffen

Once upon a time middle-class American males shared a common norm for masculinity: the Victorian patriarch. But the expanding demands of women created a confusing "crisis of masculinity" which has yet to be resolved. By the turn of the century the New Woman's insistence on public recognition deprived men of their traditional role, and her assertiveness made them feel less manly. So goes a familiar story of male gender in the United States.

A different interpretation of change in gender norms can be derived from the essays in this volume. The stern, upright patriarch was only one of a number of styles of manhood during the middle of the nineteenth century, the heyday of Evangelical Protestantism. That pluralism eroded during the late nineteenth century, gradually to be replaced by a more rigidly circumscribed set of gender expectations for middle-class males in an age of big corporations and mass-circulation magazines. This alternative interpretation reflects a difference in approach between that of most of the essays in this book, which focus on gender construction in particular groups and institutions, and that of the more generalized accounts embodying the "crisis" interpretation, which survey contemporary commentary on masculinity.[1]

The charm of the "crisis" interpretation has been its combination of simplicity and inclusiveness: everywhere traditional manhood was on the defensive. Peter Filene defines it succinctly when he claims that at the turn of the century the "concept of manliness was suffering strain in all its dimensions—in work and success, in familial patriarchy," and in sexuality. As women won recognition of the relevance of feminine values to public life, the male monopoly of that realm ended; as women complained increasingly about male behavior and inattention to the home, the masculine role generally became uncertain. The "crisis" interpretation tends to emphasize broad social trends like the end of the frontier and the declining opportunity for economic independence in an age of business bureaucratization. The impact of these trends on particular groups within the middle class is arguable and, in any case, not shown.[2]

The theme of "crisis" has the virtue of pulling together evidence of men's feelings of beleaguered resistance to women's demands, doubts about their own gender roles, and yearnings for restoration of "virility." But while the word "crisis" presupposes a turning point, it remains unclear when this crisis began, how long it lasted, and when it was resolved, if at all. The turn of the century (1880–1920) usually is singled out as a time of particular difficulty, yet worries about the state of American masculinity have been found throughout the last century and a half. In the 1950s, with no apparent challenge from women and with corporate bureaucracy long established, Arthur Schlesinger, Jr., and others wrote about the "crisis of American masculinity" in which, more than ever before, men and boys were "confused about what they should and should not do to fulfill their masculine roles."[3]

The persistence of anxiety over a long span of time stretches the idea of "crisis" and makes periodization difficult. One way out of these difficulties would be closer attention to changes in the challenge from women, which the "crisis" interpretation itself invokes as major cause. Women's historians by now have identified major shifts in the relative independence of women, in the forms and fortunes of women's cultural influence and political power, and in the means by which men fought off threats to male dominance. By elaborating the complex process of change in gender relations, women's historians have opened the way for a history of male gender which focuses more concretely on gender redefinition as adaptation to change. The adaptation has consequences for power relations, whether in family relationships, courtship and marriage, friendship, recreation, the workplace, religious, fraternal, or other voluntary associations, or politics.[4]

The emphasis in investigating masculinity at this early stage should be on identifying the variety of adaptations for different social groups in different settings. Such an emphasis should correct another limitation of the "crisis" interpretation—namely, its tendency to focus attention primarily on defensive responses, and especially on male-exclusive worlds, which can be seen as refuges from feminine influence or as peculiarly "masculine." The sports arena, battlefield, and preparatory school loom larger than they should in our picture of the construction of gender in everyday experience. Neglected are the settings which males and females share, and male-exclusive worlds like work and certain leisure activities, where gender issues, though significant, may not be paramount.[5]

By contrast, the essays in *Meanings for Manhood* do for the most part examine how masculinity was constructed by particular groups and institutions. The essays suggest how different a history of gender in the United

States may ultimately result from this shift in focus. While written independently, they lend themselves to a tentative speculative synthesis. I draw on
them to propose an interpretation of change from the antebellum period to
the Great Depression as an alternative to the "crisis of masculinity."

My essay considers change and continuity in four major dimensions of
the construction of male gender and gender relations from the antebellum
years to the 1920s: (1) style or posture: the way men express their sense of
manliness; (2) separation of male and female spheres; (3) division of labor;
and (4) dominance. I argue that styles of masculinity varied considerably
between groups and across time; that blurring of boundaries and overlapping of gender spheres increased; that a gendered division of labor was
constant over the span despite change in its rationalization; and that change
occurred in various aspects of gender relations both in the degree of male
dominance and in the ways it was maintained. My consideration is, as our
essays and the existing monographic literature largely are, confined almost
entirely to the white middle class—a major limitation which future research
on male gender urgently needs to remedy.[6]

Before the Civil War, markedly divergent conceptions and styles of masculinity coexisted, not only between social classes but within them. At one
pole within the working class was the Southern backcountry subculture of
white males in rough and dangerous occupations—like the rivermen, who
valued personal honor as much as the planter class did, and who defended it
more brutally. Preoccupation with honor and prowess also characterized
some Northern urban working-class groups, like the immigrant Irish and
those native craftsmen and laborers still imbued with preindustrial habits of
work. Such working-class males could find a reinforcing drama or literature, whether in the tall tales of Southwestern humorists, the subversive
fiction of Northern radical democrats, or the stage versions of the Bowery
b'hoy, tough and swaggering. At the other pole, some urban workers by the
1840s accepted the moral self-discipline, sobriety, and seriousness of Evangelical Protestantism.[7]

The range in styles of masculinity was just as great among the middle and
upper classes. At one extreme, as Donald Yacovone shows in this volume,
were the male abolitionists. They professed undying love for one another,
kissed, shed tears, and clasped hands, enacting a Christian "language" of
fraternal love harking back to the Middle Ages and beyond. Yacovone finds
similarly expressive male friendships among Southern secessionists. But
there was no sense among either of these embattled groups that their emotional openness represented weakness or the moral softness which republican thought stigmatized as "effeminacy."

Nor was there any fear among these celebrants of manly love that their passionate friendships would lead to homosexual acts. To the contrary, as investigations of English writings on manly love in the same period have shown, the idea that fraternity—unlike marriage—was purely spiritual, and thus the highest form of love, precluded what was then deemed "beastliness." Even in England, where an urban homosexual underworld was written about by the early eighteenth century, widespread suspicion of intense same-sex friendships as potentially sexual did not develop until the late nineteenth century.[8]

While abolitionists and secessionists created a homosociality similar in intensity of feeling to the "female world of love and ritual," at the other extreme a minority of affluent Northern urbanites preferred a thoroughly unsentimental style of masculine camaraderie. They emulated the "fancy," those English aristocrats who mixed with working-class toughs at illegal sporting events like cockfights. Other antebellum upper-class males, like the patrician Francis Parkman, longed for the restoration of the ruggedness and valor of aristocratic military heroes.[9]

Lawyers increasingly conceived of themselves as men of "action and cunning" and also preferred an unsentimental style of friendship. As Michael Grossberg indicates (this volume), they celebrated the combat of courtroom performance and the tavern conviviality of circuit riding, deriding the previous scholarly and literary pretensions of their professional forebears. Grossberg does not say whether their new emphasis on practicality and rejection of fiction, passion, and idealism involved an explicit gender contrast. But he quotes an exhortation against "fancy" which warns against "the distressing power of her wand" and calls instead for "manly submission to the sceptre of reason."

Lawyers now emphasized competitiveness, physical courage, and political realism. Their new style of manliness suited perfectly the development by the 1840 presidential campaign of the political parties as a type of male fraternal organization. Partisan rallies and processions, commonly employing military-style marching companies, were male rituals. Election day further dramatized the masculine character of electoral politics as the voting was done in saloons, barbershops, and other places frequented by men.[10]

Between the extremes of the abolitionists' manly love and the "tougher" versions of manliness of the antebellum period was an extremely influential evangelical conception of Christian manhood. This religious conception still has not received enough attention from historians of masculinity, perhaps because it does not address what seems to us peculiarly masculine. Yet women's historians, and historians of the antebellum period in general, have shown the enormous social importance of the great urban revivals from the 1820s onward.[11]

We still know relatively little about the inner lives of male converts, whether businessmen, other middle-class workers, or artisans. But examination of antebellum diaries of men as well as of women suggests not only a "prodigious appetite for religion," but also the persistence of an older, more submissive attitude toward providential workings, coupled with a strong sense of personal responsibility for doing God's work. Although evangelicals presumed male authority in the family, gender-defined division of labor, and separate spheres, they also believed devoutly that economic life must be governed by moral values, that individual and collective righteousness ought to be sustained by public policy, and that the gentler virtues should be applied wherever possible in human relationships. The wider world should be made more like the home.[12]

Zeal for becoming "my brother's keeper" came naturally to a generation of evangelical businessmen and other middle-class workers raised in a patriarchal household economy which integrated family life and labor relations. The national economy they created subsequently made their vision of a highly personalized Christian responsibility increasingly anachronistic. But as late as 1832 a convert like Lewis Tappan would roam the streets and wharves of New York City distributing religious tracts.[13]

Women, who were the majority of converts throughout the Second Great Awakening and a large majority of all church members, played a crucial role in both facilitating male conversions and initiating reform. In the realm of religion, moral reform, and charity, there was an overlapping of spheres for evangelical men and women. Furthermore, the revivals minimized gender contrasts by encouraging for both sexes the freer expression of feeling and a common standard of personal righteousness.[14]

The styles of masculinity among evangelical men probably varied somewhat. For example, the circumstances of the abolitionists, embattled as a group, and of the small businessmen, struggling to survive in increasingly competitive markets, suggest divergent tendencies. The former encouraged tender fraternal support and preoccupation with communal righteousness; the latter, prudence, calculation, and self-control, all focused on self-advancement. If the abolitionists preached emotional expressiveness and a commitment to one's fellowman, the businessmen advised: waste not, want not; be wary rather than too expressive. The same outlook, exacerbated by a timidity born of prolonged dependence at home, characterized the "new middle class" sons who came of age in evangelical homes during the 1850s.[15]

Beyond these group variations in masculine expressiveness lies a larger question of how confidently or how defensively evangelical men promoted their conception of Christian manhood. The clergymen writing for the periodicals which increasingly depended on female readership expressed concern as early as the 1840s about loss of "manliness in thought." And they worried about accusations that they had become sentimental in appealing to feminine tastes. But during the heyday of the great revivals, the evangelical businessmen and moral reformers of the old middle class displayed an extraordinary confidence in the righteousness of their cause; clarity about the virtues required for salvation, economic success, and social order; and efficiency in organizing themselves to impose their values through public policy or to persuade others to accept them. While many of these businessmen and reformers—some of them clergymen—suffered great anxiety about their individual performances and futures, they did not doubt the superiority of their standards and way of life. This group confidence was constantly reinforced by contrast with the abhorrent swaggering rowdiness, heavy drinking, and taste for brutal sports frequent among the antebellum urban working class.[16]

Overall, evangelical males do not seem to have been seriously troubled about the feminization of their world initially. Before conversion, some had resisted unprecedented incursions into public space by evangelical women seeking to purify their communities. But these men subsequently joined campaigns for temperance and moral reform and endorsed female moral authority in rearing the young and making the home a haven for the gentler virtues. Evangelical males helped transform some previously all-male institutions which had had a tradition of tavern sociability, such as the fraternal orders Mark C. Carnes analyzes herein, to sober respectability in the 1830s and 1840s. Neither they nor those who initially resisted the change regarded it as "feminizing." Among one small minority within the evangelical world, the abolitionists, there is even evidence of deliberate attempts at more egalitarian marriages.[17]

The question of how uncomfortable or threatened evangelical men were with feminization in their social universe cannot be settled yet, however. In Richmond, for example, by the 1850s men had taken over the leadership of a number of women's causes like poor relief, had created dependent female auxiliaries for new organizations, and had prevented women from speaking in public. Motives cannot be assigned confidently, but Suzanne Lebsock assumes men were anxious about women's growing autonomy in Petersburg—a discomfort first evident within the churches, where women's importance was so obvious.[18]

The most serious threat to the authority of evangelical constructions of masculinity was the waning, by the 1850s, of that powerful sense of mission—to transform society as well as to convert souls—which fueled the great revivals earlier in the century. One of the clearest signals came in the changing tone of "polite society." The insistence on sincerity as the key to etiquette gave way to a growing acceptance of formality, even theatricality, as sufficient basis for social relations among the urban middle and upper classes. The earlier emphasis on the formation of character as a difficult process of self-mastery—understood by contemporaries as a "manly" achievement—now competed with a preoccupation with external appearance and refined manners. The emerging Victorian decorousness could easily be perceived as "feminine".[19]

Concern about the feminization of polite society may help explain the growing interest in sports in the 1840s and 1850s among adults of the respectable classes generally, regardless of religious persuasion. The protracted campaign in the urban press for sports as an antidote to softness and vice in rapidly growing cities had established in the public mind a relationship between athletics and physical and mental health. By the 1850s, leading New Englanders like Emerson, Edward Everett Hale, and Thomas Wentworth Higginson had called on Americans to adopt the "muscular Christianity" which had developed earlier in England. The *New York Herald* in 1859 argued that "the absence of those athletic and muscle developing sports so common among the youth of England undoubtedly tended to reduce our young men to effeminacy." By the Civil War, even evangelicals could be heard defending the moral benefits of "innocent" and "rational" recreation.[20]

However, the frequency with which the press and leading spokesmen stressed the desirability of athletic activity for women cautions against viewing this new enthusiasm for sports simply as an antidote to perceived threats to masculinity. While admonitions on the need to check effeminacy may in some cases reflect worries that the expanding influence of women was making young men effete, they also reflected patriotic anxiety about future dangers for a "sick, flabby race." Republican fears of decadence fostered by soft living and luxury were exacerbated by the spread of a more sedentary life through an expanding urban middle class. Traditionally, expression of those fears often made use of gendered language, characterizing indulgence in luxury as "voluptuousness" and "effeminate."[21]

Explicit gendered responses to a perceived feminization of society and culture do not loom large among adult middle-class males at midcentury. The "we/they" oppositions that distressed them most were those of class and ethnicity, not of gender.

If older males in evangelical households generally seem to have acquiesced to the expanded influence of women within the home and church-related institutions, boys and young men (the former quickly, the latter less immediately and more covertly) created compensatory worlds. As Anthony Rotundo shows in this volume, boys still living at home in households where fathers were absent during the day developed a "boy culture," partly in opposition to and as an escape from the now mother-dominated home. Rotundo perceives a dialogue between the values of the two spheres: boys shuttled between the mutual dependence and self-restraint of the home and the independence and emotional release of their own world. He believes that through this dialogue, boys learned how to live with divided loyalties and so cope with the adult world of divided gender spheres.

By the 1850s, young men as well as boys had reason to be troubled by the now sharp contrast between gender spheres and the dominance of the gentle virtues within the home. In that decade the proportion of males ages fifteen through nineteen who remained at home increased dramatically in Northern cities, in marked contrast to earlier decades, when many boys left home in their early teens to begin apprenticeships—and very often to largely escape adult supervision off the job by living in boardinghouses. This prolongation of dependence reflected the desire of parents to guide sons through more uncertain and longer paths to future occupations.[22]

The resultant delay in a young man's career and marriage occurred at the very moment when Evangelical Protestantism was losing the excitement which had so powerfully attracted young converts. Optimism about reforming the world tended to be replaced by a more anxious emphasis on prudent preparation for an unpredictable economic future in which maternal and evangelical advice would be tested in a hostile male-dominated marketplace. This defensive spirit appears in the establishment of voluntary associations like the YMCA which attempted to serve as surrogate homes for young men who lived alone amid the moral perils of the city.

In a changing world where fewer sons followed their fathers' occupations and where fathers spent longer days away from home, the journey toward manhood was more tortuous. Mark C. Carnes shows us herein that young men found help through the initiation rituals of male fraternal orders, which experienced an extraordinary expansion of membership during the last half of the century. Carnes argues that these rituals helped sons raised in feminized homes to resolve a cross-gender conflict by freeing them from the emotional ties of childhood and reconciling them to the stern realities of the adult world.

Although the rituals may represent opposition to the feminization of the home, that opposition seems to have been mostly unconscious. Carnes is equally impressed by the sentimentality which the rituals superimposed on stern patriarchal themes, a sentimentality closer to the spirit of the "Christian Gentleman" model of masculinity. The enormous popularity of these secret rituals among middle-class men at midcentury, when most working-class men sought more boisterous entertainment, suggests how thoroughly

Evangelical Protestantism had transformed middle-class society. Although some occupational subcultures within that class—the legal profession, for example—maintained a more overtly "macho" masculine ideal throughout the antebellum period, the general tendency among middle-class men was to stress the sentimental values to which men and women alike should conform.[23]

The Civil War was a major turning point for middle-class attitudes toward masculinity. The war itself not only put a premium on toughness and courage among soldiers, but allowed conservative bystanders to trumpet—now as patriots—ideals of prowess for which they had had few hearers in the heyday of evangelical reformism. And the lawyer-politician's skepticism about reform and idealism of most kinds became increasingly public and strident. But the use of virile rhetoric can obscure as much as it reveals, for the last half of the nineteenth century also witnessed a loss of independence for many middle-class men, increased subordination to the regimens of others in school and in the workplace, more homogenization in consumption and recreation, and extension beyond the home of the influence of women. The rougher forms of masculinity associated with preindustrial occupations lost ground as their former settings disappeared.[24]

Middle-class men after the Civil War moved toward an accommodation with the emerging world of a bureaucratized corporate capitalism—with its greater job security, consumer options, and leisure time in more comfortable homes—and simultaneously moved toward compensatory ideas and fantasies of male independence, adventure, and virility. The New Woman and the New Man did not take shape in the 1890s as a sudden, spontaneous reaction to a stifling Victorian culture; the foundations were being laid in reconstructions of gender and gender relations in a variety of settings and groups in the postwar years.[25]

The Civil War itself was a major catalyst for change in norms of masculinity. Where the fraternal orders provided an initiation into a patriarchal manhood through a symbolic ordeal, war put many young men through actual ordeals which combined murderous male conflict with male camaraderie. The war remained "the central event of this generation's lives." Its consequences for national culture are suggested by the fusion of a previously more pacific evangelical righteousness in the Battle Hymn of the Republic with a martial imagery which would spread everywhere in the Gilded Age, from the Salvation Army to "captains of industry."[26]

We are on more speculative ground in trying to determine the extent to which the veterans' military experience shaped their return to civilian life, because almost nothing has been written about their postwar experience. We do not know how pervasive was the toughening reported by a young patrician like O. W. Holmes, Jr., nor how frequent his starker view of life, society, and manliness. Certainly his scorn for what he perceived as the cowardliness of the lower orders, and his early conservative social Darwinism, were atypical. But for the legal profession the war did seem to produce a cohort of hardened, tough-minded veterans.[27]

In national politics after the war this tough-mindedness entailed an explicit gender contrast: "real" men stood at the opposite pole temperamentally from women. Males who favored the gentler virtues or who spent much time in women's sphere were thought to be emasculated. This contrast appeared as early as 1872 in the aspersions cast by professional politicians on the patrician reformers who nominated Horace Greeley. It was followed in 1877 by Senator Roscoe Conkling's famous indictment of George William Curtis of *Harper's Weekly,* one of genteel America's favorite writers, as one of "the man milliners, the dilettanti, and carpet knights of politics" who "forget that parties are not built up by deportment, or by ladies' magazines, or gush!" The reformers were also identified with high culture, which was supposed to have made them impractical and ineffectual; in the eyes of the politicians, "culture is feminine and cultivated men tend to be effeminate."[28]

But while politicians in the 1870s could scorn those men whom they saw as identified with a feminine conception of life or feminine interests, they could not ignore the political power of women. Women proved to be formidable opponents when they could appeal to a dominant cultural value like respect for the purity of women or for protection of the family from abuse by a violent, drunken husband and father. If politicians and male writers in the Gilded Age often drew a sharp gender contrast, they did so in the face of women's increasing demands for change in male behavior and in public policy associated with it. The social purity movement's defeat of regulated prostitution—which was long preferred by the medical profession—was only the first and most dramatic evidence of the growing ability of women in the late nineteenth century to move outside their sphere to fight for protection of the home.

It is not surprising that women's first major victories occurred where traditional male prerogatives like patronage of prostitutes conflicted with public values like the sanctity of marriage. Nor is it surprising that the male medical profession succeeded in its legislative campaign against abortion, which violated the ideal of motherhood. Outside of politics, there was a similar contrast between, on one hand, men's easier approval of female missionary and charitable efforts, which contributed to social order, and, on the other hand, men's tendency to be critical of female self-improvement efforts, such as literary clubs, which might make women more independent and less concerned with home duties.[29]

The temperance movement, especially under Frances Willard's leadership of the WCTU, progressively widened the range of issues that were deemed to be women's special responsibility based on their role as mothers and guardians of the home. By the 1890s, that expanded responsibility included the community surrounding the home. The label "municipal housekeeping" expressed the increasingly successful domestication of local politics as an appropriate sphere for women. The depression of the 1890s converted women from Gilded Age antivice crusaders and mugwumps into progressive New Women who pursued a wide range of educational, labor, and neighborhood issues related to women's concern with the home and children. Well before men finally conceded suffrage, the expanded political activity of women had eroded the idea of politics, and especially the half-century-old elevation of partisanship, as a peculiarly masculine preserve.[30]

Beyond their collective actions, many women during the late nineteenth century influenced the legal balance of power in gender relations by petitioning for divorce and by serving as witnesses in divorce cases. In dealing with these petitions, as Robert Griswold shows (this volume), "judicial patriarchs" expanded the interpretation of cruelty as grounds for divorce, thereby pushing their fellowmen toward standards of considerateness in marriage that were closer to the gentle virtues expected of women. Responding to women's demands for protection against cold, rude, domineering, or violent husbands, the judges agreed that men must improve their behavior even if it meant sacrificing traditional male prerogatives.[31]

By requiring greater sensitivity to wives' expressed concerns, judges reduced earlier gender contrasts in expectations for marital behavior. Whether their increasing accommodation of the marital standards of women and of Evangelical Protestantism reflected personal persuasion or grudging acquiescence to what they could not argue against publicly, they created a new definition of responsible manhood. So far as this new definition found wider acceptance among men—and not merely as a legal norm—the foundations for a New Man who could coexist more easily with a more independent New Woman were being laid during the late nineteenth century.

The norms for a responsible manhood which appear in courtroom testimony in divorce cases and in the judges' decisions seem to have become widely diffused in the late nineteenth century. The distinctive antebellum styles of Southern manliness eroded to such a degree that John Hughes (this volume) discovers in the records of the Alabama Insane Hospital no substantial deviation from what has been found in studies of northern populations. A rather different kind of "softening" was in progress among Northern middle-class men after the Civil War, a softening of earlier attitudes toward leisure and consumption. As expanding prosperity undermined the old mentality of scarcity, spokesmen for a more relaxed attitude arose from within the ranks of Evangelical Protestantism. Characters in *Norwood* (1867), a novel by the popular preacher Henry Ward Beecher, ingeniously argue that self-indulgence is morally preferable to philanthropy: a grand home and beautiful garden provide a salutary and civilizing example for all.[32]

For young middle-class men, however, the greatest problem posed by the changing economy after the Civil War was not leisure but choice of vocation. The lingering free labor ideology presumed that most men ultimately would find self-employment in the professions, business, manufacturing, and agriculture; it did not anticipate the continued subservience of industrial workers, especially not of the middle-class employees of the burgeoning corporations. Nor did it speak to the problem of frequent, repeated failures by those entrepreneurs who did try to launch themselves independently, but increasingly found they could not withstand economic fluctuations or compete with larger firms.

The gendered implications of occupational choice after the Civil War appear in the rapidly expanding federal civil service, the first sexually integrated bureaucracy. Male applicants often viewed white-collar work as a temporary expedient, one dictated by family hardship, frequently a business failure. A writer in 1873 described the government clerk as someone who "has no independence while in office, no manhood. . . . He must openly avow his implicit faith in all his superiors, on pain of dismissal, and must cringe and fawn upon them. . . ."[33] Yet the men who remained in government service rather quickly learned to replace the traditional notion of success through self-employment with a new notion emphasizing ascent through the bureaucracy. It permitted competition with women(so long as proprieties were observed), creating a "new kind of middle-class culture— one that began to dissolve the barriers between the separate spheres of nineteenth-century middle-class America."[34]

Unlike the civil service, the ministry still promised a measure of independence as a profession—although its apparent identification with the feminization of American culture at midcentury made it seem a less manly calling for some. But here, too, in the late nineteenth century a new mentality appeared among young men who saw themselves as reforming the church's conception of its social responsibility. And as Susan Curtis shows herein, many of the leaders of the mature social gospel who came of age in the 1880s had grappled with a fear of not measuring up to their fathers. Like many of the civil service applicants, they too had seen their own or their fathers' businesses fail, despite conscientious effort, or they had worked at a variety of jobs without sufficient sense of reward.

When these men turned to the ministry, they rejected both religious and economic individualism. Initially, their social gospel made little headway among churchgoers, who continued to believe that ministers should confine their efforts to saving individual souls. But many laymen changed their minds during the depression of the 1890s, when application of the social gospel to civic crusades seemed one way of uniting a now frighteningly divided society. The ministry, threatened with increasing marginality in a secularizing society, found a new relevance. And the social gospelers themselves, as Curtis notes, found personal satisfaction in teamwork for reform, creating a host of new organizations as well as cooperating with universities, settlement houses, and other established agencies.[35]

The ministers saw neither their cooperative ethos nor the Jesus who inspired it as feminine; the Son of God was a man's man, and reform was manly work. Reacting against sentimental portrayals of Jesus, social gospelers emphasized his masculine physique and hardiness as well as his anger in denouncing evildoers. By finding a more rugged masculinity in Jesus, social gospelers provided the ministry itself—and all men engaged in religiously motivated service—with a self-image closer to other constructions of masculinity at the turn of the century. By the 1920s, men of the cloth could be great guys in Rotary and Kiwanis.

Unlike clergymen, lawyers before the 1880s had not been displaced in public leadership, nor had they suffered doubts as to their manliness. But toward the end of the century an important minority experienced a change in occupational role which threatened their traditional sense of independence. The new elite of corporate counsel not only withdrew from the old combat of courtroom litigation but also served entrepreneurs who were perceived by the public—and often by the lawyers themselves—as their masters. This elite, as Michael Grossberg suggests (this volume), compensated for this perceived loss of manliness by further emphasizing the toughness of the legal profession, and especially of initiation into it. Their preferred style of masculinity expressed their social Darwinian view of the world as an arena where men struggled for survival, in contrast to the social gospelers' view of a social environment which could be reshaped, cooperatively, by men who emulated Jesus' combination of hardiness and unsentimentality with love for others.

A further spur to emphasis on toughness among lawyers—and to hyperbole in masculine rhetoric generally—was the fight to keep women out of the bar, or at least to confine them to auxiliary work or to clearly marginal "feminine" specialties. In the typically exaggerated gender contrast employed in this fight, male lawyers insisted that their profession required strength of body and nerve, a capacity to endure insult and contact with baser natures, and an unfeeling cold-bloodedness—none of which women were thought to possess. Women's attempts to acquire these traits would cause them to lose their natural kindness, refinement, and delicacy, thus unfitting them for marriage and motherhood.

This masculine rhetoric reveals deeply held male prejudices, as well as a fear of women's gaining equality in the workplace. But whether it indicates how middle-class men, including lawyers, thought about gender spheres at the turn of the century must be questioned. The preoccupation with virility frequently coexisted in practice, as Margaret Marsh herein shows, with increased masculine participation in domesticity within more companionate marriages, especially in the suburbs. Some of the individuals frequently—and selectively—quoted in support of interpretations of hypermasculinity as reflecting a "crisis of masculinity" also supported "domestic masculinity." "Be a man," lawyer and senator Albert Beveridge exhorted in his book of advice, *The Life of a Young Man* (1906). But as Marsh notes, Beveridge also devoted a chapter to "The New Home" in the suburbs, where the young man "will spend all of his extra time, listening to his wife play the piano, reading, and not least, playing with the children."

Even without the direct testimony Marsh offers, one could infer the probable emergence of domestic masculinity from her three preconditions: a shifting ideal of marriage which emphasized companionship rather than separate spheres, sufficient job security for men to give more attention to their families, and suburban homes where that attention could be focused more easily and comfortably. In addition, as Marsh suggests in another essay, male experts on the family promoted suburban life as a means of reemphasizing the family as women's primary concern. The experts were alarmed by radical feminist proposals for collective housekeeping, which seemed to encourage individualism rather than preoccupation with the family.[36]

Late-nineteenth-century changes in recreation encouraged activities which could be shared by all members of the family. The parks movement was one of the earliest, followed by the campaign for Sunday opening of museums and other cultural activities. Ostensibly aimed at providing more uplifting recreation for the working class, Sunday opening probably was of more immediate benefit to middle-class families. By the 1880s, entertainment entrepreneurs like Tony Pastor and B. F. Keith, who promoted vaudeville, realized the potential profit in amusements cleaned up so as to be morally suitable for the whole family or for unescorted women and children. A similar commercial responsiveness to women's concerns, already so effectively expressed in the "social purity" movement, no doubt led theater owners in the 1880s to agree finally to abolish the third tier for prostitutes.[37]

Perhaps the most telling evidence of how even the most cynical entrepreneur might be drawn to cater to middle-class respectability by bringing the sexes together in recreation appears in professional baseball. As late as the Progressive years, baseball-club owners sought white-collar patrons who had the leisure to attend games on weekdays and pay the high fifty-cent admission; one means was to attract female spectators who would "enhance business by improving crowd behavior and by inducing their gentlemen friends to take them to ball games." As the century drew to an end, men and women of the respectable classes increasingly came together in public places, from parks and department stores to sporting events and vaudeville halls.[38]

They also, as Margaret Marsh shows, joined cultural, social, and recreational clubs which brought husbands and wives together, rather than separating them as was more common in the Gilded Age. This increase in heterosociality did not come quickly, easily, or without continuing criticism. But it clearly softened the boundaries between gender spheres, creating a much larger area of overlap in which men and women could participate in activities normally associated with each other's sphere. For example, by the turn of the century the connection between health, morality, and athletics had been so thoroughly accepted that physical culturists like Bernarr McFadden had a ready-made audience when they called for exercise by both sexes at all ages.

However, gender differences continued not only in those sports deemed more appropriate for men (such as football) or for women (such as tennis), but in the very approach to sports. Some of the earlier proponents of the sporting ideology deplored the new preoccupation with performance and winning. They claimed that it resulted in an extreme competitiveness which was individually and socially destructive; the proponents of athletics for women, especially women physical educators, tended to agree. They insisted that the woman athlete played "for the joy of playing" and so achieved a fuller life. Correspondingly, they favored the separation of women's sports from men's to avoid the hazards of professionalism and the subordination of the quest for health to the ideal of winning. Women were now more similar to men in their sports, but differences in gender norms persisted.[39]

In the Progressive years the ongoing reformation of gender spheres made the home seem more like the male workplace. Experts in domestic economy treated the home as an environment to be investigated and managed on scientific principles by a woman whose approach would be similar to that of any other good professional, male or female—and these professional had their own university departments. But, ironically, the very advance of specialization within academia which ensured their expert status also facilitated their sexual segregation. At the University of Chicago, for example, disciplinary boundaries in the 1890s were still ill-defined; sociology included "sanitary science," which Dean Marion Talbot hoped could become the focus for a variety of disciplines in the physical and social sciences. Those male faculty members who favored segregation of the sexes within higher education were relieved when the push toward specialization—which Talbot herself did not feel justified in opposing—eliminated sanitary science from sociology and left Talbot in charge of a new department of household administration.[40]

Combined with the continuing assumption that women were more sensitive to the needs of others, the new emphasis on the rationalization of the household carries us close to the expectations for businessmen's wives which the Lynds would find in Muncie, Indiana, in the 1920s. Maintaining the family's status and its standard of consumption, which was essential to the husband's occupational success, required women—like their husbands—to be aggressive and to appear frequently in public. The spheres of home and marketplace remained gendered, but the difference in spirit was diminished, and the expectation of an active partnership was made more explicit than it had been in the middle of the nineteenth century. A new group of family "experts" heightened expectations for marital partnership by articulating a new ideal of family democracy which called for "companionship, compatibility, equality of privilege and responsibility and mutuality in sexual gratification . . . " These experts began to evaluate the family according to the quality of interaction rather than the fulfillment of economic functions.[41]

Although the reformation of middle-class gender spheres was not complete until the 1920s, the most important components of a new set of expectations for masculinity were present by the turn of the century. Mass-circulation magazines carried these new expectations to middle-class readers everywhere; the expectations became a unifying national norm, cutting across continuing variations in gender construction in occupational and other subcultures within this class. Its ascendancy meant fewer alternative ways of defining masculinity were available, compared to the diversity of norms in the mid-nineteenth century. And because it combined divergent, potentially conflicting requirements, it could be more difficult to fulfill than some previous norms, whether of the tougher or more sentimental varieties.

In this new set of expectations the good man would be the kind of team worker required in an increasingly bureaucratized society. Yet he would maintain a virile demeanor, cool and, where necessary, tough. Work would remain crucial to his identity. He would enjoy athletics and especially competitive sports, as spectator if not as participant, and he would initiate his sons into the manly art of ball throwing. He would admire physical fitness and, generally, be as concerned as his wife with the health and recreation of family members. Above all, he would see the family as central in everyday life outside of work, expecting marriage to be companionate and, within limits, a partnership (though one in which his dominance was unchallenged). As the prudery associated with Victorian respectability eroded during the Progressive Era, one further requirement was added to this norm: the good man must be concerned also with helping his wife achieve sexual fulfillment.

How easily and frequently men lived up to the various dimensions of this norm remains to be determined. Some of the more popular accounts of men within the home early in the twentieth century, like Clarence Day's retrospective *Life with Father,* portrayed men as humorously inept in domestic activities and relations. That may help explain the tendency of men to develop masculine specialities within the domestic sphere, like master of the barbecue or director of family vacations. But the very need to define new specialities within the home also suggests the tendency to expand the areas of competence required of good spouses and parents of either sex.[42]

The new unifying norm of masculinity at the turn of the century did not, of course, immediately or completely overturn what remained of earlier constructions of masculinity, nor did it define precisely all the boundaries between manly and unmanly behavior. But it did provide a relatively pervasive common ideal, one that had profound consequences for male socialization. Coupled with changes in the passage from boyhood to adulthood, the new ideal smoothed the transition to adulthood for the majority of boys. As Anthony Rotundo observes, "boy culture" had by the late nineteenth century been co-opted and standardized by adult males; many of its lessons could now be found in books. Motivated partly by fears of "feminization" in schools staffed largely by women, adult males sought to create offsetting masculine influences in the socialization of boys by organizing their play. In the process, adults increasingly devised the rules for the games boys played, and, as formal organizations multiplied, actually began to supervise the games. The school year grew to nine months, more boys went to school, and the schools' age-graded classes discouraged older boys from playing with younger ones and teaching them the ways of the world.

From boyhood through adulthood, the careers of males now were characterized by increasing standardization, bureaucratization, and security. But male reaction to these long-term trends is insufficient to explain the frequency of expressions of hypermasculinity from the 1890s to the Great War. Long before then, men and boys of every age found compensatory excitement and means of escape, vicariously identifying with the exploits and adventures of military or fictional heroes.[43]

The more immediate provocation for hypermasculinity at the turn of the century was the growing influence and movement of women outside the home, and especially the overt rebellion of a minority against Victorian norms and ultimately against any form of male dominance. The New Woman of the 1890s had a mixed reception even among men who professed to welcome her. How much more unsettling was the openly blasphemous feminism of the avant-garde in the 1910s which "partook of the free-ranging spirit of rebellion of the time." No man could have predicted that the radical feminist vision of full economic and sexual equality, as espoused by Charlotte Perkins Gilman, Olive Schreiner, Ellen Key, and others, would give way in the 1920s to tamer prescriptions for a postsuffrage feminism, such as that of Dorothy Bromley's women, who combined marriage, career, children, and French chic.[44]

Hypermasculinity in the Progressive years was doubly reactive, to long-term change and to a very specific contemporary sense of threat to male dominance. There was indeed anxiety about what seemed to be happening to gender norms and gender relations. But calling it a "crisis" seems misleading, given the evidence we now have that a new class of experts of both sexes tended to redefine both the sexual division of labor and family relationships in ways that did not end male dominance and that in important respects perpetuated deference to male desires. Furthermore, from the 1890s onward many middle-class men were discovering that some initially upsetting aspects of women's expanding sphere—as in politics through "municipal housekeeping"—served their own concerns about social order.

More remarkable than the expressions of anxiety about masculinity in the Progressive years—and we really don't know yet how deep or widespread the concern was—is how relatively undisturbed men seem to have been in the 1920s by the dominant redefinitions of gender relations. That conclusion is not incompatible with recognition of the fierce, even vicious, hostility which women encountered when they pursued unpopular causes, like opposition to American participation in the First World War. And hostility could be just as intense when women's causes conflicted with a male group's sense of prerogative, as it did in the AMA's bitter battle against the modest recommendations of the Sheppard-Towner Act. But the anger—and especially the conviction that it was justified—with which some middle-class males attacked whatever seemed to exemplify too much independence for women suggests how conservative the new social-science conceptions of gender relations ultimately were, and how little they threatened masculine dominance.[45]

The feminism of the 1910s was undercut in the 1920s by the new ascendancy of experts, especially in psychology and family sociology. For example, the influential quantifiable measures of masculinity and femininity devised by Lewis Terman and his associates "incorporated long-standing biases that women's 'adjustment' consisted in serving men's needs and pleasures." With that bias, the new partnership of men and women in companionate marriages did not challenge male dominance. Family sociologists emphasized "psychological adjustment" through familial satisfaction of emotional needs as the means of maintaining social order.[46]

Historians of masculinity need to recognize, as women's historians already have, how much the shift from a moral to a scientific perspective undercut, by the 1920s, change in gender relations and related social reforms. Supported by Evangelical Protestantism, the ideology of domesticity gave women's reforms that could be associated with protection of the home and the family moral force, as well as legitimacy; that made it easier for women to turn their causes into crusades and made it more difficult for opponents to defend their opposition. The new social sciences tended to reify conventional gender stereotypes, reinforce gendered division of labor, and discourage moral treatment of social issues. Gone was the moral confidence and rhetoric which not only gave Victorian middle-class culture its shape for more than a century but which also had empowered the women's movement in converting others to various reforms.[47]

Although this shift to the "scientific" perspective of "experts" is beyond the scope of the new research in this book, I mention it to suggest, again, how overblown contemporary views of the "crisis of masculinity" were. Ideals of family democracy and companionate marriage preserved the gendered division of labor and male dominance while partially accommodating women's aims. The historian must take male cries of anguish about the state of manliness seriously, but not at face value. Ironically, in the very years of loudest lamentation, a change which many young women saw as a new freedom made them in important ways *more* dependent on men. When courtship had taken place in the home, women had controlled the terms; in modern dating, well-established among the middle-class by the 1920s, men had the initiative, paid the bill for entertainment, and correspondingly expected women to defer to their wishes whenever possible. The "big spender," seated in an expensive sports car with a girl at his side, would become an icon of modern masculinity.[48]

The middle-class definition of manliness in the twentieth century seemed to encompass easily virility, domestic comfort, and constantly expanding consumption. What little we know so far about constructions of masculinity among the working class by the turn of the century suggests no such comfortable accommodation of ideals with changing circumstances. Instead, as the essays in this volume by Mary Blewett and Ava Baron indicate, through the late nineteenth century different groups of workers found themselves increasingly unable to maintain older ideals against the onslaughts of employers. Sometimes, as Baron shows, a group of workers adopted a new definition of masculinity which seemed immediately useful in contesting employers' arguments, but which in the long run would trap the workers themselves. The general tendency seems to have been toward a narrower and less secure definition, which had unhappy implications for gender relations within the working class.

When workers defined the man as the sole provider for his family, they made his wife's employment a disgrace to him. The Victorian notion of gender spheres was adopted where it was least feasible. Working-class families too often needed more than one wage earner; moreover, as standards of consumption rose during the twentieth century, so did pressures for wives to work. Increasingly, working-class wives faced the struggle of combining a job with full responsibility for child rearing and housekeeping while yet deferring to the ultimate authority of their husbands even in the home—and this during the same period when companionate marriages became the norm for the business class.[49]

Mass media threatened male wage earners' dignity by constantly exposing them to middle-class standards of achievement, consumption, and leisure. Moreover, the class bias of those standards increasingly was obscured by national heroes—from Theodore Roosevelt to Ronald Reagan—whose style of masculinity seemed to cut across class lines. On the other hand, the commercialization of leisure was a slow process which the working class itself shaped to some extent before the Great Depression; the movies, for example, provided characters and themes with which male wage earners could identify, even in depictions of upward mobility. And the saloon, the church, and the ethnic community probably continued to reinforce previous norms of masculinity for the immigrant working class in the 1920s. It was these immigrants' children and grandchildren who led the way toward fuller participation in the mainstream consumer culture depicted in the movies and who felt resentment that they could afford so little.[50]

Male wage earners in the twentieth century might doubt their manliness as providers for their families, but they never as a group confronted a general perception that they were unmasculine. Male homosexuals increasingly did. By the turn of the century, urban homosexual underworlds began to attract attention both from sensational journalism and from the medical profession. That attention was focused especially on men who adopted women's sexual and cultural roles and had a well-developed collective life.

Medical conceptualization of the "invert" who reversed gender roles was built on the folk wisdom that males who desired sex only with other males therefore wished to be women and were effeminate.

The identification of effeminacy with homosexuality was not complete as late as World War I; for example, expressions of intimacy which the U.S. Navy identified as both effeminate and perverted continued to be regarded by many clergymen as fraternal and Christian. The Navy's prosecution of homosexuals at its Newport, Rhode Island, training center in 1919–20 revealed "a series of disputes over the boundaries between homosociality and homosexuality in the relations of men and over the standards by which their masculinity would be judged." But given the already heightened emphasis on virility in middle-class constructions of male gender, the historian can surmise an increasing tendency from the 1920s onward to worry about effeminacy in any form as symptomatic of homosexuality—increasingly perceived as a biological deviation from "normal" masculinity.[51]

Summary generalization of a new middle-class norm for masculinity in the twentieth century necessarily oversimplifies. It ignores, for example, continuing variations in gender construction among occupational subcultures, such as those of doctors, salesmen, bookkeepers, and engineers. And it ignores the room for variation within any gender norm which historian Charles Rosenberg has so persuasively analyzed for the Victorian norms of "Masculine Achiever" and "Christian Gentlemen." Beyond more obvious—and extreme—variations such as the sexual athlete and the "big spender," we need to learn more about, for example, the way businessmen by the 1920s incorporated what previously had been seen as women's distinctive contribution of service into male-exclusive organizations like the Rotary, Kiwanis, and Lions clubs.[52]

It is sufficient for this argument that the twentieth-century definition of masculinity was, most obviously by comparison with multiple alternative conceptions at midcentury, a compromise or at least a balancing act which brought together apparently contradictory elements: domestic masculinity and the preoccupation with virility. However complementary these elements were in some ways, they clearly invited different emphases in different male personalities.

The linking during the twentieth century of virility and domesticity in one broadly unifying norm does have an exclusionary consequence for males. The man who fails in Christian love can ask forgiveness, and he who fails in business can try again. But the boy or man who dislikes competitive sports or virile postures has little choice but to affect "manly" interests and behavior, and to hope that these affectations will not be exposed. Options which existed in nineteenth-century concepts of masculinity vanished during the early twentieth century, and in some cases came to be stigmatized as abnormal. The prudent Victorian clerk or shopkeeper who regarded sports as a waste of time, and perhaps as immoral, would now be obliged to keep his views to himself. The abolitionists' variant of the female world of love and ritual would by the 1920s be viewed as "sissy" at best, "queer" at worst. On the other hand, there was always the possibility that the values and activities associated with domesticity would be given more emphasis at the expense of preoccupation with virility. The abolitionists' hopes for fraternalism and for truly egalitarian marriages might be resurrected in modern forms.

TWELVE

On Men's History and Women's History

Nancy F. Cott

The founding assumption of this collection of essays on masculinity must be the same as the basic premise of women's studies—that gender *matters* in social and historical analysis. Gender matters because the disparate situations of the sexes cause them to experience or perceive events or circumstances differently. The differences, similarities, and overlap between men's and women's experiences and viewpoints must be systematically investigated if we are to understand the fullness of human culture, development, and society. For two decades women's history has aimed to institute these perceptions in place of the assumption in traditional scholarship that the male is sufficient to represent the human norm. Now it is up to "men's history" to show that the latter assumption has also obscured or distorted the historical record we thought we knew about men's lives.

This generation's scholarship in women's history can be described as having two vectors, as being about women *and* about gender. It has intended to uncover women "hidden from history"—their lives, thoughts, and accomplishments—*and* it has intended to discover and analyze the patterns of social organization of the sexes that we now call gender or the sex/gender system.[1] Both efforts have been necessary, and complementary: without investigation into women's lives, the functions and meanings of sex in the social order could not be explained; and without examination of the social aspects and power relations of women's and men's interactions, women's lives could not be understood. Besides new empirical research, women's history has also required reconsideration of conventional historical concepts, methods, and data in light of women's experiences, and the formulation of new paradigms which will include both sexes and take seriously the analytical concept of gender.

If scholars in women's history have been addressing two lacks—the need to know about women, and the need to know about gender—scholars in "men's history" do not seem to face the same double task. There is little motive to unmask or uncover, since the history of men as human individuals has been constantly investigated. There is, however, a great need to

• 205 •

NANCY F. COTT

situate men's history in an explication of the sex/gender system. In contrast to women—who are too often seen only in terms of their sex—men have been the *un*marked sex. Since we know so little about men as gendered beings, "men's history" must be about the social construction of masculinity and manhood rather than simply about men as a group.

There is every opportunity for salutary intersection between "men's" and women's history. Focused work in "men's history" should make the history of the social relations of the sexes more feasible. As much as practitioners in women's history have in theory embraced their double task,[2] the awesome work of uncovering women's lives has often taken precedence. But where practitioners in women's history had to invent the use of gender as a category of historical analysis, current writers of men's history find the concept already set before them. Too, historians considering the construction of masculinity can be wary of the false steps of early ventures in women's history: the mistaking of images for realities, the mistaking of ideology for social life, or the assumption of universal gender definitions unmodified by markers of ethnicity or class or race or region.

The risk that gender will be defined in falsely universalizing ways seems less in men's than in women's history. Where historians of women may be predisposed to assume that gender was the significant determinant of whatever they investigate, in men's history other, more familiar, competing categories—politics, race, region, and class, to name just a few—crowd the frame of reference in any consideration of motivation or causation. These, crosscutting the category of male gender, induce a healthy, constructive skepticism and force the historian to ask: Which men are we talking about? How does male gender intersect with other analytic categories? Common recognition of diversity among males makes unlikely any assumption that all men as men share the same consciousness or behavior, even if the salience of gender in socialization or social organization is being stressed. A universalizing gender definition makes no more sense applied to women than to men. Free of such Platonic ideals, we can move toward a history which makes clear that social relations and power relations between the sexes interact with other social categorizations.

The tendency of essays in this collection to describe the "man's sphere" and the "woman's sphere" as though these were distinct physical sites— rather than ideological constructions about propriety—can probably be pinned on the earlier historiography in women's history. Women's historians are leaving behind this peculiar reification. The understanding of "spheres" as geographical more than ideological—as though life was physically divided into two arenas—was a reductive move, further exaggerated by equating the man's sphere with the "public," the woman's sphere with

(margin note: warnings?)

(margin note: False universalization)

the "private." Most recently, investigation of women outside the prosperous circles of the urban Northeast, and greater stress on women's combination of market-oriented work with social reproduction and on the two sexes' sharing of familial economic burdens, has got beyond the notion that "woman's sphere" was a defined point to which every woman was manacled. (I am thinking here of such work as Elizabeth Pleck's, Joan Jensen's, Nancy Hewitt's, Tom Dublin's, and Nancy Osterud's.)[3] Historians of women have lately been trying to distinguish between "woman's sphere" and women's culture—the latter something more portable or pervasive than geographical.[4] Perhaps men's historians ought to do the same.

We certainly have to distinguish between what is exclusively male culture and what is "public"—the two are not coterminous, although a male viewpoint, past or present, might conflate them. An early exemplar (not to say pioneer) of gendered history, John Faragher's *Women and Men on the Overland Trail,* explicitly pointed out this fallacy. Reading through men's documents, Faragher found that women rarely appeared salient in the collective work of the overland emigrants; but by reading women's documents he discovered that women composed an essential working half of the collective, *public,* effort.[5] The public, of course, may stretch far and wide, to religion and recreation as well as the market and politics. To equate the public with the "man's sphere" is to posit that all women were behind the closed doors of home. This is an absurdity easily countered by pictorial evidence, such as the nineteenth-century paintings of rural and urban life displayed at the Whitney Museum several years ago.[6] These genre paintings frequently pictured women outdoors (peddlers, for instance), directly contradicting the many contemporaneous texts in which women dwelled only at the private domestic hearth. The language of men's and women's "spheres" had as much to do with the ruling fiction of differentiation between the sexes as it did with physical sites—perhaps more. In the dominant prescription of gender complementarity, whatever characteristics or activities pertained to one sex were not to pertain to the other.

When using the terms "woman's sphere" and "man's sphere" we ought to ask in what sense, really, that possessive ending is meant—men's and women's. The sense of exclusive possession? or of belonging? or of domination? It is important to stress the extent to which women *were* present in public—on the street, in the workplace, in the courts. But one must also ask, *Which* women were in public, when, and why? and Who saw them there?[7] Conversely, men were not absent from the "private" realm. Several papers here emphasize the private household as a female space from which men felt excluded or alienated, to an extent that seems to me to exaggerate an ideological and psychological construction into a physical reality. The notion that there was a concrete "woman's sphere"—i.e., the private home—that was not also "man's sphere" is not tenable. Even where nineteenth-century men might feel the effect of their womenfolk's standards of taste, they held legal and patriarchal power. Through decades of paeans to women's halo of domesticity, the maxim "a man's home is his castle" stood firm, all of its implications about women's and children's duty and service intact. Men's dominion over the home was perhaps even more readily enforced legally than was their dominion in the state and the market.

The essays here are rather more about men than about gender, but they indicate routes toward the goal of a "gendered history." The essays begin to remove the "unmarked" quality of men and illuminate them as gendered subjects. Yacavone, for instance, re-views "friendship" in the mid-nineteenth century and makes it clear that what is at issue is *male* friendship, intimacy between men which informs male identity and definition. Rotundo prevents us from generalizing about boyhood as simply an age-group experience and attunes us to boyhood as male socialization, dynamically related to the circumstances of adult men and women. Carnes forces reevaluation of all-male voluntary organizations as constituted not merely circumstantially *of* men but substantively *about* men, and about rituals of affirming maleness. What should our path of reasoning be, once the unmarkedness of the male sex is ended? Beyond the fascination of the new perspective, what is the significance of finding that the construction of manliness is involved in a phenomenon being investigated, whether that phenomenon be friendship, childhood, or voluntary organization? How should we assign causal priority or significance to gender determination, as compared, for instance, to region or class? To raise such questions is to ask what is the justification or promise of looking into the history of men as men. How does it parallel or differ from the promise of women's history?

The engine driving women's history is the possibility of transforming history as a whole, by means of seeing the formerly unseen, looking from women's viewpoints. The promise is that coming around from the conventional perspective to that of women's history will equip us to discover what *really* happened, or what it really meant. Perhaps the justification for a history of manhood will be parallel. Finding gender the decisive variable, a history of men as gendered subjects may promise to be truly transformative, making known elements fall together—as in a kaleidoscope—in an entirely new pattern. An alternative reasoning is that acknowledging the gendered nature of men's activities will illuminate all their arenas of life, but emphasize the contingency of gender determination, making it one influential variable among others. A third possible justification, stressing method more than narrative, might be to argue that emphasis on the gendered nature of male beings is the best way to bridge the categories of the private and the public.

This last points directly to the advantages of focusing on men in order to get to the sex/gender system. The public and the private are more obviously inseparable when we look at men's lives than when we look at women's lives—if only because we tend more readily to focus on men's participation in public, while admitting they have private character. If the boundary between private and public does become more elusive when men are studied as gendered subjects, that may focus needed attention on it. Demarcation between "public" and "private" has been a basic premise of modern life, but without consistent or unanimously shared definitions or boundaries. In Anglo-American law, and therefore in much of our common usage, "public" means what pertains to the state (the public interest), and "private" means what pertains to individual property rights (a private interest). In equally common usage, "public" includes both sides of the dichotomy just mentioned—includes both the state and the market—and "private" designates the personal and familial. For historians to subject this vexed area to historical scrutiny through the sign system of gender would be a great leap forward.

In doing so historians might clarify other large themes regarding American society and culture—themes such as individualism. The essays in this collection have—for the time being—made me think about individualism and the construction of social order in the United States in a certain fashion of gendered inquiry. Tony Rotundo's point about the internal hierarchy of boys' worlds started my thinking. Rotundo points out that "boy culture" was divided by ethnicity, geography, and class, as well as by size and skill; he remarks on the "pecking orders" that boys established through constant competition and individual striving and combat. (Michael Grossberg's depiction of the competitive construction of pecking order among lawyers in the late nineteenth century echoes this image, too.) Rotundo reasons that the competitive interaction in "boy culture" replicated (or presaged) the entrepreneurial marketplace: despite the ways in which "boy culture" poised itself against the values of the middle-class adult male world, he suggests, it ultimately prepared middle-class boys to function in individualistic, competitive, entrepreneurial society.

Since I found Rotundo's portrayal of "boy culture" solid and persuasive, I wondered if it was relevant also to working-class boys. If, however, a similar "boy culture" existed for working-class boys—a big *if*—then how did it produce the male adult outlook that Ava Baron found among unionized printers, an outlook not entirely individualistic but rather conjoining self-interest in a shared community of interest? Not only Baron's depiction but others in recent labor history—for instance, David Montgomery's writing on skilled workers in urban industrial areas, or Steven Hahn's writing on rural yeomanry—show those adult men's values to be not strictly individualistic but connected to the welfare of a class of men as a whole.[8]

We tend to posit individualism and group culture as mutually exclusive, but I think this deserves reconsideration.[9] Rotundo's evidence for "boy culture," for instance, shows "herding" activities (protective of the group) as well as individualistic competition. Of course, one gains individual identity by belonging in, being "like," a certain group—as well as by being unlike other groups. Boy culture was (ironically) as much created by domesticity as restricted by it; the boys relied on distinguishing themselves from the "home" group and from adult men. (Similarly, the unionized printers who are Baron's subjects knew who they were as men by distinguishing themselves both from women and from boys.)

If groups are, as I would assert, constitutive of individual identity, groups have to have some kinds of bonds to compose themselves. What kinds of ties bound the groups that gave rise to male individuals? Rotundo contrasted the nature of domestic bonds—love, nurturance, and so on—with boy culture's self-assertion, multiple conflicts, and friendships. I would stress that the multiple conflicts, and the friendships, may not necessarily have been so different in kind. Their functions merged in the creation of "pecking orders," the shifting hierarchies that boys were always creating and revising. *Fixed* social hierarchies compose social bonds, of course: the lord and the serfs, the master and the slaves, the king and the subjects, are held together by being thus distanced from each other; perhaps repeated successive *shifting* hierarchies accomplish the same business of social ordering, but with more turbulence.

Hierarchies of wealth, status, and power had not disappeared in the nineteenth-century United States, but were understood to be up for grabs, subject to change or even to constant redrawing. The resulting opportunity and anxiety, as seen through this volume's essays, created a tension between the model of the free individual man and men's need for certainty that a group existed in which to anchor male identity. Several of this volume's essays suggest men's anxieties about how to achieve individual capacity without becoming isolated, and show men caught between desire for individuation and need for escape into some form of male group. In fraternal societies men enacted their ambivalence and literally ran away from individualism. The Red Men ritual described by Carnes appears to me a repetition-compulsion ritual, in which the individual is made more isolated, more alone, more vulnerable than ever, and after experiencing the depth of isolation is reincorporated into the male group. That is repeated over and over in order to exhaust the fear of being the isolated individual.

Perhaps the more typical means of expressing male ambivalence about the individual/group relation lies in the formation and re-formation of pecking orders or shifting hierarchies (an adult version of "boy culture"). Baron's paper provides fascinating evidence of a shift from a stable and predictable age-defined progression from boyhood to manhood to the less predictable, more testable, ramified, and performance-defined hierarchy of "competence." Grossberg argues that the advent of the case method meant that lawyers, through their training and practice, were constantly having to battle out a pecking order among themselves. The absence of father figures in many of these investigations is relevant here too. (Rotundo, for instance, found few fathers represented in the autobiographies he used for source material, and Susan Curtis found "God the Father" on the wane.) Blanking out the father symbolically gets rid of the established hierarchy. It thus appears to free the son who comes to manhood. But it requires, for the maintenance of some social order, an alternative form of male cohesion. That is what male "pecking orders," although contested and shifting by their very definition, provide: a statement of male bonds and group belonging.

The speculations on my part suggest how the various specialized investigations of male groups in these essays may contribute to a thorough reconsideration of fundamental themes in nineteenth-century U.S. history. Men's history may thus not only make male gender matter but also, by identifying certain "national" or "era" characteristics more particularly as male, open these to thorough re-viewing and new theorizing.

Fits w/ Riley.

Notes

Introduction

1. Gerda Lerner, "The Challenge of Women's History," from a lecture given at the Aspen Institute for Humanistic Studies, 25 August 1977, published in *The Majority Finds Its Past* (New York: Oxford University Press, 1979), pp. 178, 180. See also Natalie Zemon Davis, who told the Berkshire Conference on Women's History in 1975 that "we should now be interested in the history of both women and men. We should not be working on the subjected sex any more than a historian of class can focus exclusively on peasants." In "Women's History in Transition: The European Case," *Feminist Studies* 3 (1976): 83–103.

2. Women tended to be overlooked in the early works of the new social history. For example, Stephan Thernstrom's pioneering study of Newburyport, Massachusetts, dealt with "the lives of hundreds of obscure men" at the "very bottom of the social ladder" of American society. It perhaps goes without saying that yet another rung existed further down, occupied by the wives of these men. The point is that Thernstrom failed to say it. *Poverty and Progress: Social Mobility in a Nineteenth-Century City* (Cambridge: Harvard University Press, 1964); 1972 reprint, p. 3.

3. Gerda Lerner, *The Creation of Patriarchy* (New York: Oxford University Press, 1986). "One of the most challenging tasks" of women's history, she notes, is to "trace with precision" the various forms and historical transformations of patriarchy (p. 239).

4. David G. Pugh, *Sons of Liberty: The Masculine Mind in Nineteenth-Century America* (Westport, Conn.: Greenwood Press, 1983), p. 31.

5. Joe L. Dubbert, *A Man's Place: Masculinity in Transition* (Englewood Cliffs, N.J.: Prentice-Hall, 1979), p. 122.

6. George B. Forgie, *Patricide in the House Divided: A Psychological Interpretation of Lincoln and His Age* (New York: Norton, 1979), pp. 253–56.

7. Rupert Wilkinson, for example, suggests that the American preoccupation with "tough guys"—whether in politics or popular culture—was a "long-standing reaction against luxury and consumer self-indulgence" (*American Tough: The Tough-Guy Tradition and American Character* [New York: Harper and Row, 1984], p. 102). Carroll Smith-Rosenberg argues that the Davy Crockett myth offered Jacksonian men "an outlet for hostility and frustration in the violence of jingoism and racism"

(*Disorderly Conduct: Visions of Gender in Victorian America* [New York: Alfred A. Knopf, 1985], p. 108).

8. G. J. Barker-Benfield, *The Horrors of the Half-Known Life: Male Attitudes toward Women and Sexuality in Nineteenth-Century America* (New York: Harper and Row, 1976), p. 120.

9. Christine Stansell, *City of Women: Sex and Class in New York, 1789–1860* (New York: Knopf, 1986), pp. 36, 99.

10. Stansell, *City of Women,* pp. 23–30.

11. The assessment of the field has not changed substantially in recent years. Nearly a decade ago, Pleck and Pleck wrote that the history of masculinity was then a new subject of inquiry with a "small but growing literature." Elizabeth H. Pleck and Joseph H. Pleck, *The American Man* (Englewood Cliffs, N.J.: Prentice-Hall, 1980), p. 1. The volume of essays edited by Mangan and Walvin often suffers from an overemphasis on literary or prescriptive materials and exclusively male domains such as public schools, team sports, and the military. J. A. Mangan and James Walvin, *Manliness and Morality: Middle-Class Masculinity in Britain and America, 1800–1940* (Manchester: Manchester University Press, 1987).

12. Peter N. Sterns, *Be a Man! Males in Modern Society* (New York: Holmes & Meier, 1979), p. 5. A revised edition of this seminal work has been published in 1990.

13. John Demos, *Past, Present, and Personal: The Family and the Life Course in American History* (New York: Oxford University Press, 1986), p. 43.

14. Ellen K. Rothman, *Hands and Hearts: A History of Courtship in America* (New York: Basic Books, 1984); Elaine Tyler May, *Great Expectations: Marriage and Divorce in Post-Victorian America* (Chicago: University of Chicago Press, 1980); Beth Bailey, *From Front Porch to Back Seat: Courtship in Twentieth-Century America* (Baltimore: Johns Hopkins University Press, 1988); Robert L. Griswold, *Family and Divorce in California, 1850–1890: Victorian Illusions and Everyday Realities* (Albany: State University of New York Press, 1982); John Modell, *Into One's Own: From Youth to Adulthood in the United States, 1920–1975* (Berkeley: University of California Press, 1989).

15. Elliott Gorn, *The Manly Art: Bare-Knuckle Prize Fighting in America* (Ithaca, N.Y.: Cornell University Press, 1986); Steven A. Reiss, *Touching Base: Professional Baseball and American Culture in the Progressive Era* (Westport, Conn.: Greenwood Press, 1980); Donald J. Mrozek, *Sport and American Mentality, 1880–1910* (Knoxville: University of Tennessee Press, 1983); David Macleod, *Building Character in the American Boy: The Boy Scouts, YMCA, and Their Forerunners, 1870–1920* (Madison: University of Wisconsin Press, 1983); Lynn Dumenil, *Freemasonry in American Culture, 1880–1930* (Princeton: Princeton University Press, 1984); Mark C. Carnes, *Secret Ritual and Manhood in Victorian America* (New Haven: Yale University Press, 1989).

16. Mary P. Ryan, *Cradle of the Middle Class: The Family in Oneida County, New York, 1790–1865* (Cambridge: Cambridge University Press, 1981), p. 231.

17. This dominant culture retained its cohesiveness through extraordinary economic, religious, and intellectual change and the major shifts in mood which John Higham has identified around the Civil War and at the end of the century. Although

Victorian Americans became less optimistic and religious and more preoccupied with perpetuating their values through institutions during the Gilded Age, we do not believe that Victorian culture was limited to the sexual prudery with which later generations would identify it. See Higham, "The Reorientation of American Culture in the 1890's," in John Weiss, ed., *The Origins of Modern Consciousness* (Detroit: Wayne State University Press, 1965); see also Daniel Howe, "Victorian Culture in America," in *Victorian America* (Philadelphia: University of Pennsylvania Press, 1976).

18. See Mark C. Carnes and Clyde Griffen, "Men's History: Whither and Whether?" *Organization of American Historians Newsletter* (August 1988).

19. See Nancy Cott, *The Bonds of Womanhood: "Woman's Sphere" in New England, 1780–1835* (New Haven: Yale University Press, 1977), and Suzanne Lebsock, *Free Women of Petersburg: Status and Culture in a Southern Town, 1784–1860* (New York: W. W. Norton, 1984).

20. Solid beginnings in these fields are found in James Horton, "Freedom's Yoke: Gender Conventions among Antebellum Free Blacks," *Feminist Studies* 12 (spring 1986), and George Chauncey, Jr., "Christian Brotherhood or Sexual Perversion? Homosexual Identities and the Construction of Sexual Boundaries in the World War One Era," *Journal of Social History* 19 (winter 1985).

21. The citation is from Eleanor Maccoby and Carol Jacklin, *The Psychology of Sex Differences* (Stanford: Stanford University Press, 1974). The debate is succinctly summarized in James A. Doyle, *The Male Experience* (Dubuque, Iowa: Wm. C. Brown, 1989), pp. 46–99; see also Perry Treadwell, "Biologic Influences on Masculinity," in Harry Brod, ed., *The Making of Masculinities* (Boston: Allen & Unwin, 1987).

Lionel Tiger emphasized the role of "behavioural propensities" or "inborn biological programmes" in shaping male attitudes, in *Men in Groups* (New York: Random House, 1969), p. 58. Susan Brownmiller believed that a propensity for men to commit rape resulted from men's greater size and physical strength (*Against Our Will: Men, Women and Rape* [New York, 1975]). The Freudian explanation that male identity is formed when a son's fear of his father displaces oedipal attachments has been turned on its head by Nancy Chodorow, who emphasizes the role of the mother, in *The Reproduction of Mothering: Psychoanalysis and the Sociology of Gender* (Berkeley, 1978).

22. For further discussion, see Clyde Griffen, "Reconstructing Masculinity from the Evangelical Revival to the Waning of Progressivism," this volume.

Chapter One

1. "Mrs. Manners," *At Home and Abroad; or, How to Behave* (New York, 1853), pp. 40–41.

2. The phrase is from Charles Dudley Warner, *Being a Boy* (Boston, 1897 [1877]), pp. 66–67, but similar imagery appears throughout the source material: Lewis Wallace, *Lew Wallace: An Autobiography* (New York, 1906), pp. 54–55; Daniel Carter Beard, *Hardly a Man Is Now Alive: The Autobiography of Dan Beard* (New York, 1939),

p. 379; Ray Stannard Baker, *Native American: The Book of My Youth* (New York, 1941), pp. 30, 85, 208; Warner, pp. 49, 87, 91, 150–151.

3. Henry Seidel Canby, *The Age of Confidence: Life in the Nineties* (New York, 1934), p. 46.

4. This essay is drawn from a larger study of middle-class manhood in nineteenth-century America. The middle-class is defined broadly here to mean those men who worked in business (not including commercial farming or small-scale independent artisanry), the professions, or the arts. Since the study examines the lives of those men who arrived at middle-class status in adulthood, it includes the boyhoods of many men who grew up in small farming communities. Few of these people with rural roots, however, were the sons of simple farmers. Rather, their fathers tended to be the lawyers, judges, journalists, merchants, and land speculators who formed the elites of small towns in the nineteenth-century North.

The study from which this essay is drawn is based on private letters and diaries. For the exploration of boyhood, however, autobiographies have proven to be a more fruitful source and thus provide the chief reservoir of primary material for this essay. Autobiographies have their limits, so the concept of boy culture developed here has been corroborated with the scattered evidence on boyhood available in nineteenth-century letters, diaries, novels, and prescriptive literature. Those sources do little to contradict the bare facts about boyhood presented in the autobiographies, but they remove the glow of affectionate approval that surrounds men's recollections of their earliest years.

5. Edward Everett Hale, *A New England Boyhood* (Boston, 1964 [1893]), pp. 22–23, 31.

6. E. Anthony Rotundo, "Manhood in America: The Northern Middle Class, 1770–1920" (Ph.D. diss., Brandeis University, 1982), pp. 180–97, 347–56; Nancy Cott, *The Bonds of Womanhood: "Woman's Sphere" in New England, 1780–1835* (New Haven, 1977), pp. 44–47, 57–60, 84–92; Mary Ryan, *Cradle of the Middle Class: The Family in Oneida County, New York, 1780–1865* (New York, 1981), pp. 157–65.

7. James R. McGovern, *Yankee Family* (New Orleans, 1975), p. 73; Ryan, p. 162; "Mrs. Manners," p. 40.

8. Beard, p. 76.

9. Philip Greven, *The Protestant Temperament: Patterns of Child-Rearing, Religious Experience, and the Self in Early America* (New York, 1977), pp. 45–46; Leonard Ellis, "Men among Men: An Exploration of All-Male Relationships in Victorian America" (Ph.D. diss., Columbia University, 1982), p. 395.

10. This approximate age is based on several pieces of evidence: Henry Dwight Sedgwick, *Memoirs of an Epicurean* (New York, 1942), p. 43; Beard, p. 79; Hale, pp. 16–17; Kenneth S. Lynn, *William Dean Howells: An American Life* (New York, 1970), p. 43.

11. Gender segregation was not unique to middle-class Victorian children. Psychologists Eleanor Maccoby and Carol Jacklin, in their research on group play among children, found that boys and girls nearly always segregated themselves when they could. Their findings held true across all cultural bounds (Eleanor Mac-

coby and Carol Jacklin, "Gender Segregation in Childhood," in Hayne W. Reese, ed., *Advances in Child Development and Behavior* 20 [New York, 1987]). The virtual universality of gender-segregated play raises the possibility—but does not prove—that this phenomenon has biological roots.

The evidence from a single historical study like this one cannot by itself support theories of physical origins in gendered behavior. Indeed, the data on which this essay is based can explain the existence of segregated play in the middle-class Victorian setting without relying on biology as a causal mechanism. Starting in the earliest years of childhood, a middle-class boy in the nineteenth century encountered evidence of male superiority at every turn—from his first Bible lesson about a male God and a male Savior to his experience of his father as the ultimate source of punishment in his family. In spite of the feminine clothing he wore and the feminine population of his daily world, a boy learned lessons about the importance of gender difference from the toys he and his sisters were given, the tasks he saw grown men and women perform, and the clothes he saw adult males and females wearing. Under these circumstances, a boy came to associate maleness with superiority, and also learned to associated gender differentiation with the power and prerogatives of manhood. Thus, when a boy was given his first pair of trousers and the freedom of movement which his sisters were not allowed (in itself a message about the broader privileges of maleness), it could not be a surprise that he would opt for male companions and reject the feminine world, which meant confinement and powerlessness.

This reading of the evidence is obviously speculative and does not rule out biological influence or determination in the explanation of gender-segregated play. But it does suggest that biology is not necessary to explain segregated groups in this case.

12. The "city states" quotation is from Canby, p. 35. See also Canby, pp. 42–46; Wallace, p. 55; Sedgwick, p. 31; Lynn, p. 42; and Howard Doughty, *Francis Parkman* (Cambridge, Mass., 1983 [1962]), pp. 14–15.

13. See, for example, Hale, pp. 45, 53–54, 57–59.

14. Sedgwick, p. 31.

15. There is a danger of overstating the similarities between girls' and boys' lives before age six. They were given different toys to play with (McGovern, p. 73), and mothers were kept keenly aware of the different worlds for which they were raising their toddlers (James Barnard Blake, Diary, 3 August 1851, American Antiquarian Society; Kirk Jeffrey, "Family History: The Middle-Class American Family in the Urban Context, 1830–1870" [Ph.D. diss., Stanford University, 1972], pp. 202–3), so they must have treated their children differently according to sex. Still, the early domestic life of boys zealously discouraged basic "male" virtues like aggression and self-assertion in favor of "feminine" kindness and submission.

16. Beard, p. 76; Greven, pp. 45–46.

17. Alphonso David Rockwell, *Rambling Recollections: An Autobiography* (New York, 1920), pp. 30–31, 56; Wallace, pp. 55, 121; Beard, p. 203; Baker, p. 85; Hale, pp. 22–23, 40, 66–67, 86, 88, 151; Warner, p. 49; Doughty, pp. 14–15; Wheaton J. Lane, *Commodore Vanderbilt: An Epic of the Steam Age* (New York, 1942), pp. 11, 13, 162;

Sedgwick, pp. 20–21, 28–29; Ellis, pp. 252–53; Irving Bartlett, *Daniel Webster* (New York, 1978), p. 288; Samuel Hastings to Thomas Russell, 21 December 1835, Charles Russell Papers, Massachusetts Historical Society.

18. Thomas Russell to John Brooks, 9 November 1836, Charles Russell Papers; Massachusetts Historical Society; Wallace, p. 55; Beard, pp. 78, 92; Lynn, pp. 54–55; Ellis, pp. 251–53; Samuel McChord Crothers, "The Ignominy of Being Grown-Up," *Atlantic Monthly* 98 (1906): 47. It is worth noting that much of the harshest violence seemed to take place in areas of the Midwest that were not many decades removed from frontier status and that were settled by Southern as well as Yankee stock.

19. Hale, pp. 55, 151; Warner, pp. 127–28; Doughty, pp. 14–15; Lynn, p. 45.

20. Beard, pp. 92, 110; Hale, pp. 23, 200–201; James Lovett, *Old Boston Boys and the Games They Played* (Boston, 1906); William Wells Newell, *Games and Songs of American Children* (New York, 1883).

21. Ellery Clark, *Reminiscences of an Athlete; Twenty Years on Track and Field* (Boston, 1911), p. 6; Beard, pp. 102–3; Wallace, p. 22.

22. Warner, pp. 89–91; Beard, p. 92; Clark, p. 6.

23. Beard, p. 79; Hale, pp. 82–83, 136–37; Lynn, p. 45; Ryan, pp. 164–65; Joseph Kett, *Rites of Passage: Adolescence in America, 1790 to the Present* (New York, 1977), pp. 91–92. There is a literature on volunteer fire companies as a part of urban working-class culture; see, for example, Bruce Laurie, *Working People of Philadelphia, 1800–1850* (New York, 1980).

24. Even the businessmen and professionals of the small towns kept farms, and they relied on menial labor from their sons. See Charles Russell to Theodore Russell, 26 January 1830, Charles Russell Papers, Massachusetts Historical Society. Charles's instructions to Theodore are included in many letters to his wife Persis. See, for example, 25 January and 31 May 1830; 14 March, 8 December, and 16 December 1831. See also Baker, p. 20.

25. Hale, pp. 36–37.

26. Warner, p. 50.

27. Rockwell, p. 31.

28. Given the ephemeral nature of these bonds it is not surprising that the strongest and most enduring friendships were forged at home between brothers and cousins. Kin friendships like this one built on a foundation of love and familiarity that already existed (see Rockwell, p. 31). But such relationships could be both loyal and turbulent at the same time. See Theodore Russell to Persis Russell, 25 March and 31 October 183[4?], and Theodore Russell to Charles Russell, 21 September and 14 December 183[4?], Charles Russell Papers, Massachusetts Historical Society.

29. An interesting exception to this nation-state model of boyhood friendships is the passionate bond between Pierre and his cousin Glen Stanly in Herman Melville's novel *Pierre*. The open devotion and confiding intimacy of their relationship could readily be found in the ties between male youths in their late teens and twenties, but were extremely rare between nineteenth-century boys. Herman Melville, *Pierre; or, The Ambiguities* (New York, 1971).

30. On Roosevelt and his museum, see Kathleen Dalton, "The Early Life of The-

odore Roosevelt" (Ph.D. diss., Johns Hopkins University, 1979), pp. 171–72. A club that stole fruit is described in Wallace, p. 55.

31. Warner, p. 50.

32. Lynn, p. 44; Beard, p. 78.

33. Lynn, p. 43; Sedgwick, pp. 32–33; Canby, pp. 42–45; W. S. Tryon, *Parnassus Corner: A Life of James T. Fields, Publisher to the Victorians* (Boston, 1963), p. 9. These antagonisms between towns and neighborhoods became the basis for the high school sports rivalries that blossomed late in the century.

34. Canby, pp. 42–43, and more generally pp. 40–45; see also Sedgwick, pp. 32–33, Rockwell, pp. 56–57, and Newell, p. 176.

35. Canby, p. 37; Ellis, pp. 251-53; Beard, pp. 92, 103, 110–11; see also Stephen Salisbury, Jr., to Betsy Salisbury, 27 October 1810, Salisbury Family Papers, 1674–1906, American Antiquarian Society; Theodore Roosevelt, *The Strenuous Life: Essays and Addresses* (New York, 1902), pp. 162–64.

36. Canby, p. 40; Sedgwick, p. 33; Rockwell, p. 31.

37. Male autobiographers who grew up in the nineteenth century sometimes talked about the democracy that existed among boys. What they meant in modern terms is that their boy culture was a meritocracy in which a boy's demonstrated abilities, not his family's status, determined his standing among his peers. See Canby, p. 40, and Hale, pp. 32–33.

38. Lynn, p. 45; on stoicism, see also Beard, p. 96.

39. Wallace, p. 122; see also John Doane Barnard, "Journal of His Life, 1801–1858," MS, Essex Institute, pp. 3–4; Beard, p. 47; Rockwell, p. 56; Canby, p. 44.

40. Ryan, p. 161; Canby, p. 235; also pp. 192–94.

41. Crothers, p. 47. For examples of boys who combined affection with hostility, see Lynn, p. 45; Wallace, p. 55. Henry Seidel Canby even claimed that bullying, while it represented "primitive sadism," was laced with pleasure because it gave the victims "delicious terrors" (Canby, p. 37).

42. Hale, p. 37; Wallace, p. 55; Barnard, pp. 3–4; Canby, pp. 43–44.

43. Beard, p.78.

44. Ibid., pp. 73–74; Rockwell, pp. 35–36. Younger boys could—and sometimes did—use pranks for the same purposes against older boys (Beard, pp. 76, 78–79).

45. Beard, p. 78.

46. Kett, pp. 46–50.

47. In the era before compulsory education, playing hooky was a very common form of boyish rebellion (Wallace, pp. 26–27; Beard, p. 78).

48. See, for example, Lynn, p. 47. Insolence and disorder were common even at prestigious urban schools (Hale, pp. 17, 34–35).

49. Hale, p. 58; Warner, pp. 48–49.

50. See Kett, pp. 124–27, on age grading.

51. Even in small towns, where fathers were more likely to work nearby, mothers were the ones who intervened in boys' daily activities with friends. See Wallace, p. 22, and Lynn, pp. 42, 44.

52. Theodore Russell to Charles Russell, 26 January 1830, Charles Russell Papers,

Massachusetts Historical Society; Elisha Whittlesey to William Whittlesey, 13 December 1830, and Elisha Whittlesey to Comfort Whittlesey, 20 January 1840, William W. Whittlesey Papers, Western Reserve Historical Society; Baker, p. 20; Warner, pp. 41–43.

53. Wallace, pp. 77–79; Barnard, pp. 3–4.

54. Beard, p. 102.

55. Ibid.; Mark Twain, *The Adventures of Huckleberry Finn* (New York, 1968), p. 346.

56. Sedgwick, p. 23; Warner, p. 161; "Mrs. Manners," pp. 42–43.

57. This extension of the female ethical domain out into a male world is a modest, personal version of the moral reform crusades which women conducted in the nineteenth century. See Ryan, pp. 83–98, 105–36, 210–18, and Carroll Smith-Rosenberg, *Religion and the Rise of the American City* (Ithaca, N.Y., 1971), chaps. 4, 7.

58. Beard, pp. 111, 157–58; Lynn, p. 44.

59. Lynn, pp. 42, 44; Beard, pp. 157–58; Wallace, p. 22.

60. Rotundo, pp. 193–97.

61. Hale, p. 55; Baker, p. 85.

62. Beard, pp. 157–58. See also Sedgwick, pp. 20–21; Wallace, p. 27.

63. Beard, p. 111; see also Warner, pp. 80–81.

64. "Mrs. Manners," p. 43. See also Warner, pp. 73–74, and the comments in Mark Carnes, "The Making of the Self-Made Man: The Emotional Experience of Boyhood in Victorian America," unpublished, p. 11.

65. Beard, p. 199.

66. The vituperation heaped on "sissies" not only reflected boys' insecurity about their own tendencies to follow their mothers' advice and their desire to maintain the integrity of their subculture, but may also have represented a way for boys to deflect their own anger from their mothers (who, after all, were trying to frustrate them) onto more acceptable targets.

67. Some boys grew conscious of this pulling and tugging. Dan Beard wrote in his autobiography: "Life was beginning to become complicated to an earnest and well-meaning little chap who wished to understand and to do what was right but was troubled by the difference between the teachings of his wise mother, the example of the older boys, and the incomprehensible talks of the preachers" (Beard, pp. 71–72).

68. A useful discussion of the indefinite language of age in the early nineteenth century (and the indefinite phases of life which the language indicated) is in Kett, pp. 11–14.

69. See, for example, Doughty, pp. 15, 18.

70. Rockwell, p. 63; see also Wallace, pp. 80–82.

71. The average age of puberty for boys in this era was about sixteen (Kett, p. 44).

72. Beard, p. 199.

73. A squabble between brothers over the use of the suit provides good evidence of clothing as a badge of "'civilized' manhood." See Theodore Russell to Persis Russell, 31 October 183[4?], Charles Russell Papers, Massachusetts Historical Society.

74. Warner, p. 1; Rockwell, p. 63; nn. 29–32 herein.

75. E. Anthony Rotundo, "American Fatherhood: A Historical Perspective," *American Behavioral Scientist* 29 (1985): 7–25.

76. For direct testimony on this point, see Hale, pp. 36–37.

77. Linda Kerber has written a searching review of this research as part of her "Separate Spheres, Female Worlds, Woman's Place: The Rhetoric of Women's History," *Journal of American History* 75 (1988): 9–39.

78. Rotundo, "Manhood in America," pp. 75–110.

79. Ryan, pp. 155–62; Rotundo, "Manhood in America," pp. 180–97, 347–56.

80. For similar thoughts, see Ryan, pp. 162–65.

81. Hale, pp. 54–55.

82. Ellis, pp. 501–604; Lovett, pp. 80–175.

83. Jeffrey Hantover, "Sex Role, Sexuality, and Social Status: The Early Years of the Boy Scouts of America" (Ph.D. diss., University of Chicago, 1976); David Macleod, *Building Character in the American Boy: The Boy Scouts, Y.M.C.A., and Their Forerunners, 1870–1920* (Madison, Wis., 1983); Peter Filene, *Him/Her/Self: Sex Roles in Modern America,* 2d ed. (Baltimore, 1986), pp. 95–96; Kett, pp. 193–204, 223–24.

84. Kett, pp. 122–31.

85. Ibid., pp. 124–27, 152–58.

Chapter Two

1. See Stuart Blumin, "The Hypothesis of Middle-Class Formation in Nineteenth-Century America: A Critique and Some Proposals," *American Historical Review* 90 (April 1985): 299–338. For the consensus position, see esp. Louis Hartz, *The Liberal Tradition in America: An Interpretation of American Political Thought since the Revolution* (New York: Harcourt, Brace, 1955), pp. 51–52. The revisionist position is stated most directly in Paul Johnson, *A Shopkeeper's Millennium: Society and Revivals in Rochester, New York, 1815–1837* (New York: Hill and Wang, 1978), and Anthony F. C. Wallace, *Rockdale: The Growth of an American Village in the Early Industrial Revolution* (New York: Knopf, 1978).

2. Mary P. Ryan, *Cradle of the Middle Class: The Family in Oneida County, New York, 1790–1865* (Cambridge: Cambridge University Press, 1981), pp. 231–32.

3. W. S. Harwood, "Secret Societies in America," *North American Review* 164 (May 1897): 620, 623; Albert C. Stevens, *Cyclopaedia of Fraternities* (New York: E. B. Treat, 1907 [1897]). The preface for the 1897 edition gave somewhat higher totals than Harwood, p. xv. Stevens estimated that 40 percent of the adult male population belonged to a lodge; see *Cyclopaedia of Fraternities,* p. xvi.

4. Tiger recognizes that not all societies have formal initiations, but he suggests that men perform the "functional equivalents" of such ceremonies. But these are defined so broadly—sports, politicking, etc.—as to render the concept of "initiation" meaningless (*Men in Groups* [New York: Random House, 1969], p. 154).

5. By the late nineteenth century, membership in ritualistic organizations was so widespread as to make generalization impossible. It is possible to discern a membership shift in the Red Men and the Odd Fellows, during the formative 1830s and 1840s, from laborers and artisans to clerks, shopkeepers, and lawyers; membership

in the Freemasons differed from region to region and from lodge to lodge. On the essentially middle-class character of fraternal orders, see Lynn Dumenil, *Freemasonry and American Culture, 1880–1939* (Princeton: Princeton University Press, 1984), p. 229; Mary Ann Clawson, "Brotherhood, Class and Patriarchy: Fraternalism in Europe and America" (Ph.D. diss., State University of New York at Stony Brook, 1980), pp. 393–99; John Gilkeson, "A City of Joiners: Voluntary Associations and the Formation of the Middle Class in Providence, 1830–1920" (Ph.D. diss., Brown University, 1981), p. 121; Don Harrison Doyle, *The Social Order of a Frontier Community: Jacksonville, Illinois, 1825–1870* (Urbana: University of Illinois Press, 1978), pp. 182–83, 187, 269; and Brian Greenberg, *Worker and Community: Response to Industrialization in a Nineteenth-Century American City, Albany, New York, 1850–1884* (Albany: State University of New York Press, 1985), pp. 89-101. On the infusion of the middle classes into the Odd Fellows, see James L. Ridgely, *History of American Odd Fellowship* (Baltimore: Grand Lodge, I.O.O.F., 1878), pp. 7, 32, 142–43.

6. Harwood, "Secret Societies in America," pp. 620–22; one year later another observer proposed an inquiry into the cause of this strange "attraction," adding that it raised the question of "whether the mystical side to our natures has not expanded relatively more rapidly than that which looks mainly to material comfort"; in Stevens, *Cyclopaedia of Fraternities* (from the preface to the first [1897] edition, p. xvi).

7. Stevens, *Cyclopaedia of Fraternities,* pp. 238–43; Charles Litchman, *Official History of the Improved Order of Red Men* (Boston: Fraternity Publishing Co., 1893), p. 249.

8. Litchman, *Official History,* pp. 252–55, 292.

9. Stevens, *Cyclopaedia of Fraternities,* p. 244; also Litchman, *Official History,* pp. 294–96.

10. Thomas K. Donnalley, *Handbook of Tribal Names of Pennsylvania* (Philadelphia, 1908), pp. 231–49; Litchman, *Official History* pp. 294–320.

11. Nearly forty years later, in 1908, elderly Red Men recalled that the "whole desire" of members of the order was to perform the adoption ceremony; Donnalley, *Handbook of Tribal Names of Pennsylvania,* p. 231.

12. *Record of the Great Council of New York: Improved Order of Red Men* (Elmira, N.Y.: Gazette Co., 1890), p. 315.

13. See Stevens, *Cyclopaedia of Fraternities,* p. 246; also Noel P. Gist, "Secret Societies: A Cultural Study of Fraternalism in the United States," *University of Missouri Studies* 15 (October 1940): 42.

14. Litchman, *Official History,* pp. 298–354; Stevens, *Cyclopaedia of Fraternities,* pp. 244–46.

15. Donnalley, *Handbook of Tribal Names of Pennsylvania,* pp. 231–40.

16. Verbatim accounts of the Adoption Degree were published by the National Christian Association, an organization that sought to diminish the appeal of secret ritual by making it public. The description is from [Ezra A. Cook], *Red Men Illustrated: The Complete Illustrated Ritual of the Improved Order of Red Men* (Chicago: Ezra A. Cook, 1896), pp. 13–61. Its accuracy was verified by comparing it to the extensive commentaries on the degree by scholars and historians of the order.

17. "Freemasonry in the Forest," *Masonic Review* (November 1870); "Masonry

among the Indians," *Masonic Signet and Mirror* (May 1852); "Eli Parker," *Masonic Review* (September 1858); "New Race of Men," *Masonic Review* (September 1869); "Savages and Symbolism," *Masonic Review* (April 1856). See also Albert Pike, the preeminent Masonic ritualist, who argued that the pure meaning of "Divine Truth" could be found in the "sacred traditions of all the primitive Nations" (*Morals and Dogma of the Ancient and Accepted Scottish Rite of Freemasonry* [Charleston, S.C.: Supreme Council of the A.A.S.R., 1872]), pp. 105, 576, 598–99; also Albert Mackey, *Encyclopaedia of Freemasonry* (Philadelphia; L. H. Everts, 1886), p. 547.

18. Roscoe Pound, "Lectures on the Philosophy," in *Masonic Addresses and Writings* (Richmond, Va.: Macoy Publishing Co., 1953), pp. 99–100.

19. J. M. W. Whiting, Richard Kluckhohn, and Albert Anthony, "The Function of Male Initiation Ceremonies at Puberty," in Eleanor E. Maccoby, T. M. Newcomb, and E. L. Hartley, eds., *Readings in Social Psychology* (New York: Henry Holt and Co., 1958). For a criticism of the study on technical grounds see Edward Norbeck, D. E. Walker, and M. Cohen, "The Interpretation of Data: Puberty Rites," *American Anthropologist* 64:3 (1962).

20. Robert V. Burton and J. M. W. Whiting, "The Absent Father and Cross-Sex Identity," *Merrill-Palmer Quarterly* 7 (1961): 87–90.

21. See Frank W. Young, "The Function of Male Initiation Ceremonies: A Cross-Cultural Test of an Alternative Hypothesis," *American Journal of Sociology* 68 (January 1962): 381–86.

22. The literature is substantial, and increasing rapidly. The early or most influential works include: Anne L. Kuhn, *The Mother's Role in Childhood Education* (New Haven: Yale University Press, 1947); Barbara Welter, "The Cult of True Womanhood: 1820–1860," *American Quarterly* 18 (summer 1966); Ruth Bloch, "American Feminine Ideals in Transition: The Rise of the Moral Mother," *Feminist Studies* 4 (June 1978); Ann Douglas, *The Feminization of American Culture* (New York: Knopf, 1977); Nancy Cott, *The Bonds of Womanhood* (New Haven: Yale University Press, 1977); and Ryan, *Cradle of the Middle Class*.

23. Rev. John S. C. Abbott, "Paternal Neglect," *Parents' Magazine* (March 1842), cited in Kuhn, *The Mother's Role in Childhood Education*, p. 4; also Bernard W. Wishy, *The Child and the Republic: The Dawn of Modern American Child Nurture* (Philadelphia: University of Pennsylvania Press, 1968), pp. 26–29.

24. See G. R. Bach, "Father-Fantasies and Father-Typing in Father-Separated Children," *Child Development* 17 (1946): 63–80; David B. Lynn, "A Note on Sex Differences in the Development of Masculine and Feminine Identification," *Psychological Review* 66 (1959): 126–35; R. R. Sears, M. H. Pintler, and P. S. Sears, "Effect of Father Separation on Pre-School Children's Doll Play Aggression," *Child Development* 17 (1946): 219–43. Talcott Parsons believed that when fathers were mostly absent during child rearing, sons would be deprived of the essential connections to society; conversely, excessive maternal affection would discourage sons from entering into the instrumental world inhabited by men. Talcott Parsons and R. F. Bales, *Family, Socialization and Interaction Process* (Glencoe, Ill., 1955).

25. For a forceful exposition of this argument, see Joseph H. Pleck, *The Myth of Masculinity* (Cambridge: Massachusetts Institute of Technology Press, 1984).

26. Some learning theorists insist that children identify with nurturing and affectionate parents rather than with those who are perceived as powerful; see E. M. Hetherington and G. Frankie, "Effects of Parental Dominance, Warmth, and Conflict on Imitation in Children," *Journal of Personality and Social Psychology* 6 (1967): 119–25; P. H. Mussen and L. Distler, "Masculinity, Identification,and Father-Son Relationships," *Journal of Abnormal and Social Psychology* 59 (1959): 350–56; A. Bandura and R. H. Walters, *Adolescent Aggression: A Study of the Influence of Child-Training Practices and Family Interrelationships* (New York: Ronald Press Co., 1959).

27. See E. Anthony Rotundo, this volume; see also Mark C. Carnes, "The Making of the 'Self-Made Man': The Emotional Experience of Boyhood in Victorian America," paper presented at the annual meeting of the Organization of American Historians, April 1984.

28. *Lectures and Charges of the Degrees of the Independent Order of Odd Fellows in the United States* (Philadelphia: J. Royer, 1833), p. 7.

29. *Odd Fellowship Illustrated* (Chicago: Ezra Cook, 1875), p. 44; see also *Dr. Willis's Exposé of Odd Fellowship* (Boston: 1846), p. 35.

30. James R. Carnahan, *Pythian Knighthood: Its History and Literature* (Cincinnati: Pettibone Mfg. Co., 1890), pp. 222–23; J. J. Fultz, Grand Dictator, *Infancy, Youth and Manhood; or, How to Work the "K of H" Ritual* (Mount Vernon, Ohio: Knights of Honor, 1889).

31. No account of the 1845 Patriarchal Degree could be located; the version cited here is based on the 1875 NCA exposé, *Odd Fellowship Illustrated*. Henry L. Stillson noted that from 1845 until 1880 there was only one revision (1873) of the ritual and that if offered no important modifications; in Henry L. Stillson, ed., *The Official History and Literature of Odd Fellowship* (Boston: Fraternity Publishing Co., 1898), p. 552.

32. H. L. Haywood compared the initiation experience to the "crisis of adolescence when a boy finds himself passing through a mysterious change that throws his whole being into turmoil . . . " Like the man who has experienced a religious conversion, the fraternal initiate understands that "he can never become with he was." In *The Great Teachings of Freemasonry,* pp. 30–31.

33. Greenberg, *Worker and Community,* p. 92; Clawson, "Brotherhood, Class and Patriarchy," pp. 245–46, 415.

34. Victor Turner, *The Ritual Process: Structure and Anti-Structure* (Ithaca, N.Y.: Cornell University Press, 1969), pp. 111–13, 125–29 (129n); *Process, Performance and Pilgrimage* (New Delhi: Concept Publishing Co., 1979), pp. 38, 129; and *The Forest of Symbols: Aspects of Ndembu Ritual* (Ithaca, N.Y.: Cornell University Press, 1967), pp. 93–111.

Chapter Three

1. James T. Searcy, "Self-Adjustability," pp. 12–13 (pamphlet printed privately in the hospital print shop in 1895), Alabama Collection, University of Alabama Library, Tuscaloosa, Alabama. Capitalization in the original.

2. Ibid., p. 54. Searcy had expressed these ideas as early as 1888, explaining that

competition was the key to manliness, which he described at that time as "progressive and inventive." Females, he continued, were less "inventive, aggresive [*sic*], and constant; true to tradition, habits, fashions and customs of society. She is less sinful, less vicious on this account, and more moral, more constant, more consistent, more conservative, more religious." (See Searcy's "Heredity," *Transactions of the Medical Association of the State of Alabama* 40 [1888]: 364–65.) In 1916, near the close of his career, he showed that the passage of three decades had altered his ideas hardly at all. (See his "Humanity—Biologically Considered," pamphlet printed privately in the hospital print shop in 1916, p. [12]; Alabama Collection.)

3. John S. Hughes, "Alabama's Families and Involuntary Commitment of the Insane, 1861–1900: New Solutions to Old Problems," Working Papers, Series 2 (May 1987), Legal History Program, Institute for Legal Studies, University of Wisconsin Law School, Madison, Wisconsin. This account provides a more detailed analysis of commitment. For an example of Alabama's commitment statues, see *Revised Code of Alabama* (Montgomery: Reid and Screws, 1867), sections 1040–74.

4. In 1865, when the asylum was still quite small, it admitted twenty-one patients. For this group the average duration of their present attack was over four years, roughly the length of time that the institution had been open. In 1870 the average length of patients' current attacks of insanity remained high at slightly over five years. In 1880 it fell to only four months, reflecting that the hospital was extremely crowded and that the superintendent had succeeded in keeping away all but acute cases. By 1890, after some of the crowding had been relieved by expansion, the average length of stay had risen to two and a half years. In short, most patients sent to the hospital had suffered with the disease for a long while before their families finally decided to commit them. This data is compiled from the Admissions Book, Staff Library, Bryce Hospital, Tuscaloosa, Alabama. Statistics on all admissions were recorded in this book on the date of the patient's admission. The Alabama Insane Hospital is now called Bryce Hospital in honor of Dr. Peter Bryce, its first superintendent, whose tenure lasted from its opening in 1861 to his death in 1892.

5. *Code of Alabama*, 1876 (Montgomery: W. W. Screws, 1876), section 1482.

6. For examples of these causes, see the Admissions Book. Patients are listed there in order of their admission by the number assigned to their case and by the date of their admission.

7. See, for example, Admissions Book, patients nos. 6, 9, 47, 131, 147, 527, 1499, and 1504. Women did commonly enter the hospital for reasons relating to pregnancy, childbirth, menstruation, and other female complaints. These conditions were all partially biological, however, and not rooted in "jobs" as were the men's conditions. See n. 12 below.

8. Ibid., patients nos. 1, 2, 21, 34, 36, 58, 135, 151, and 152.

9. It is possible too that, for reasons of propriety and caution, families were reluctant to send women members to an unproved institution far from home. Later, when the hospital became better known, these factors diminished.

10. Admissions Book, passim. The case history of one woman did include claims of masturbation, but neither her husband (who committed her) nor the hospital identified this as a source of her insanity. Doctors at the hospital in fact did not learn

of this until after the woman had been released and her husband informed them of her continuing mental problems. (See file of patient no. 2770, admitted 17 December 1886, Records Office, Bryce Hospital.) See also the records for patient no. 1073 for another example of a woman suspected of masturbation. In this case the general practitioner who treated her at home in 1875 performed a surgical procedure to end the "self-abuse."

11. A good summary of Victorian ideas about masturbation is found in Robin and John Haller, *The Physician and Sexuality in Victorian America* (New York: Norton, 1974), pp. 195–211. See also H. Tristam Englehardt, Jr., "The Disease of Masturbation: Values and the Concept of Disease." *Bulletin of the History of Medicine* 48 (summer 1974): 234–48.

12. Admissions Book. For an example of a woman with insanity related to "erotic ideas," see file of patient no. 2669, letter of sister to patient, 3 June 1886, Records Office.

13. Admissions Book for the years 1880 and 1890. In 1880 the hospital admitted sixty-five women. Seventeen, or 26 percent, of that number suffered from insanity attributed to childbirth, pregnancy, menopause ("climacteric" insanity), or uterine troubles. In 1890, 30 of the 155 women admitted (19 percent) suffered from insanity attributed to a similar feminine complaint.

14. Ibid., patient nos. 18, 54, 67, 92, 136, 146, 168, and 207. Later samples are not very reliable. Whoever kept the Admissions Book in the 1870s and after seldom used the term "grief." By the 1890s the book was haphazardly kept with regard to exciting causes and forms of patients' insanity.

15. The third man deranged by grief had been in his early thirties when his wife died unexpectedly. His grief therefore stemmed from a powerful domestic loss. What distinguished this man's case was its very uniqueness. In an age of high maternal mortality, many other relatively young men were no doubt left widowed, yet few of them seem to have found in this circumstance the sort of grief that led to derangement.

16. Ibid., passim. From the sample of cases during the first five years see, for example, patient nos. 14, 119, and 192.

17. A few cases of sexual abuse also appear in the records. In one case, for example, a young woman complained that her father had impregnated her and that her mother had performed an abortion to hide the fact from the public. Her charge was officially listed as a delusion, but her admitting physician believed her story because she so accurately described a septic abortion. See patient no. 4627, Case History Book no. 7, p. 289, Records Office.

18. The doctors were never certain whether to consider alcoholics and drug addicts as insane like other inmates. In 1869 the trustees actually established a policy of forbidding the admission of "inebriates and opium eaters." Their intention was to lobby for a special institution for these patients; when the state refused to establish one, the Alabama Insane Hospital resumed admitting them. See "Proceedings of the Board of Trustees," Trustees Record Book, 1:39–40, Staff Library.

19. Admissions Book, passim.

20. For examples of mixed dependencies, see files of patient nos. 2273, 3171, 3832, 4418, and 5794. Some women did mix opium with morphine (see file of patient no. 1364, for example). Any mixing was rare among women; on those occasions where it did occur, only once was alcohol involved (see file of patients no. 946), and in that case alcohol dependency was clearly secondary to opium addiction.

21. For an excellent discussion of this kind of addiction see David T. Courtwright, *Dark Paradise: Opiate Addiction in America before 1940* (Cambridge: Harvard University Press, 1982). The Hallers' *Physician and Sexuality,* pp. 273–303, also summarizes drug addiction. Neither account considers alcoholism in detail.

22. *Annual Report* (Tuscaloosa: Alabama Insane Hospital print shop, 1872), p. 24; emphasis in original.

23. Patient no. 4627, Case History Book no. 7, p. 289.

24. *Annual Report,* 1872, p. 34. By the 1890s the reports no longer mentioned moral treatment by name, but Bryce's policies continued largely unaltered when Searcy took over in 1893.

25. *Annual Report,* 1876 (Montgomery: W. W. Screws, 1876), p. 32. For good discussions of moral treatment see Gerald Grob, *Mental Institutions in America: Social Policy to 1875* (New York: Free Press, 1973), and David J. Rothman, *The Discovery of the Asylum: Social Order and Disorder in the New Republic* (Boston: Little, Brown, 1971).

26. For examples of statistics on recovery see *Annual Report,* 1876, p. 12; *Annual Report,* 1878 (Montgomery: Barret & Brown, 1878), p. 10; *Annual Report,* 1880 (Montgomery: Barret & Brown, 1880), p. 9; *Annual Report,* 1882 (Montgomery: Allred & Beers, 1882), p. 11; *Biennial Report,* 1884 (Montgomery: Barret & Co., 1884), p. 11; *Biennial Report,* 1888 (Montgomery: Brown & Co., 1888), p. 14; and *Biennial Report,* 1890 (Montgomery: Brown Printing Co., 1890). p. 15.

27. "Proceedings of the Board of Trustees," 5 October 1895, Trustees Record Book 1:[220], Staff Library; emphasis added.

28. *Biennial Report of the Alabama Insane Hospital,* 1888 (Montgomery: W. D. Brown & Co., 1888), p. 17. In 1890 Bryce said that he had always tried "to make the Hospital a home in its truest sense for the unfortunate class committed to its care." See *Biennial Report,* 1890, p. 18; emphasis added. A legislative investigative committee used the same language in 1879: "In all of its apartments it [the asylum] presents the appearance of a pleasant and well regulated home." See *Report of the Special Joint Committee Appointed to Visit the Insane Hospital at Tuskaloosa. . . [sic]* (Montgomery: Barret & Brown, 1879), p. 3.

29. *Annual Report,* 1870 (Montgomery: John G. Stokes & Co., 1870), p. 32, passim. For more on punishment, specifically the revocation of chapel privileges, see Joseph Camp, *An Insight into an Insane Asylum* (published privately by the author, 1882), pp. 30–31. Camp, the guilty party and a minister, was punished for shouting out "Amen." Camp's exposé also discussed putting patients in the "cross-hall," or seclusion room, for violations of the rules.

30. Bryce reported that one of his male patients jokingly told him that "a crazy man and a wheel-barrow must have been made for each other." The superintendent did not dispute the wisdom of this. See *Biennial Report,* 1890, p. 17. Some black

women did work outdoors, but white women never did. Until 1903 the hospital housed both blacks and whites (though the races occupied separate wards), but thereafter most blacks were sent to a new hospital north of Mobile designed only for them. A few blacks, several dozen of each sex, continued to be held in Tuscaloosa largely because they could perform jobs in the institution that whites would not.

31. "Proceedings of the Board of Trustees," 4 October 1893, Book 1:[204], Staff Library.

32. Robert O. Mellown, "The Construction of the Alabama Insane Hospital, 1852–1861," *Alabama Review* 38 (April 1985): 83–104. The Kirkbride design was named after Dr. Thomas Kirkbride of the Pennsylvania Hospital in Philadelphia.

33. In 1871 one doctor from Jackson County treated a "perfectly wild & frenzied" patient by bleeding from the arm and "cup[ping] freely in the temples." (See statement of case history by John F. Clarke, M.D., 4 October 1871, in file of patient no. 709, Records Office.) As late as 1890 a twenty-seven-year-old patient who had developed "severe neuralgia" only four days after her marriage was treated by her family doctor in a similarly interventionist way. Her "Exam" form (a hospital document filled out by the examining physician on admission) states that "she was blistered behind each ear, and nearly all of her teeth [were] extracted." (See file of patient no. 3999, admitted 21 October 1890, Records Office.)

34. Physician, researcher, and medical writer René Dubos observed more than thirty years ago that two distinct points of view have competed in medicine. One, symbolized by the Greek goddess Hygeia, strove for health through prevention and a moderate life-style. The other, symbolized by the god Asclepius, intervened only after illness or injury occurred. Significantly, the first was feminine and the latter masculine. Moral treatment as practiced in the Alabama Insane Hospital clearly followed more logically from the Hygeia model than from the Asclepius, despite the fact that most Victorian physicians clearly worshiped in the temple of Asclepius. See Dubos, *Mirage of Health: Utopias, Progress, and Biological Change* (New York: Harper & Row, 1959), esp. chap. 5, "Hygeia and Asclepius."

35. *Annual Report,* 1875 (Montgomery: W. W. Screws, 1875), p. 28. Rothman's *Discovery of the Asylum* first explored this quality of American asylums, arguing that their founders consciously tried to set a social example.

36. For biographical sketches of the superintendents, see Thomas M. Owen, *History of Alabama and Dictionary of Alabama Biography* (Chicago: S. J. Clarke Publishing Co., 1921), pp. 224, 1518.

37. See Barbara Sicherman, "The Quest for Mental Health in America, 1880–1917" (Ph.D. diss., Columbia University, 1967), and "The Uses of a Diagnosis: Doctors, Patients, and Neurasthenia," *Journal of the History of Medicine and Allied Sciences* 32 (1977): 33–54; Rosenberg, *The Trial of the Assassin Guiteau* (Chicago: University of Chicago Press, 1968), and "The Place of George M. Beard in Nineteenth-Century Psychiatry," *Bulletin of the History of Medicine* 36 (1962): 245–59; and Haller and Haller, *The Physician and Sexuality in Victorian America.* The quotation is from the Hallers' *Physician and Sexuality,* p. 42.

38. Sicherman, in "The Uses of a Diagnosis," discusses fully the often contradictory ends to which a diagnosis of neurasthenia could be put.

39. Sicherman's "Quest for Mental Health" (pp. 35–45) and her "Uses of a Diagnosis" both discuss this intraprofessional tension. Rosenberg's *Trial of the Assassin Guiteau* likewise addresses this issue clearly. More recently, Gerald N. Grob (*Mental Illness and American Society, 1875–1940* [Princeton, N.J.: Princeton University Press, 1983]) has considered this division in a larger context. For an excellent primary account of this professional split see S. Weir Mitchell, "Address before the Fiftieth Annual Meeting of the American Medico-Psychological Association," *Proceedings of the American Medico-Psychological Association* 50 (1894): 101–21, in which Mitchell politely but roundly condemned the state of institutional psychiatry.

40. See, for example, Bertram Wyatt-Brown, *Southern Honor: Ethics and Behavior in the Old South* (New York: Oxford University Press, 1982); Philip Thomason, "The Men's Quarter of Downtown Nashville," *Tennessee Historical Quarterly* (spring 1982): 48–66; and Elliot Gorn, "'Gouge and Bite, Pull Hair and Scratch': The Social Significance of Fighting in the Southern Backcountry," *American Historical Review* 90 (February 1985): 18–43.

Chapter Four

1. Ann Douglas, *The Feminization of American Culture* (New York: Knopf, 1977). Other works that suggest that American life was in the midst of change include the following: T. Jackson Lears, *No Place of Grace* (New York: Pantheon, 1981); Daniel Rodgers, *The Work Ethic in Industrial America, 1850–1920* (Chicago: University of Chicago Press, 1974); Elaine May, *Great Expectations: Marriage and Divorce in Post-Victorian America* (Chicago: University of Chicago Press, 1980); Christopher Lasch, *Haven in a Heartless World* (New York: Basic Books, 1977); Lears, "From Salvation to Self-Realization: Advertising and the Therapeutic Roots of the Consumer Culture, 1880–1930," in Lears and Richard Wightman Fox, ed., *The Culture of Consumption* (New York: Pantheon, 1983); and Warren Susman, "'Personality' and the Making of Twentieth Century Culture," in John Higham and Paul Conkin, eds., *New Directions in American Intellectual History* (Baltimore: Johns Hopkins University Press, 1979).

2. Stephen Mintz (*A Prison of Expectations* [New York: New York University Press, 1983]), Mary Ryan (*Cradle of the Middle Class* [New York: Cambridge, 1981]), and Paul Johnson (*A Shopkeeper's Millennium* [New York: Hill & Wang, 1978]) all speak to different dimensions of this ideal in the early to mid-nineteenth century. This view is corroborated by autobiographies such as P. T. Barnum, *Struggles and Triumphs,* edited and abridged by Carl Bode (New York: Penguin, 1981); August Rauschenbusch, *Leben und Wirken* (Cassel, Germany: J. G. Oncken Nachfolger, GmbH, 1901); Elizabeth Stuart Phelps Ward, *Austin Phelps: A Memoir* (New York: Schribner's, 1891); Washington Gladden, *Recollections* (Boston: Houghton Mifflin, 1909); Lyman Abbott, *Reminiscences* (Boston: Houghton Mifflin, 1923); David Riesman, *The Lonely Crowd* (New Haven: Yale University Press, 1950); and Philip Rieff, *Triumph of the Therapeutic: The Uses of Faith after Freud* (New York: Harper & Row, 1966).

3. Josiah Strong, *The Times and Young Men* (New York: Baker & Taylor, 1901), p. 179.

4. By the early twentieth century, it was difficult to find a book on the subject of religion that did not deal in some way with the issues of social religion. Indeed, Ferenc Szasz found that many of the ministers, who later became part of the Fundamentalist movement in the 1920s, engaged in social reform in the early part of the century. In 1908, when Frank Mason North read a paper titled "The Church and Modern Industry," which included the Methodists' Social Creed, the Federal Council of Churches endorsed it virtually unanimously as the Social Creed of the Churches. This body in 1908 represented more than seventeen million American Protestants. Jacob Dorn, *Washington Gladden: Prophet of the Social Gospel* (Columbus: Ohio State University Press, 1968), along with Dores Sharpe, *Walter Rauschenbusch* (New York: Macmillan, 1942); Howard Wilson, *Mary McDowell, Neighbor* (Chicago: University of Chicago Press, 1928); George B. Nash, III, "Charles Stelzle: Apostle to Labor," *Labor History* 11 (spring 1970): 151–74; Robert Crunden, *Ministers of Reform* (New York: Basic, 1982); John P. McDowell, *The Social Gospel in the South: The Woman's Home Mission Movement in the Methodist Episcopal Church, South, 1886–1939* (Baton Rouge: Louisiana State University Press, 1982); William Hutchison, "Cultural Strain and Protestant Liberalism," *American Historical Review* 76 (April 1971): 386–411; Hutchison, *The Modernist Impulse in American Protestantism* (New York: Oxford, 1982); and Ferenc Szasz, "The Progressive Clergy and the Kingdom of God," *Mid-America* 55 (January 1973): 3–20, all suggest how pervasive the social gospel had become by the early twentieth century.

5. This essay is based on an examination of the childhood, adolescent, and adult experiences of the following men, according to their autobiographical writings: Gladden, *Recollections;* Lyman Abbot, *Reminiscences* and *What Christianity Means to Me* (New York: Macmillan, 1921); Francis Greenwood Peabody, *A Little Boy in Little Boston* (Cambridge, 1935); Shailer Mathews, *New Faith for Old* (New York: Macmillan, 1936); Sharpe, *Walter Rauschenbusch,* and the Walter Rauschenbusch Papers, American Baptist Historical Society, Rochester, New York (hereinafter WRP, ABHS); Charles Stelzle, *A Son of the Bowery* (New York: Doran, 1926); Charles Sheldon, *Charles Sheldon: His Life Story* (New York: Doran, 1925); Charles Macfarland, *Across the Years* (New York: Macmillan, 1936); Francis John McConnell, *By the Way* (New York: Abingdon-Cokesbury Press, 1952); Harry Emerson Fosdick, *The Living of These Days* (New York: Harper & Row, 1956); and Josiah Strong, *My Religion in Everyday Life* (New York: Baker & Taylor, 1910). For collective biographies of social gospelers, see Hutchison, "Cultural Strain and Protestant Liberalism," and Janet F. Fishburn, *The Fatherhood of God and the Victorian Family* (Philadelphia: Fortress, 1981).

6. Robert Moats Miller, *Harry Emerson Fosdick* (New York: Oxford, 1984), pp. 7–8; Fosdick, *The Living of These Days,* p. 36; McConnell, *By the Way,* pp. 23–36, 57; Mathews, *New Faith for Old,* p. 10; Sharpe, *Walter Rauschenbusch,* p. 43.

7. Mathews, *New Faith for Old,* and Creighton Lacy, *Frank Mason North: His Social and Ecumenical Mission* (Nashville: Abingdon Press, 1967), discuss the boys' fathers and their businesses. Sharpe, *Walter Rauschenbusch,* opens with a lengthy discussion of Rauschenbusch's ancestors and of his father's achievements. Rauschenbusch's *Leben und Wirken,* which was begun by August Rauschenbusch and completed by

Walter Rauschenbusch, revealed even more about his father than Walter realized as a child. Macfarland, *Across the Years,* and Sheldon, *His Life Story,* open with recollections of their fathers' industry and example.

8. Abbott, *Reminiscences,* pp. 23–40, 61–64, 93; Rauschenbusch, *Leben und Wirken,* pp. 228–29; Macfarland, *Across the Years,* pp. 5–6; Gladden, *Recollections,* p. 11; Stelzle, *A Son of the Bowery,* p. 30.

9. Sharpe, *Walter Rauschenbusch,* pp. 35–39, 58; Peabody, *A Little Boy in Little Boston,* pp. 14, 22; Macfarland, *Across the Years,* p. 19.

10. In recent years a number of works have appeared exploring the various dimensions of this emerging culture of consumption and the demise of Victorianism. See Harry Braverman, *Labor and Monopoly Capital* (New York: Monthly Review Press, 1974); David Brody, *Steelworkers in America* (New York: Harper & Row, 1960); John Cawelti, *Apostles of the Self-Made Man* (Chicago: University of Chicago Press, 1965); Louis Galambos, *Competition and Cooperation* (Baltimore: Johns Hopkins University Press, 1966); James Gilbert, *Designing the Industrial State* (Chicago: Quadrangle, 1972); Gilbert, *Work without Salvation* (Baltimore: Johns Hopkins University Press, 1977); Lears, *No Place of Grace;* Mintz, *A Prison of Expectations;* Lears and Fox, *The Culture of Consumption;* Daniel Horowitz, *The Morality of Spending* (Baltimore: Johns Hopkins University Press, 1985); Warren Susman, *Culture as History* (New York: Pantheon, 1973); John Higham, "The Reorientation of American Culture in the 1890s," in *Writing American History* (Bloomington: Indiana University Press, 1970); Stanley Coben and Lorman Ratner, *The Development of an American Culture* (Englewood Cliffs, N.J.: Prentice-Hall, 1970); and Douglas, *The Feminization of American Culture.* For specific discussions of the important place of leisure in this consumer culture, see Lewis A. Erenberg, *Steppin' Out* (Chicago: University of Chicago Press, 1981); Lary May, *Screening Out the Past* (Chicago: University of Chicago Press, 1980); and John F. Kasson, *Amusing the Million* (New York: Hill & Wang, 1978). Inspired in part by Rieff's *Triumph of the Therapeutic* and Riesman's *Lonely Crowd,* both of which discussed America's changing social relations and evolving cultural values in the modern period, these more recent examinations of consumer culture explore the new ways people learned the cultural messages of their society, the emphasis on immediate gratification, and some of the contradictions this emerging cultural system raised.

11. Mathews, *New Faith for Old,* chap. 1; Lacy, *Frank Mason North,* chap. 1; Gladden, *Recollections,* pp. 268, 273; Stelzle, *A Son of the Bowery,* chap. 1.

12. Henry A. Atkinson, *Men and Things* (New York: Missionary Education Movement, 1918), pp. 191–92; Gladden, "The Labor Question," *Century* 32 (June 1886): 328; Sheldon, *His Life Story,* pp. 81–89.

13. Fosdick, "The Trenches and the Church at Home," *Atlantic Monthly* 123 (January 1919): 27, and Fosdick, *The Living of These Days,* pp. 63, 77; Sharpe, *Walter Rauschenbusch,* p. 43; Mathews, *New Faith for Old,* pp. 10–13.

14. Authors responsible for the standard picture of the social gospel include the following: Charles Hopkins, *The Rise of the Social Gospel in American Protestantism, 1865–1915* (New Haven: Yale University Press, 1940); Aaron Abell, *The Urban Impact on American Protestantism, 1865–1900* (Cambridge: Harvard University Press, 1943);

Robert Handy, *The Social Gospel in America, 1870–1920* (New York: Oxford, 1966); Henry May, *Protestant Churches in Industrial America* (New York: Harper, 1949); Ronald White, *The Social Gospel* (Philadelphia: Temple, 1976); and Dorn, *Washington Gladden.* While I agree with the authors of the social gospel that their ideas and programs represented a significant departure from the religion of their parents, I also believe that they were not the first and only advocates of Christian reform. Paul Johnson, Ronald Walters, David Rothman, and Anne Rose, for example, have written of reform movements in the early nineteenth century that were organized to address pervasive social ills. Most of these reforms, however, continued to focus on individual regeneration. See Walters, *American Reformers, 1815–1860* (New York: Hill & Wang, 1978); Johnson, *A Shopkeeper's Millennium;* Rose, *Transcendentalism as a Social Movement, 1830–1850* (New Haven: Yale University Press, 1981); Rothman, *The Discovery of the Asylum* (Boston: Little, Brown, 1971). From developing Unitarianism in the early nineteenth century to transcendentalism in the 1830s and to ministers like Henry Ward Beecher and Horace Bushnell, liberal Protestants had been assailing the Calvinism of earlier centuries and even the uncertainty of the "anxious bench" in evangelical Protestant revivals before the Civil War. Certainly, the social gospelers were not the first to undermine orthodox Protestantism. The difference between those scattered expressions and the social gospel is that the latter had become dominant by the turn of the century. Therefore, while one might be able to point to an early spokesman for social responsibility in the early nineteenth century, that person likely had a limited audience. To give some idea of the change in acceptability of the social gospel, I refer to the work of Washington Gladden. When he first published books that challenged Victorian culture and Evangelical Protestantism, he was denounced by local and national critics. By the 1880s and 1890s, when others began to question Victorian formulas for success and salvation, Gladden's work reached a wide audience. While conditions in his life led him to question the demands placed on him as a child, those conditions were not general until later in the century, at which time his work struck a responsive chord among many American Protestant men.

15. For standard work on the cooperative enterprises of the social gospel, see Hopkins, *The Rise of the Social Gospel in American Protestantism, 1865–1915;* Abell, *The Urban Impact on American Protestantism, 1865–1900;* May, *Protestant Churches in Industrial America;* Dorn, *Washington Gladden;* Sharpe, *Walter Rauschenbusch;* Crunden, *Ministers of Reform;* and Allen Davis, *Spearheads for Reform* (New York: Oxford University Press, 1967).

16. Galley proof of "Jesus and the Social Problems of Our Age," in WRP, ABHS, box 41; Sharpe, *Walter Rauschenbusch,* p. 322; Gladden, *Tools and the Man* (Boston: Houghton Mifflin, 1893), p. 38; Macfarland, *Spiritual Culture and Social Service* (New York: Revell, 1912), p. 23.

17. Strong, *The Times and Young Men,* pp. 45–46.

18. Harriet Beecher Stowe, *In the Footsteps of the Master* (New York: Ford, 1877); Thomas De Witt Talmage, *From Manger to Throne* (Philadelphia: Historical Publishing Co., 1890); Frederick W. Farrar, *The Life of Christ* (New York: World, 1874); George Gordon, *The Christ of Today* (Boston: Houghton Mifflin, 1896); E. S. Ames,

The Divinity of Christ (Chicago: New Christian Century, 1911); Lyman Abbott, *Jesus of Nazareth* (New York: Harper, 1869); Thomas Hughes, *The Manliness of Christ* (Boston: Houghton Mifflin, n.d.); Mathews and Burton, *The Life of Christ* (Chicago: University of Chicago Press, 1901); Charles Jefferson, *The Character of Jesus* (New York: Crowell, 1908); Peabody, *Jesus Christ and the Christian Character* (New York: Macmillan, 1908); Bouck White, *The Call of the Carpenter* (Garden City: Doubleday, 1914); Herbert Willett, *The Call of the Christ* (New York: Revell, 1912); George Wendling, *The Man of Galilee* (Washington, D.C.: Olcott, 1907); Herbert Gates, *The Life of Jesus* (Chicago: University of Chicago Press, 1908); Fosdick, *The Manhood of the Master* (New York: Association Press, 1913); G. W. Fiske, *Jesus' Ideals of Living* (New York: Abingdon Press, 1922); Bruce Barton, *The Man Nobody Knows* (Indianapolis: Bobbs-Merrill, 1925); Robert Norwood, *The Man Who Dared to Be God* (New York: Scribner's, 1929); Walter Denny, *The Career and Significance of Jesus* (New York: Nelson, 1934). For discussions of hymns see Sandra Sizer, *Gospel Hymns and Social Religion* (Philadelphia: Temple, 1978), and Henry Cope, *One Hundred Hymns You Ought to Know* (New York: Revell, 1906).

19. Talmage, *From Manger to Throne,* pp. 217–18. See also Herbert Gutman, "Protestantism and the American Labor Movement: The Christian Spirit in the Gilded Age," *American Historical Review* 72 (October 1966): 74–101.

20. White, *Call of the Carpenter,* p. 312; Gates, *The Life of Jesus;* Mary Austin, *The Man Jesus* (New York: Harper & Bros., 1915); Robert Coyle, *Workingmen and the Church* (Chicago: Winona, 1903); Wendling, *The Man of Galilee;* Willett, *The Call of the Christ;* Burgess, *The Life of Jesus;* Mathews, *New Faith for Old,* pp. 123–34.

21. Fosdick, *The Manhood of the Master,* p. 161.

22. Niese, *The Newspaper and Religious Publicity* (New York: Doran, 1925), pp. 15–16; Stelzle, *Principles of Successful Church Advertising* (New York: Revell, 1908), pp. 56–57.

23. Susan Curtis Mernitz, "The Disintegration of Faith: The Social Gospel and Modern American Culture" (Ph.D. diss., University of Missouri, 1986), esp. chap. 4. The following show evidence of both the social gospel and commercial interests: Stelzle, *Principles of Successful Church Advertising;* Clarence Barbour, ed., *Making Religion Efficient* (New York: Association Press, 1912); W. B. Ashley, *Church Advertising: Its Why and How* (Philadelphia: Lippincott, 1917); Francis Case, *Advertising the Church* (New York: Abingdon Press, 1925); Case, *A Handbook of Church Advertising* (New York: Abingdon Press, 1921); Elliott, *How to Advertise a Church* (New York: Doran, 1920); Christian Reisner, *Church Publicity* (New York: Eaton & Mains, 1910); Mathews, *Scientific Management in the Churches* (Chicago: University of Chicago Press, 1912).

24. Anderson, *Man of Nazareth,* pp. vii, 22; Fiske, *Jesus' Ideals of Living,* p. 3; Rufus Jones, *The Life of Christ,* p. 9; Charles Fiske and Burton Easton, *The Real Jesus: What He Taught, What He Did, Who He Was* (New York: Harper, 1929), p. 73; Barton, *The Man Nobody Knows;* Denny, *The Career and Significance of Jesus;* Norwood, *The Man Who Dared to Be God.*

25. Henry Cope, *The Friendly Life* (New York: Revell, 1909), p. 50; William Dawson, *Threshold of Manhood* (New York: Revell, 1909), p. 242.

26. Strong, *My Religion in Everyday Life,* p. 44; Abbott, *What Christianity Means to Me,* pp. 5–10; and Sharpe, *Walter Rauschenbusch,* p. 322.

27. "Messages of the Men and Religion Forward Movement," *Boys' Work,* vol. 5 (New York: Association Press, 1912), pp. 5–6

28. Richardson, *Religious Education of Adolescents* (New York: Abingdon Press, 1918), pp. iv, 58–61; Walter Rauschenbusch to Hilmar Rauschenbusch, 1 May 1917, WRP, ABHS, box 50; Macfarland, *Across the Years.*

29. Rauschenbusch became more sensitive to the role of fathers in the twentieth century as he struggled to provide guidance and a good example for his children while permitting them great latitude in their lives. In 1917 he was asked to address the graduating class at Simmons College on the subject "the issues of life." Rauschenbusch decided to "put in a good word for fathers" who, he believed, were maligned by popular cultural media. See "The Issues of Life" (commencement address delivered in Harvard Church, Brookline, Mass., 11 June 1917), *Simmons Quarterly* 7 (July 1917): 1–9. See also a document dated 31 March 1918 in WRP, ABHS, box 39.

The Macfarland children did not follow in their father's footsteps. Upon graduation from Columbia University, Charles Stedman Macfarland, Jr., began working as an advertising and publicity agent. James M. Macfarland studied at Princeton and earned an advanced degree in business administration at New York University. He ran the Northern New Jersey News Bureau, and then became a newspaper correspondent for the Associated Press, the New York dailies, and regional newspapers. Lucia M. Macfarland became deputy director of the Morris County Welfare Board and began supervising the "problem" cases in the county. The Macfarland children's activities and successes would suggest that their upbringing helped prepare them for the secular world that was dominated by big business.

Chapter Five

1. I am exploring the wider cultural ramifications of fraternal relations in "'Surpassing the Love of Women': A reinterpretation of Victorian Masculinity."

2. David G. Pugh, *Sons of Liberty: The Masculine Mind in Nineteenth-Century America* (Westport, Conn.: Greenwood Press, 1983), pp. xv, xvi, 14 cited, 130–53; Michael Kimmel, "The Contemporary 'Crisis' of Masculinity in Historical Perspective," in Harry Brod, ed., *The Making of Masculinities: The New Men's Studies* (Boston: Allen & Unwin, 1987), pp. 121, 122–23 cited, 124–35, 137–40; Peter N. Stearns, *Be a Man! Males in Modern Society* (New York: Holmes & Meier, 1979), pp. 39–58, 113.

3. Representative studies are Pugh, *Sons of Liberty;* Joe L. Dubbert, *A Man's Place: Masculinity in Transition* (Englewood Cliffs, N.J.: Prentice-Hall, 1979); Peter N. Stearns, *Be a Man;* Elizabeth H. Pleck and Joseph H. Pleck, eds., *The American Man* (Englewood Cliffs, N.J.: Prentice-Hall, 1980); Peter Filene, "'Between a Rock and a Soft Place': A Century of American Manhood," *South Atlantic Quarterly* 84 (autumn 1985): 339–55; Peter Cominos, "Late Victorian Sexual Respectability and the Social System" *International Review of Social History* 8 (1963): 18–43; Kimmel, "Contemporary 'Crisis' of Masculinity."

4. Helpful studies are Jeffrey Richards, "'Passing the Love of Women': Manly Love and Victorian Society," in *Manliness and Morality: Middle-Class Masculinity in Britain and America, 1800–1940* (New York: St. Martin's Press, 1987), pp. 92–119. See also E. Anthony Rotundo, "Manhood in America: The Northern Middle Class, 1770–1920" (Ph.D. diss., Brandeis University, 1982) and "Body and Soul: Changing Ideals of American Middle Class Manhood," *Journal of Social History* 16 (summer 1983): 23–38; Drew Gilpin Faust, *A Sacred Circle: The Dilemma of the Intellectual in the Old South, 1840–1860* (Baltimore, Md.: Johns Hopkins University Press, 1977); and Pat Caplan, ed., *The Cultural Construction of Sexuality* (London and New York: Tavistock, 1987).

5. Authors who assume that romantic, ritualistic lives were unique to women are Carroll Smith-Rosenberg, "The Female World of Love and Ritual: Relations between Women in Nineteenth-Century America," *Signs* 1 (autumn 1975): 1–30 and *Disorderly Conduct: Visions of Gender in Victorian America* (New York: Alfred A. Knopf, 1985); Nancy Cott, *The Bonds of Womanhood: "Woman's Sphere" in New England, 1780–1835* (New Haven: Yale University Press, 1977); and Martha Vicinus, "Distance and Desire: English Boarding-School Friendships," *Signs* 9 (summer 1984): 600–622.

6. Our understanding of Victorian sexuality has changed radically in recent years, sparking a reconsideration of male sexual roles. See F. Barry Smith, "Sexuality in Britain, 1800–1900: Some Suggested Revisions," in Martha Vicinus, ed., *A Widening Sphere: Changing Roles of Victorian Women* (Bloomington: Indiana University Press, 1977), pp. 182–98; Peter Gay, *The Bourgeois Experience*, 2 vols. to date (New York: Oxford University Press, 1984–); Michel Foucault, *The History of Sexuality*, vol. 1, trans. Robert Hurley (New York: Pantheon, 1978); Phillippe Ariès and André Béjin, eds., *Western Sexuality: Practice and Precept in Past and Present Times* (New York: Basil Blackwell, 1985); and Peter Gardella, *Innocent Ecstasy: How Christianity Gave America an Ethic of Sexual Pleasure* (New York: Oxford University Press, 1985).

7. Thomas R. Dew, "Dissertation on the Characteristic Differences between the Sexes and on the Position and Influence of Woman in Society," *Southern Literary Messenger* 1 (May/July 1835): 493–512, 621–32; Barbara Welter, *Dimity Convictions: The American Woman in the Nineteenth Century* (Athens: Ohio University Press, 1976); Cott, *The Bonds of Womanhood*.

8. Historians have employed a variety of words ranging form the awkward to the odd, to describe the phenomenon of intimate friendship: "homosocial behavior," "male bonding," even the Whitmanesque creation "adhesiveness" (borrowed from phrenology). I believe the phrase "language of fraternal love" captures the sentimentality of the nineteenth century and stresses the form in which most of the phenomenon found expression.

9. On the abolitionist movement, see Lawrence J. Friedman, *Gregarious Saints: Self and Community in American Abolitionism, 1830–1870* (Cambridge: Cambridge University Press, 1982); Aileen S. Kraditor, *Means and Ends in American Abolitionism, 1834–1850* (New York: Pantheon, 1969); and Lewis Perry, *Radical Abolitionism: Anarchy and the Government of God in Antislavery Thought* (Ithaca, N.Y.: Cornell University Press, 1973). I have treated the relationship between gender roles and radical reform in my *Dilemmas of the Liberal Persuasion: Samuel Joseph May, Antebellum*

Religion and Reform (Philadelphia: Temple University Press, forthcoming), chap. 7–9. Dorothy Hammond and Alta Jablow "Gilgamesh and the Sundance Kid: The Myth of Male Friendship," in Brod, ed., *The Making of Masculinities,* pp. 241–58 seek to connect male friendship to the history of "patriarchy."

10. *Unitarian Review,* cited in Douglas Stange, *Patterns of Antislavery among American Unitarians, 1831–1860* (Cranbury, N.J.: Associated Universities Press, 1977), p. 46; Lydia Maria Child to Caroline Weston, 7 March 1859, *Microfiche of the Collected Correspondence of Lydia Maria Child* (Millwood, N.Y.: Kraus, 1980), 7/172k.

11. Parker Pillsbury, *Acts of the Antislavery Apostles* (Concord, N.H., 1883), p. 104.

12. Octavius Brooks Frothingham, *Recollections and Impressions, 1822–1890* (New York: G. P. Putnam's Sons, 1891), pp. 49–50; Samuel Joseph May to Sidney Howard Gay, 27 July 1846, Sidney Howard Gay Papers, Columbia University (May refers to his cousin Samuel May, Jr., as an "Israelite"); Elizabeth Cady Stanton, "Speech before the American Anti-Slavery Convention," 1860(?), Elizabeth Cady Stanton Papers, microfilm, reel II, Library of Congress (she proclaimed, "I have always regarded Garrison as the great missionary of the gospel of Jesus to this guilty nation"); Maria Weston Chapman, "Line," in *Liberty Bell* (Boston: Massachusetts Anti-Slavery Fair, 1839), p. 5; Lawrence Friedman, *Gregarious Saints,* p. 3; Perry, *Radical Abolitionists,* pp. 107–8; Angelina Grimké to Abby Kelley, 15 April 1837, Abigail Kelley Foster Papers, American Antiquarian Society.

13. Anders Nygren, *Agape and Eros,* trans. Philip S. Watson (London: SPCK, 1953), pp. 41, 63, 75–78; James Freeman, "Sermon 11, God Pardons Penitent Sinners," in Freeman, *Sermons and Charges* (Boston: Carter, Hendee, 1832), pp. 126–27.

14. "Agape," in Samuel Macauley Jackson, ed., *The New Schaff-Herzog Encyclopedia of Religious Knowledge,* 15 vols. (Grand Rapids, Mich.: Baker Book House, 1964), 1:80–81; Nygren, *Agape and Eros,* pp. 148, 308–9; Tillich quoted in Jean H. Hagstrum, *Sex and Sensibility: Ideal and Erotic Love from Milton to Mozart* (Chicago: University of Chicago Press, 1980), p. 4; Charles Stuart to Theodore Dwight Weld, 8 March 1838, in Gilbert H. Barnes and Dwight L. Dumond, eds., *Letters of Theodore Dwight Weld, Angelina Grimké Weld and Sarah Grimké, 1822–1844,* 2 vols. (1934; reprint, Gloucester, Mass.: Peter Smith, 1965), 2:589; Anthony Barker, *Captain Charles Stuart* (Baton Rouge: Louisiana State University Press, 1986). pp. 152, 265.

15. Friedman, *Gregarious Saints,* pp. 134–35; William Lloyd Garrison to Oliver Johnson, 14 August 1837, in Walter Merrill and Louis Ruchames, eds., *Letters of William Lloyd Garrison,* 6 vols. (Cambridge: Harvard University Press, 1971–81), 2:281 (hereafter *LWLG*); Lewis Perry, "'We Have Had Conversation in the World': The Abolitionists and Spontaneity," *Canadian Review of American Studies* 6 (1975): 3–26. I think "timelessness" rather than "spontaneity" characterizes the Garrisonians, better linking the movement's religious foundations to its abolitionism and group dynamics.

16. James C. Jackson to William Lloyd Garrison, 6 March 1840, in *Liberator,* 20 March 1840.

17. Lydia Maria Child, *Isaac T. Hopper: A True Life* (Boston: John P. Jewett, 1853), p. 466; John A. Alexander, "The Ideas of Lysander Spooner," *New England Quarterly* 23 (June 1950): 202; Wendell Phillips to Lydia Maria Child, 21 February 1842, in E. Lewis,

ed., "Letters of Wendell Phillips to Lydia Maria Child," *New England Magazine* 5 (February 1892): 731–32; Oliver Johnson, *William Lloyd Garrison and His Times* (Boston: Houghton Mifflin, 1881), p. 53; William Lloyd Garrison to John Greenleaf Whittier, 21 January 1868, *LWLG* 6:36–39; Friedman, *Gregarious Saints*, pp. 43–44. The biblical story of David and Jonathan has long been a transcendent theme in Western culture. For example, George Frideric Handel employed it in *Saul*, a 1739 oratorio, wherein he idealized love between men: "And more than woman's love thy wond'rous love to me." (Hagstrum, *Sex and Sensibility*, pp. 303–5).

18. Friedman, *Gregarious Saints*, p. 50; *Liberator*, 28 August 1840; Pillsbury, *Acts*, p. 104.

19. On the relationships between May and Garrison, see *Dilemmas of the Liberal Persuasion*, esp. chap. 7; William Lloyd Garrison to Samuel Joseph May, 18 February 1834, *LWLG* 1:114–15; *Frederick Douglass' Paper*, 9 October 1857, Yale University Microfilm.

20. "Fifth Annual Report of the Massachusetts Anti-Slavery Society (1837)," in *Proceedings of the Massachusetts Anti-Slavery Society at Its Fifth Meeting, 27 January 1837* (Boston: Massachusetts Anti-Slavery Society, 1837), p. 33; Samuel Joseph May to Amos A. Phelps, 7 September 1835, and to William Lloyd Garrison, 23 November 1851, Samuel Joseph May MS, Boston Public Library (hereafter BPL); Samuel Joseph May Diary, 31 October 1865, May Antislavery Collection, Cornell University Library; *Journal of Charlotte L. Forten*, ed. Ray A. Billington, (New York: Collier-Macmillan, 1961), pp. 23, 77; Samuel Joseph May to William Lloyd Garrison, 25 September 1860, quoted in Friedman, *Gregarious Saints*, p. 52; see also Samuel Joseph May to William Lloyd Garrison, 18 January 1841, Samuel Joseph May MS, BPL.

21. William Lloyd Garrison to Anna E. Benson, 20 May 1834, in *LWLG*, 1:345; W. Freeman Galpin, "God's Chore Boy: Samuel Joseph May," unpublished MSS, Syracuse University Archives, 1947, p. 224; William Lloyd Garrison, *Selections from the Writings and Speeches of William Lloyd Garrison* (Boston: R. F. Wallcut, 1852), p. 200; William Lloyd Garrison to Samuel Joseph May, 9 December 1867, *LWLG*, 5:309, microfiche supplement.

22. Thomas J. Mumford, George B. Emerson, and Samuel May, Jr., eds., *Memoir of Samuel Joseph May* (Boston: Roberts Brothers, 1873), pp. 5–10; Sigmund Freud, "Screen Memories" (1899), in *Complete Psychological Works, Standard Edition*, 24 vols., ed. and trans. James Stachey and Anna Freud (London: Hogarth Press, 1953–62), 3:302–22; Freud, *The Psychopathology of Everyday Life*, trans. A. A. Brill (New York: Macmillan, 1915), pp. 57–68. On childhood loss and grief see John Bowlby, *Attachment and Loss*, vol. 3 : *Loss, Sadness, and Depression* (New York: Basic Books, 1980), pp. 14–16, 276, 290–91.

23. Jonathan Katz, *Gay American History* (New York: Thomas Y. Crowell, 1976), Emerson cited p. 459.

24. Mumford et al., eds., *Memoir*, pp. 35–36, 39, 50; Joseph May, *Samuel Joseph May, a Memorial Study by His Son* . . . (Boston: G. H. Ellis, 1898), p. 28.

25. Mumford et al., eds., *Memoir*, pp. 51–58.

26. Mumford et al., eds., *Memoir*, pp. 169–70; William P. Tilden, "Rev. Samuel J. May," *Monthly Religious Magazine* 46 (August 1871): 170–78.

27. Thomas J. Mumford to Samuel Joseph May, 20 February 1862, in *Life and Letters of Thomas J. Mumford, with Memorial Tributes,* ed. Mrs. Thomas J. Mumford (Boston: George H. Ellis, 1879), pp. 67–69; also pp. 40, 42–44, 59, 60, 83, 132.

28. David Brion Davis, "The Emergence of Immediatism in British and American Antislavery Thought," in Davis, ed., *Antebellum Reform* (New York: Harper & Row, 1967), pp. 139–52. On women in the antislavery movement see Blanch G. Hersh, *The Slavery of Sex: Feminist-Abolitionists in America* (Chicago: University of Illinois Press, 1978); Gerda Lerner, *The Grimké Sisters from South Carolina: Rebels against Slavery* (Boston: Houghton, Mifflin, 1967); William H. Pease and Jane H. Pease, "The Role of Women in the Antislavery Movement," *Canadian Historical Association: Historical Papers Presented at the Annual Meeting Held in Ottawa, June 7–10, 1967,* pp. 167–83. Lydia Maria Child, *Letters from New York* (New York: Charles S. Francis, 1843), pp. 233–34.

29. Samuel Joseph May to Henry W. Bellows, 9 February 1847, Henry Whitney Bellows Papers, Massachusetts Historical Society; Samuel Joseph May to Edgar Buckingham, 8 February 1865, in Mumford et al. eds., *Memoir,* pp. 283–84; Samuel Joseph May, *On the Redemption by Christ* . . . (Boston: Wm. Crosby and H. P. Nichols, 1847), pp. 3–4; "A Discourse Preached at Syracuse on the Evening of November 1, 1846," *National Anti-Slavery Standard,* 10 December 1846; "Nonresistance," *Monthly Miscellany* 2 (October 1839): 23–24; and "On the Treatment of Enemies," *The Liberal Preacher* 4 (1830): 83–97; *Syracuse Daily Standard,* 7 July 1871; Samuel Joseph May to Woman's Rights Convention, held at Worcester, Massachusetts, October 1850, in *Woman's Rights Tract No. 8* (Syracuse, N.Y.: Masters' Print, 1852?), p. 8; Samuel Joseph May, *Rights and Condition of Women; Considered in "The Church of the Messiah," November 8, 1846* (Syracuse, N.Y.: Stoddard and Babcock, 1846).

30. Barker, *Captain Charles Stuart,* pp. 31, 34–35, 65.

31. Theodore Dwight Weld to Sarah and Angelina Grimké, 28 December 1837, in Barnes and Dumond, eds., *Letters of Weld-Grimké,* 1:509.

32. Theodore Dwight Weld to James G. Birney, 10 July 1837, in Dwight L. Dumond, ed., *Letters of James Gillespie Birney, 1831–1857,* 2 vols. (New York: Appleton-Century, 1938), 1:394–95; also 1:130–32, 292–93; Theodore Dwight Weld to Angelina Grimké, 28 December 1837, cited in Barker, *Stuart,* pp. 110–18, 142.

33. Kraditor, *Means and Ends in American Abolitionism,* pp. 39–117.

34. Robert H. Abzug, *Passionate Liberator: Theodore Dwight Weld and the Dilemma of Reform* (New York: Oxford University Press, 1980), pp. 91–92, 214–15; James A. Thome to Theodore Dwight Weld, 18 May 1839, and Augustus Wattles to Angelina Grimké, 7 May 1838, in Barnes and Dumond, eds., *Letters of Weld-Grimké,* 2:666, 764–65, 837–38.

35. James A. Thome to Theodore Dwight Weld and Angelina Grimké Weld, 18 May 1839 and 29 May 1840, in Barnes and Dumond, eds., *Letters of Weld-Grimké,* 2:764–65, 837–38; Abzug, *Passionate Liberator,* p. 214.

36. Charles Stuart to James G. Birney, 6 March 1855, in Dumond, ed., *Letters of Birney,* 2:1169–71.

37. Milton A. Rugoff, *The Beechers: An American Family in the Nineteenth Century*

(New York: Harper & Row, 1981), p. 124; William Leach, *True Love and Perfect Union: The Feminist Reform of Sex and Society* (New York: Basic Books, 1980), pp. 103–4.

38. For other nonabolitionist groups that practiced similar bonding rituals, see Jonathan Butler, "From Millerism to Seventh Day Adventism: 'Boundlessness to Consolidation,'" *Church History* 55 (March 1968): 50–64, and Faust, *Sacred Circle,* pp. 15, 17, 26, 43.

39. George Chauncy, Jr., "Christian Brotherhood or Sexual Perversion? Homosexual Identities and the Construction of Sexual Boundaries in the World War One Era," *Journal of Social History* 19 (winter 1985): 189–211; Vern L. Bullough and Martha Voght, "Homosexuality and Its Confusion with the 'Secret Sin' in Freudian America," *Journal of the History of Medicine* 28 (April 1973): 144–49.

40. Studies that have failed to heed Carroll Smith-Rosenberg's warnings about the social construction of sexuality before Freud include John Boswell's *Christianity, Social Tolerance, and Homosexuality* (Chicago: University of Chicago Press, 1980), esp. pp. 133–34 and 218–26; Katz's *Gay American History;* and Robert K. Martin's *Hero, Captain, and Stranger: Male Friendship, Social Critique, and Literary Form in the Sea Novels of Herman Melville* (Chapel Hill: University of North Carolina Press, 1986). Lillian Faderman, in *Surpassing the Love of Men: Romantic Friendship and Love between Women from the Renaissance to the Present* (New York: William Morrow, 1981); Nancy Sahli, in "Smashing: Women's Relationships before the Fall," *Chrysalis* 8 (summer 1979): 17–21; and Vicinus, in "Distance and Desire," pp. 601–2, assume that all Romantic female friendships are in some way homoerotic or lesbian. Michael Lynch's "'Here is Adhesiveness': From Friendship to Homosexuality" (*Victorian Studies* 29 [autumn 1985]: 67–96) also misreads the nineteenth century in general and Walt Whitman in particular by assuming homoerotic desire and intent. For a corrective to Boswell, see Caroline Walker Bynum, *Jesus as Mother: Studies in the Spirituality of the High Middle Ages* (Berkeley: University of California Press, 1982), pp. 162–63.

41. Cited in Robert B. Martin, *With Friends Possessed: A Life of Edward FitzGerald* (New York: Atheneum, 1985), pp. 72–73, 117; cited in Hagstrum, *Sex and Sensibility,* p. 3. My interpretation of fraternalism differs from that of Richards ("'Passing the Love of Women'"); he also argues for a heterosexual tradition of affectionate male relations.

42. Mumford et al., eds., *Memoir,* pp. 84–86, 254–55; Samuel Joseph May Diary, 11 May 1865, May Antislavery Collection, Cornell University.

43. Smith-Rosenberg, "Love and Ritual," passim; William R. Taylor and Christopher Lasch, "Two 'Kindred Spirits': Sorority and Family in New England, 1839–1846," *New England Quarterly* 36 (March 1963): 23–41; Lynch, "Here Is Adhesiveness," p. 70; François Joseph Gall, *The Influence of the Brain on the Form of the Head . . . ,* 6 vols. trans. Winslow Lewis, Jr. (Boston: Marsh, Capen & Lyon, 1835), 3:200–316.

44. John Higham, "The Reorientation of American Culture in the 1890s," in Higham, ed., *Writing American History: Essays on Modern Scholarship* (Bloomington: Indiana University Press, 1970), pp. 74–102; Joe L. Dubbert, "Progressivism and

the Masculinity Crisis," *Psychoanalytic Review* 61 (fall 1974): 443–55; Sean Wilentz, *Chants Democratic: New York City and the Rise of the American Working Class, 1788–1850* (New York: Oxford University Press, 1984); Mary Ann Clawson, "Nineteenth-Century Women's Auxiliaries and Fraternal Orders," *Signs* 12 (autumn 1986): 40–61; Leonard Harry Ellis, "Men among Men: An Exploration of All-Male Relationships in Victorian America" (Ph.D. diss., Columbia University, 1982).

45. Christopher Ricks, in *Tennyson* (New York: Macmillan, 1972), pp. 215–30, indicated that Tennyson's son excised his father's writing to avoid the possible taint of homosexuality. Samuel J. May's son Joseph rejected his father's feminized values; see Joseph May, *The Heroes of Today: A Sermon . . .* (Philadelphia, 1881?); *Jesus: A Study in Ideal Manhood* (Philadelphia, 18?); and *Manliness: A Sermon Preached in the First Unitarian Church of Philadelphia . . .* (Philadelphia, 1881?).

46. Jeffrey Weeks, *Coming Out: Homosexual Politics in Britain, from the Nineteenth Century to the Present* (London: Quartet Press, 1977), pp. 11–22, 68–83 (21 quoted); Robert A. Nye, "Honor in Transition: Masculinity an Male Codes of Honor in Modern France," paper delivered at the French Historical Society meeting, 1985, 7–13; Henry Abelove, "Freud, Male Homosexuality, and the Americans," manuscript essay kindly supplied by the author; Phyllis Grosskurth, *Havelock Ellis: A Biography* (New York: Alfred A. Knopf, 1980). The rise of psychoanalysis, and the growing popularity of sexologists like Ellis, to a large degree resulted from their desires to relieve society of personal repression. Sex reformers may have diminished feelings of guilt, but at the price of heightened awareness of presumed sexual deviation.

Chapter Six

1. *Parker v. Parker,* Case 403, San Mateo County, 1882 (testimony of Annie Parker). On the expansion of legal conceptions of matrimonial cruelty, see two essays by Robert L. Griswold: "The Evolution of the Doctrine of Mental Cruelty in Victorian American Divorce, 1790–1900," *Journal of Social History* 20 (fall 1986): 127–48, and "Law, Sex, Cruelty, and Divorce in Victorian America, 1840–1900," *American Quarterly* 38 (winter 1986): 721–45. For the complete text and an analysis of an intriguing nineteenth-century cruelty case, see Robert L. Griswold, "Sexual Cruelty and the Case for Divorce in Victorian America," *Signs* 11 (spring 1986): 529–41.

2. *Pfeiffer v. Pfeiffer,* 9 *New York Supplement* 31 (1889).

3. Kai T. Erickson, *Wayward Puritans: A Study in the Sociology of Deviance* (New York: John Wiley and Sons, 1966), pp. 4, 6–7, 11, 13, 15–16.

4. A detailed analysis of the sample and the setting is found in Robert L. Griswold, *Family and Divorce in California, 1850–1890: Victorian Illusions and Everyday Realities* (Albany: State University of New York Press, 1982), pp. 18–38. Every divorce case in San Mateo County was examined; every fifth case in Santa Clara County was examined. California's relatively expansive divorce statutes, and especially its appellate-court interpretations of matrimonial cruelty, made it a harbinger of legal developments to come, and therefore particularly worthy of study.

5. Although domesticity—and its power to redefine manhood—first took shape

within the middle class, the legal redefinition of manhood and the function of the court as moral theater were certainly not confined to the middle class. In the two California counties, 17 percent of the families involved in divorce proceedings came from the upper class, 17 percent from the middle class, 14 percent from farming, 19 percent from skilled trades, 9 percent from unskilled trades, and 24 percent from the laboring class. For a full discussion of the class background of the litigants see Griswold, *Family and Divorce in California, 1850–1890*, pp. 24–26.

6. *Caroline v. John Peters*, Case 784, San Mateo County, 1871 (formal complaint and testimony of Peter Monotti and William Nelson); *Alice v. Edward Kilday*, Case 736, San Mateo County, 1886 (formal complaint); *Polly v. James Haun*, Case 2417, Santa Clara County, 1866 (formal complaint). The point is not that women received divorces solely because of such indignities; rather, they received divorces if a pattern of such behavior undermined the health of the wife or if such behavior was linked to more serious evidence of cruelty.

7. *Vicenta v. Daniel Wilson*, Case 2353, Santa Clara County, 1866 (testimony of Mrs. H. S. Hanson).

8. *Emma v. Joseph Tuers*, Case 2161, Santa Clara County, 1856 (testimony of William Spencer).

9. *Ellen v. Minor Havely*, Case 3024, Santa Clara County, 1869 (testimony of Ellen Havely).

10. *Mary v. David Savage*, Case 6065, Santa Clara County, 1880 (formal complaint).

11. *Ann v. Thomas Warhurst*, Case 2231, Santa Clara County, 1865 (formal complaint); *Vicenta v. Daniel Wilson* (formal complaint); *Alice v. Edward Kilday* (formal complaint).

12. *Ottilia v. Herman Kottinger*, Case 4505, Santa Clara County, 1876 (testimony of S. Strauss); *Susan v. Nicholas Dodge*, Case 2829, Santa Clara County, 1869 (testimony of Deborah McGowen); *Jane v. Fred Sayers*, Case 595, San Mateo County, 1869 (testimony of Clara Spaulding).

13. *Ellen v. Minor Havely* (testimony of Carrie Armstrong); for an extended discussion of such cases see Griswold, *Family and Divorce*, pp. 131–35.

14. *Eliza v. J. P. Noyes*, Case 1304, San Mateo County, 1878 (formal complaint); *Margaret v. Michael Maloney*, Case 597, San Mateo County, 1868 (formal complaint). Although a discussion of child-custody decisions is beyond the scope of this essay, data from the California counties and the nation in general suggest that a judicial redefinition of fatherhood was under way as well. In the early nineteenth century, children routinely went to the father in divorce and separation disputes, but in the ensuing decades jurists increasingly awarded children to mothers. In the closing years of the century, courts almost always awarded young children to mothers; perhaps more telling, mothers and not fathers now held the presumptive right to custody. Even mothers who were successfully sued for divorce more often than not received custody. In the two California courts, 91 percent of female divorce petitioners who requested custody received it; by contrast, only 37 percent of male petitioners were successful in this regard. See Griswold, *Family and Divorce in California, 1850–1890*, p. 153, and Michael Grossberg, "Who Gets the Child? Custody,

Guardianship, and the Rise of a Judicial Patriarchy in Nineteenth-Century America," *Feminist Studies* 9 (1983): 235–60.

15. *Brainard v. Brainard,* 1 *Brayton* 55 (Vermont, 1816).

16. *Butler v. Butler,* 1 *Parsons* 344 (Pennsylvania, 1849).

17. *Carpenter v. Carpenter,* 30 *Kansas Reports* 744 (1883).

18. *Waldron v. Waldron,* 24 *Pacific Reporter* 654 (California, 1890).

19. Lawrence Friedman, "The Two Faces of Law," *Wisconsin Law Review* 1 (1984): 13–35. In this article, and at greater length in another, Friedman argues that a form of consensual divorce was emerging by the late nineteenth century; see "Rights of Passage: Divorce Law in Historical Perspective," *Oregon Law Review* 63 (1984): 649–69.

20. Men, too, increased their use of cruelty suits. Divorces granted to men on grounds of cruelty were in fact the fastest-growing category in the nation for either sex. This trend suggests that men shared in the redefinition of family life that was under way in the nineteenth century. Many men's as well as women's expectations for marriage were unfulfilled, and rather than muddle through, thousands looked to the courts for relief. For these men, this admission of their wives' cruelty must have been difficult. After all, it was one thing for a woman to complain of cruelty, but quite another for a man to do so. Many men undoubtedly found it difficult to complain about the physical mistreatment, rudeness, or callousness of their wives. Such complaints surely seemed "unmanly" to many men: a "real" man should be able to control his wife, and if he could not, far be it from him to seek redress from agents of the state. Better to suffer in silence, withdraw to the masculine environs of a saloon, dominate his wife by brute force, or simply desert. This inhibiting aspect of male culture, however, diminished as the century came to a close. Between 1867 and 1871, men nationwide received only 800 divorces on grounds of cruelty; between 1902 and 1906, by contrast, husbands received 13,678 such divorces, an increase of 1,610 percent. See U.S. Bureau of the Census, *Special Reports: Marriage and Divorce, 1867–1906,* part 1 (Washington, D.C.: Government Printing Office, 1909), p. 27.

21. Ibid., pp. 28–29.

22. Ibid., pp. 86–89.

23. *Harriett v. Stephen Purdy,* Case 3298, Santa Clara County, 1870 (testimony of A. Chubbuck).

24. *Polly v. James Haun* (testimony of J. M. Owen).

25. *Mary v. William Allen,* Case 823, San Mateo County, 1872 (testimony of Mary Hull).

26. *Martha v. Samuel Brisbine,* Case 3632, Santa Clara County, 1872 (testimony of George and Exa Loss); *Kate v. Edward Bliven,* Case 4574, Santa Clara County, 1876 (testimony of Kate Bliven and John Turner); *Elaika v. Marlin Mattson,* Case 214, San Mateo County, 1876 (testimony of F. M. Hale); *Michael v. Catharine Ryan,* Case 931, San Mateo County, 1888 (defendant's cross-complaint).

27. *Amilla v. Joseph Kelly,* Case 1375, Santa Clara County, 1860 (formal complaint); *Elizabeth v. Egbert Etts,* Case 684, San Mateo County, 1871 (formal complaint).

28. *Brown v. Brown,* 38 *Arkansas Reports* 328 (1881).

29. *Walton v. Walton,* 34 *Kansas Reports* 197–98 (1885).

30. *Mahone v. Mahone,* 19 *California Reports* 626–28 (1862).

31. *Mack v. Handy,* 39 *Louisiana Annotated Reports* 491–99 (1887).

32. *Azbill v. Azbill,* 14 *Kentucky Law Reports* 106 (1892).

33. *McGill v. McGill,* 19 *Florida Reports* 345 (1882).

34. U.S. Bureau of the Census, *Special Reports: Marriage and Divorce, 1867–1906,* vol.1, p. 29.

35. *Berryman v. Berryman,* 59 *Michigan Reports* 607–9 (1886).

36. *Susan v. David Trayer,* Case 4379, Santa Clara County, 1875 (testimony of George Plank); *Elizabeth v. Jerome Hill,* Case 4295, Santa Clara County, 1875 (testimony of Sebastian Shaw).

37. *Elizabeth v. Orrin Dennis,* Case 623, San Mateo County, 1869 (testimony of D. Hoag).

38. *Seward v. Nellie Jones,* Case 366, San Mateo County, 1882 (testimony of P. M. Davenport).

39. Michael Grossberg, *Governing the Hearth: Law and the Family in Nineteenth-Century America* (Chapel Hill: University of North Carolina Press, 1985), pp. 289–307. The term "judicial patriarchy" is Grossberg's.

40. *Inskeep v. Inskeep,* 5 *Iowa Reports* 208 (1857).

41. Ibid., 209; see also William T. Nelson, *A Treatise on the Law of Divorce and the Annulment of Marriage* (Chicago: Callaghan and Co., 1895), p. 191, and Joel Prentiss Bishop, *Commentaries on the Law of Marriage and Divorce,* vol. 2, 4th ed. (Boston: Little, Brown and Co., 1864), p. 487. Legal writers also argued that the character and social class of the litigants—"the peculiar modes of life of the parties, and the habits of the community wherein they dwell"—had to be taken into account when assessing evidence. Bishop boldly suggested that behavior acceptable in lower-class communities would generate strong suspicions of adulterous intent among more refined sorts; in his judgment, there were "many freedoms which, in the unreserved contact of humble life, continually take place without imputation; whilst an equal license in classes of a higher order, and a more refined education, would naturally lead to a very different conclusion." See Bishop, *Commentaries on the Law of Marriage and Divorce,* vol. 2. p. 500; *Pollock v. Pollock,* 71 *New York Reports* 137 (1877).

42. On jurists' suspicions of vague moral allegations against a defendant's character, see *Washburn v. Washburn,* 5 *New Hampshire Reports* 195 (1830); *Evans v. Evans,* 93 *Kentucky Reports* 518 (1892); *Brooks v. Brooks,* 145 *Massachusetts Reports* 575 (1888); *Carter v. Carter,* 62 *Illinois Reports* 626 (1873).

43. *O'Bryan v. O'Bryan,* 13 *Missouri Reports* 17 (1850); see also *Blake v. Blake,* 70 *Illinois Reports* 626 (1873).

44. *Beadleston v. Beadleston,* 2 *New York Supplement* 811 (1888); see also *Stevens v. Stevens,* 8 *New York Supplement* 47 (1889); *Thomas V. Thomas,* 51 *Illinois Reports* 164 (1869).

45. *Osborn v. Osborn,* 44 *New Jersey Equity Reports* 258–61 (1888); see also *Pfeiffer v. Pfeiffer,* 9 *New York Supplement* 31 (1889), and *Steffens v. Steffens,* 11 *New York Supplement* 424–29 (1890). Judges also warned about accepting the testimony of a *particeps criminis* unless supported by strong corroborating evidence; otherwise, as Georgia Justice Ebenezer Starnes cautioned in 1855, "It would be to place the reputation of every lady at the mercy of any foul-mouthed reprobate, who, casting upon her a

lustful eye, might falsely seek to sully her reputation." See *Leary v. Leary,* 18 *Georgia Reports* 702 (1855); *Lewis v. Lewis,* 9 *Indiana Reports* 109 (1857); *Payne v. Payne,* 42 *Arkansas Reports* 236 (1883); *Evans v. Evans,* 93 *Kentucky Reports* 516–17 (1892).

46. *Baxter v. Baxter,* 1 *Massachusetts Reports* 345 (1805); *Holland v. Holland,* 2 *Massachusetts Reports* 154 (1806).

47. *Derby v. Derby,* 21 *New Jersey Equity Reports* 38 (1870).

48. Ibid., p. 49.

49. Ibid., p. 50.

50. *Hedden v. Hedden,* 21 *New Jersey Equity Reports* 61–66 (1870); *Cane v. Cane,* 39 *New Jersey Equity Reports* 149 (1884).

51. For a complete discussion of the relationship between false allegations of adultery and more expansive definitions of matrimonial cruelty, see Griswold, "Law, Sex, Cruelty, and Divorce in Victorian America," pp. 721–45.

52. *Coble v. Coble,* 5 *North Carolina Reports* 395 (1856). This suit was for a legal separation.

53. *Graft v. Graft,* 76 *Indiana Reports* 138 (1881). Courts were less certain about the impact on men unfairly accused of adultery. Nevada and Michigan, for example, made no distinction, while other courts (Texas, for one) argued that men suffered less from such calumnies than women; see *McAlister v. McAlister,* 71 *Texas Reports* 696–97 (1886); *Kelly v. Kelly,* 18 *Nevada Reports* 53 (1883); and *Whitmore v. Whitmore,* 49 *Michigan Reports* 417–18 (1882).

54. Bureau of the Census, *Special Reports: Marriage and Divorce, 1867–1906,* part 1, p. 27.

55. Ibid.

56. Elizabeth Cady Stanton, "Address at the Decade Meeting on Marriage and Divorce," in Pauline Davis, *A History of the National Woman's Rights Movement for Twenty Years* (New York: Journeymen Printers' Co-operative Association, 1871; reprint 1971, Kraus Reprint Company).

Chapter Seven

1. John Higham, "The Reorientation of American Culture in the 1890s," in Higham, ed., *Writing American History* (Bloomington, Ind., 1970), p. 79.

2. For example, E. Anthony Rotundo, "Body and Soul: Changing Ideals of Middle-Class Manhood, 1770–1920," *Journal of Social History* 16 (summer 1983): 32; Peter Gabriel Filene, *Him/Her/Self: Sex Roles in Modern America* (New York, 1974), esp. pp. 105–6. Colleen McDannell ("True Men as We Need Them," *American Studies* [fall 1986]: 19–36) breaks new ground in both her analysis of masculinity and her focus on Catholic men.

3. Kenneth Jackson, in *The Crabgrass Frontier: The Suburbanization of the United States* (New York, 1985), pp. 97–99, has a good discussion of suburban leisure; on pp. 41–44 is a look at mid-nineteenth-century commuting by horsecar and omnibus. Jon Teaford, in *The Twentieth Century American City* (Baltimore, 1986), p. 21, gives commuting times for the early twentieth century: eighteen minutes from suburban Queens to midtown Manhattan; twenty-three minutes from Riverside to Chicago.

Suburban Philadelphians, unless they chose the true countryside, could expect to be downtown in thirty minutes or less. *Thirty Miles around Philadelphia on the Lines of the Pennsylvania Railroad* (Philadelphia, 1913). Since the deterioration of the railroad and mass transit, and the advent of large-scale traffic jams caused by automobile commuting, Americans have forgotten the convenience of early-twentieth-century rail commuting. See also John R. Stilgoe, *Metropolitan Corridor* (New Haven, 1983), pp. 267–82.

4. The term "masculine domesticity" is my own. Contemporaries would have used words like "manly" and (by 1910 or so) "virile" rather than "masculine." They also would not have used the word "domesticity" in the context in which historians use it. Progressive Era Americans would have spoken of the role of the "manly" man in the home.

5. The question of what is or is not feminist has become quite complicated in the last few years; for example, Karen Blair, in *The Clubwoman as Feminist: True Womanhood Redefined, 1868–1914* (New York, 1980), argues that women's-club members who upheld many aspects of conventional domesticity were nevertheless feminists. In that sense, there are feminist aspects to masculine domesticity: men's and women's spheres merged in perceptible ways. My own view of feminism is less encompassing: Feminism is an ideology that begins with a recognition that women are denied full participation in the society, and demands equal rights and opportunities for women within the larger society. In this view, masculine domesticity was not so much feminist as it was an alternative to, or substitution for, feminism. See Nancy Cott, *The Grounding of Modern Feminism* (New Haven, 1987), pp. 4–5.

6. Carl Degler has argued that middle-class families had become "companionate" by the mid-nineteenth century, but I think his dating is too early. Most of his data is drawn from letters between husbands and wives who spent long periods of time (months, occasionally years) apart. What the letters indicate to me is that husbands and wives *loved* each other, not that men were involved in the details of the household. See Carl Degler, *At Odds: Women and the Family in America from the Revolution to the Present* (New York, 1980), pp. 33–42. William Alcott, a very widely read writer of marital advice in the mid-nineteenth century who was considered an advocate of greater family intimacy, told his readers that if a husband spent the dinner hour with his family, that was quite enough. See Alcott, *The Young Husband* (Boston, 1839), p. 136. On Alcott's influence, see Degler, *At Odds*, p. 269. Joan Seidl, in "Consumers' Choices: A Study of Household Furnishings, 1880–1920," *Minnesota History* 48 (spring 1983): 183–97, demonstrates how the pattern of male domestic involvement in the house itself developed in Minnesota.

7. The term "literary domestic" is Mary Kelley's, in *Private Woman, Public Stage: Literary Domesticity in Nineteenth Century America* (New York, 1984), pp. vi–xiii.

8. Kathryn Sklar, *Catharine Beecher: A Study in Domesticity* (New Haven, Conn., 1973), p. 163. Sklar's biography of Beecher remains perhaps the best analysis of the ideology of domesticity.

9. Some historians have become skeptical of the reality of the doctrine of separate spheres, because of their beliefs that the affectional marriage had triumphed by the mid-nineteenth century and that marriages of affection were necessarily compan-

ionate. In particular, Carl Degler (for the United States) in *At Odds* and Laurence Stone (for England) in *The Family, Sex, and Marriage* (London, 1977) make this claim. But so far the weight of the evidence, it seems to me, is on the side of those who maintain that gender separation was a reality at midcentury. Historians are well aware of Carroll Smith-Rosenberg's work on women's relationships; her older essays, with her new work, recently appeared as *Disorderly Conduct: Visions of Gender in Victorian America* (New York, 1985). Suzanne Lebsock, in *The Free Women of Petersburg* (New York, 1984), argues that "the evidence from Petersburg suggests that marriage was fundamentally asymmetrical" (p. 18; see also pp. 19–29). Mary Ryan makes much the same argument in *Cradle of the Middle Class* (New York, 1981), pp. 189–97. The quotation is from p. 191.

10. Listing all of the works about the changing roles of women would require a bibliographic essay in itself. For an overview, see Sheila Rothman, *Woman's Proper Place* (New York, 1978). Work on the history of men continues to follow the Higham interpretation. The best of these analyses is Peter Filene's *Him/Her/Self*. See also Elizabeth Pleck and Joseph Pleck, *The American Man* (Prentice-Hall, 1980).

11. William Alcott's marital advice tract, *The Young Husband,* is a typical example. But books that offered general advice rarely concerned themselves with such topics.

12. Henry Ward Beecher, *Lectures to Young Men* (New York, 1849), pp. 41, 120–127, 152; John Angell James, *The Young Man's Friend* (New York, 1860), esp. p. 50; Karen Halttunen, *Confidence Men and Painted Women* (New Haven and London, 1982), esp. pp. 25–26 and 47–48.

13. Quoted in J. A. Banks, *Victorian Values* (London, 1981), p. 81.

14. Catharine Sedgwick, *Home* (New York, 1890 [1835]).

15. *Godey's Lady's Book* (January 1855): 37–40.

16. *Godey's* (February 1855): 110–12.

17. *Godey's* (March 1855): 206–8. Arthur argued that domestic happiness (or misery) was in the hands of the husband. The belief in the power of men to wreck the happiness of women is an important theme of the domestic novels of the mid-nineteenth century as well. Susan Warner's *Wide, Wide World* (New York, 1852) makes this point explicitly, esp. pp. 12, 23.

18. Harriet Beecher Stowe, *My Wife and I* (New York, 1967; reprint of Riverside ed., esp. p. 478. The other novel referred to is *We and Our Neighbors: or, The Records of an Unfashionable Street* (New York, 1875).

19. Stowe, *My Wife and I*, p. 98.

20. A good brief introduction to Diaz and her work is Jane Benardete, "Abby Morton Diaz," in Langdon Lynne Faust, ed., *American Women Writers,* vol. 1 (abridged) (New York, 1983), pp. 161–63.

21. Abby M. Diaz, *A Domestic Problem* (New York, 1974; reprint of 1875 ed.), pp. 36–37.

22. Margaret Sangster, *The Art of Being Agreeable* (New York, 1897), p. 22. Sangster was a popular domestic writer whose works appeared in many of the women's magazines of the period.

23. The "sear and palsy" quotation is from L. H. G. Abell, *Woman in Her Various*

Relations (New York, 1851), p. 214; the "just as important" quotation is from Sangster, pp. 272–73. See also Sangster, p. 49.

24. "A Father's View of the Home," *Independent* 61 (1906): 912.

25. James Canfield, "The Philosophy of Staying in Harness," *Cosmopolitan* 39 (May 1905): 10–11.

26. I am indebted to Mark Carnes for informing me that the heyday of male fraternal associations was in the nineteenth century; there was a relative decline in the early part of the twentieth. The community data are from Haddonfield, New Jersey, which became an important railroad suburb of Philadelphia in the last years of the nineteenth century and continued so into the twentieth. *Minutes of the Haddonfield Sewing Society* (handwritten MS, 1896–1903); *Minutes of the Penn Literary Society* (handwritten MS, 1897–1918); *Papers of the Haddonfield Natural Science Club* (miscellaneous materials, 1901–1914). Materials on the Debating Society are mixed in with the Natural Science Club's papers. All are in the Haddonfield Historical Society, whose librarian, Kathy Tassini, shared with me the information on the early vicissitudes of the (male) Civic Club. Interestingly, later in the century Haddonfield men did organize such a club quite successfully, which may be a clue that masculine domesticity perhaps did not long outlive this period.

27. It may seem surprising that in what we have come to see as the golden age of domesticity, domestic advice-givers themselves urged women not to "build a wall around" the "sphere of domestic duties," because that would render them "narrow" and incapable of having "prospects, interests, hopes or enjoyment beyond it." These are L. H. G. Abell's words, from *Woman in Her Various Relations*, p. 22. Abell, although a conservative advocate of domesticity, believed that women needed "society" for their own emotional well-being; husbands did not come into the matter.

28. See Sangster, p. 39. My point about the new significance of the husband-wife bond can be illustrated by two stories that focus on the same theme—whether a woman should put her husband or her child first—which appeared some sixty years apart. The first, in *Godey's Lady's Book* (August 1843) ended with a child maimed because of her mother's decision to leave her with a nurse for *one evening* to go out with her husband. After the child's injury, the father's business failed, and the author concluded that there was "little prognostic of a brighter day" (p. 69). Contrast that attitude with a *Ladies Home Journal* story (April 1908) in which a young mother becomes so attached to her first baby that she neglects her husband. The young woman's mother advises her: "You should go out more and try to forget the baby for a time" (p. 16). Although shocked by her mother's advice, she follows it, and is rewarded by a better relationship with her husband and a happier child. The difference between the stories, which have nearly exactly the same subject, is very important for understanding the changes in attitudes toward marriage and parenthood that occurred during this period.

29. Martha Bruère and Robert Bruère, *Increasing Home Efficiency* (New York, 1912), pp. 291–92; Anne Morgan, *The American Girl* (New York, 1916), p. 24.

30. The male advice-givers will be discussed later in the essay. The Richard Hard-

ing Davis piece is "Our Suburban Friends," *Harper's* 89 (January 1894): 55–57.

31. When historians use the term "companionate" to describe marriages in the twentieth century, they run the risk of confusion, because in the 1920s the term "companionate marriage" came to mean a specific type of marriage urged especially by Judge Ben Lindsay of Colorado, who argued for trial marriages that could be easily dissolved, and in which people would agree not to have children. It should be clear that in this essay, "companionate" refers to a marriage in which the partners are, quite literally, companions.

32. Bruère and Bruère, p. 292; see also pp. 173–74 and 177–78. For a first-rate analysis of the implications of the Bruères' work for our understanding of middle-class patterns of consumption, see Daniel Horowitz, "Frugality or Comfort: Middle Class Styles of Life in the Early Twentieth Century," *American Quarterly* 37 (summer 1985): 239–59. See also his *Morality of Spending* (Baltimore, 1985).

33. Stowe, *My Wife and I,* p. 229.

34. Ibid., p. 478.

35. Ibid., p. 38. On p. 447, Eva proposes to "introduce the country sitting room into our New York house." Stowe described the Hendersons' house, which was physically within the city limits, in unmistakably suburban terms. See pp. 468–69.

36. Claudia Bushman is the author of a study of the Robinson family which focuses on Harriet Hanson Robinson. It is a carefully researched work, rich in both material and understanding. See *A Good Poor Man's Wife* (Hanover, Conn., 1981). For the specific information cited here, see pp. 86–87.

37. Lydia Maria Child to her sister-in-law Lydia B. Child, 11 February 1875, in Milton Meltzer and Patricia Hollan, eds., *Lydia Maria Child: Selected Letters* (Amherst, Mass., 1982), p. 530.

38. Bushman, pp. 146, 200. I should note here that my interpretation of Hattie Shattuck's growing resentment toward her husband's business failures differs form that of the family's biographer. Claudia Bushman argues that "Sid provided neither a living nor a home. Hattie had no children and cleaved to her mother rather than her husband. Yet the family functioned well as a unit. All three pooled their resources and did not blame the others for their lacks" (p. 200). Hattie Shattuck's own behavior implied quite different feelings; she grew bitter and angry, and she refused to live with her husband during the long years of his reversals. I would guess she was dissatisfied with her marriage.

39. Michael Katz, Michael Doucet, and Mark Stern, *The Social Organization of Early Industrial Capitalism* (Cambridge, Mass., 1982), p. 29. Carroll Smith-Rosenberg makes much the same point in *Disorderly Conduct,* pp. 167–70.

40. Mary Augusta Carr Cumings diaries, the Schlesinger Library, Radcliffe College. Entries for the following dates: 4 January 1869; 28 January 1872; 7 and 11 February 1876; 1877 passim (this is the year they had their house built in Jamaica Plain); 3 May 1878; and dated notes in the memoranda section, 1876. The daybooks are sketchy, but revealing.

41. For example, we can look at one suburb at the turn of the century. Overbrook Farms, an upper-middle-class Philadelphia suburb, was built in 1893. In 1900, of its male heads of households (154 out of 173), 51 percent worked as corporate officers,

business executives, and bankers; another 10 percent were managers or other nonexecutive-level corporate employees; and 24 percent were physicians, lawyers, and other professionals. The majority of the men in this community belonged to the "new" middle class, albeit in the upper reaches of it. Manuscript Census Records, Enumeration District 904, 1900. See also Elaine Tyler May, *Great Expectations: Marriage and Divorce in Post-Victorian America* (Chicago, 1980), p. 49; and Peter Filene, *Him/Her/Self,* pp. 80–83.

42. Diaz, pp. 115–16; see also p. 99.

43. Stowe, *My Wife and I,* p. 40.

44. Sangster, p. 137.

45. Bruère and Bruère, pp. 291–92.

46. *American Homes and Gardens* (November and December 1905), editorials.

47. Seidl, "Consumers' Choices," p. 186.

48. Seidl, p. 189.

49. Kate Wiggin, *Children's Rights* (Boston, 1890), pp. 63–67.

50. See Filene, *Him/Her/Self,* pp. 86–88. Allen Davis has an interesting analysis of manliness in relation to war in *American Heroine* (New York, 1973), pp. 228–31, 240–41.

51. Albert J. Beveridge, *The Young Man and the World* (Buffalo, New York, 1907).

52. Ennis Richmond, *Boyhood: A Plea for Continuity in Education* (London and New York, 1898), pp. 71–72; Carl Werner, *Bringing up the Boy* (New York, 1913), esp. pp. 69–83; Kate Upson Clark, *Bringing up Boys* (New York, 1899), p. 35; Sangster, *The Art of Being Agreeable,* p. 55. The issue of the impact of Boy Scouting on father-son relations is problematic. David Macleod (*Building Character in the American Boy* [Madison, Wisconsin, 1983]) has some information on the number of fathers who were troop leaders; he says (p. 268) that the organization made "ritual gestures" toward closer father-son relations. Boy Scouting was popular in the suburbs, and we need to know more about the participation of fathers.

53. Beveridge, *The Young Man and the World,* pp. 64–66.

54. Bernarr Macfadden, *Manhood and Marriage* (New York, 1916), p. 81.

55. Clement Wood, *Bernarr Macfadden: A Study in Success* (New York, 1929), p. 14.

56. Macfadden, *Manhood and Marriage,* pp. 25–26; Wood, *Bernarr Macfadden,* p. 14.

57. Beveridge, *The Young Man and the World,* pp. 164–66.

58. David P. Handlin, *The American Home: Architecture and Society, 1815–1915* (Boston, 1979), pp. 116–20; Jackson, *Crabgrass Frontier,* p. 152.

59. Papers and Proceedings, *Third Annual Meeting, American Sociological Society,* esp. pp. 167–68 and 181–90.

60. See Foster Rhea Dulles, *America Learns to Play: A History of Popular Recreation, 1607–1940* (New York, 1940), chap. 11, esp. pp. 194–201. Dulles's book remains the most comprehensive national study of recreation. His study shows that in the last years of the nineteenth century and the early years of the twentieth, the most popular forms of recreation were those that families could enjoy together. He says of football (which, along with baseball and boxing, was an important spectator sport) that "few adults found themselves able or willing to play football. . . . The

game was primarily for boys." (p. 198). For the institutionalization of family to-getherness in one suburb, see Tello J. Apery, *Overbrook Farms* (Philadelphia, 1936), pp. 76–80, and Wendell and Smith, *Overbrook Farms: A Suburb Deluxe* (Philadelphia, 1905). *Bylaws of the Haddon Field Club* (Haddonfield, N.J. [c. 1910]). For baseball on the suburban lawn, see Handlin, *American Home,* p. 181.

61. Cordelia Drexel Biddle, *My Philadelphia Father* (New York, 1955), pp. 1, 40.

62. There *were,* of course, some single-sex societies, including the Colonial Dames, the Daughters of the American Revolution, and the prestigious Fortnight-ly, a women's club modeled on the New Century Club of Philadelphia (but tailored for suburban women with a special "section" for "mothers"). Men had a few frater-nal organizations, including the Masons, and a "gun club" that held target shoots. (One of the most amusing things about the gun club was that its target-shoot pro-gram reminds one of nothing so much as a women's club printed program.) *Haddonfield Gun Club: Second Annual Shoot at Targets* (Haddonfield, 1908); the *Haddon Monthly* (March and April 1901) has information on the Haddon Fort-nightly and other clubs; for the Mothers and Teachers Club, see *Programme, the Haddonfield Mothers and Teachers Club* (Haddonfield, 1906).

63. Peter Stearns, *Be a Man! Males in Modern Society* (New York and London, 1979), p. 107.

64. Elaine Tyler May, *Great Expectations,* p. 54; Robert Fogelson, *The Fragmented Metropolis: Los Angeles, 1850–1930* (Cambridge, Mass., 1967), pp. 104–5.

65. Gwendolyn Wright, *Building the Dream* (New York, 1981), pp. 109–11, and *Moralism and the Model Home* (Chicago, 1980), pp. 9–46.

66. In order to determine the changes and continuities in house design between the 1860s and 1870s, on the one hand, and the first decade of the twentieth century, on the other, I examined 151 interior and exterior designs from these sources: Cal-vert Vaux, *Villas and Cottages* (New York, 1970 [1864]); E. C. Hussey, *Home Building: A Reliable Book of Facts* (Watkins Glen, N.Y., 1976 [1875]); Palliser, Palliser & Co., *Palliser's Model Homes* (Fenton, California, 1972 [1878]); *American Homes and Gar-dens,* 1906–1912; and the *Craftsman,* 1901–1906. I deliberately stayed away from "bungalow books" in order to make sure that I included large numbers of designs that appealed to the upper middle class. The question might be raised: Did builders use pattern books and house designs? The answer appears to be that they did. See Catherine Bisher, "Jacob W. Holt: An American Builder," originally published in the *Winterthur Portfolio* (spring 1981) and reprinted in Dell Upton and John Michael Vlach, *Common Places* (Athens, Georgia, 1986), pp. 447–81.

67. David Handlin, *The American Home,* pp. 306–10, analyzes the shift in Frank Lloyd Wright's architectural emphasis from the family to the individual as the cen-tury progressed. In the early twentieth century, when Wright was designing houses for the *Ladies Home Journal,* he emphasized family. Gwendolyn Wright, *Moralism and the Model Home,* pp. 139 and 249–53; Jan Cohn, *The Palace or the Poorhouse* (East Lansing, Michigan, 1979), pp. 106–7; Joy Wheeler Dow, "The Fascination of an En-glish Cottage," *American Homes and Gardens* (February 1911): 50. See also *American Homes and Gardens* (March 1906): 161–62, and Frank Lloyd Wright, "The Card-board House," in *The Future of Architecture* (New York, 1953), pp. 152–53.

68. This whole area is a difficult one to understand. On the one hand, the popularity of children's designs (they pervaded the *Craftsman* as well as *American Homes and Gardens* in the first decade of the twentieth century) suggests recognition of children as individuals. On the other hand, it shows that they are being set off from their parents, and seems to indicate that they are no longer automatically part of women's space. Questions of child and parental space need more attention from historians.

69. Rothman, *Woman's Proper Place,* pp. 68–69; Charlotte Perkins Gilman, *The Home* (New York, 1903).

70. For example, Beveridge, in *Young Man and the World,* pp. 175–77, makes it explicit that he does not expect women and men to take on identical socioeconomic roles.

Chapter Eight

1. Charles Moore, "The Woman Lawyer," reprinted in *Green Bag* 26 (1914): 525–31.

2. Duncan Kennedy, "Toward an Historical Understanding of Legal Consciousness: The Case of Classical Legal Thought in America, 1850–1940," *Research in Law and Society* 3 (1980): 6.

3. For a helpful introduction to the question of legal autonomy see Sally Falk Moore, *Law as Process: An Anthropological Approach* (London, 1978).

4. For valuable discussions on the use of gender in historical analysis see Joan W. Scott, "Gender: A Useful Category of Historical Analysis," *American Historical Review* 91 (1986): 1053–75; Linda Nicholson, *Gender and History: The Limits of Social Theory in the Age of the Family* (New York, 1986).

5. My approach to the issue of professionalization has been influenced by Thomas Haskell, ed., *The Authority of Experts: Studies in History and Theory* (Bloomington, Ind., 1984), esp. Haskell's introduction, and by Magali Sarfatti Larson, *The Rise of Professionalism* (Berkeley, 1977).

6. Lawrence M. Friedman, *A History of American Law,* 2d ed. (New York, 1985), pp. 303–22; Maxwell Bloomfield, *American Lawyers in a Changing Society, 1776–1876* (Cambridge, Mass., 1976), esp. chaps. 1–5. For discussions of the emergence of an indigenous American legal literature see Charles Warren, *A History of the American Bar* (Boston, 1911), chaps. 1, 12, and 20; Friedman, *History of American Law,* pp. 322–33; and Morton Horwitz, "Part 3—Treatise Literature," *Law Library Journal* 69 (1976):461.

7. Robert A. Ferguson, *Law and Letters in American Culture* (Cambridge, Mass., 1984), part 2.

8. Law student, cited in ibid., p. 135.

9. Parsons, cited in ibid., p. 93.

10. Ferguson has conducted the most thorough study of the impact of antiliterary influences on the bar; see, for example, *Law and Letters,* pp. 87–95.

11. Friedman, *History of American Law,* p. 304.

12. Timothy Walker, "Professional Success," *Western Law Journal* 1 (1844): 544.

13. Alexis de Tocqueville, *Democracy in America,* trans. Henry Reeve (New York,

1973), pp. 48–56, 102–7, 247–50, 256–58, 282–90; Daniel Boorstin, *The Americans: The National Experience* (New York, 1965), pp. 35–42.

14. Ann Douglas, *The Feminization of American Society,* esp. chap. 4.

15. Joseph Story, "Value and Importance of Legal Studies," in William Wetmore Story, ed., *The Miscellaneous Writings of Joseph Story* (New York, 1852), p. 548.

16. For an evocative assessment of circuit riding and its relation to legal professionalism see Daniel Calhoun, *Professional Lives in America: Structure and Aspiration, 1750–1850* (Cambridge, Mass., 1965), chap. 3.

17. John P. Kennedy, *Memoirs of the Life of William Wirt, Attorney General of the United States* (Philadelphia, 1849), vol. 1, pp. 66–67.

18. DuPonceau, quoted in Friedman, *History of American Law,* p. 310.

19. For the most thorough study of conviviality see William R. Johnson, *Schooled Lawyers: A Study in the Clash of Professional Cultures* (New York, 1978).

20. Butterfield, quoted in Johnson, *Schooled Lawyers,* p. 27.

21. For a discussion of the depiction of lawyers in obituaries see Bloomfield, pp. 147–50.

22. For an introduction to recent analyses of the masculine ideals of the era see E. Anthony Rotundo, "Body and Soul: Changing Ideals of American Middle Class Manhood," *Journal of Social History* 16 (1983): 23–38.

23. Sullivan, cited in Charles Warren, *A History of the American Bar* (Boston, 1911), p. 206.

24. Robinson, cited in ibid., p. 511.

25. See, for example, Johnson, *Schooled Lawyers,* p. 38.

26. Warren, *A History of the American Bar,* chaps. 10–12.

27. For a discussion of the professional implications of the Lincoln myth see Jerold Auerbach, *Unequal Justice: Lawyers and Social Change in Modern America* (New York, 1976), chap. 1.

28. Robert Wiebe, "Lincoln's Fraternal Democracy," in John L. Thomas, ed., *Abraham Lincoln and the American Political Tradition* (Amherst, Mass., 1986), p. 19. I would like to thank Michael Holt for bringing this article to my attention.

29. Ibid., p. 17.

30. David Field, "The Study and Practice of the Law," *Democratic Review* 14 (1844): 345.

31. Stephen Botein, "'What We Shall Meet Afterwards in Heaven': Judgeship as a Symbol for Modern American Lawyers," in Gerhard Grieson, *Professional Ideologies* (New York, 1982), p. 50; for a comparative assessment of the power of American judges see Patrick S. Atiyah, "Lawyer and Rules: Some Anglo-American Comparisons," *Southwestern Law Journal* 37 (1983): 545–62.

32. Maxwell Bloomfield, "The Supreme Court in American Popular Culture," *Journal of American Culture* 5 (1982): 3; see also Bloomfield, "Law and Lawyers in American Popular Culture," in *Law and American Literature* (Chicago, 1980), pp. 22–25. For a fictional depiction of this veneration see Thomas Wolfe, "How Certain Joyners Went to Town," in *The Hills Beyond* (New York, 1943), p. 258.

33. For a discussion of the history of women judges see Beverly Cook, "Women Judges: A Preface to Their History," *Golden Gate Law Review* 14 (1984): 573–610.

34. George Sharswood, *Professional Ethics* (Philadelphia, 1854), p. 55.

35. Joseph Baldwin, *The Flush Times of Alabama and Mississippi: A Series of Sketches* (1853, reprinted Gloucester, Mass., 1974), p. 241.

36. "Law and Lawyers in American Popular Culture," p. 25. For Story's depictions of the law as religion see Perry Miller, ed., *The Legal Mind in America: From Independence to the Civil War* (Garden City, N.Y., 1962), p. 180; for Lincoln's statement on law as religion see "Address before the Young Men's Lyceum of Springfield, Illinois," In John G. Nicolay and John Hay, eds., *The Complete Works of Abraham Lincoln,* vol. 1, 2d ed. (New York, 1905), pp. 42–43; see also Thomas C. Grey, "The Constitution as Scripture," *Stanford Law Review* 37 (1984): 1–25.

37. "The Independence of the Judiciary," *North American Review* 46 (1843): 411.

38. Jerome Frank, *Law and the Modern Mind* (New York, 1930) pp. 3–11, 14–19, 253–60.

39. Philip Hone, cited in Charles Haar, ed., *The Golden Age of American Law* (New York, 1965). Haar's collection is a very useful introduction to primary documents of the era.

40. *The Pioneers, or the Sources of the Susquehanna: A Descriptive Tale,* intro. James Franklin Beard (Albany, N.Y., 1980). p. 344. For valuable assessments of the book, see Brook Thomas, "*The Pioneers,* or the Sources of American Legal History: A Critical Tale," *American Quarterly* 36 (1986): 87; see also Henry Nash Smith, *Virgin Land* (Cambridge, Mass., 1950), pp. 66–68, and Perry Miller, *The Life of the Mind in America* (New York, 1965), pp. 99–104.

41. For an insightful discussion of the courtroom as moral theater, see Robert L. Griswold, "Adultery and Divorce in Victorian America, 1800–1900," Legal History Program Working Papers, series 1, no. 6 (School of Law, University of Wisconsin at Madison), pp. 14–17.

42. Aviam Soifer, "The Paradox of Paternalism and Laissez-Faire Constitutionalism: United States Supreme Court, 1888–1921," *Law and History Review* 5 (1987): 250.

43. For a discussion of Shaw and *Billy Budd* see Brook Thomas, "The Legal Fictions of Herman Melville and Lemuel Shaw," *Critical Inquiry* 11 (1984): 24–51.

44. Botein, "Judgeship as a Symbol," pp. 53–54; for the general shift from pulpit to courtroom see John Murrin, "The Legal Transformation: The Bench and Bar of Eighteenth Century Massachusetts," in Stanley N. Katz and John Murrin, eds., *Colonial America: Essays in Politics and Social Development,* 3d ed. (New York, 1983), pp. 540–72.

45. *Farwell v. Boston and Worcester R.R.,* 4 Metcalf 49 (Massachusetts, 1842); *Commonwealth v. York,* 9 Metcalf 93 (Massachusetts, 1845); *Commonwealth v. Briggs,* 16 Pickering 203 (Massachusetts, 1834). For a thorough discussion of Shaw's jurisprudence see Leonard Levy, *The Law of the Commonwealth and Chief Justice Shaw* (Cambridge, Mass., 1957).

46. Blackwell, cited in Elizabeth Clark, "Religion, Rights and Difference: The Origins of American Feminism, 1848–1860," Legal History Program Working Papers, series 2, no. 2 (School of Law, University of Wisconsin at Madison), p. 18.

47. For varying assessments of the new professionalism see Auerbach, *Unequal*

Justice, chaps. 1–3; Robert Stevens, *Law School: Legal Education in American from the 1850s to the 1980s* (Chapel Hill, N.C., 1983), chaps. 1–7; Johnson, *Schooled Lawyers,* chaps. 4–7.

48. For discussions of these questions see Robert Gordon, "The Ideal and the Actual in the Law," in Gerald Gawalt, *The New High Priests: Lawyers in Late Nineteenth Century America* (Westport, Conn., 1984), pp. 160–72; Auerbach, *Unequal Justice,* chaps. 2–4; Johnson, *Schooled Lawyers,* chaps. 5–7; Michael Schudson, "Public, Private, and Professional Lives: The Correspondence of David Dudley Field and Samuel Bowles," *American Journal of Legal History* 21 (1977): 191–211; Peter Filene, "Between a Rock and a Hard Place: A Century of American Manhood," *South Atlantic Quarterly* 84 (1985): 339–55.

49. Stevens, *Law School,* p. 54.

50. *Centennial History of the Harvard Law School, 1817–1917* (Cambridge, Mass., 1917), p. 130.

51. James Barr Ames, *Lectures on Legal History and Miscellaneous Essays* (Cambridge, Mass., 1913), p. 362.

52. Statements in this paragraph are cited in Auerbach, *Unequal Justice,* pp. 96–98.

53. Strong cited in Friedman, *History of American Law,* p. 638; Needham cited in Auerbach, *Unequal Justice,* p. 37.

54. Freidman, *A History,* p. 639; see also D. Kelly Weisberg, "Barred from the Bar: Women and Legal Education in the United States, 1870–1890," *Journal of Legal Education* 28 (1977): 485–507.

55. Southward, cited in Karen Berger Morello, *The Invisible Bar: The Woman Lawyer in America, 1639 to the Present* (New York, 1986), p. 173.

56. California legislator, quoted anonymously in Moritmer D. Schwartz, Susan L. Brandt, and Patience Milrod, "Clara Shortridge Foltz: Pioneer in the Law," *Hastings Law Journal* 27 (1976): 548.

57. *Bradwell v. State,* 16 Wallings 141 (1872); see also Nancy Gilliam, "A Professional Pioneer: Myra Bradwell's Fight to Practice Law," *Law and History Review* 5 (1985): 105–33.

58. *In re Goodell,* 39 Wisconsin 245, 242 (1875); for a stinging critique of the decision see Ada M. Bittenbender, "Woman in Law," reprinted in Annie Nathan Meyer, ed., *Woman's Work in America* (New York, 1891), pp. 227–28; for Bittenbender's assessment of all the cases of women attempting to practice law see pp. 218–44; for a decision in favor of a woman becoming a lawyer see *In re Hall,* 1 Conn. 131 (1882) (this case apparently inspired Charles Moore to write his tale of Mary Padelford).

59. For a rather dogmatic assertion of judicial disdain for lawyers-turned-legislators see Isaac Redfield, "The Responsibilities and Duties of the Legal Profession," *American Law Register,* New Series 10 (1871): 547. In regard to the issue of varying voices of masculinity, it is important to acknowledge the point made by Elizabeth Pleck and Joseph Pleck: "There has no model American man but a range of manhoods." Bradley and Ryan illustrate part of that range and its institutionalized expression. Pleck and Pleck, eds., *The American Man* (Englewood Cliffs, N.J., 1980), p. 7.

60. 9 *Court of Claims Reports* 346 (1873). After being granted the right to practice

before the United States Supreme Court, Lockwood also secured the right to practice before the claims court.

61. *In re Lockwood,* 154 U.S. 116 (1893).

62. "Women and the Constitution," American Political Science Association *News for Teachers of Political Science* 46 (summer 1985): 13; see also Weisberg, "Barred from the Bar," pp. 486–87.

63. University of Iowa officials cited in Morello, *The Invisible Bar,* p. 52.

64. Ibid., p. 54.

65. James Harrison Kennedy and Wilson M. Day, eds., *The Bench and Bar of Cleveland* (Cleveland, 1889), p. 124.

66. Antonio Gramsci, *Letters from Prison,* ed. and trans. L. Lawner (New York, 1973), p. 204. My thinking on this topic has been greatly influenced by T. Jackson Lears, "The Concept of Cultural Hegemony: Problems and Possibilities," *American Historical Review* 90 (1985): 567–93, and by Maureen Cain, "Gramsci, the State, and the Place of Law," in David Sugarman, ed., *Legality, Ideology, and the State* (New York, 1983), pp. 95–117.

67. Ada Bittenbender, "Women in Law," *Chicago Law Times* 2 (1888): 291–305; Weisberg, "Barred from the Bar," pp. 502–3; Stevens, *Law School,* pp. 82–84.

68. Hastings official cited in Morello, *The Invisible Bar,* pp. 62–63.

69. Friedman, *History of American Law,* p. 641.

70. *Beyond Her Sphere: Women and the Professions in American History* (Westport, Conn., 1978), p. 110. Legal historian Robert Stevens also points to specific professional barriers that distinguished law from medicine: "Women found it more difficult to become lawyers than doctors, for example, because the legal profession was institutionalized and had, in general, been granted licensing powers earlier than the medical profession" (Stevens, *Law School,* p. 82).

71. Cynthia Fuchs Epstein, *Women in Law* (New York, 1981), p. 4; Mary Roth Walsh, *"Doctors Wanted: No Women Need Apply": Sexual Barriers in the Medical Profession, 1835–1875* (New Haven, 1976), pp. 107–8. Walsh argues, though, that the professionalizing reforms initiated in the 1920s after the Flexner Report made entrance into medicine much more difficult for women and began to reduce the number of women physicians. Walsh, *"Doctors Wanted,"* chap. 6.

72. Couzins, quoted in Morello, *The Invisible Bar,* p. 83.

73. Darrow, quoted in E. Harris Drew, "Women and the Law," *Women's Law Journal* 47 (1961): 21.

74. Nicholson, *Gender and History,* p. 25; Nancy Hartsock, *Money, Power and Sex* (New York, 1983), pp. 230–47; Catherine MacKinnon, *Feminism Unmodified: Discourses on Women and the Law* (Cambridge, Mass., 1987), pp. 74–77.

75. Smith, cited in Michael Grossberg, "Altruism or Professionalism: Boston and the Rise of Organized Legal Aid, 1900–1925," *Boston Bar Journal,* 22 (1978): 22, 29.

76. Florence Ellinwood Allen, *To Do Justly* (Cleveland, 1965), pp. 45–46.

77. Weisberg, "Barred from the Bar," p. 504.

78. *Law as Process,* p. 55.

79. "The Changing Faces of Fatherhood," in John Demos, ed., *Past, Present, and Personal: The Family and the Life Course in American History* (New York, 1986), p. 42.

80. Elizabeth Fox-Genovese and Eugene Genovese, "The Political Crisis of Social History," in Fox-Genovese and Genovese, eds., *The Fruits of Merchant Capitalism* (New York, 1984), pp. 179–212; Tony Judt, "A Clown in Regal Purple: Social History and the Historians," *History Workshop* 7 (1979): 66–94; Olivier Zunz, "The Synthesis of Social Change: Reflections on American Social History," in Zunz, ed., *Reliving the Past: The Worlds of Social History* (Chapel Hill, 1985).

Chapter Nine

1. A large body of research documents various facets of gender antagonism at work and men's efforts to exclude women from skilled jobs, as well as gender cooperation. See, for example, Ava Baron, "Women and the Making of the American Working Class: A Study of the Proletarianization of Printers," *Review of Radical Political Economics* 14:3 (fall 1982): 23–42; Mary H. Blewett, *Men, Women, and Work: A Study of Class, Gender and Protest in the New England Shoe Industry, 1780–1910* (Urbana: University of Illinois Press, 1988); Patricia Cooper, *Once a Cigar Maker: Men, Women, and Work Culture in American Cigar Factories, 1900–1919* (Urbana: University of Illinois Press, 1987); Sonya O. Rose, "Gender Antagonism and Class Conflict: Exclusionary Strategies of Male Trade Unionists in Nineteenth Centry Britain," *Social History* 13:2 (May 1988): 191–208; Barbara Taylor, "'The Men Are as Bad as Their Masters . . .': Socialism, Feminism and Sexual Antagonism in the London Tailoring Trade in the Early 1830's," *Feminist Studies* 5:1 (spring 1979): 7–40; and Susan Levine, *Labor's True Woman: Carpet Weavers, Industrialization and Labor Reform in the Gilded Age* (Philadelphia: Temple University Press, 1984).

2. The literature on working-class masculinity is sparse but growing. See, for example, Ava Baron, "Contested Terrain Revisited: Technology and Gender Definitions of Work in the Printing Industry, 1850–1920," in Barbara Wright, et al., eds., *Women, Work, and Technology: Transformations* (Ann Arbor: University of Michigan Press, 1987), pp. 58–83; Ileen DeVault, "'Give the Boys a Trade': Gender and Job Choice in the 1890's," in Baron, ed., *Work Engendered: Toward a New History of Men, Women, and Work* (Ithaca, N.Y.: Cornell University Press, forthcoming); Paul Willis, *Learning to Labor: How Working Class Kids Get Working Class Jobs* (Westmead, U.K.: Saxon House, 1977); Willis, "Shop-Floor Culture, Masculinity, and the Wage Form," in John Clarke, Charles Critcher, and Richard Johnson, eds., *Working-Class Culture: Studies in History and Theory* (New York: St. Martin's Press, 1979); David Halle, *America's Working Man: Work, Home, and Politics among Blue-Collar Property Owners* (Chicago: University of Chicago Press, 1984); David Bensman, *The Practice of Solidarity: American Hat Finishers in the Nineteenth Century* (Urbana: University of Illinois Press, 1985); Cynthia Cockburn, *Brothers: Male Dominance and Technological Change* (London: Pluto Press, 1983); Mary Ann Clawson, "Brotherhood, Class and Patriarchy: Fraternalism in Europe and America" (Ph.D. diss., State University of New York at Stony Brook, 1980); and Mary Blewett, "Masculinity and Mobility: The Dilemma of Lancashire Weavers and Spinners in Late-Nineteenth-Century Fall River, Massachusetts," this volume.

3. Most research on apprenticeship focuses on the early colonial craft system and the master-apprentice relation. The few recent studies on the nineteenth-century

United States do not examine the gender implications of apprenticeship. See W. J. Rorabaugh, *The Craft Apprentice: From Franklin to the Machine Age in America* (New York: Oxford, 1986); William Mulligan, Jr., "From Artisan to Proletarian: The Family and Vocational Education of Shoemakers in the Handicraft Era," in Charles Stephenson and Robert Asher, eds., *Life and Labor: Dimensions of American Working-Class History* (Albany: State University of New York Press, 1986), pp. 22–36; Charles More, *Skill and the English Working Class, 1870–1914* (London: Croom Helm, 1980); and Charles F. Sabel, *Work and Politics: The Division of Labor in Industry* (New York: Cambridge University Press, 1982), pp. 57–72.

4. Circular letter to the Master Printers of the City of New York, 13 July 1811, in George A. Stevens, *New York Typographical Union No. 6, Study of a Modern Trade Union and Its Predecessors,* New York State Department of Labor, Bureau of Labor Statistics (hereafter NYSBLS), 1911 (Albany: J. B. Lyon Co., 1913), p. 68. For a discussion of artisan character and the significance of a competence, see Ric Northrup, "Character, Competence, and Culture among Philadelphia Artisans, 1785–1820" (paper presented at the Conference of the Transformation of the Delaware Valley Project, 1750–1850, Philadelphia Center for Early American Studies, University of Pennsylvania, May 1987).

5. George Barnett, "The Introduction of the Linotype," in *Chapters on Machinery and Labor* (Cambridge: Harvard University Press, 1926), p. 11.

6. *Workingman's Advocate* 2:47 (16 June 1866): 4. For historical analyses of the "family wage" in the United States, see Martha May, "The Historical Problem of the Family Wage: The Ford Motor Company and the Five Dollar Day," *Feminist Studies* 8:2 (summer 1982): 399–424; Blewett, *Men, Women, and Work,* esp. chap. 5.

7. Report of Franklin Typographical Society, 22 July 1844, in Ethelbert Stewart, *A Documentary History of the Early Organization of Printers,* U.S. Department of Labor, vol. 11, bulletin no. 61 (Washington, D.C., 1905), p. 928.

8. "Mass Meeting of Printers," in Joel Munsell, comp., *Printers' Scraps,* vol. 9 (Albany, 1860), p. 77.

9. Journeymen couched demands for wage increases in terms of their ability to fulfill their roles as family providers. See, for example, "Remonstrance of Printers in Boston, Re: Remuneration Now Received for Their Labor," Massachusetts Legislature, House Document 44 (February 1949): 2–3; and *The Printer* (August 1864): 116.

10. Stevens, *New York Typographical Union,* p. 454; United States Industrial Commission, "Report of the Industrial Commission on the Relations and Conditions of Capital and Labor," 7: Manufacturers and General Business and Testimony Taken 1 November 1899 (Washington, D.C., 1901): 583. There is no evidence that an apprentice was required to demonstrate his ability by making or exhibiting a "masterpiece" to prove his competence. James Motley, *Apprenticeship in American Trade Unions* (Baltimore: Johns Hopkins University Press, 1907), p. 28.

11. NYSBLS, 4th *Annual Report,* 1886, quoted in E. Bemis, "Relation of Labor Organizations to the American Boy and to Trade Instruction," *Annals of the American Academy of Political and Social Science* 5 (1894–95): 85.

12. *Typographical Journal* 47:5 (November 1915): 609.

13. *Typographical Journal* 43:6 (December 1913): 673.

14. Local typographical societies attempted to limit apprenticeship throughout the 1830s and 1840s, but these efforts were ineffective. NYSBLS, 4th *Annual Report* (Albany, 1886). The apprenticeship problem was largely responsible for the formation of the National Typographical Association in 1836, and was considered critical by the founders of the National Typographical Union in 1850. Motley, *Apprenticeship in American Trade Unions*, p. 36.

15. Circular letter to the Master Printers of the City of New York, 13 July 1811, in Stevens, *New York Typographical Union*, p. 68; see also Stewart, *A Documentary History*, pp. 66–67; *Printers' Circular* 1:9 (1 November 1866): 113–14. Controversies over apprenticeship were visible even in the first decades of the nineteenth century. See George A. Tracy, *History of the Typographical Union, Its Beginnings, Progress, and Development* (Indianapolis: International Typographical Union, 1913), pp. 34–36.

16. Circular letter to master printers by New York Typographical Society, 13 July 1811, in Stevens, *New York Typographical Union*, pp. 67–68.

17. Addison B. Burk, *Apprenticeship as It Was and Is* (Philadelphia: Philadelphia Social Science Association, 1882), pp. 7–8.

18. Charles More, *Skill and the English Working Class*, pp. 139–42, and More, "Skill and the Survival of Apprenticeship," in Stephen Wood, ed., *The Degradation of Work? Skill, Deskilling and the Labour Process* (London: Hutchinson, 1982), pp. 109–21.

19. *Inland Printer* 8:3 (December 1890): 200.

20. NYSBLS, 4th *Annual Report*, p. 123.

21. Ibid., pp. 233–37. Bernard Bailyn, in *Education in the Forming of the American Society* (New York: Vintage, 1962), sees the decline of apprenticeship as part of the general movement of removing education from the family to more formal institutions; but this too was part of a general change in class relations.

22. Burke, *Apprenticeship as It Was and Is*, pp. 11–12; NYSBLS, 4th *Annual Report*, pp. 99, 100, 122; and Stevens, *New York Typographical Union*, p. 456.

23. *Typographical Advertiser* 12:4 (July 1867): 342.

24. Tracy, *History of the Typographical Union*, p. 1098.

25. NYSBLS, 4th *Annual Report*, pp. 203–4.

26. Stevens, *New York Typographical Union*, p. 417; Barnett, "Introduction of the Linotype," p. 6; NYSBLS, 1913–14, No. 3, Whole No. 56 (Albany, September 1913), p. 359.

27. Harry Kelber and Carl Schlesinger, *Union Printers and Controlled Automation* (New York: Free Press, 1967), pp. 11–14.

28. For an analysis of these conflicts, see Baron, "Contested Terrain Revisited," pp. 58–83.

29. United States Industrial Commission, *Hearings* 7:583.

30. American Newspaper Publishers Association, bulletin no. 1249 (25 January 1904).

31. Jacob Loft, *The Printing Trades* (New York: Farrar and Rhinehart, 1944), p. 45; Barnett, "Introduction of the Linotype," p. 10.

32. Charles Francis, *Printing for Profit* (New York: Bobbs-Merrill, 1917), p. 300; *Editor and Publisher* 1 (9 November 1901): 8; United States Congress, House, *Regulation and Restriction of Output*, 11th Special Report of the Commissioner of

Labor, 58th Congress, 2d Session, House Document 734 (Washington, D.C., 1904), p. 43.

33. *Typographical Journal* 43:6 (December 1913): 673–74.

34. *Typographical Journal* 32:3 (March 1908): 253.

35. *Typographical Journal* 50:2 (February 1917): 115.

36. Loft, *The Printing Trades,* p. 123.

37. For a discussion of the relationship between this shift in masculinity and relations between men and women printers, see Baron, "Contested Terrain Revisited," pp. 58–83.

38. *Typographical Journal* 39:5 (November 1911): 525.

39. Report of the President, *Typographical Journal* supplement 39:4 (October 1911): 32.

40. Report of the Machine Committee, Chicago Typographical Union, *Minutes* 5 (29 September 1895): 307.

41. Chicago Typographical Union, *Minutes* 8 (29 July 1906): 305.

42. ANPA *Bulletin* 358 (1 July 1911); for discussion of rules on discharge and incompetence established by the union, see Arthur R. Porter, Jr., *Job Property Rights: A Study of the Job Controls of the International Typographical Union* (New York: King's Crown Press, 1954), pp. 36–44.

43. *Typographical Journal* 50:2 (February 1917): 115.

44. Chicago Typographical Union, *Minutes* 4 (27 March 1892): 313–14; Porter, *Job Property Rights,* pp. 36–44; Stevens, *New York Typographical Union,* p. 529.

45. Chicago Typographical Union, *Executive Committee Minutes* 12 (22 November 1914): 130.

46. Tracy, *History of the Typographical Union,* p. 1099.

47. *Inland Printer* 15:6 (September 1895): 594.

48. *Typographical Journal* 12:7 (1 April 1898): 271.

49. NYSBLS, 4th *Annual Report,* pp. 216–17, 297; *Inland Printer* 20:3 (December 1897): 303.

50. Report of the President, *Typographical Journal* supplement 39:4 (October 1911): 32.

51. *Inland Printer* 20:3 (December 1897): 303.

52. *Typographical Journal* 32:3 (March 1908): 251.

53. Report of the President, *Typographical Journal* supplement 39:4 (October 1911): 32.

54. *Typographical Journal* 43:6 (December 1913): 678.

55. Report of the President, *Typographical Journal* supplement 39:4 (October 1911): 32.

56. Ibid.

57. *Inland Printer* 5:7 (April 1888): 516.

58. Employers had attempted to supplant apprenticeship with training schools in previous decades. Such efforts, however, were largely unsuccessful. See Baron, "Women and the Making of the American Working Class." By the end of the nineteenth century, the development of scientific management, the passage of state compulsory-education laws, and new work processes bolstered employers' efforts to

train printers outside the apprenticeship system. The number of manual training schools grew rapidly in the 1890s, from fifteen schools with 3,300 students in 1894 to forty schools with 13,900 students in 1897. Paul H. Douglas, *American Apprenticeship and Industrial Education* (New York: Longmans, Green & Co., 1921), p. 179.

59. Douglas, *American Apprenticeship,* pp. 9, 179.

60. United States Commissioner of Labor, 17th *Annual Report,* "Trade and Technical Education" (Washington, D.C., 1902), p. 422; *Typographical Journal* 49:5 (November 1916): 604; see also NYSBLS, 4th *Annual Report,* p. 337. Employers often used their schools as a way to recruit and train strikebreakers. Douglas, *American Apprenticeship,* pp. 315–16; Oswald, *Printing in the Americas,* chap. 28; Loft, *The Printing Trades,* p. 214.

61. *Typographical Journal* 12:11 (1 June 1898): 471–72.

62. For examples of different positions on and various proposed solutions to the advent of trade schools by the national union, see Tracy, *History of the Typographical Union,* pp. 1098–1100; NYSBLS, 4th *Annual Report,* pp. 159–63; Report of Officers, 61st Session of the International Typographical Union, *Typographical Journal* supplement 47:2 (August 1915): 256–59.

63. Quoted in Tracy, *History of the Typographical Union,* p. 909.

64. International Typographical Union communication, 11 January 1915, in Chicago Typographical Union, *Minutes* 12 (28 February 1915): 200–201.

65. *International Printer* 19:4 (July 1897): 410.

66. American Newspaper Publishers' Association, *Labor Bulletin* 28 (11 April 1908).

67. Douglas, *American Apprenticeship,* p. 317.

68. By 1912, employers and organized labor together supported a federal bill for public funds for industrial education. This was part of a general movement supported by the National Association of Manufacturers and the American Federation of Labor. Douglas, *American Apprenticeship,* p. 326.

69. Report of Officers, 63d Session of the International Typographical Union, *Typographical Journal* supplement 51:2 (August 1917): 206.

70. Even after the development of publicly funded vocational schools, publishers and printers continued to dispute apprenticeship limitations. American Newspaper Publishers' Association, *Bulletin* 5063 (6 May 1925).

71. Report of Officers, 66th Session of International Typographical Union, Quebec, Canada, 8–13 August 1921, *Typographical Journal* supplement 59:2 (August 1921): 216–17.

72. *Inland Printer* 20:5 (February 1891): 629.

73. *Typographical Journal* 9:11 (1 December 1896): 425–26.

74. *Typographical Journal* 32:3 (March 1908): 253.

75. United States Industrial Commission, *Hearings,* 620–21.

76. *Typographical Journal* 34:6 (June 1909): 658.

77. On printers' job property rights, see Porter, *Job Property Rights.* On generational inheritance among printers in Canada and Britain, see Wayne Roberts, "The Last Artisans: Toronto Printers, 1896–1914," in Gregory S. Kealy and Peter Warrian, eds., *Essays in Canadian History* (Toronto: McClelland & Steward, Ltd., 1976), pp.

125–42; Cockburn, *Brothers,* p. 114. For discussion of inheritance of skilled positions in other trades, see Taka Matsumura, *The Victorian Flint Glass Makers: The Labour Aristocracy Revisited* (Manchester, U.K.: Manchester University Press, 1983), and Stephen Hill, *The Dockers: Class and Tradition in London* (London: Heinemann, 1976).

78. *Typographical Journal* 45:2 (August 1914): 200.

79. See printers' debate on this subject in *Typographical Journal* during 1914, esp. 44:6 (June 1914): 760 and 45:2 (August 1914): 199–200.

80. *Inland Printer* 20:5 (February 1898): 629.

Chapter Ten

1. On the "strenuous life," see Elizabeth H. Pleck and Joseph H. Pleck, *The American Man* (Englewood Cliffs, N.J.: Prentice-Hall, 1980). For a more developed class analysis of the material in this essay, see Mary H. Blewett, "Manhood and the Market," in Ava Baron, ed., *Work Engendered: Toward a New History of Men, Women, and Work* (Cornell University Press, forthcoming). The anonymous clergyman is quoted in Massachusetts Bureau of Labor Statistics, *Second Annual Report* (1871), p. 474.

2. The work of David Montgomery, David Bensman, Patricia Cooper, and Nick Salvatore explores masculinity in the workplace and the meaning of manliness in the life of Eugene Debs. For treatments of working-class masculinity that suggest cultural continuity and cross-class continuities, see Peter N. Stearns, *Be a Man! Males in Modern Society* (New York: Holmes and Meier, 1979), esp. chap. 4, and Judith A. McGaw, *Most Wonderful Machine: Mechanization and Social Change in Berkshire Paper Making, 1801–1885* (Princeton: Princeton University Press, 1987), esp. chap. 9.

3. On the emigrations, see Charlotte Erickson, "The Encouragement of Emigration by British Trade Unions, 1850–1900," *Population Studies* 3 (1949): 248–73. On managers' views of insubordination, see *Fall River News,* 6 March 1875. For conservative assessments of this radical challenge, see *Commercial Bulletin,* 28 August and 2 October 1875; *Providence Journal,* 29 September 1875; *Fall River News,* 22 October 1875. For the nature of popular radicalism in Lancashire, see Edward P. Thompson, "Class Consciousness," in *The Making of the English Working Class* (1963), pp. 669–729. On Lancashire radicalism among textile workers in the early nineteenth century, see Cynthia Shelton, *The Mills of Manayunk: Industrialization and Social Conflict in the Philadelphia Region, 1787–1837* (Baltimore: Johns Hopkins University Press, 1986). The mule spinners in New England and Lancashire have been studied comparatively by William Lazonick, in "Industrial Relations and Technical Change: The Case of the Self-Acting Mule," *Cambridge Journal of Economics* 3 (1979): 231–62; by Isaac Cohen, in "Workers' Control in the Cotton Industry: A Comparative Study of British and American Mule Spinning," *Labor History* 26 (winter 1985): 53–85; and by Mary Freifeld, in "Technological Change and the 'Self-Acting' Mule: A Study of Skill and the Sexual Division of Labor," *Social History* 11 (1986): 319–43.

4. *Boston Herald,* 24 February 1875. Between 1870 and 1872, eighteen corporations in Fall River built five additional cotton mills, while fifteen new corporations con-

structed seventeen more mills, enormously increasing the city's productive capacity, which by 1870 had already surpassed that of Lowell. This expansion of production required six thousand more workers by 1872; the work force more than quadrupled between 1865 (2,654) and 1875 (11,514). By 1880, Fall River produced 32 percent of all the cotton print cloth in the country, which, combined with the production of mills in Rhode Island, Connecticut, and southern Massachusetts, dominated the national market with 57 percent of production; see Thomas Russell Smith, *The Cotton Textile Industry of Fall River, Massachusetts* (New York, 1944), pp. 50–65, and Frederick M. Peck and Henry H. Earl, *Fall River and Its Industries* (Fall River, 1877), p. 68. In contrast, see William Lazonick on the intense competition, small firm size, and specialization of the textile industry in England ("Competition, Specialization, and Industrial Decline," *Journal of Economic History* 41 [March 1981]: 31–38).

5. Mule spinning involved huge machines that moved back and forth on tracks in the mill floor. The spinner manipulated the frame to draw and twist the yarn to specification and then, as the forward action reversed, allowed the spun yarn to be wound on bobbins. Weavers tended power-driven looms that required frequent interventions to assist the weaving process. On the development of the spinners' and weavers' unions in Lancashire, see H. A. Turner, *Trade Union Growth Structure and Policy* (University of Toronto Press, 1962), pp. 108–68.

6. Turner, pp. 128–29; Lazonick, "The Case of the Self-Acting Mule," pp. 231–62. Mule spinners in Fall River had made regional organization their goal since 1858; see David Montgomery, *The Fall of the House of Labor: The Workplace, the State, and American Labor Activism, 1865–1925* (Cambridge: Cambridge University Press, 1987), pp. 156–59. However, the Fall River mule spinners lost most of their local strikes, and the regional goal remained visionary until serious attempts were made in 1875.

7. Patrick Joyce, in *Work, Society and Politics: The Culture of the Factory in Later Victorian England* (Brighton, U.K.: Harvester Press, 1980), analyzes midcentury Lancashire as a culture of class harmony and cooperation based on two key structural elements in the experience of modern factory work: the convergence of home and work in the family wage economy of factory workers, and the maturation of mechanization. Lancashire workers came to Fall River in different waves of immigration and therefore represented somewhat different experiences. Many of those who arrived in the 1840s and 1850s served in the Civil War fighting for the Union cause, while later arrivals from England endured the Preston strike of 1853–54 and the "cotton famine" of the early 1860s. On the cotton famine in Lancashire during the American Civil War, see William O. Henderson, *The Lancashire Cotton Famine, 1861–65* (Manchester University Press, 1934), and Edwin Waugh, *Home-Life of the Lancashire Factory Folk during the Cotton Famine* (Manchester, University Press, 1867). For an overview of the transformation to a male breadwinner wage norm (family wage) in mid-nineteenth-century Britain, see Wally Seccombe, "Patriarchy Stabilized: The Construction of the Male Breadwinner Wage Norm in Nineteenth-Century Britain," *Social History* 11 (1986): 53–76. For an overview of British immigrants, see Rowland T. Berthoff, *British Immigrants in Industrial America, 1790–1950* (Cambridge: Harvard University Press, 1953). On the role of New England textile workers in late-nineteenth-century labor politics, see Montgomery, *Fall of the House of Labor,* pp. 154–

70. John T. Cumbler's study of Fall River explored the social institutions—such as lodges, pubs, and workingmen's clubs—that textile workers brought with them from Lancashire to Fall River, but not the ideology and politics; see *Working-Class Community in Industrial America: Work, Leisure, and Struggle in Two Industrial Cities, 1880–1930* (Westport, Conn.: Greenwood Press, 1979), pp. 148–53.

8. On the 1870 strike, see Massachusetts Bureau of Labor Statistics (hereafter MBLS), *Second Annual Report* (1871), pp. 41–93; *Fall River News,* 21 July–16 September 1870; *Boston Herald,* 26–30 August 1870.

9. MBLS (1871), pp. 76–82, esp. p. 78.

10. Ibid.

11. Ibid., pp. 57–62. On the women's role, see pp. 68–74, 84.

12. See the debate between the Spinners' Committee and "Mill Operative" and "Main Street" who supplied the manufacturers' view of the strike, letters to the editor, *Fall River News,* 23, 26, and 30 July 1870; 8, 13, 15, 16, 18, and 20 August 1870.

13. *Fall River News,* 16 and 20 August 1870.

14. Lillian Chace Wyman, "Studies of Factory Life: Black-listing at Fall River," *Atlantic Monthly* 62 (November 1888): 605–12. On the blacklist, see MBLS, *First Annual Report* (1870), p. 326; *Second Annual Report* (1871), pp. 80–82.

15. *Fall River News* 16 and 20 August 1870; 8 and 16 September 1870; MBLS (1871), p. 90.

16. MBLS (1871), pp. 476–79, 481.

17. On the ten-hour protest, see *Fall River News,* 3 April 1874; *Boston Herald,* 3 April 1874; *Boston Advertiser,* 3 April 1874; *Lawrence American,* 4 April 1874; and *Lawrence Journal,* 11 April 1874. On post-Civil War labor politics, see David Montgomery, *Beyond Equality: Labor and the Radical Republicans, 1862–1872* (Urbana: University of Illinois Press, 1981).

18. MBLS (1871), pp. 49, 469–70, 476–86. For budgets and diets of Fall River mule spinners and weavers in 1874, see MBLS (1875), pp. 284–90; in 1875, *Fall River News,* 6 March 1875. On beer drinking, see MBLS (1882), pp. 209, 220, 254–60.

19. On "sick" spinning, see MBLS (1871), p. 482; Wyman, "Studies of Factory Life," p. 611; and *Fall River News,* 16 August 1870. On "lashing the help," see MBLS, *Thirteenth Annual Report* (1882), pp. 348–54. On competition in the spinning rooms that caused a disastrous fire in 1874, see MBLS, *Sixth Annual Report* (1875), pp. 142–77; *Labor Journal,* 26 September and 3 October 1874 (Fall River Historical Society).

20. *New York Times,* 23 January and 15 March 1875. On the exclusion of women weavers from the key meeting of male weavers, see letter to the editor, *Boston Globe,* 23 February 1875.

21. *Fall River News,* 18 January, 22 February, 8 March, and 17 March 1875. The terms of the contracts with the cloth printers for Fall River goods in the spring of 1875 made it impossible for the manufacturers to respond with a lockout. When they negotiated subsequent contracts, the Fall River agents insisted on reserving the right to close all the mills if there was a strike in any one mill; see *Commercial Bulletin,* 28 August 1875. On the women's meeting, see *Fall River News,* 18 January and 22 February 1875.

22. *Boston Globe,* 18 January 1875.

23. *Fall River News,* 15 and 22 February 1875; 1, 8, 13, 15, and 17 March 1875; 5 April 1875. A female representative of the women weavers of Fall River, Miss Cassie O'Neil, advocated the organization of women weavers and ring spinners, as well as equal pay for equal work, during a mule spinners' strike in Lowell shortly after the successful weavers' strike; see *Boston Herald,* 25 April 1875; *Lowell Courier,* 26 April 1875. For O'Neill on child labor, see *Fall River News,* 1 March 1875. Women strikers formed their own organization for a few weeks and adamantly refused to accept any compromise with the manufacturers; see *Boston Journal,* 18 January 1875; *Boston Herald,* 1 February 1875. Their public activities during the events of 1875 were described as more violent and "disgusting" than those of the men; see *New York Times,* 29 September 1875.

24. *Fall River News,* 22 February 1875; *Boston Globe,* 23 February 1875.

25. Quote is from MBLS (1882), p. 300. The *Sixth Annual Report* of the MBLS (1875) advocated a major reform of factory legislation along the lines of English law (pp. 186–87); see also *Fall River News,* 30 April 1875; see also *Fall River News,* 5 April 1875. On the regional convention, see *Fall River News,* 22 May 1875; *Boston Herald,* 21 and 22 May 1875. For an assessment of the success of the weavers' strike from the conservative press, see *Commercial Bulletin* (Boston), 26 August 1875. Since the 1840s, native-born textile workers in Fall River had feared the degraded conditions of English workers; see "To the Employers of Fall River" (1841) (Fall River Historical Society). On the pre–Civil War period, see Norman Ware, *The Industrial Workers, 1840–1860* (New York: Quadrangle Books, 1924, reprint 1964), pp. 76–78, 116–118; Phillip T. Silvia, Jr., "The Spindle City: Labor, Politics and Religion in Fall River, 1870–1905" (Ph.D. diss., Fordham University, 1973), pp. 12–58; and Sylvia Chace Lintner, "A Social History of Fall River, 1859–1879" (Ph.D. diss., Radcliffe College, 1945), pp. 123–30.

26. *New York Herald,* 13 and 19 October 1875.

27. *New York Herald,* 25 September 1875.

28. *Fall River News,* 19, 22, 24, and 30 July 1875; 2 August 1875. On the radical challenge of the vacation movement, see *Commercial Bulletin,* 28 August 1875. During their vacation, the weavers formally joined the national union of textile operatives and agitated for a ten-hour law in Rhode Island; see *Fall River News,* 10 and 17 August 1875.

29. *Fall River News,* 14 August and 4, 11, 13, and 16 September 1875. Some of the strike rhetoric was cast in terms of the rights of American citizens in a free country, but the actions were inspired by the Lancashire past; see Edward P. Thompson, "The Moral Economy of the English Crowd in the Eighteenth Century," *Past and Present* 50 (February 1971): 76–136. One of the chief sources of this inspiration was seventy-five-year-old labor activist Jonathan Biltcliffe; see *New York Herald,* 25, 26, 27, and 28 September 1875; *Boston Herald,* 28 September 1875. On the events of 27 September see *Fall River News,* 27 September; the testimony in the cases of those accused of participating in a riot, 29 September and 2 and 6 October 1875; and reports from special correspondents in the *New York Times,* 28 and 29 September 1875, and in the *New York Herald,* 25, 26, 27, and 28 September 1875. For statements by William H. Jennings of the Merchants Mill on the "peculiar" and intolerable ac-

tivities of the Lancashire weavers, see *Fall River News,* 22 October 1875. For the conservative press, see *Providence Journal,* 29 September 1875, and *Commercial Bulletin,* 2 October 1875.

30. On 2 October 1875, *L'Echo du Canada,* the French Canadian newspaper in Fall River, described the events of the bread riot on 27 September as dangerously violent and led by a "ridiculous mob"; see Lintner, pp. 158–59. One of the defense lawyers for the six men arrested for rioting, a Yankee labor reformer, strongly denied any "premeditation or collusion or purpose" on the part of the crowd that besieged city hall for bread, and defended his clients on the basis of their American right to peaceable assembly; *Fall River News,* 2 October 1875. On the return of the "vacationers" to the mills, see *New York Herald,* 13, 16, and 19 October 1875; on operatives' attitudes, see MBLS (1882), p. 361; on labor reformers, see *Fall River News,* 1 October 1875. On anger and masculinity, see Peter N. Stearns, "Men, Boys and Anger in American Society, 1860–1940," in M. A. Mangan and James Walvin, eds., *Manliness and Morality: Middle-Class Masculinity in Britain and America, 1800–1940* (Manchester, U.K.: Manchester University Press, 1986).

31. *Boston Globe,* 18 August 1879.

32. Quote is from the *Boston Globe,* 10 July 1879. On the 1879 strike, see *Providence Journal,* 9 and 13 May 1879; *Boston Herald,* 16 July–7 October 1879; *Boston Globe,* 13 June–25 August 1879; MBLS, *Eleventh Annual Report* (1880), pp. 53–68. On the conservative policies of the spinners after 1879, see Cumbler, pp. 173–94. Beginning in the 1890s, ring spinning replaced mule spinning for all yarn in American cotton-textile production. The mule spinners made no serious attempt to organize the female ring spinners until too late.

33. Wyman, p. 611.

34. Some of these activists may have been the wives of spinners, suggesting an additional family dimension to their rebellion. Along with the work of Carol Morgan and Sonya Rose, this analysis of the 1870s in Fall River provides new evidence on gender politics among Lancashire workers and on the militancy and historic agency of English women textile workers. The official *History of the Fall River Strike* (Fall River, 1875), by "A Workingman," acknowledged only the initial role of the women weavers.

35. *Fall River News,* 22 February 1875.

Chapter Eleven

1. The first statement of the interpretation is Joe Dubbert's "Progressivism and the Masculinity Crisis," reprinted in Elizabeth Pleck and Joseph Pleck, eds., *The American Man* (Englewood Cliffs, N.J.: Prentice-Hall, 1980), p. 307; see also Dubbert's survey, *A Man's Place: Masculinity in Transition* (Englewood Cliffs, N.J.: Prentice-Hall, 1979), and David Pugh's *Sons of Liberty: The Masculine Mind in Nineteenth-Century America* (Westport, Conn.: Greenwood Press, 1983). More sophisticated in relating gender and social change, but largely concerned with the twentieth century, is Peter Filene's *Him/Her/Self: Sex Roles in Modern America,* 2d ed. (Baltimore: Johns Hopkins University Press, 1986).

2. Filene, *Him/Her/Self,* 69–80; on causal explanation for the crisis, see, for example, Michael S. Kimmel, "The Contemporary 'Crisis' of Masculinity in Historical Perspective," in Harry Brod, ed., *The Making of Masculinities: The New Men's Studies* (Boston: Allen & Unwin, 1987).

3. Beth Bailey, *From Front Porch to Back Seat: Courtship in Twentieth-Century America* (Baltimore: Johns Hopkins University Press, 1988), p. 102. The role of these crises prior to the 1960s in producing new definitions of masculinity is uncertain given the similarities over time in some types of proposals for restoring "manliness," like Theodore Roosevelt's summons to the "strenuous life."

4. See, for example, Mary Ryan, *Cradle of the Middle Class: The Family in Oneida County, New York, 1790–1865* (New York: Cambridge University Press, 1981); Rosalind Rosenberg, *Beyond Separate Spheres: Intellectual Roots of Modern Feminism* (New Haven: Yale University Press, 1982); Nancy Cott, *The Grounding of Modern Feminism* (New Haven: Yale University Press, 1987). Interpretive essays which show the richness of the monographic literature that women's historians have created on two major aspects of gender relations are Linda Kerber's "Separate Spheres, Female Worlds, Woman's Place: The Rhetoric of Women's History," *Journal of American History* 75 (June 1988): 9–39, and Paula Baker's "Domestication of Politics: Women and American Political Society, 1780–1920," *American Historical Review* 89 (June 1984): 620–47.

5. This bias is evident in the recent collection of essays edited by J. A. Mangan and James Walvin, *Manliness and Morality: Middle-Class Masculinity in Britain and America, 1800–1940* (New York: St. Martin's Press, 1987). Refreshingly free of that bias is Jock Phillips's exemplary survey of masculinity in another part of the English-speaking world, New Zealand: *A Man's Country: The Image of the Pakeha Male* (Aukland, New Zealand: Penguin Books, 1987).

6. The monographic literature on masculinity for the white working class is cited in the essays by Baron and Blewett in this book. Exemplary beginnings for historical analysis of gender for black males and for male homosexuals are James Horton, "Freedom's Yoke: Gender Conventions among Antebellum Free Blacks," *Feminist Studies* 12 (spring 1986): 51–76, and George Chauncey, Jr., "Christian Brotherhood or Sexual Perversion? Homosexual Identities and the Construction of Sexual Boundaries in the World War One Era," *Journal of Social History* 19 (winter 1985): 190–211.

7. Divergence in conceptions of manhood is evident from colonial times, as Philip Greven's typology of three "temperaments" among white Protestants suggests (*The Protestant Temperament: Patterns of Child-Rearing, Religious Experience, and the Self in Early America* [New York: Alfred A. Knopf, 1977]). It is unclear whether colonial Americans were as self-conscious about divergence in norms from masculinity as Americans at midcentury were. E. Anthony Rotundo postulates a unifying emphasis on the useful citizen in the late eighteenth century in "Body and Soul: Changing Ideas of American Middle-Class Manhood, 1770–1920," *Journal of Social History* 16 (summer 1983).

For antebellum working-class ideas of masculinity, see Elliot Gorn, "'Gouge and Bite, Pull Hair and Scratch': The Social Significance of Fighting in the Southern

Backcountry," *American Historical Review* 90 (February 1985); David Reynolds, *Beneath the American Renaissance: The Subversive Imagination in the Age of Emerson and Melville* (New York: Alfred A. Knopf, 1988), chap. 6; Sean Wilentz, *Chants Democratic: New York City and the Rise of the American Working Class, 1788–1850* (New York: Oxford University Press, 1984); and Bruce Laurie, *Working People of Philadelphia, 1800–1850* (Philadelphia: Temple University Press, 1980).

8. Mangan and Walvin, eds., *Manliness and Morality,* pp. 103–7. John Gillis claims that in England by 1860 "men no longer dared embrace in pubic or shed tears"; quoted in David Greenberg, *The Construction of Homosexuality* (Chicago: University of Chicago Press, 1988), p. 388. Because of literary description of the "molly houses," homosexuality in England had become identified with effeminacy before the nineteenth century (Greenberg, pp. 330–34). There is no comparable evidence for the United States before the 1890s.

9. Bertram Wyatt-Brown, *Honor and Violence in the Old South* (New York: Oxford University Press, 1986), chaps. 2–3; George Fredrickson, *The Inner Civil War: Northern Intellectuals and the Crisis of the Union* (New York: Harper & Row, 1965), pp. 33–35.

10. Baker, "Domestication of Politics," p. 629.

11. Important exceptions are E. Anthony Rotundo, "Manhood in America: The Northern Middle Class, 1770–1920" (Ph.D. diss., Brandeis University, 1981), and Charles Rosenberg, "Sexuality, Class and Role in Nineteenth-Century America," in Pleck and Pleck, eds., *The American Man.* On more specialized subjects, such as advice books for young men and male sexual reform, the influence of evangelicalism has received more attention.

12. Lewis Saum, *The Popular Mood of Pre–Civil War America* (Westport, Conn.: Greenwood Press, 1980), part 1.

13. Paul Johnson, *A Shopkeeper's Millennium: Society and Revivals in Rochester, New York, 1815–1837* (New York: Hill and Wang, 1978), p. 47; Bertram Wyatt-Brown, *Lewis Tappan and the Evangelical War against Slavery* (Cleveland: Case Western Reserve University Press, 1969), p. 53. Another leading New York City merchant, W. E. Dodge, would join the pastor of a smaller community during an 1856 revival in "house-to-house visits, inviting men to the mercy seat" (Allan Horlick, *Country Boys and Merchant Princes: The Social Control of Young Men in New York* [Lewisburg, Pa.: Bucknell University Press, 1975], p. 81).

14. Susan Juster, "'In a Different Voice': Male and Female Narratives of Religious Conversion in Post-Revolutionary America," *American Quarterly* 41 (March 1989), p. 36.

15. Ryan, *Cradle of the Middle Class,* pp. 161, 183–84. Whether sons growing up in a time of declining religious enthusiasm—or men of the preceding generation who had never been caught up in that enthusiasm—were in fact more exhilarated by economic change and ambivalent, at best, about the new moral discipline has yet to be determined. Carroll Smith-Rosenberg suggests that bourgeois men expressed their ambivalence toward the emerging social order of Jacksonian America through the "two competing mythic dramas" of male moral reformers and the Davy Crockett almanacs. The "joke" of the almanacs provided an "outlet for hostility and frustra-

tion in the violence of jingoism and racism", which it defined as the natural characteristic of the young white American male" (*Disorderly Conduct: Visions of Gender in Victorian America* [New York: Oxford University Press, 1986], pp. 90–92, 107–8). In the absence of any specification of who the almanac readers were, this interpretation remains inspired speculation. One could as easily guess that most men with strong religious commitments did not spend much time reading the almanacs, and that many men with weaker religious inclinations may have read them with less engagement and identification than Smith-Rosenberg suggests.

16. Ann Douglas, *The Feminization of American Culture* (New York: Alfred A. Knopf, 1977), chap. 7; John Gilkeson, *Middle-Class Providence, 1820–1940* (Princeton: Princeton University Press, 1986), chap. 2.

17. Blanche Hersh, *The Slavery of Sex: Feminist-Abolitionists in America* (Urbana: University of Illinois Press, 1978), chap. 7.

18. Suzanne Lebsock, *The Free Women of Petersburg: Status and Culture in a Southern Town, 1784–1860* (New York: W. W. Norton, 1984), pp. 225–36.

19. Karen Halttunen, *Confidence Men and Painted Women: A Study of Middle-Class Culture in America, 1830–1870* (New Haven: Yale University Press, 1982), chap. 4; John Higham, "The Reorientation of American Culture in the 1890s," in John Weiss, ed., *The Origins of Modern Consciousness* (Detroit: Wayne State University Press, 1965), p. 27.

20. Quoted in Melvin Adelman, *A Sporting Time: New York City and the Rise of Modern Athletics, 1820–70* (Urbana: University of Illinois Press, 1986), p. 284.

21. For examples of gendered republican descriptions of decadence and corruption, see Michael Lienesch, *New Order of the Ages: Time, the Constitution, and the Making of Modern American Political Thought* (Princeton: Princeton University Press, 1988), p. 43 and passim. Harriet Beecher Stowe argued that the "women of America can, if they choose, hold back their country from following in the wake of an old, corrupt, worn-out, effeminate European society . . . " (quoted in Alan Trachtenberg, ed., *Democratic Vistas: 1860–1880* [New York: George Braziller, 1970], p. 136).

22. Ryan, *Cradle of the Middle Class,* pp. 167–69.

23. Judging by the evidence for Providence, Rhode Island, the fraternal orders had special appeal for that portion of the middle class which Mary Ryan portrays as prolonging their sons' dependence in order to improve their opportunities: the lodges in that city "attracted large numbers of shopkeepers, clerks, artisans, and other men from the lower middle class and the upper strata of the working class." Gilkeson, *Providence,* p. 159.

24. Fredrickson, *Inner Civil War,* pp. 69–78. Roger Lane shows for Philadelphia during the last half of the nineteenth century that violence against others waned while suicide rates increased; see his *Violent Death in the City: Suicide, Accident, and Murder in Nineteenth Century Philadelphia* (Cambridge: Harvard University Press, 1979).

25. John Higham sees both sexes as rejecting Victorian restraint and decorum in the 1890s in favor of a "masculine" vigor, boldness, and adventuresomeness: "women became more manly, men became more martial" ("Reorientation," p. 27).

26. Eric Foner, *Reconstruction: America's Unfinished Revolution, 1863–1877* (New York: Harper & Row, 1988), p. 34.

27. Maris Vinovskis, "Have Social Historians Lost the Civil War?" *Journal of American History* 76 (June 1989): 50; Fredrickson, *Inner Civil War*, pp. 168–70.

28. Quoted in Matthew Josephson, *The Politicos, 1865–1896* (New York: Harcourt, Brace, 1938), pp. 246–47; Richard Hofstadter, *Anti-intellectualism in American Life* (New York: Alfred A. Knopf, 1963), p. 186. The politicians could have found reinforcement for their view of culture as feminine among many supporters of culture, such as Horace Bushnell and the Beecher sisters; they saw women working in the home as representing the "beauty principle" and the strongest influence for refining as well as redeeming man (Alan Trachtenberg, *The Incorporation of America: Culture and Society in the Gilded Age* [New York: Hill and Wang, 1982], pp. 145–46).

29. "The Abortion Movement and the AMA, 1850–1880," in Smith-Rosenberg, *Disorderly Conduct;* Karen Blair, *The Clubwoman as Feminist: True Womanhood Redefined, 1868–1914* (New York: Holmes & Meier, 1980), chap. 4, esp. pp. 70–71. For an overview of women's expanding activities outside the home, see Carl Degler, *At Odds: Women and the Family in America from the Revolution to the Present* (New York: Oxford University Press, 1980), chap. 13.

30. David Pivar, *Purity Crusade: Sexual Morality and Social Control, 1868–1900* (Westport, Conn: Greenwood Press, 1974); John D'Emilio and Estelle Freedman, *Intimate Matters: A History of Sexuality in America* (New York: Harper & Row, 1988), chap. 7; Ruth Bordin, *Women and Temperance: The Quest for Power and Liberty, 1873–1900* (Philadelphia: Temple University Press, 1981), chaps. 6–7; David Thelen, *The New Citizenship: Origins of Progressivism in Wisconsin, 1885–1900* (Columbia: University of Missouri Press, 1972), p. 99.

31. The judicial patriarchs' intervention in domestic relations did not support women's drive for greater independence through statutory modification. As Nancy Cott notes, the judiciary's role "seems often to have been to limit the extent to which wives could establish independent economic personae despite such statutes" ("Patriarchy in America Is Different: Grossberg's *Governing the Hearth*," *American Bar Foundation Research Journal* [fall 1987]: 813).

32. William McLoughlin, *The Meaning of Henry Ward Beecher: An Essay on the Shifting Values of Mid-Victorian America, 1840–1870* (New York: Alfred A. Knopf, 1970), chap. 5.

33. Quoted in Cindy Aron, *Ladies and Gentlemen of the Civil Service: Middle-Class Workers in Victorian America* (New York: Oxford University Press, 1987), p. 36.

34. Ibid., p. 188.

35. Thelen, *The New Citizenship*, p. 99.

36. Margaret Marsh, "From Separation to Togetherness: The Social Construction of Domestic Space in American Suburbs, 1840–1915," *Journal of American History* 76 (September 1989): 512–15.

37. Gunther Barth, *City People* (New York: Oxford University Press, 1980); Lewis Erenberg, *Steppin' Out: New York Nightlife and the Transformation of American Culture, 1890–1930* (Westport, Conn: Greenwood Press, 1981), pp. 67–69; Russell Nye, *The Unembarrassed Muse: The Popular Arts in America* (New York: Dial Press, 1970),

chap. 6; Claudia Johnson, "That Guilty Third Tier," in Daniel Howe, ed., *Victorian America* (Philadelphia: University of Pennsylvania Press, 1976).

38. Steven A. Reiss, *Touching Base: Professional Baseball and American Culture in the Progressive Era* (Westport, Conn.: Greenwood Press, 1980), p. 27.

39. Donald Mrozek, *Sport and American Mentality, 1880–1920* (Knoxville: University of Tennessee Press, 1983), p. 158.

40. Rosenberg, *Beyond Separate Spheres,* p. 49.

41. Robert and Helen Lynd, *Middletown: A Study in American Culture* (New York: Harcourt, Brace and Company), part 2; Paula Fass, *The Damned and the Beautiful: American Youth in the 1920s* (New York: Oxford University Press, 1977), pp. 71–72, 109–10.

42. John Demos, *Past, Present, and Personal: The Family and the Life Course in American History* (New York: Oxford University Press, 1986), p. 61. Warren Belasco, in *Americans on the Road: From Autocamp to Motel, 1910–1945* (Cambridge, Mass: Massachusetts Institute of Technology Press, 1979), p. 67, notes that "for fathers, autocamping offered unquestioned family leadership, both as camper and camp guide. Tent, khakis, and camp fire, all were comfortably within the male sphere."

43. Daniel Rodgers, *The Work Ethic in Industrial America, 1850–1920* (Chicago: University of Chicago Press, 1978), chap. 5.

44. Cott, *Modern Feminism,* pp. 36, 42; *Harper's Monthly* 155 (1927): 552–60.

45. Kerber, "Separate Spheres," pp. 27–28.

46. Cott, *Modern Feminism,* p. 154; Fass, *The Damned and the Beautiful,* p. 98.

47. Kathryn Sklar, "Religious and Moral Authority as Factors Shaping the Balance of Power for Women's Political Culture in the Twentieth Century," paper presented at the annual meeting of the Organization of American Historians, April 1989. Linda Gordon notes an increasing reluctance among the new "experts" and professionalized charity workers to condemn men guilty of family violence as the "old feminist diatribes came to seem moralistic and unscientific" (*Heroes of Their Own Lives: The Politics and History of Family Violence, Boston, 1880–1960* [New York: Viking, 1988], pp. 19–22).

48. Bailey, *Front Porch,* pp. 13–24; on encouragement for the "big spender" in cabarets and nightclubs, see Erenberg, *Steppin' Out,* pp. 199–202.

49. This struggle was especially problematic for wives who previously, as single workers, had known the freedom and excitement of the new heterosocial amusements of dance halls, skating rinks, and amusement parks. These pleasures often ended with marriage or motherhood in working-class families strained by low income, few community services, and lack of labor-saving appliances. (Kathy Peiss, *Cheap Amusements: Working Women and Leisure in Turn-of-the-Century New York* [Philadelphia: Temple University Press, 1986], p. 188).

50. As late as the 1970s, sociologist Lillian Rubin found that working-class wives did not challenge this conception of male prerogative in the home partly because they recognized their husbands' need to compensate for lack of authority in the workplace. See her *Worlds of Pain: Life in the Working-Class Family* (New York: Basic Books, 1976), chap. 5–6, and Roy Rosenzweig's *Eight Hours for What We Will: Work-*

ers and Leisure in an Industrial City, 1870–1920 (Cambridge: Cambridge University Press, 1983), pp. 172, 216–18.

51. Chauncey, "Christian Brotherhood," p. 206; Jonathan Katz, ed., *Gay American History: Lesbians and Gay Men in the U.S.A.* (New York: Thomas Y. Crowell, 1976),pp. 39–43. Chauncey argues elsewhere that "the changing focus of medical inquiry into sexual deviance . . . can be analyzed as a response to particular changes in and challenges to the Victorian sex/gender system such as the women's movement, the growing visibility of urban gay male subcultures, and the changing gender structure of the economy" ("From Sexual Inversion to Homosexuality: Medicine and the Changing Conceptualization of Female Deviance," *Salmagundi* 58–59 [fall 1982–winter 1983]): 114–16.

52. Rosenberg, "Sexuality, Class and Role," esp. pp. 240–42. During the Progressive years men already had moved to assume leadership in domestic missionary work through the Laymen's Missionary Movement and the Men and Religion Forward Movement. See, for example, "Ending Women's Monopoly of Religion," *Literary Digest* 44 (6 January 1912): 23–24.

Chapter Twelve

1. *Hidden from History*—by Sheila Rowbotham—was the title of one of the first texts in women's history issuing from the women's liberation movement (London: Pluto Press, 1973). The usage "sex/gender system" originated, so far as I know, in Gayle Rubin's germinal essay, "The Traffic in Women: Notes on the 'Political Economy' for Sex," in *Toward an Anthropology of Women,* ed. Rayna Reiter (New York: Monthly Review, 1975).

2. For example, two early and highly inspiring essays explicitly outlined the aims of women's history to reveal the social relation of the sexes: Natalie Zemon Davis, "Women's History in Transition: The European Case," *Feminist Studies* 3 (winter 1975–76): 83–103, and Joan Kelly, "The Social Relation of the Sexes: Methodological Implications of Women's History," *Signs* 1:4 (summer 1976): 809–23. For a more recent discussion, see Joan W. Scott, "Gender: A Useful Category of Historical Analysis," *American Historical Review* 91:5 (December 1986): 1053–75.

3. Elizabeth H. Pleck, "Two Worlds in One: Work and Family," *Journal of Social History* 10:2 (1976): 178–95; Joan Jensen, "Cloth, Butter and Boarders: Women's Household Production for the Market," *Review of Radical Political Economics* 12 (summer 1980): 14–24, and *Loosening the Bonds: Mid-Atlantic Farm Women, 1750–1850* (New Haven: Yale University Press, 1986); Nancy Hewitt, "Feminist Friends: Agrarian Quakers and the Emergence of Women's Rights in America," *Feminist Studies* 12 (spring 1986): 27–49, and "Beyond the Search for Sisterhood: American Women's History in the 1980s," *Social History* 10:3 (October 1985): 299–321; Thomas Dublin, "Women and Outwork in a Nineteenth-Century New England Town," in *The Countryside in the Age of Capitalist Transformation,* ed. Steven Hahn and Jonathan Prude (Chapel Hill: University of North Carolina Press, 1985); Nancy Grey Osterud, "'She Helped Me Hay It as Good as a Man': Relations among Women and

Men in an Agricultural Community," in *"To Toil the Livelong Day": America's Women at Work, 1780–1980,* ed. Carol Groneman and Mary Beth Norton (Ithaca, N.Y.: Cornell University Press, 1987).

4. E.g., Suzanne Lebsock, *The Free Women of Petersburg: Status and Culture in a Southern Town, 1784–1860* (New York: Norton, 1984).

5. John Mack Faragher, *Women and Men on the Overland Trail* (New Haven: Yale University Press, 1979).

6. Patricia Hills, *The Painters' America: Rural and Urban Life, 1810–1910* (New York: Praeger, 1974).

7. These questions are addressed very effectively in Christine Stansell's "Origins of the Sweatshop," in *Working-Class America,* ed. Michael Frisch and Daniel Walkowitz (Urbana: University of Illinois Press, 1938); "Women, Children, and the Uses of the Street: Class and Gender Conflict in New York City, 1850–1860," *Feminist Studies* 8:1 (summer 1982): 309–37; and *City of Women: Sex and Class in New York, 1789–1860* (New York: Knopf, 1986).

8. David Montgomery, *The Fall of the House of Labor* (New York: Cambridge University Press, 1987); Steven Hahn, *The Roots of Southern Populism* (New York: Oxford, 1983).

9. The ideas of Martha Minow have influenced me greatly on this point. See e.g., Minow, "The Supreme Court, 1986 Term, Foreword: Justice Engendered," *Harvard Law Review* 101:1 (November 1987). Related and stimulating points of view are contained in Drucilla Cornell, "The Poststructuralist Challenge to the Ideal of Community," *Cardozo Law Review* 8:5 (April 1987), and *Reconstructing Individualism,* ed. Thomas Heller et al. (Stanford: Stanford University Press, 1986).

Contributors

Ava Baron, professor of sociology, Rider College, has written extensively on women and the law, and on women employed in the sewing and printing industries and in working in the legal profession. She is editor of *Work Engendered: Toward a New History of Men, Women, and Work* (Cornell University Press, forthcoming), and is completing work on a book-length manuscript entitled "Men's Work and the Woman Question: Work and Gender in the Printing Industry, 1830–1920."

Mary H. Blewett, professor of history at the University of Lowell, in Massachusetts, is the author of *Men, Women, and Work: Class, Gender, and Protest in the New England Shoe Industry, 1780–1910* (University of Illinois Press, 1988), awarded the Herbert G. Gutman Prize in Social History, the New England Historical Association Book Award, and the Joan Kelly Prize in 1989. She has also published *The Last Generation: Work and Life in the Textile Mills of Lowell, Massachusetts, 1910–1960* (University of Massachusetts Press, 1990), and is working on a study of the culture and politics of Lancashire immigrants in the textile mills of southern New England in the mid-nineteenth century.

Mark C. Carnes, associate professor of history, Barnard College, Columbia University, the author of *Secret Ritual and Manhood in Victorian America* (Yale University Press, 1989), is co-editor of the *Dictionary of American Biography* (Charles Scribner's Sons, 1988), and managing editor of the 20-volume *American National Biography* (Oxford University Press, forthcoming). He has also published *The Compensations of War: The Diary of an Ambulance Driver during the Great War* (University of Texas Press, 1983). He is exploring primitive imagery in urban-industrial contexts in late nineteenth-century America.

Nancy F. Cott, professor of American studies and history at Yale University, is the author of *The Bonds of Womanhood: "Women's Sphere" in New England, 1780–1835* (1977), *The Grounding of Modern Feminism* (1987), and the forthcoming *A Woman Making History: Mary Ritter Beard through Her Letters,* all published by Yale University Press.

Susan Curtis, assistant professor of history, Purdue University, is completing a book on the social gospel and modern American culture. Her current research interest is generational experience in the Gilded Age.

Clyde Griffen, the Lucy Maynard Salmon Professor of History at Vassar College, is the author, with Sally Griffen, of *Natives and Newcomers: The Ordering of Opportunity in Mid-Nineteenth-Century Poughkeepsie* (Harvard University Press, 1978). He is now working on a study of the ideas, perceptions, and realities of success in America from the Colonial period to the present.

Robert L. Griswold, associate professor of history, University of Oklahoma, is the author of *Family and Divorce in California, 1850–1890: Victorian Illusions and Everyday Realities* (State University of New York Press, 1982). He has recently published several articles on the history of divorce in *Signs, American Quarterly,* and the *Journal of Social History,* and is completing a study of the history of fatherhood in America from 1920 to the present.

Michael Grossberg, associate professor of history and law, Case Western Reserve University, has published *Governing the Hearth: Law and the Family in Nineteenth Century America* (University of North Carolina Press, 1985), as well as several articles on the legal history of the family. He is currently writing *The Search for Justice: A Social History of American Law,* forthcoming from Indiana University Press.

John Starrett Hughes, assistant professor of history, University of Texas at Austin, author of *In the Law's Darkness: Isaac Ray and the Medical Jurisprudence of Insanity in Nineteenth-Century America* (Linden Series in Legal History, New York University School of Law, 1986), is finishing a case history of madness and society in the Victorian South.

Margaret Marsh, professor of history at Stockton State College, is the author of *Anarchist Women, 1870–1920* (Temple University Press, 1981), and *Suburban Lives* (Rutgers University Press, 1990). Her articles have appeared in edited collections and in several journals, including the *Journal of American History,* and the *American Quarterly.* Her current research, a collaboration with gynecologist Wanda Ronner, is on the medical and cultural history of infertility in the United States.

E. Anthony Rotundo, instructor in history at Phillips Academy, Andover, whose articles on the male role in historical perspective have appeared in the *Journal of Social History, American Behavioral Scientist,* and elsewhere, has received a fellowship from the National Endowment for the Humanities to complete a book on manhood in nineteenth-century America.

Donald Yacovone, an assistant editor at the Black Abolitionist Papers Project, is author of *Dilemmas of the Liberal Persuasion: Samuel Joseph May, Antebellum Religion and Reform* (Temple University Press, forthcoming). He has also published articles on black temperance and antebellum reform in *Journal of the Early Republic,* and *Perspectives in American History.* He is writing a biographical introduction for *"Better to Die Free than Live Slaves": The Civil War Writings of George E. Stephens,* and is engaged in research on the subject of masculinity in Victorian America.

Index